Sociology for Nurses

Second edition

Sociology for Nurses

Second edition

Edited by

Elaine Denny and Sarah Earle

polity

The right of Elaine Denny and Sarah Earle to be identified as Authors of this
Work has been asserted in accordance with the UK Copyright, Designs and
Patents Act 1988.

First published in 2009 by Polity Press

Polity Press
65 Bridge Street
Cambridge CB2 1UR, UK

Polity Press
350 Main Street
Malden, MA 02148, USA

ISBN-13: 978-0-7456-4624-4
ISBN-13: 978-0-7456-4625-1 (pb)

A catalogue record for this book is available from the British Library.

Typeset in 10.5/13pt Quadraat-Regular
by Servis Filmsetting Ltd, Stockport, Cheshire
Printed and bound in China by 1010 Printing International Ltd.

For further information on Polity, visit our website: www.politybooks.com

Contents

Contributors

Geraldine Brown is a research fellow in the Applied Research Centre in Sustainable Regeneration, Coventry University. She has extensive experience of undertaking research for the voluntary, community and public sectors. Her interests include the working relationships between partners in health provision and the relationship between the experience of social exclusion and institutional attempts at inclusion across a range of social policy areas. A key aim of her work is to promote the voices of those who tend to be marginalized.

Pat Chambers is a senior lecturer in the School of Public Policy and Professional Practice and director of postgraduate research in the Research Institute of Life Course Studies, both at Keele University. Her research interests are located within social gerontology, in particular family relationships in later life and the intersection of critical gerontology and social work with older people.

David Cox is emeritus professor, Faculty of Health, at Birmingham City University. Since 2002 he has been chair of South Birmingham Primary Care Trust. He teaches and has written about the sociology of policy implementation and reorganization in childcare and the NHS.

Lorraine Culley is professor of social science and health and associate director of the Mary Seacole Research Centre in the Faculty of Health and Life Sciences at De Montfort University, Leicester. A sociologist by background, Lorraine has published widely in the social sciences in the areas of education, gender and ethnicity. She is currently researching several aspects of cultural diversity and health, including work on infertility and reproductive technologies, endometriosis and the educational implications of sickle cell.

Elaine Denny is professor of health sociology at Birmingham City University. Her research interests focus around women as recipients and providers of health care, in particular reproductive health, and she has published work on women's experience of IVF, the experience of endometriosis, and the occupation of nursing. Her current research is a Research for Patient Benefit-funded collaborative study on endometriosis and cultural diversity aimed at improving services for minority ethnic women.

Simon Dyson is professor of applied sociology and director of the Unit for the Social Study of Thalassaemia and Sickle Cell at

De Montfort University, Leicester. He is the author of *Ethnicity and Screening for Sickle Cell* (Elsevier, 2005) and, with Brian Brown, of *Social Theory and Applied Health Research* (Open University Press, 2006). He has worked with local and national sickle cell support groups for over twenty years and is an advisor to the Sickle Cell Society.

Sarah Earle is senior lecturer in the Faculty of Health & Social Care at the Open University. Her research interests include women's reproductive health, the sociology of sexuality and the role of sociology within health care education and practice. She has published widely in these areas.

Mike Filby was formerly associate dean and professor in the Faculty of Health at Birmingham City University, where his main teaching and research interests were in the sociology of work and organizations. He had a particular interest in the sociology of health work and undertook research into the organization of ancillary work, teamwork in primary care and interprofessional relationships in community nursing. Since retiring from higher education, he has been undertaking research and policy analysis for a voluntary sector organization.

Barbara Green is a senior lecturer at Birmingham City University with a first degree in sociology with history and a masters degree in nursing. The theme of her research dissertation was the relationship between sociology and nursing. Her clinical background is as a registered nurse in acute medicine, having worked as a ward sister in this speciality for eight years. She currently teaches sociology to pre-registration student nurses.

Alistair Hewison is senior lecturer in the School of Health and Population Sciences at the University of Birmingham. His research and teaching interests centre on management and policy in health care. Recent work includes an evaluation of the management of end-of-life care in care homes and an examination of new models of care delivery in an acute trust. He is associate editor of the *Journal of Nursing Management* and is a regular contributor to scholarly journals and books.

Gayle Letherby is professor of sociology and school research coordinator at the School of Law and Social Science, University of Plymouth. Her scholarly interests include reproductive and non-parental identity and experience; and feminist research and epistemology. Among recent relevant publications are, with Paul Bywaters, *Extending Social Research: Application, Implementation and Presentation* (Open University Press, 2007); with Jennifer Marchbank, *An Introduction to Gender: Social Science Perspectives* (Pearson, 2007); and, with Sarah Earle (eds), *The Sociology of Health Care: A Reader for Health Professionals* (Palgrave, 2008).

Douglas McCarrick is head of social and community studies at Coventry University. He has a background in local politics, where he has chaired housing and urban renewal committees and served as a scrutineer of health services. He has also been active in community work and welfare campaigns and supported the movement Defend Council Housing. He has led a number of voluntary organizations, including a local housing association.

Terry O'Donnell is senior lecturer at Leeds Metropolitan University. Her main interests are in the sociology of the physically active and sporting body and the sociology of public health. She is researching aspects of young women's embodiment in relation to clothing choices and is collaboratively exploring the dominance of body image discourses in the social construction of anorexia nervosa.

Keith Sharp is dean of the Faculty of Education, Humanities and Sciences at the University of Gloucestershire. He is interested in the sociology of sexuality and social theory and is co-author of Sociology in Focus (1995) and Psychology in Focus (Causeway Press, 2002) and, with Sarah Earle, of Sex in Cyberspace (Ashgate, 2007).

Philip Shelton is senior lecturer in health sociology and policy lecturer at Birmingham City University. He also works as an associate lecturer at the Open University. His current interests focus on the application of sociological knowledge to nursing practice and student approaches to learning on placement.

Nick Watson is professor of disability studies and director of Strathclyde Centre for Disability Research at the University of Glasgow. He has published widely on a range of disability issues, including disabled childhoods, disability and identity, disability and technology and disability theory. He is editor of a four-volume series entitled Disability: Major Themes in Health and Social Welfare, published by Routledge in 2007.

Corinne Wilson is a senior sociology lecturer at Coventry University. She teaches on a number of modules which explore the relationship between gender, the family and health. Her research interests include teenage pregnancy, lone motherhood, feminist methodology and epistemology. Since 2001 she has been involved in a number of qualitative research projects around the experiences of young pregnant women and young parents.

Acknowledgements

The editors and publisher are grateful to the following for permission to reproduce copyright material:

Blackwell Publishing for the extract in Activity 6.4 on p. 129.
Controller of HMSO and the Queen's Printer for Scotland for table 9.1 on p. 189, figure 6.1 on p. 124 and the figures in activity 8.1 on p. 168 and in box 15.1 on p. 315. Crown copyright material reproduced under class licences no. CO1W0000283 and no. P2008000352.
The Independent UK for the extract in Activity 4.5 on p. 89.

Illustration Credits

The publisher would like to acknowledge permission to reproduce the following images:

Chapter 1:
© Jacky Fleming; © Brad Killer/iStock; ©Schwadron, Harley; © Jean Schweitzer/iStock

Chapter 2:
Roman Milert/iStock; © Anette Romanenko/iStock; © Chris Schmidt/iStock.

Chapter 3:
Maria Perry; © Keith Brofsky/Getty; www.sijetaisseropositif.com;

Chapter 4:
Getty Images; Annett Vauteck/iStock;

Chapter 5:
David Monniaux/Wikimedia Commons; ©Marilyna/Dreamstime; www.keepyoureyeontheball.org; © Haynes Publishing

Chapter 6:
©Jui Chen/iStock; © Robert Cocquyt/iStock; National Statistics Online; © Olegseleznev/Dreamstime.

Chapter 7:
© Shariffc /Dreamstime; James o. Jenkins; © Andres Balcazar/iStock; © Sean Locke/iStock.

Chapter 8:
©Pete Saloutos/iStock; © Tomas Bercic/iStock; © anne de Haas/iStock.

Chapter 9:
© Vikram Raghuvanshi/iStock; © poco_bw/iStock; ©Arekmalang/Dreamstime.

Chapter 10:
©Jaymast/iStock; ©Pawel Kierzkowski/iStock; Mikhail Fomichev/Wikimedia Commons; ©Paul Prescott/iStock.

Chapter 11:
©Duncan Walker/iStock; © Alexander Raths/iStock.

Chapter 12:
© Dean Mitchell/iStock; © Darren Baker/iStock; © Andresr/iStock.

Chapter 13:
© Dr Heinz Linke/iStock; ©Anetta/Dreamstime.

Introduction

Sarah Earle and Elaine Denny

Teaching sociology to nurses has become a significant issue within health sociology, as reflected in the workshop 'Teaching Sociology to Healthcare Professionals in Training' at the British Sociological Association's Medical Sociology Conference in York in 2001, and in subsequence conferences and events. The essential skills clusters (ESC) of the Nursing and Midwifery Council (NMC, 2007) demonstrate the need for the twenty-first-century nurse to utilize knowledge from a range of disciplines when assessing patients/clients and deciding on an approach to care. Nursing is no longer (if it ever was) the sum of its tasks – or what nurses 'do' – but has become a complex set of relationships. Society has changed since the inception of the NHS, deference towards health professionals has lessened and individuals are more willing to challenge 'experts'. Professional boundaries are becoming less rigid, and many client groups are demanding a more active part in decision-making. The NHS itself has seen many reorganizations, and nurses, along with other health care workers, have had to adapt to changing structures and ideologies of health care.

The impact of these changes has been immense, and many nurses have found themselves at a loss to know how to prepare themselves for the new demands made of them. There are probably few nurses who would turn to sociology to provide answers, as it is a discipline frequently perceived to be not of direct relevance to nursing work. This book has, therefore, deliberately set out to demonstrate the usefulness of sociology by relating the concepts and theories of sociology and health policy to nursing practice, with examples from all four branches of nursing. The aim of the book is to provide an accessible sociological textbook on health, illness and health care based on the needs of pre-registration nursing courses. It is also of relevance to post-registration students on 'top-up' degree programmes, particularly those who are new to the study of sociology.

The book is divided into four parts:

Part I considers the contribution that sociological knowledge can make to the delivery of nursing care. It starts by introducing the key sociological theories and approaches that underpin many of the concepts discussed later in the book. It then turns to the frequently raised question of why nurses need to study sociology, and how a knowledge of these theories may make a difference to nursing practice. One of the tasks of sociology is to encourage us to apply a 'sociological imagination' to things we may take for granted; the concepts of 'health' and 'nursing' are explored here using just such an approach.

Part II explores diversity and inequality in health and health care, demonstrating the link between client groups and the structures of society. These structures will advantage some groups and disadvantage others, resulting in wide variations in the incidence and experience of morbidity and mortality. A continuing theme here will be the role of nurses in challenging inequality and becoming advocates for patients and clients. Confronting and questioning your own beliefs and values may be the result of engaging with the issues raised in this section.

Part III questions where care takes place, and, although the hospital is the visible face of the NHS, it is argued here that increasingly the location for health care is outside of institutions. Formal care in the primary and community care setting is providing a much wider range of services than ever before, and nurses are expanding their role in these settings, particularly within the fields of mental health and learning disability. The family has always been a major source of informal health work, although the relationship between the family, health and illness is a complex, and not necessarily a positive, one.

Part IV moves on to policy influences on health and health care, and considers the relevance of policy and management issues to nurses at all levels, not just those in senior roles, and the opportunity for nurses to engage in policy debate. The book finishes by moving outside of the NHS and direct patient/client care and introducing the reader to the crucial link between the environment and health, particularly the importance of housing.

The chapters are similarly structured and designed to enable you to reflect on the sociological issues raised and to relate them to nursing practice:

- each chapter begins with the key issues, giving you signposts on what to expect;
- learning outcomes enable you to assess whether you have understood and learned from what you have read;
- key terms are explained in the glossary boxes to aid understanding at a glance;
- there are activities to carry out with colleagues from your own, or different, branches of nursing, enabling reflection and encouraging you to relate theory to practice;
- at the end of each chapter there are summary points;
- to expand your knowledge, annotated further reading and questions for discussion are included at the end of the chapter;

- and there is also a website accompanying this volume, providing further reading, questions for discussion, and links to internet resources.

Once you have read this book, and engaged with the activities and discussion questions, we hope that you will feel equipped to use a sociological approach as one of your tools for formulating and delivering optimum nursing care. You may also wish to enter into the debates about the future of nursing and its place in determining health policy. Most of all you should be able to look beyond the simple explanations of everyday issues and problems to gain a deeper, more meaningful understanding.

References

NMC 2007: Mapping of Essential Skill clusters to the *Standards of Proficiency for Pre-Registration Nursing Education* (Annexe 3) (NMC 2004); www.nmc-uk.org [last accessed 15 December 2008].

Part I

Nursing and the Sociology of Health and Health Care

Sociology is not always easy to understand – even for sociology students – and its relevance to nursing, and nurses, is not readily apparent. There is considerable controversy regarding whether nurses should study sociology, and we have attempted to reflect this within part I of this book. Some commentators have suggested that sociology should not be included in the nursing curriculum, arguing that it can add no value to nurse education and training. Others have suggested that sociology is vital to nurse education and to the future of nursing as a profession!

Student nurses often ask 'Why do we have to do sociology?', and it is as a response to this question that we have written this book and, more specifically, chosen to include the chapters in this part. Each of these chapters examines key concepts and debates in relation to nursing and to the sociology of health and health care.

The first chapter, 'What is Sociology?', introduces you to key sociological approaches, concepts and theories. With this in mind, you may find it useful to start with this chapter, or to come back to it after reading the other chapters within this part. It begins by outlining the distinction between sociological knowledge and other forms of knowledge and considers the role of sociology within society. Sociology is often criticized as 'just common sense', and this chapter challenges this interpretation. It examines the distinction between social 'structure' and social 'action', outlining key sociological theories and their relevance to our understanding of health and health care. The chapter then explores methodological approaches and some of the research methods commonly used by sociologists to explore health and illness.

In chapter 2, we specifically address the question 'Why Should Nurses Study Sociology?' and explore the role of sociological knowledge within nursing practice. Following on from the discussion begun in chapter 1, this chapter examines how, far from being 'just common sense', sociology can help to develop a range of thinking skills which are vital to contemporary nursing. It highlights the problem of the 'theory–practice gap' and focuses on the sociology of nursing as well as the role of sociology in nursing. By drawing on a variety of empirical studies, the chapter explores the value of sociological knowledge to nurses. We also look at the importance of sociological research methods as both a tool for carrying out research and a resource for evaluating published research.

Nurses are involved in caring for people who are ill or dying, as well as in promoting health and well-being. Whichever is the case, understanding what being 'healthy' means is important – although it is a challenging task, to say the least. In chapter 3, 'What is Health?', we consider the range of ways that health has been defined, looking at 'social' definitions as well as the distinction between professional and lay definitions. Models of health are explored and, here, we contrast the biomedical model, which has been influential within medicine and health care, with the social model, which focuses on the social causes of disease. We consider the social construction of health and illness, examining how normal healthy processes become medicalized, and discuss the iatrogenic effects of medicalization on individuals and on society. The chapter also considers a more holistic approach to care within nursing and offers some sociological reflections on this.

Chapter 4, 'Nursing as an Occupation', provides a brief historical overview of nursing, mapping the development of nursing and nurse registration from the nineteenth century onwards. Just as other chapters within this section consider issues of definition, this one explores the debates which attempt to define what nursing is: is it an art or a science? We consider the process of becoming a nurse and the socialization of students into nursing. Following on from the debate identified in chapter 2, this chapter further highlights the tension of the 'theory–practice gap' within the socialization of student nurses. The gendered nature of nursing is considered together with the role and status of men within nursing. Power relations are explored and elitism within nursing and the relationships between nurses and other health care workers are considered. Drawing on the concept of emotion work, relationships between nurses and patients are also discussed.

What is Sociology?

Keith Sharp

Key issues in this chapter

- The nature of sociological inquiry and the role of sociology
- Sociology and 'common sense'
- An introduction to sociological theory
- An introduction to research methods

By the end of this chapter you should be able to . . .

- understand some of the debates concerning the role of sociology within society;
- recognize the distinction between sociology and 'common sense';
- discuss some of the different sociological theories;
- recognize the different research methods and understand the relationship between theory and method.

1   Introduction

Sociology is concerned, in the broadest sense, with the study of human society. As this implies, its scope is almost limitless: it is possible, in principle, to have a *sociology of* any activity in which human beings engage. Inevitably the sorts of things which have concerned sociologists have changed somewhat over time. The principal concerns of the 'founding fathers' of sociology, writing in the nineteenth century, were the major social, political and economic changes which had taken place across Europe since the late Middle Ages. Early sociological writing was dominated, for example, by attempts to chart and explain the rise of industrial capitalism, to explain the changing nature and role of religion in society and to understand the new forms which social and political institutions had taken since the Industrial Revolution (Giddens, 2001). Today, the concerns of sociologists have altered in ways which largely reflect the changing nature of society. Changing sexual attitudes and behaviours, changing gender relations, globalization, new communications technologies, changing patterns of criminality and social aspects of health and illness – the subject of this book – have all loomed large in recent sociological literature (see, for example, Letherby et al., 2008; Earle and Sharp, 2007; Sassen, 2007; and Nettleton, 2006).

There are a number of key questions and issues which lie at the heart of sociological inquiry, whatever the specific topic to which it is directed. The aim of this chapter is to introduce the most important of these. Before we do this it is important to make a few general points about the nature of sociological inquiry, and how it may differ somewhat from other disciplines. The remainder of this chapter is devoted to two main issues. The first is the range of what can be called 'theoretical debates' in sociology. We shall consider the main competing theoretical positions adopted by sociologists, and illustrate the implications of these different positions for the ways in which sociology can shed light on the nature of society and its institutions. An appreciation of these debates will be helpful in understanding many of the chapters which follow and in evaluating the contribution which sociology can make to nursing practice. The second issue is the methodological tools which are used in sociological research, and some of the debates which surround them. We shall introduce the main approaches to the conduct of sociological research and the controversies which surround these.

2   The nature of sociological inquiry

The first thing we need to note about the discipline of sociology is that it is characterized by diversity. Whilst in any discipline we will find a degree of disagreement between practitioners, this is especially marked in the case of sociology. Unlike disciplines such as chemistry or biology, sociologists disagree even over the most fundamental principles of how to go about their work. We shall examine some of these disagreements later in this chapter. What this means is that sociology cannot, in general, be used to 'solve' technical problems in the way that knowledge from other 'scientific' disciplines may be able to do.

Sociology and other disciplines

A second point worth noting about sociology is that many of the things it is concerned with are also of interest to researchers from other disciplines. It is therefore prone to 'boundary disputes'. A good example of this is the relationship between sociology and psychology. In broad terms it is possible to say that, whilst sociology is concerned with understanding *societies*, psychology is concerned with understanding *individuals*. But very quickly the value of this distinction starts to break down. Rather obviously, societies are made up of individuals and so it seems silly to suggest that societies can be understood entirely without reference to individuals. Let us take a concrete example. Sociologists often like to use the term socialization. However, the processes by which individuals are socialized seem fairly clearly to fall within the domain of psychology, and the whole subfield of learning has a great deal to say about this. Unfortunately, sociologists rarely seem to take much notice of the wealth of psychological literature which details the complexity of the socialization process; similarly, psychologists are often accused of failing to give proper attention to the insights of sociologists on the complex effects of wider social processes on individual learning.

socialization processes by which individuals acquire the roles, norms and cultures of society

The role of sociology within society

Finally, we should note that sociology must confront a particularly wide range of ethical issues. Not only must sociologists deal with the sorts of issues around the avoidance of individual harm in the course of conducting research which any human scientist must confront, but there are also a wider set of ethical concerns about the role of sociology in society. Is it the role of sociology, for example, to make recommendations about the kinds of social arrangements which are most desirable? Or should it, as the sociologist Max Weber argued, avoid such essentially political questions and focus, instead, on developing a neutral understanding of the social world, leaving questions of how society *should* be organized to politicians? As you will see from part II of this book, sociology has been particularly influential in identifying social inequalities in health. Is it the role of sociology to comment on the extent to which such inequalities *should* be eradicated (bearing in mind that even beginning to do so would entail massive costs which would have to be funded somehow) or should sociologists be content merely to describe and explain the extent of the inequality that exists?

Sociology versus 'common sense'

An often voiced criticism of sociology is that it is just 'common sense', and that sociologists do little more than state the obvious. So it is important to explain why sociology is, and must be, more than just common sense (see also chapter 2). The first point to make about this is that there is often more than one 'common-sense' view on any given issue. For some people it is just 'common sense' that the poor are poor because they are lazy, stupid and work-shy. For others, it is just common sense that poverty results from historical inequalities in society, and hence has nothing to do with individual attributes. Clearly both views cannot be correct, and so little will be gained in this case by relying on common sense. In fact the explanation of poverty is a highly complex example, which requires sophisticated sociological research and analysis (see chapter 8).

Similarly, 'common sense' often conceals positions of self-interest. It might be common sense for the rich to regard the poor as lazy, stupid and work-shy, but it seems most unlikely that such a view would be regarded as common sense by someone in poverty.

The role of sociology is to challenge the obvious, and to assess the evidence and arguments for and against any particular position which is advanced.

Genetically

3 Major theoretical debates in sociology

The aim of this section is not to provide you with a comprehensive summary of debates in sociological theory, but rather to highlight some of the most important and to sketch out their implications for how sociologists concerned with health and illness go about their work. The distinction between structure, on the one hand, and action, on the other, is fundamental to theoretical debates within sociology and these are discussed below.

structure organized patterns of social behaviour and the social institutions within society

action purposeful and conscious behaviour

Structural theories

A question often posed by sociologists is: what is society? Although this may appear rather simple at first sight, we can quickly see that it does in fact raise a number of different possibilities. One general view of society can be called structural. This view tends to see societies as systems of interconnected parts which influence each other in a variety of complex ways. The focus is less on the specific actions of individuals than on the roles which they occupy and the ways in which these roles relate to each other.

Let us consider the example of a hospital. A structural view of a hospital might focus, first of all, on how power and authority are distributed throughout the organization. At the top of the hospital (or in modern Britain the NHS Trust) might be a chief executive who has ultimate responsibility for the operational and strategic management of the hospital. The hospital's administration might be organized into a number of departments – human resources, finance, estates, etc. – each of which has a head, who is accountable to the chief executive and to whom staff of the department are responsible. The various clinical services provided by the trust will similarly be organized into units, with heads, each of whom will be responsible to the chief executive for the effective and efficient delivery of their own particular service.

role   the expected behaviours of holders of particular positions within society ◄

Within these structures individuals occupy a particular **role**. Notice that, in talking about roles, we are not talking about the individuals who occupy them. Take, as an example, the role of a consultant surgeon employed by an NHS Trust in a large metropolitan hospital. To a very significant extent, the behaviour and performance of any consultant surgeon employed in such a context will be substantially the same. The same job needs to be done, the same standard of professional performance is expected, even similar codes of dress and personal demeanour are expected (and usually found) amongst the individuals who occupy these roles. Plainly these similarities do not derive from essentially similar personalities just happening to find themselves in the same job; rather they derive from the expectations associated with the role in question.

We can see, too, that there are a variety of social mechanisms which tend to ensure that individuals conform to the expectations of the roles they occupy. Some of these are very formal. For example, it is an expectation (not unreasonable) that anyone occupying the role of consultant surgeon will take all reasonable steps to ensure that their patients are operated on in a safe and competent manner. If in a particular case a surgeon does not do this, then there exist various formal and legal sanctions which either ensure future conformity to this aspect of the role or remove the individual from that role altogether. Others are much more informal. For example, a surgeon who reports to work unshaven, unwashed and dressed in a dirty track suit will probably suffer the disapproval of his colleagues and superiors, which may or may not be enough to cause a change in behaviour before more formal sanctions are invoked.

The concept of role allows sociologists to think about societies and organizations within societies as having a life independent of the individuals who constitute them. In a very real sense, then, individual people, their hearts, minds and personalities, do not really figure in the sort of sociology that emphasizes structure. Hospitals, governments, prisons, families, or whatever, operate in the way they do, with the consequences they have, not because of anything to do with the individuals who constitute them, but because of the structures, rules and roles which define them.

'Structural' sociologists share a common view of how we should conceptualize society. Whilst at one level this is true, it is important to point out that there are a number of different approaches, exhibiting some quite fundamental differences, that fall under the general umbrella of structural sociology. We shall now consider two of these: functionalism and Marxism.

Functionalism   The origins of sociology lie in the nineteenth century, and no one was more significant in its development than the Frenchman Émile Durkheim (1858–1917). Although the term 'sociology' had been coined by the French philosopher Auguste Comte, it was Durkheim who established it as a serious academic discipline. It was, moreover, Durkheim who established the principles of the theoretical approach known as functionalism.

The starting point for Durkheim, and for functionalist sociology in general, is the idea that societies are complete systems and that their component parts cannot be viewed in isolation from each other. Sometimes an analogy with a living organism is used. Consider a dog. It is composed of various limbs, organs, connective tissues, etc. In itself, each of these constitutive parts does very little; it is only when they are all connected together to form an actual living dog that we can appreciate the functions of each part and, crucially, how each part contributes to the overall functioning and performance of the dog. For functionalists such as Durkheim, this is how we should view societies. We cannot take each part in isolation but rather need to consider each element of a society in relation to the whole.

Durkheim was fond of illustrating this point with seemingly unpromising examples. For example, in his classic text *The Rules of Sociological Method* (1964), he sought to illustrate that even crime – something we are accustomed to regarding as a social problem – makes a positive contribution to the overall functioning of society. Durkheim makes two important points about crime: first, that without crime (that is, the breaking of legally sanctioned social norms) there would be no innovation and societies would stagnate; second, that crime (and, importantly, its punishment) serves to heighten society's collective commitment to certain core values without which no society could exist. In other words, by punishing law-breakers, societies reinforce the boundaries of acceptable conduct and the commitment of their members to upholding these.

Although Durkheim had little to say about health care (he was, after all, writing at the turn of the twentieth century), later 'functionalist' sociologists have applied the idea of 'function' to various aspects of health and its management. Most famously, perhaps, was the work of Talcott Parsons (1902–79) on the 'sick role'. This is explored in more detail in chapter 3, but in essence Parsons argued that there was a socially defined 'role' which, in modern societies, individuals adopt when they become sick. The sick role has both rights and obligations attached to it: the sick individual has the *right* to refrain from work and other normal social duties, but also the *obligation* to seek appropriate medical advice and a speedy return to full health. For Parsons, this role – and, note, it is the *role* and not the individuals who occupy it – ensures the smooth functioning of society. Disease and ill-health are potentially disruptive to society, and so the existence of the sick role ensures that this disruption is kept to a minimum.

To what extent is ill-health socially constructed?

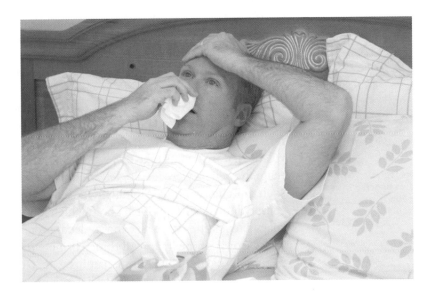

Whilst there is something very appealing about the functionalist view of the world, it is not without criticisms. First of all, by concentrating almost exclusively on the positive social functions of institutions and roles, functionalists such as Parsons have been accused of ignoring their negative or harmful consequences. For example, we might criticize the sick role by pointing out that in cases of chronic illness and disability, the adoption of this role discourages full participation in society and encourages dependency (see chapter 7). Similarly, the prestige and independence accorded to the medical profession might encourage the abuse of medical power and the exploitation of patients for personal gain. Functionalism tends to ignore conflict at all levels. Secondly, functionalism – like other structural theories – can be accused of playing down the degree of independence which social actors actually possess. They tend to be treated as 'pawns' in a larger game, and are assumed to be unable to alter social institutions or roles as a result of their own independent actions.

Marxism   A second structural theory within sociology is Marxism – named after its founder, Karl Marx (1818–83). If functionalism can be accused of understating the degree of conflict in society, the same cannot be said of Marxism. According to Marx, the starting point for social analysis was the inherent conflicts – economic in origin – which exist between social classes. For Marx, a social class is a group of people who share a common economic position. In all forms of pre-socialist society, Marx claimed, there were essentially two classes: those who owned the **means of production** and those who did not. Much of Marx's analysis concentrated on capitalist society. Under capitalism the two classes for Marx are the **bourgeoisie** and the **proletariat**.

means of production the means by which surpluses are extracted

bourgeoisie   those who own the means of production

proletariat   those who sell their labour

Marx claimed that the relationship between the two classes was inevitably exploitative. Wage labourers (the proletariat) generate more wealth for their employers than they are allowed to keep: in short, the rich get richer at the expense of the poor. For Marx, this relationship (part of the economic *infrastructure*) was fundamental to explaining the nature of society. For him, and his followers, the nature of the institutions and roles which make up a society can be explained with reference to these fundamental inequalities and their inherently volatile nature. Let us take the example of religion. For Marx, religious beliefs were **ideologies** and form part of the *superstructure* of society. Religion under capitalism (at least the sort of nineteenth-century industrial capitalism about which Marx wrote) stressed that social inequalities were just and, indeed, ordained by God. Just think of the words of the hymn 'All things bright and beautiful': 'The rich man in his castle, The poor man at his gate, God made them, high or lowly, And ordered their estate.' These words epitomize the ideological function of religion: it encourages the poor to accept their condition and to tolerate, graciously, the superior economic position of the bourgeoisie.

ideologies   system of ideas underlying social action

There have been many attempts to apply Marxist thought to the study of health and illness, for example, the theory of **commodification**. One such account is offered by McKinlay (1985), who suggests that, under modern capitalism, medicine, like any other good or service, has become commodified. In other words, medicine has become just another product which is bought and sold, and out of which significant profits are generated for those who own the means of production. Although McKinlay's analysis focuses on the

commodification   when economic value is given to something not previously ascribed any economic value

United States, where health care is explicitly provided primarily by the private sector, it may still have resonance in countries such as the UK where health care is provided principally by the state. One illustration of this is the way in which medical practice is influenced by the activities of the large pharmaceutical companies. It could well be argued that drugs are developed and marketed to medical practitioners not out of a sense of social responsibility, but primarily as a means of making profits – and pretty huge ones at that. Thus, the motivating factor for the development of a drug therapy is not *need* (or, arguably, far more research would have been done to develop drugs to combat diseases of the developing world) but the potential to generate profit. There is simply more money to be made from treating 'diseases' of the rich than diseases of the poor (see, for example, Williams, Gabe and Davis, 2009; Law, 2006).

It can be argued that the basis of drug discovery is making profit, not furthering our ability to promote and improve health.

PHARMACEUTICAL CONVENTION

" IF WE CAN'T CURE CANCER, OUR HOPE IS to AT LEASt TURN IT INto A LONG-TERM PROFITABLE DISEASE. "

Action theories

Both of the approaches considered above have in common the idea that wider social forces exert powerful influences on individual behaviour. Although there are stronger and weaker formulations of the idea, the essential assumption shared by structural approaches is that they seek to explain patterns of individual behaviour in terms of the location of individuals within wider social structures. It is perhaps not surprising, therefore, that some sociologists have criticized these approaches for underestimating the role of individual action in society.

One of the first sociologists to develop a critique of what he saw as the overemphasis on structural determinants of action was Max Weber (1864–1920). Weber's sociology is rich and complex and encompasses

Activity 1.1   The commodification of health

Read the case study below and then answer the questions.

Alison is a student nurse in her second year. She is currently on placement and has just finished a morning shift. Although she's exhausted she decides to pop in to her local health club for a swim before heading off home (she gets a specially discounted rate). After her swim, Alison remembers that there is almost nothing in the fridge, so she drives to the nearest supermarket to get some food. It's difficult to know what to buy; there are lots of offers. She buys – amongst other things – some yoghurts and margarine which promise to 'lower cholesterol', some cereal bars packed with 'all 9 essential amino acids', and some bread which claims to be 'medium GI' and 'low in fat'. She also buys a newspaper and a women's magazine. She sets off home and does some work on her next assignment before preparing something to eat. Later that evening, she switches on the television to wind down and watches a programme on celebrity diets. She picks up the magazine that she bought earlier that day and skims through it; there are lots of adverts for teeth whitening, eye laser treatment and cosmetic surgery. Eventually the programme ends, Alison puts down her magazine and goes up to bed.

(a)   Drawing on the case study, make a list of the different ways in which health can be described as commodified.

(b)   Do you agree that health and medicine have been commodified?

(c)   Who benefits from the commodification of health?

a recognition that human beings do not act merely in response to wider social forces, but rather for conscious reasons and towards certain purposes. At its simplest it was not enough, for Weber, to say that events occur because social structures ordain them; instead he was concerned to understand how individuals come to see the world in such a way that they voluntarily choose a particular course of action. To capture the importance of this dimension, Weber used the term *Verstehen*, which translates, approximately, as 'empathetic understanding'. This means, in essence, that, to gain a full understanding of an individual's action, we must look at the world from their point of view and, as it were, step into their shoes. This approach is evident in Weber's analysis of the origins of capitalism (Weber, 1958). Unlike Marx, who saw capitalism as the inevitable outcome of an economically driven process, Weber insisted that it was essential to put oneself in the shoes of the early capitalist entrepreneurs and to try to understand how their view of the world differed from those which had gone before. By doing this, Weber develops a theory of how a particular interpretation of the world – that of the early Calvinist Protestants – led to patterns of behaviour which resulted, eventually, in the emergence of capitalism as an economic system.

Taking patients' actions at face value can lead to limited and one-dimensional nursing practice. What value might there be in the concept of *Verstehen*, or stepping into a patient's shoes to understand fully the reasons for their actions?

Symbolic Interactionism   Whilst Weber was responsible for sensitizing sociologists to the need to account for social action from the point of view of the actor, it was a group of philosophers and sociologists from the University of Chicago who developed a major theory of social action which became known as *symbolic interactionism*. Undoubtedly the most significant figure in the development of this approach was George Herbert Mead (1863–1931).

The starting point for Mead's analysis was his recognition that human beings are fundamentally different from animals, not only because their behaviour is more complex, but because it is of a fundamentally different kind. Take a simple example. If a man kicks a dog, the response of the dog is predictable. It may be that the dog's previous experiences will influence its response, and that, because of this, all dogs will not react in exactly the same way. Nevertheless, the essential feature of its response is that it is predictable and, in a genuine sense, automatic. Now imagine that you are standing at a bus stop and someone walks up to you and kicks you. How will you react? Your immediate reaction might be to say you would kick them back, but a moment's reflection will reveal that the situation is more complicated than this. In fact your reaction will be influenced by a wide range of factors. Who kicked you? If it was your best friend, you might assume either that it was intended as a prank, or perhaps that you had upset them and the kick was intended maliciously. Which you choose will depend on a further set of factors: what is the expression on their face, was the kick accompanied by any words, are there any background circumstances which might explain their anger with you, etc.? If the kick was from a stranger, then a whole new set of factors will need to be considered before you can decide how to react. The point is that, unlike the dog – who reacts automatically – a human being can, and indeed must, *choose* how to react. And, in making that choice, they must place themselves in the position of the kicker and interrogate their motives. We ask the question: why did that person kick me? Only when we have done that do we select a course of action, and, as this example illustrates, that could vary from laughter, if we decide it was a prank by a friend, to extreme fear and panic, if we decided it was an assault by a malicious stranger. This contrasts very sharply with the reaction of the dog, which is completely oblivious to the point of view of its attacker.

Mead (1934) describes this process as *taking the role of the other*. Human beings do not merely react to situations in automatic and predictable ways (as both functionalists and Marxists might be accused of assuming) but rather *interpret* situations and select courses of action according to this interpretation. For Mead this is because we possess a social *self*. Mead's concept of self has two parts: the *I* and the *Me*. Although this idea is rather abstract, in essence it is quite simple. Think of the *Me* as the public part of yourself, which you place on display to others, and the *I* as the private part, which is accessible only to yourself. Now think about how you choose a course of action: what you are going to wear to an interview for example. You imagine yourself in your pinstripe suit, or your floral dress, and imagine how others will react to you. In other words, your *Me* has a 'conversation' with your *I* and, on the basis of taking the role of the other, you choose a course of action which suits your goals.

Activity 1.2   **Taking the role of the other**

(a)   Describe what is meant by 'taking the role of the other'.

(b)   Is taking the role of the other important to the provision of good nursing practice? What role does it play in developing reflective practice?

(c)   How easy is it to take the role of the other when nursing children, people with mental health problems or people with learning disabilities?

What all of this means is that symbolic interactionists tend to reject theories which see human beings as passive pawns in the play of wider social forces. Rather they are concerned with understanding how people interpret situations and how these interpretations influence their future conduct. It should be obvious that this approach introduces a significant element of uncertainty in our understanding of human action: indeed, for interactionists, human conduct is to a large extent unpredictable.

In summary, sociology is often described as multi-paradigmatic; this means that there are many different competing sociological explanations. Sociological theories are generally divided into theories of social structure, such as functionalism, or theories of social action, such as symbolic interactionism. The other chapters within this book will introduce you to some other important sociological theories, and it is worth remembering that all theories are concerned with the relationship between structure and action. For example, see chapters 5 and 11 for a discussion of feminist theories, chapter 6 for theories of ageing, chapter 7, which focuses on disability theory, and chapter 9, in which you will find a theoretical discussion of 'race' and 'ethnicity'.

Activity 1.3   **Nursing: menial and mundane?**

If nursing involves anything more complex than the most menial of tasks, and if nurses enjoy any sort of decision-making capacities independent of medicine, then they require . . . knowledge on which to base their decisions about what sort of actions they should be taking, and when they should be taking them. In other words, nurses require a theoretical grounding for their actions. This, of course, says nothing about the sort of theory that should underpin nursing practice, specifically whether or not sociology is an appropriate theoretical source . . . The point to be made at this stage of the argument is that, given that nurses deal with a myriad of different people and a multiplicity of problems, using various, often complex methods, it is inconceivable that they would be capable of making informed decisions about care if they were not in possession of some sort of overarching model of their professional activity. In short, given the nature of their job, it is axiomatic that nurses require theoretical knowledge of some sort . . . The deprecation of nursing as mundane work is often articulated by identifying it as 'women's work' . . . nothing more than a public extension of private domestic labour, which in itself is seen as requiring little thought or skill. (Porter, 1995, p. 1131)

(a)   Do you agree with the position expressed by Porter?
(b)   Should nurses just know how to do things or should they also understand the theory behind what they are doing?
(c)   Do you think that sociology can provide nurses with the theoretical underpinnings for practice?

4   Methods of sociological research

It is important to emphasize that the theoretical debates in sociology which have just been introduced have implications for how sociologists try to explore the social world and, indeed, for the kinds of 'facts' which they assume can be discovered. Whilst we cannot directly map a particular theory onto a method of research, we can nevertheless say that different theories lead much more naturally to one method than to another. There are various ways in which we can classify methods of sociological research, but probably the most helpful is to distinguish between quantitative and qualitative approaches.

Quantitative research

As the name suggests, quantitative research methods are those which concentrate on measurement. There are many different things which sociologists can try to measure. An obvious example is 'health', and this can be approached in a variety of ways. One way is to rely on data which are routinely collected by governments, such as public records of deaths. At its simplest (and this is essentially how much research on inequalities in health is carried out) we count the number of deaths per 1,000 of the population, and compare death rates between different social groups. The numerical differences between groups then become the facts for sociologists to explain. Of course, we must be careful with this, because, although the data are likely to be very reliable, we might question the extent to which merely being alive is equivalent to 'health'!

We might also choose to measure such things as 'attitudes' and behaviour. Commonly, attitudes are measured using *questionnaires* or *surveys* which ask respondents to place their response to various statements on a scale ranging from one extreme to another – these are called *Lickert* scales (see box 1.1). Although this is a quick and

---

Box 1.1	A Lickert scale

Lickert scales are used in surveys and usually contain between three and nine categories, although five categories is the most common.

To what extent do you agree with the following statement?

I enjoy learning about the sociology of health.

Strongly agree	Agree	Undecided	Disagree	Strongly disagree
(1)	(2)	(3)	(4)	(5)

efficient method of gathering large amounts of data, we might question the extent to which the way in which someone responds to such a statement reflects how they would actually behave.

Behaviour can be measured either directly or indirectly. Direct measurement refers to actual *observations* of behaviour (see for example Hutchinson and Johnston, 2008). For example, a researcher interested in nurse–patient interaction might simply count the number of interactions which take place between a particular group of patients and a nurse over a set period of time. The researcher may be present for this – in which case their presence may affect the behaviour of the nurse and patients – or it could be done using covert recording equipment. Although this is likely to give a more accurate picture, it does raise the ethical question of whether researchers *should* observe behaviour without the knowledge of those they are observing. Such studies also tell us very little about the *quality* of the interactions which take place. In the UK, health research, especially that involving NHS patients and staff, is regulated by a Research Governance Framework to ensure that it is conducted to the highest ethical standard (see box 1.2). England, Northern Ireland, Scotland and Wales each have their own Research Governance Framework (see www.dh.gov.uk). Behaviour may also be measured indirectly, for example by relying on accounts given by respondents through self-completed questionnaires or structured interviews (interviews in which a limited range of possible answers is offered to the interviewee) (see Blaxter, 1990). Although such an approach would allow us to explore aspects of behaviour which are not usually directly observable – such as an individual's pattern of drinking alcohol or smoking – the reliability of such responses may need to be questioned. Merely because an individual admits to drinking between 15 and 20 units of alcohol a week, it does not follow that they actually do! It would consequently be unwise always to assume that quantitative data gathered in this way is necessarily a faithful representation of how people actually behave.

Qualitative research

An alternative approach, which has a close affinity with social action theories, is to obtain qualitative data. Here the emphasis is not upon measurement, but rather on attempting to understand the world from the point of view of social actors. Qualitative researchers use a variety of data collection techniques but are generally united by their concern to understand the meanings which underlie the behaviour of those they study. For example, a qualitative researcher interested in nurse–patient interaction would be unlikely to want to count the number of interactions which take place, but rather would be interested in discovering what the interactions mean to both parties.

Activity 1.4   **A national survey on young patients**

Table 1.1 draws on data from the 2004 Patient Survey Report on young patients. This survey was carried out in 150 NHS acute and specialist trusts, and 62,277 young patients took part.

Table 1.1 Patient Survey Report on young patients

	National average (%)		
	Yes	Sometimes	No
Did nurses give you the patient information about your care and treatment in a way that you could understand?	64	29	7
Did doctors give you the patient information about your care and treatment in a way that you could understand?	57	33	10
While you were in hospital, did nurses give you emotional support and comfort when you needed it?	60	30	10
Did nurses talk in front of you as if you were not there?	3	12	85
Did doctors talk in front of you as if you were not there?	5	18	77
In your opinion, were there enough nurses on duty to care for you in hospital?	64	29	7
Were you given enough privacy when you were being examined or treated?	80	16	4

Source: Adapted from Healthcare Commission, 2004, pp. 28–33.

(a)   What does the table tell you about young patients' experiences of health care?

(b)   What do you think might be the advantages of using a survey method of data collection? What are the disadvantages of this method?

(c)   What sort of data would emerge if qualitative methods were used and how would they differ from the data presented above?

This is because, from a social action point of view, it is these meanings which explain the actions of those involved.

There are a number of ways in which qualitative researchers attempt to understand the points of view of social actors. First there is *interviewing*. Qualitative researchers tend to employ either semi-structured interviews or unstructured interviews (for example, see O'Baugh et al., 2008). The first of these employs a predetermined

Box 1.2   **Research governance**

- Sets out principles, requirements and standards;

- Defines mechanisms to deliver them;

- Describes monitoring and assessment arrangements;

- Improves research and safeguards the public by:
  - enhancing ethical awareness and scientific quality
  - promoting good practice
  - reducing adverse incidents and ensuring lessons are learned
  - preventing poor performance and misconduct;

- Is for all those who:
  - design research studies
  - participate in research
  - host research in their organization
  - fund research proposals or infrastructure
  - manage research
  - undertake research;

- Is for managers and staff, in all professional groups, no matter how senior or junior;

- Is for those working in all health and social care research environments, including:
  - primary care
  - secondary care
  - tertiary care
  - social care
  - public health.

Source: Department of Health, 2005, p. v.

list of questions which is put to each respondent and the second is based more loosely on a general set of issues. In both cases, the interviewer asks open-ended questions and allows the respondent to answer in his or her own words. In both cases, too, the interviewer can respond to the answers given and ask additional or supplementary questions as appropriate. These forms of interviewing are more akin to a guided conversation than anything else, and the object is to allow the respondent to explore an issue or topic as it affects them. The intention is to allow the respondent's own emphases to come to the surface and for the researcher to grasp the world from the respondent's point of view. Thus, in the case of nurse–patient interaction, a researcher might ask a patient simply: 'How do you find the nurses here?', and allow the respondent to talk freely about the things that are important to them.

Qualitative researchers also sometimes employ *participant observation* (see, for example, Allan, 2006). This means, essentially, that the researcher participates in the activity being studied in order to grasp it from the point of view of those involved. Participant observation may be either overt – in which the researcher's identity as a researcher is made known to all concerned – or covert – in which they conceal their identity. An overt participant observer interested in nurse–patient interaction might come to work on a particular ward as a nurse, and make observations from that standpoint, but only after declaring their research activity to their colleagues and patients. A covert observer might enter a ward posing as a patient, and observe the activity from that point of view. Clearly, the former runs the risk of influencing the behaviour of those they are studying. Conversely, whilst the covert observer might obtain a more faithful view of events, the ethical issues alluded to above are once again raised.

methodological pluralism   use of more than one method of data collection

Some researchers use what is called **methodological pluralism**. This approach recognizes that each method of data collection has its own strengths and weaknesses, and it can be used to build a fuller picture of social life (for example, see Lehna and McNeil, 2008). Whether one adopts a quantitative or qualitative strategy, or both, it is important that social researchers pay attention to issues of representativeness. Most research is carried out on samples, and, on the basis of data collected from a sample, generalizations are made to a wider population. A researcher who observes interactions between Nurse Jones and Mrs Smith, Mr Jenkins and Miss Shepherd will want to say something general about the relationship between nurses and patients, not merely about these four particular individuals. It is important, therefore, that in some sense the interactions observed are shown to be typical of interactions of that kind – or, if they are not, how they differ from the typical should be explained.

Activity 1.5   **Nursing and sociological research methods**

(a)   Consider the research issues below and think about which research methods you might adopt to explore these.

Children's perceptions of going into theatre
The housing needs of people with mental health problems who are being discharged from hospital
Patients' views of hospital food
Student nurses' perceptions of people with learning difficulties

(b)   Think of other research issues and identify which research methods you would use to investigate them.

So, whilst there are many research methods available to social researchers, the methods chosen, and whether they are quantitative or qualitative, will depend upon the theoretical approach that has been adopted. The internet has also opened up other opportunities for social research (for example, see Hine, 2005). In the following chapter you will be able to explore the role of sociological research within nursing in more depth (see, in particular, part IV).

Summary and Resources

Summary

- Sociology is concerned with the study of human societies.

- Sociology is distinct from 'common sense' because it challenges the obvious and assesses evidence for and against any position taken. However, there is debate concerning the role of sociology within society. That is, should sociologists simply report what they see or should they be concerned with changing the social world around them?

- Research methods are generally described as either quantitative – which include methods such as questionnaires – or qualitative – which include semi-structured or unstructured interviews and participant observation.

- The choice of sociological research methods depends largely upon the theoretical approach adopted by the researcher.

Questions for Discussion

1 Should sociologists develop neutral understandings of the social world or should they seek to influence change?

2 Next time you are on placement, ask yourself, 'What is going on here?' Describe what you are doing, or seeing, and then try to explain it.

3 What do you think are the main advantages and disadvantages of adopting methodological pluralism?

Further Reading

A. Bowling: *Research Methods in Health: Investigating Health and Health Services.* 2nd edn, Buckingham: Open University Press, 2002. This is a popular book which will guide you further in understanding research methods as applied to health and health care services.

S. Earle and G. Letherby (eds): *The Sociology of Healthcare: A Reader for Health Professionals.* Basingstoke: Palgrave, 2007. This is an excellent collection of readings exploring many aspects of the sociology of health care, including: sociological theory; sociological research; inequalities and diversity; the body and the mind; and power and professional practice.

A. Giddens: *Sociology.* 6th edn, Cambridge: Polity, 2009. This is a comprehensive sociological text which explores a wide range of useful topics. It is well illustrated and easy to read.

References

Allan, H. T. 2006: 'Using participant observation to immerse oneself in the field: the relevance and importance of ethnography for illuminating the role of emotions in nursing'. *Journal of Research in Nursing*, 11(5), 397–407.

Blaxter, M. 1990: *Health and Lifestyles*. London: Tavistock Routledge.

Department of Health 2005: *Research Governance Framework for Health and Social Care*. 2nd edn, London: HMSO.

Durkheim, E. 1964: *The Rules of Sociological Method*. New York: Free Press.

Earle, S., and Sharp, K. 2007: *Sex in Cyberspace: Men who Pay for Sex*. Aldershot: Ashgate.

Giddens, A. 2001 [1971]: *Capitalism and Modern Social Theory*. Cambridge: Cambridge University Press.

Healthcare Commission 2004: *Patient Survey Report, 2004: Young Patients*. London: Healthcare Commission; www.healthcarecommission.org.uk [last accessed 14 August 2008].

Hine, C. 2005: *Virtual Methods: Issues in Social Research on the Internet*. Oxford: Berg.

Hutchinson, A. M., and Johnston, L. 2008: 'An observational study of health professionals' use of evidence to inform the development of clinical management tools'. *Journal of Clinical Nursing*, 17(6), 2203–11.

Law, J. 2006: *Big Pharma*. London: Robinson.

Lehna, C., and McNeil, J. 2008: 'Mixed-methods exploration of parents' health information understanding'. *Clinical Nursing Research*, 17(2), 133–44.

Letherby, G., Williams, K., Birch, P., and Cain, M. (eds) 2008: *Sex as Crime*. Cullompton, Devon: Willan.

McKinlay, J. B. (ed.) 1985: *Issues in the Political Economy of Healthcare*. London: Tavistock.

Mead, G. H. 1934: *Mind, Self, and Society: From the Standpoint of a Social Behaviourist*. London: University of Chicago Press.

Nettleton, S. 2006: *The Sociology of Health and Illness*. 2nd edn, Cambridge: Polity.

O'Baugh, J., Wilkes, L. M., Luke, S., and George, A. 2008: 'Positive attitude in cancer: the nurses' perspective'. *International Journal of Nursing Practice*, 14(2), 109–14.

Porter, S. 1995: 'Sociology and the nursing curriculum: a defence'. *Journal of Advanced Nursing*, 21(6), 1130–5.

Sassen, S. 2007: *A Sociology of Globalization*. London: W. W. Norton.

Weber, M. 1958: *The Protestant Ethic and the Spirit of Capitalism*. New York: Charles Scribner's Sons.

Williams, S., Gabe, J., and Davis, P. 2009: *Pharmaceuticals and Society: Critical Discourses and Debates*. Oxford: Wiley-Blackwell.

2 Why Should Nurses Study Sociology?

Barbara Green and Sarah Earle

Key issues in this chapter

- The difference between sociology in nursing and sociology of nursing
- The value of developing sociological skills
- Using sociological skills in nursing practice
- Sociological knowledge: policy, practice and change

By the end of this chapter you should be able to . . .

- discuss the reasons why nurses should study sociology;
- understand the distinction between sociology of nursing and sociology in nursing;
- understand the value of sociological skills;
- discuss the role of sociological knowledge and the future of nursing practice.

1 Introduction

As your experience in clinical practice develops you will come across patients with a wide range of concerns and from a diversity of social backgrounds. The main aim of this chapter is to demonstrate the practical relevance of sociology to nursing, and to explore how sociology may provide you with exciting new ways with which to understand the needs of your patients.

The next section discusses conceptual differences between sociology in nursing and sociology of nursing. Section 3 focuses on the cognitive skills that an appreciation of sociology may encourage, enabling you positively to shape and influence practice. Section 4 draws on empirical studies to demonstrate

cognitive relating to thinking processes

the role of sociology in exploring social issues in health and the social worlds of patients, nurses and other health care workers. The final section addresses the role of sociological knowledge in policy, practice and the future of nursing.

2   Sociology in nursing and sociology of nursing

There are two main types of sociological knowledge relevant to nurses: one is identified as sociology in nursing and the other as the sociology of nursing. Each type of knowledge has the scope to enable the 'ordinary' day-to-day work of nurses to be seen in a different light; it is this alternative perspective which is characteristic of sociology. Sociology encourages us to view everyday phenomena in a different way. It is like being given a new pair of glasses. This is sometimes referred to as problematizing; that is, what at first sight might seem unremarkable becomes problematic. More will be said about this later, but first let us turn to the distinction between sociology in and of nursing.

phenomena   states or processes that can be observed

problematizing   looking beyond the obvious to seek an explanation

Sociology can be defined most simply as the study of 'human social life' (Giddens, 2006, p. 4) (also see chapter 1 for a further discussion of defining sociology). A sociological approach to nursing locates the work of individual nurses squarely within a social context rather than considering it in isolation. In general terms, when a sociological analysis is applied to the essence of individual health care experience, whether it be that of patients or health care workers, this is termed 'sociology in nursing'. 'The sociology of nursing' usually refers to issues affecting the profession as a whole, such as its occupational status, or recruitment and attrition problems (see chapter 4 for further discussion of nursing as an occupation). The role of sociology in relation to nursing is continuously debated within the literature. However, as Pinikahana (2003) has argued, the most important thing to remember is that sociology is only relevant to nurses if it is *applied* to nursing.

3   Sociology: helping develop skills

Is sociology just 'common sense'?

It is important to clarify exactly how a knowledge of sociology can be of value to practising nurses. Can sociology be described as 'just common sense'? Let us consider what sociology does have to offer nursing practice.

In her treatment of the question, Hannah Cooke (1993, p. 215) describes sociology as an 'emancipatory discipline'. By this she means that nurses need to be self-critical and to question the long-held assumptions of the profession. This may seem difficult in the light of your limited practical experiences, or an unfamiliarity with academic study. Although 'training' still has a valuable part to play in nurse education, for example in the learning of practical skills such as aseptic or injection techniques, it is important to distinguish between this and the acquisition of a higher education, of which the study of sociology is an example. It is argued by Ross (1981), for example, that the concept of learning in education, as opposed to training, is characterized by discovery and transformation of thought, which suggests personal growth and a radical shift in previously held beliefs and values. Ellis (1992) describes this as a 'personal education'. Arguably, any academic discipline in its authentic form is a valuable experience for students on vocational courses, but classical authors of sociology, notably Wright Mills (1959) and Berger (1963), would argue that the subject holds a unique fascination and distinctiveness.

Learning practical skills such as taking blood are central to becoming a nurse – but is this the limit of nursing?

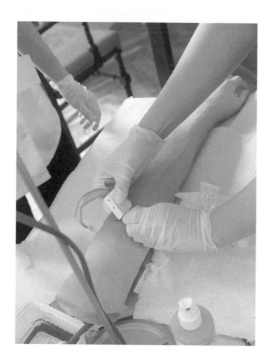

Activity 2.1

Sociology *in* nursing or sociology *of* nursing?

Read Items A and B and answer the questions below. Item A is an extract from a study exploring the views of district nurses who work with clients who misuse substances. Item B is an extract from a study exploring the emergence of professional identity amongst nurses.

Item A   All the district nurses drew upon a discourse of 'risk' rather than 'need' when describing working with clients who misuse substances. This is illustrated in the following accounts, which emphasize the aggressive behaviour of clients. While participants acknowledged that this is a result of drug dependency, it is constructed as a risk to the service provider, rather than considering the drug dependency to be problematic or harmful to the client:

> 'From the experiences that we've had, it can be sort of the aggression. The aggression that can come if they're not getting the drugs that they want, or they're not getting the treatment. We've experience that firsthand up here and that is quite daunting, quite scary. And for us going in to visit people on our own.'
> 'There was one chap who wanted a dressing doing at one stage, and we didn't know he had a drug problem at the time. I went in as a first visit, as a one-off they wanted me to go there and then. So I went, but on getting there, it wasn't really the dressing he wanted doing, it was some methadone he wanted. So I felt very vulnerable in that position because he was quite aggressive. So then we went in twos after that, even though it didn't really warrant it once he'd settled down. But I think the stigma was there and it was, "We'd better go in twos just to be on the safe side."' (Peckover and Chidlaw, 2007, p. 241)

Item B   The most extensive sociological examination of nursing is found in the literature on professions, which has sought to answer the question of whether nursing is a profession by locating it in an occupational hierarchy based on education, self-regulation and autonomy. Here, nurses have been primarily compared to physicians as the model for a classic professional. Researchers have found that nursing has historically sought to achieve an occupational identity by upgrading skills, increasing educational credentials, recruiting from the middle class, and establishing licensing requirements to regulate practice, thus leading many to grant it a professional status. As the most common strategy to advance their professional standing, nursing education and training has moved from apprenticeships in the hospital to university programs. . . . The establishment of academic programs emphasizing science, theory, and research has served to validate a core body of knowledge by which nursing claims institutional recognition. (Adapted from Apesoa-Varano, 2007, p. 250)

(a)   Identify whether items A and B portray sociology in nursing or sociology of nursing and explain why.

(b)   What type of sociology most interests you and why?

Wright Mills (1959, p. 7) coined the term 'sociological imagination' to describe his particular view of the sociological enterprise in his classic work of the same name. What he meant by this is the ability to shift one's thinking from one perspective to another, or possession of a certain quality of mind, open to different interpretations of phenomena. This can also be applied to the difference between education and training. As previously stated, we do need elements of training in nurse education, but there is an often quoted saying that 'dogs can be trained to jump through hoops', referring to the fact that people can be trained to do tasks without really having to think very much about them. The consequences of this in nursing can be, and have been, disastrous.

Conversely, the possession of this difference in quality of mind and approach to practice, when transferred into appropriate action by nurses, will arguably ensure the evidence base for practice required by the profession. But, more than this, it represents an approach to practice, underpinned by critical thinking, analytic and questioning skills, which is crucial to achieve the 'new futures for nursing' envisioned by Cooke (1993, p. 215) and supported by government initiatives and reports (for example, see DH, 2006, 2008b).

So, what are these new futures likely to be? Why do nurses always seem to come 'back to basics'? What are the essentials of nursing care and do you need a degree to give a bedpan? The following subsection will demonstrate how knowledge of sociology can help you in addressing such questions.

Activity 2.2   **Sociology and 'common sense'**

(a) Explain your understanding of the term 'common sense'. Do you think that sociology is 'just common sense'? How useful is this term when talking to patients?

(b) Imagine a patient experiencing quite severe wound pain two days post-operatively following a cholecystectomy (gall bladder removal). Leaving aside the intervention of prescribed analgesia, what kind of social influences do you think might affect this person's reaction to pain?

(c) 'It is the capacity of sociology to take nurses temporarily "out of nursing" that represents one of its strongest attributes' (Mulholland, 1997, p. 850). What do you think that Mulholland means by this statement?

Nursing skills and reflective practice

Arguably, the development of reflective practice can bridge the theory–practice gap and there is a wealth of literature suggesting that sociology can play an important role in the development of reflective skills within nursing (see for example Aranda and Law, 2007).

However, all of this relates to the broader question of what nursing is and how it might be defined. This is at a time when policy changes from both the government (DH, 2000, 2002b, 2006) and professional bodies (RCN, 2008) indicate trends which lead away from the identification of 'hands-on' care as important, in terms of both status and financial reward. It is not a new issue: Christine Hancock (1991, p. 174), then the general secretary of the Royal College of Nursing, suggested that, 'If qualified nurses are content to delegate the heart of their role to others, they should not be surprised if they are supplanted in the workforce'. This reflects a legitimate concern about the future of nursing, reiterated by Castledine (1998, p. 225), who argued that nurses should 'not become the technical substitutes of physicians'.

The changes in 'core' nursing tasks are attributed to increased patient turnover, a shortage of qualified nurses, the present system of nurse training, and the fact that nurses are being constantly encouraged to take on more tasks currently carried out by doctors. Contemporary policy documents (DH, 2006, 2008a, 2008b) appear to reflect this latter scenario (see box 2.1), yet it is highly questionable how far such apparent merging of traditional professional boundaries is in the best interests of future nursing practice and, ultimately, the care of patients.

It is worth considering the question of why, despite the promotion of holistic care in nurse education for decades, nurses sometimes persist in attaching more importance to those aspects of care underpinned by medical science than to those influenced by social,

paradigms systematic and coherent bodies of knowledge ◄ cultural, psychological, spiritual and emotional **paradigms** of knowledge (this is discussed further in chapter 4).

Box 2.1	**Vision of the future of the registered nurse**
Role of nurses	• Practitioners, partners and leaders at the heart of care, coordinating multidisciplinary teams and resources, across care settings and agencies.
	• Carers, advocates, and managers of care pathways, working in partnership with patients.
	• Influence and credibility from point of care to boardroom.
	• Accountable for quality of nursing care, and an accountable partner in the whole patient experience.

Values and mindsets	• Clarity about, and commitment to, the values of the profession: integrity, compassion, continuous improvement, advocacy and partnership working.
	• Continually challenging and improving care quality and championing patient experience.
	• Pride in the work of nurses and ambition for nursing as a profession.
	• Confident innovators, keen for our contribution to be demonstrated.
Careers	• Respected, socially valuable profession offering inspiring, rewarding and fulfilling careers.
	• Degree-level education and training, balancing practice with theory, with continuous career development.
	• Flexible, personalized career paths across practice areas and fields (practice, academia, practice development, management).
Public perception	• Highly qualified, competent professionals with relevant experience and expertise.
	• Conscientious, competent, safe, compassionate, care-focused and patient-orientated.

Source: DH, 2008a, p. 6.

Activity 2.3 **The 'stark reality' of care?**

Few care processes are more complex than terminal care of the distressed, incontinent elderly patient. When I and my loved ones are sick or dying, I want our nurses to be caring, patient and tolerant – and well-educated into the bargain. But perhaps most policy-makers have not experienced such situations and cannot imagine why a trained intellect is crucial, even when wiping a bottom. (Salvage, 2001, p. 21)

(a) Can you think of other examples of what Salvage describes as the 'stark reality' of hands-on care?

(b) Why do you think that Salvage uses this term?

(c) Do you agree that a trained intellect is crucial, even when wiping a bottom?

A routine blood glucose test: however, further information can be gained by empathetic understanding on the nurse's part to consider why a patient's diabetic control might be poor, thus leading to better solutions.

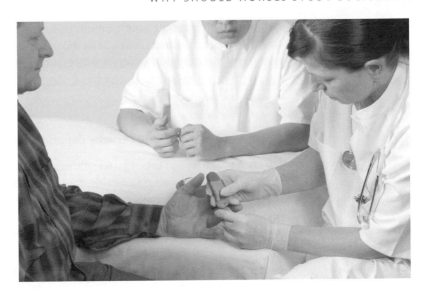

4 The role of sociological knowledge

The aim of this section is to illustrate the value of sociological knowledge and the role it plays in examining the realities of nursing practice. Recognizing the significance of an evidence base within modern nursing, this section draws on a range of empirical studies, all of which have something to tell nurses about their relationships with patients, informal carers and other health professionals, or about their role in the workplace. Building on the discussion of research methodologies presented in chapter 1, the two specific themes addressed below are:

1 in what ways sociological methods can be adopted within nursing research;
2 why an understanding of sociological research methodology will aid nurses to interpret the validity and reliability of published research.

A key feature underpinning sociological research methods is the idea that things may not be what they seem. As Berger (1963) suggests, you are 'looking behind', or 'seeing through' and generally unmasking the common façades of everyday life. As Earle (2001) argues in her discussion of the role of sociology within the therapies, sociologists take the everyday and the taken-for-granted and try to look beyond obvious explanations to gain a deeper understanding of contemporary social issues.

Ellis (1992) attempts to integrate knowledge from various academic disciplines with the theory and practice bases of interpersonal professions. Following on from his discussion of a 'personal education', his model of 'semantic conjunction' can also be useful. In application to nursing, this term simply suggests that the subject matter of sociology is useful to nurses because sociologists and nurses share some common interests and concerns. Nowhere is this more clearly illustrated than in the piece of classic sociological research – described in Jeffery's 'Normal rubbish' (1979) – a study based on interviews with doctors and observation of three English casualty departments.

Perceptions of patients in casualty departments

Jeffery's study has as much to tell nurses, doctors and anyone working with vulnerable or health-compromised individuals about the truth of their work today as when it was published. It provides insight into perceptions of patients and demonstrates at best a lack of care, and at worst the wholesale neglect of and infliction of (further) damage on certain groups of patients. Via a process of social construction, particular patients became categorized by doctors as 'normal rubbish' (see box 2.2). This is a good example of an interactionist approach to research (see chapter 1), in which individual actions are subject to scrutiny.

social construction   the way in which social reality is constructed by individuals and groups

---

Box 2.2   **'Normal rubbish'**

Trivia
Patients who 'casually' pop into casualty with conditions neither traumatic nor urgent are described as 'normal trivia'. They trivialize the emergency services by presenting with conditions which should be taken to the GP.

Drunks
'Normal drunks' are abusive and usually appear in the middle of the night. If they are brought in unconscious, normal drunks are often kept in as it is unclear whether they are sleeping off the drink or whether they have received a blow to the head.

Overdoses
A 'normal overdose' is usually female and perceived as a self-harmer rather than as a 'genuine' suicide. She is usually a regular and 'does it for attention'.

Tramps
'Normal tramps' smell and wear layers of rotten clothing. They usually come in during the night in winter and are just trying to find a bed for the night. They often pretend to be sick in order to achieve this.

(Other patients defined as 'normal rubbish' include 'nutcases', and smelly, dirty and obese people.)

Source: Jeffery, 1979, pp. 106–7.

Significant for the sociological study of nursing is that although Jeffrey confined his interviewing to doctors, it is made clear that other staff working in the department – such as nurses and porters – were in a process of collusion with the medical staff about the way these particular patients were viewed. It is shown in the following comment made by a porter to a doctor after a person identified by the department staff as a 'tramp' was seen in the casualty department and discharged by the doctor. A short time later he collapsed and died outside on the pavement. In order to allay the worries of the doctor concerned, the porter says: 'It's alright, sir, I've turned him round so that it looks as though he was on his way to Casualty.' This seminal piece of sociological research, which so clearly demonstrates the interface between sociology and nursing, has a tremendous amount to say to nurses.

Before the results of published research can be used as evidence for practice it must be scrutinized in an informed way for reliability and validity – terms which will become more familiar and

seminal research is seminal if it has a determining influence on sociological thought

reliability research is reliable if it can be repeated to produce the same results

validity research is valid if it measures what it has set out to measure

---

Activity 2.4

Normal rubbish: deviant patients in casualty departments

In Jeffery's study (1979), 'rubbish' was a category generated by the staff themselves. It was commonly used in discussions of the work and of the patients seen within the casualty environment:

'It's a thankless task, seeing all the rubbish, as we call it, coming through.'

'I wouldn't be making the same fuss in another job – it's only because it's mostly bloody crumble like women with insect bites.'

'I think the [city centre hospital] gets more of the rubbish – the drunks and that.'

(a) It is clear from this research that nurses working in the casualty department shared the same attitude towards some patients as the doctors. If twenty-first-century nurses are educated to underpin their practice with theory, which specific aspects of the latter do you consider that the nurses of 1979 might not have been aware of?

(b) The full title of the article appears at the top of this extract. In what sense do you think that some patients are identified by the author as 'deviant'?

(c) It is clear from Jeffrey's study that some patients are regarded as 'legitimately sick' while others are not. How do you think this impacts on the concept of 'holistic' assessment and care within contemporary nursing?

meaningful to you in the future. For now, you are strongly advised to consolidate your knowledge by reading – or re-reading – chapter 1 and perhaps carrying out some further reading on research methods of your own.

The remainder of this section continues the theme of exploring the realities of nursing work by focusing on more contemporary sociological research (but, for a more recent study of 'problem patients', see the work by Shaw, 2004, who explores attitudes to patients with psychiatric diagnoses). Some comparisons between the studies will be self-evident as the chapter progresses, and it is not the remit here to focus on them, but rather to identify and emphasize the value of sociological knowledge for practising nurses.

Researching the experiences of clients with learning difficulties

Richardson (2000) explores the social context of people with learning difficulties by interviewing six people living in nurse-managed community homes over a period of eighteen months (group living is discussed further in chapter 13). Drawing on the social model of disability, which is discussed at length in chapter 7, he asks three questions (p. 1384):

1   What do people with learning difficulties, living in the community, have to say about their lives and experiences?
2   What are their views about the differences between their lives and those of non-disabled people?
3   How do disablist assumptions influence the lives of people with learning difficulties and nursing practice?

The significance of this research undoubtedly lies, in part, in its inclusion of people with learning difficulties as participants, thereby reversing the stereotypical notion that 'People corralled within the frame of learning difficulties are deemed incompetent, unable to adequately speak for themselves, and thus requiring care, protection and treatment' (Richardson, 2000, p. 1384).

As well as giving nurses valuable insight into participants' views, the research reflects current policy initiatives for people with learning difficulties which are based on the principles of rights, independence, choice and inclusion. It is a useful illustration of the way that sociological research methods can be used by nurses to explore the experiences of specific client groups, enriching the practice base of nurses and others (for another interesting study on end-of-life care and people with learning difficulties, see the study by Todd, 2009). The concept of research validity is implicit in Richardson's work through his focus on autobiographical voice.

autobiographical voice methodological approach which allows participants to tell their own stories

Whereas the two articles explored so far have addressed the experiences of patients or clients, the next takes a broader perspective and explores the role of nurses in the workplace, and their relationships with other health care workers.

Relationships between nurses and health care assistants

A study by Daykin and Clarke (2000) explores the relationships between nurses and health care assistants (HCAs) in the NHS. It is based on interviews in two English hospital wards providing medical care for older adults. A sociological account of nursing is given in which various perspectives are brought to bear on aspects of the individual nursing role and the profession as a whole.

The research was carried out to evaluate a new skill-mix project which increased the number of HCAs in proportion to registered nurses and simultaneously phased out the role of primary nurses. The aim of the research was to discover what impact the project had on the staff in relation to care delivery and working conditions.

The research identified a dichotomy between professional rhetoric and professional practice (Holt and Warne, 2007) – that is, what nurses *should* do and what *really* happens in practice. Despite nurses heralding the concept of holistic care as reflecting best practice, the researchers found that, in the context of the new skill mix described above, a hierarchical division of labour emerged between the two groups. This resulted in care organization by selectivity of work and task allocation. Box 2.3 outlines some of the key findings.

Box 2.3   **Rhetoric vs reality**

Perceptions of the skill-mix project

- a threat to the holistic delivery of care;

- detrimental to the quality of care;

- a threat to the ability to apply sophisticated skills of assessment and analysis.

Realities of the skill-mix project in practice

- staff shortages and resource constraints prevented skill-mix teams;

- qualified nurses worked below their actual skill levels;

- a hierarchical division of labour emerged.

Source: Daykin and Clarke, 2000, pp. 353–4.

The exposure of some of the realities of nursing practice necessarily suggests that the registered nurses did not want to deliver the essentials of hands-on care in keeping with the philosophy of primary nursing and holistic care delivery, but rather that, when faced with the realities of financial constraints, staffing shortages, and so on, there is a clear theory–practice gap.

From these observations, the authors provide significant insights into the perceived value of nursing's professionalization project, described by the authors as an attempt by nurses to 'renegotiate their relationship with the state and secure greater recognition and professional status' (Daykin and Clarke, 2000, p. 349). A key factor in this has traditionally been the claim to a distinct knowledge base from which to develop theoretical models of holistic care, professional autonomy, the selection and ownership of higher-status technical skills, and the scope to renegotiate role boundaries between nursing and doctoring.

Taking up this issue, Daykin and Clarke suggest that, given the current social context for care, where the likelihood is that nurses and HCAs will continue to do a significant proportion of the 24-hour, round-the-clock work, the profession might serve itself better by adopting an inclusive rather than a hierarchical 'outgroup' attitude towards this group of co-workers. Not only would this help to preserve the knowledge and ownership of nursing care for nurses, but it would also acknowledge the crucial contribution to care made by health care assistants.

A further useful insight to emerge from this research is that, although the two groups were generally united in their opposition to the skill-mix project, a range of 'multiple and apparently contradictory viewpoints' (Daykin and Clarke, 2000, p. 353) was expressed about respective workplace roles; health care assistants were, on the whole, far more enthusiastic than the nurses. Daykin and Clarke attribute this again to the dichotomy between ownership of a perceived appropriate theoretical stance for nursing and the social reality of the care context, steeped as it is in day-to-day issues of staff shortages, economies of scale and financial stringency. Using a structural analysis, they suggest that a possible effect of this apparent disunity of ideas and purpose (expressed in the article as 'ambivalence') is that it represents potential for exploitation by managers if perceived as a weakness of nursing systems. Likely manifestations could be (further) imposition of routinized, ritualistic, deskilled, task-based work systems onto hospital staff in direct contradiction to the concept of professional autonomy so prized by some sections of the contemporary nursing workforce.

Daykin and Clarke (2000) challenge some of the existing premises on which current nursing practice is based and make an invaluable contribution to the sociology of nursing. For example, they explore issues that have the potential to raise awareness of professionalization among practising nurses; such awareness is a prerequisite for the necessary action to achieve future changes, which will ultimately improve the experiences of both patients and health care workers (also, for an interesting study on the relationship between operating theatre nurses and operating department practitioners, see Timmons and Tanner, 2004).

5 Sociological knowledge: policy, practice and change

The final section of this chapter considers the role of sociological knowledge in achieving change through policy and practice. The idea of change is perhaps daunting to those of you as yet unfamiliar with many aspects of the nursing role, yet today it is endemic to health care – the pace is relentless and the future likely to be characterized by increasing complexity and paradox (UKCC, 1999; NMC, 2005). In this chapter the significance of sociological knowledge and its unique capacity to expose areas of both nursing practice and policy where positive change might be achieved has been emphasized, but important questions remain about how far this fundamental truth is likely to be either recognized or acted upon. The issues are considered here as a critical future challenge to you as students of nursing on the threshold of dynamic and fulfilling careers.

Being a student nurse

The role of a student nurse is often not easy; Wakefield (2000) has explored some of the tensions. The 'old-school' traditional structural hierarchy of sister, staff nurse, enrolled nurse and nursing auxiliary, where student nurses at least had the security of a clearly defined role, has been replaced by an alternative system in which students and HCAs compete for authority, status and knowledge – a situation at times characterized by discord and friction (ibid.). Qualification is not likely to herald the disappearance of these conflicts, as the anomalies between the latter group and qualified nurses described by Daykin and Clarke (2000) demonstrate.

In this context, then, what price change? As inexperienced practitioners in the nursing environment and in relation to clinical competency, you may feel relatively powerless within practice settings (see Bradbury-Jones, Sambrook and Irvine, 2007), a less than ideal situation from which to think about the possibilities for practice and policy change in relation to sociology. The fact that the issues *are* raised here, however, clearly presupposes critical thinking skills and reflects a protracted debate in nurse education about the relative merits of theory and practice in the curriculum, and how they should be organized.

The role of sociology

The problem of theory–practice integration in the nursing curriculum is particularly pertinent in relation to sociology. One reason for this is that sociology is concerned with the exposure of key issues such as health inequalities. Not only do these have a detrimental effect on individual health care, but they may be constructed and maintained at an institutional level and subject to covert structural processes of which individual practitioners may be unaware. It is useful here to return to Wright Mills (1959), who argued that the sociological imagination is at its most effective in making the distinction between personal troubles and public issues, the idea that what may appear to be an individual phenomenon is actually highly determined by social structures. This is demonstrated to very good effect in chapter 7. Consequently it can be argued that the crux of the sociological enterprise for nursing should be a focused concern with the concept of power and power relations at all levels of health care practice, an area where nurses have traditionally been invisible.

All this implies that, in order for nurses to use sociological knowledge effectively both in nursing and at the broader policy level, a more overtly political focus and agenda for the inclusion of sociology in the nursing curriculum is required. My guess is that this may be immediately problematic to some students in terms of their own current values and beliefs about educational requirements for nursing, and it is worth thinking at this stage how comfortably (or not) these ideas about sociology sit with your own views as novice practitioners. Clifford (2000), in her discussion of international politics and nurse education, suggests that, although issues of politics, power and control have been of concern to nurses, there has, to date, not been a framework in place to integrate one with the other. Important questions of direction and focus remain, as professional boundaries become blurred and traditional roles disappear.

Nursing – the future

Meeting the physical, psychological, social, cultural, emotional and spiritual needs of others, often at times of their greatest vulnerability and distress, has been misnamed the 'dirty work' of nursing (for example, see Shaw, 2004). Arguably, this 'dirty work' is, in fact, a privilege, and yet it is precisely these uniquely caring aspects of nursing which seem currently to be under threat.

The structural location of nurse education in universities, its dance with academia, professionalizing agendas and new role developments coterminous with interdisciplinary working (DH, 2006, 2008a) should not be allowed to detract from the core humanistic value of care on which nursing has historically been built. This is in the context of increasing numbers of medical tasks being undertaken by nurses, arguably at a cost to true role *expansion* as opposed to mere extension by default. Encouragingly, there is now some evidence that the argument 'while there is much to be gained from humanizing medicine, there is nothing to be gained from medicalizing nursing'

(Farmer, 1995, p. 794) is being recognized at policy level (RCN, 2008). Acknowledgement in the NHS job evaluation scheme, Agenda for Change, that 'emotional effort' – or emotional labour – is assessed as one of sixteen factors to determine revised pay scales is significant (DH, 2002a). Indeed there is a considerable body of sociological work focusing on the emotional labour carried out by nurses and other health professionals. Drawing on the groundbreaking work of Hochschild (1983), writers such as James (1992) – who writes about nursing – and Hunter (2001) – who writes about midwifery – argue that providing emotional support to patients and families is very skilled work. However, emotion work is not always recognized, and sometimes nurses can feel ill-equipped to meet the emotional needs of patients, particularly at times of acute distress or following bereavement.

emotional labour
regulation of one's own and other people's feelings

Emotional labour, such as setting patients' minds at ease or consoling patients in distress, is a definite skill that needs to be carefully developed.

If in the future nurses are to develop the critical awareness and analytic skill that will prepare them for action to rescind this situation, there has never been a greater need to embrace sociology as a means of illuminating their unique position for determining and influencing the overall quality of health care, practice and policy. As stated earlier, it is an issue of power relations; this is the stance taken by Clifford (2000), arguing that in an age of globalization nurses need to think politically, beyond their own boundaries of practice and towards becoming the key health policy makers of this century (also see Davidson et al., 2003). Sociology has a great deal to contribute to the knowledge base for this role expansion in nursing, but it is also a truism that 'nursing as knowledge remains unrevealed to many people' (Hegyvary, 2003, p. 104), and this is where we return to the perennial issue of nursing definition. There have been many books and policy documents

Activity 2.5   Nursing and emotional labour

Read the case study and then answer the questions below.

Laura was a student midwife on a busy labour ward. She arrived on duty one afternoon for a late shift to discover that there had been a stillbirth and that the baby's mother was critically ill following a post-partum haemorrhage. She had just been transferred to the intensive care unit. The staff members on duty were quiet and subdued by the traumatic events of the delivery. The family were still in the visitors' room on the labour ward and had requested to see the baby. Laura's first job was to wash and dress the baby and take her to the family. She had been asked to do this because she was a trained counsellor and she agreed.

As she washed and dressed the baby, Laura talked to her and then took her to meet the other members of her family. There were four people in the room, the baby's father, grandmother and grandfather and an aunt. Laura said, 'Hello, I have brought the baby to meet you', and lifted the baby girl out of the cot to show her to them. The baby's grandmother stepped forward and took her in her arms. Laura asked the family if they wanted to be alone with her and they nodded agreement, and she left them for half an hour before returning to see if they needed anything. She noted that the family had returned the baby to her cot and were sitting in silence. With their consent, she took the baby from the room, telling the family that they could see her at any time while she was in the hospital. They asked to be taken to the intensive care unit and Laura allocated another member of support staff to go with them.

Laura returned the baby to the small treatment room where she was being kept prior to transfer to the hospital mortuary. One of the midwifery managers entered the room and spoke to Laura. On seeing her, Laura burst into tears. The manager reached out and touched Laura's arm. Laura apologized and explained that she had not realized how distressing this would be – it was her first experience in caring for a woman who was experiencing stillbirth. The midwifery manager said, 'That makes no difference, it never gets any easier.' Laura found this very comforting.

When Laura reflected on this later she knew that she had felt confident that she would be able to respond sensitively to the needs of the family and therefore was not afraid of having to find the 'right' words. However, in the whole of her training as a nurse, and so far in midwifery, she had not received any professional development in bereavement care. Without her own development in this area she would have continued to feel unqualified to help.

Source: Komaromy et al., 2007.

(a) How does Laura engage in emotional labour?
(b) Reflect on your own practice experiences and consider how, when and to whom you provide emotional labour.
(c) Do you always feel equipped to provide for the emotional needs of patients or clients?

addressing the question of how nursing is to be defined, but it will all remain at the level of paper, policy and a superficial political correctness unless nurses are prepared to *act powerfully* to reclaim their professional role in the delivery of essential, humanistic care. It must be professional nurses who, first, identify these unique elements of best practice and, second, exert the power and influence to control the resources necessary to claim and deliver it.

Summary and Resources

Summary

- The difference between education and training is identified, as is the role of sociology in facilitating the development of reflexivity in nurses.

- The 'sociological imagination' can enable nurses to move beyond common-sense explanations to the development of a more critical approach to nursing practice.

- Sociological research and research methods are useful for nurses both in conducting their own research and in being able to evaluate research to help inform evidence-based practice.

- Nurses can use sociological knowledge as a means of empowerment and to help determine the future of the profession for the advantage of patients.

Questions for Discussion

1 In Jeffery's (1979) study, good patients were defined in terms of their medical characteristics and whether they fulfilled at least one of the following criteria:

   (a) they allowed the doctor to practise the skills necessary for passing exams;
   (b) they allowed the doctor to practise his/her speciality;
   (c) they tested the doctor's competence and maturity.

   Reflect on this and consider the extent to which nurses and other health care workers categorize patients in this way.

2 Do you agree with Daykin and Clarke (2000), amongst others, who argue that there is a discrepancy between nursing practice and professional rhetoric?

3 Try to identify other sociological studies and explore the contribution they make to your nursing practice in particular, and to nursing as a profession more generally.

Further Reading

There is continuous debate in the literature on whether nurses should or should not study sociology. You may be interested in reading around this debate and, if so, you might like to look at one or more of the following.

H. Cooke: 'Why teach sociology?' Nurse Education Today, 13(3) (1993), 210–17; **K. Sharp: 'Why indeed should we teach sociology? A response to Hannah Cooke'**, Nurse Education Today, 15 (1995), 52–5; **S. Porter: 'Why teach sociology? A contribution to the debate'**, Nurse Education Today, 16(3) (1996), 170–4; **J. Mulholland: 'Assimilating sociology: cultural reflections on the "sociology in nursing" debate'**, Journal of Advanced Nursing, 25(4) (1997), 844–52; **D. Allen: 'Review article: nursing and sociology: an uneasy marriage?'** Sociology of Health & Illness, 23(3) (2001), 386–96; **K. Aranda and K. Law: 'Tales of sociology and the nursing curriculum: revisiting the debates'**, Nurse Education Today, 27(6) (2007), 561–7.

References

Apesoa-Varano, E. C. 2007: 'Educated caring: the emergence of professional identity among nurses'. Qualitative Sociology, 30, 249–74.

Aranda, K., and Law, K. 2007: 'Tales of sociology and the nursing curriculum: revisiting the debates'. Nurse Education Today, 27(6), 561–7.

Berger, P. 1963: Invitation to Sociology: A Humanistic Perspective. London: Penguin.

Bradbury-Jones, C., Sambrook, K. S., and Irvine, F. 2007: 'The meaning of empowerment for nursing students: a critical incidence study'. Journal of Advanced Nursing, 59(4), 342–51.

Castledine, G. 1998: 'The future of specialist and advanced practice'. In G. Castledine and P. McGee (eds), Advanced and Specialist Nursing Practice. Oxford: Blackwell, pp. 225–32.

Clifford, C. 2000: 'International politics and nursing education: power and control'. Nurse Education Today, 20, 4–9.

Cooke, H. 1993: 'Why teach sociology?' Nurse Education Today, 13, 210–16.

Davidson, P. M., Meleis, A., Daly, J. and Douglas, M. 2003: 'Globalisation as we enter the 21st century: reflections and directions for nurse education, science, research and clinical practice'. Transcultural Nursing, 15(3), 162–74.

Daykin, N., and Clarke, B. 2000: '"They'll still get the bodily care." Discourses of care and relationships between nurses and health care assistants in the NHS'. Sociology of Health & Illness, 22(3), 349–63.

DH (Department of Health) 2000: The NHS Plan. London: HMSO.

DH 2002a: Agenda for Change. London: HMSO.

DH 2002b: Delivering the NHS Plan: Next Steps on Investment, Next Steps on Reform. London: HMSO.

DH 2006: Modernising nursing careers – setting the direction. London: HMSO.

DH 2008a: *Framing the Nursing and Midwifery Contribution: Driving up the Quality of Care*. London: HMSO.

DH 2008b: *High Quality Care for All: NHS Next Stage Review Final Report*. London: HMSO.

Earle, S. 2001: 'Teaching sociology within the speech and language therapy curriculum'. *Education for Health*, 14(3), 383–91.

Ellis, R. 1992: 'An action-focused curriculum for the interpersonal professions'. In R. Barnett (ed.), *Learning to Effect*. Buckingham: Open University Press, pp. 69–86.

Farmer, E. 1995: 'Medicine and nursing: a marriage for the 21st century?' *British Journal of Nursing*, 4(14), 793–4.

Giddens, A. 2006: *Sociology*. 5th edn. Cambridge: Polity.

Hancock, C. 1991: 'Support workers in the UK'. *International Nursing Review*, 38(6), 172–5.

Hegyvary, S. T. 2003: 'Foundations of professional power'. *Journal of Nursing Scholarship*, 2, 104.

Hochschild, A. R. 1983: *The Managed Heart: Commercialization of Human Feeling*. Berkeley: University of California Press.

Holt, M., and Warne, T. 2007: 'The educational and practice tensions in preparing pre-registration nurses to become future health promoters: a small exploratory study'. *Nurse Education in Practice*, 7, 373–80.

Hunter, B. 2001: 'Emotion work in midwifery: a review of current knowledge'. *Journal of Advanced Nursing*, 34(4), 436–44.

James, N. 1992: 'Care = organisation + physical labour + emotional labour'. *Sociology of Health & Illness*, 14(4), 489–509.

Jeffery, R. 1979: 'Normal rubbish: deviant patients in casualty departments'. *Sociology of Health & Illness*, 1(1), 90–108.

Komaromy, C., Earle, S., Foley P., and Lloyd, C. 2007: 'Reproductive loss and the moment of death'. *Practising Midwife*, 10(7), 27–30.

Mulholland, J. 1997: 'Assimilating sociology: critical reflections on the "sociology in nursing" debate'. *Journal of Advanced Nursing*, 25, 844–52.

NMC (Nursing and Midwifery Council) 2005: *Assuring Fitness for Practice. A Policy Review commissioned by the Nursing and Midwifery Council Nursing Task and Finish Group*. London: NMC.

Peckover, S., and Chidlaw, R. G. 2007: 'Too frightened to care? Accounts by district nurses working with clients who misuse substances'. *Health and Social Care in the Community*, 15(3), 238–45.

Pinikahana, J. 2003: 'Role of sociology within the nursing enterprise: some reflections on the unfinished debate'. *Nursing and Health Sciences*, 5(2), 175–80.

RCN (Royal College of Nursing) 2008: *Nursing Futures, Future Nurses*. London: RCN.

Richardson, M. 2000: 'How we live: participatory research with six people with learning difficulties'. *Journal of Advanced Nursing*, 32(6), 1383–95.

Ross, S. 1981: *Learning Discovery*. London: Gordon & Breach.

Salvage, J. 2001: 'New year revolution'. *Nursing Times*, 97(1), 21.

Shaw, I. 2004: '"Dirty work" patients and "revolving doors"'. *Qualitative Health Research*, 14(8), 1032–45.

Timmons, S., and Tanner, J. 2004: 'A disputed occupational boundary: operating theatre nurses and operating department practitioners'. *Sociology of Health and Illness*, 26(5), 645–66.

Todd, S. 2009: 'The absence of death and dying in intellectual disability research'. In S. Earle, C. Komaromy and C. Bartholomew (eds), *Death and Dying: A Reader*. London: Sage, pp. 245–51.

UKCC 1999: *Fitness for Practice: Report of the Commission for Education*. London: UK Central Council for Nursing, Midwifery and Health Visiting.

Wakefield, A. 2000: 'Tensions experienced by nurses in a changed NHS culture'. *Nurse Education Today*, 20(7), 571–8.

Wright Mills, C. 1959: *The Sociological Imagination*. London: Oxford University Press.

3 What is Health?

Sarah Earle

> **Key issues in this chapter**
> - Defining health
> - Models of health
> - Social influences on health and disease
> - Experiences of illness, sickness and disease
> - Nursing, health and holism
>
> **By the end of this chapter you should be able to . . .**
> - review official and lay definitions of health;
> - compare and contrast the biomedical and social models of health;
> - give an account of how health and disease are influenced by social factors;
> - understand illness behaviour, sickness and stigma;
> - evaluate a holistic approach to nursing practice.

1 Introduction

Did you know that poorer people will die sooner and suffer more ill-health than those who are wealthier? Did you know that women are more likely than men to be diagnosed with mental illness, and that older and disabled people are the two groups in society most likely to be refused life-saving treatment? Arguably, these facts are social rather than biological, and, although the majority of sociologists would not deny the biological nature of disease, most would agree that our understanding, treatment and experience of health and ill-health are socially influenced. Sociologists would also agree that the production and distribution of disease are social, rather than biological, matters. The purpose of this chapter is to explore how sociology can help us to understand health better, taking as its foundation the position put forward by Turner, who argues that health and ill-health are 'fundamentally a social state of affairs' (1995, p. 37).

2 Defining health

It may seem easy, but defining health is actually quite hard. Before you read on, think about what health means to you. Is your definition of health the same as that of your colleague? Kelman has argued that 'perhaps the most perplexing and ambiguous issue in the study of health since its inception centuries or millennia ago, is its definition' (1975, p. 625), but defining health is essential if we are to understand it and deliver appropriate services. It is an important issue for nurses because, to help the patient achieve health, nurses should have some understanding of the factors that contribute to 'healthiness'.

Official definitions of health

Health is often defined quite simply as an 'absence of disease'. This has been one of the most pervasive official definitions of health in the modern Western world and is one that can be frequently found within medical documentation, government reports and legislation.

Do you believe that this is a good way of defining health? How does it compare with your own definition? Health as an 'absence of disease' is also the cornerstone of the biomedical model – discussed in more detail below – which, in spite of its limitations (Barbour, 1995), is the most influential model of health within modern medicine. To describe health in this way is to define it in extremely negative terms; that is, you are considered healthy only if you are not suffering from any disease. However, research suggests that, just as it

worried well individuals ◄— is possible to feel unwell when one is healthy (for a discussion of the
who are otherwise
physically and mentally
healthy but are concerned
about their health and
well-being

'worried well', see Weatherhead and Lawrence, 2006), it is possible to feel healthy even when suffering from chronic or terminal illness (for example, see Falk, Wahn and Lidell, 2007).

Another commonly used definition is that of the World Health Organization, which defines health as 'not merely the absence of disease, but a state of complete physical, mental, spiritual and social well-being' (WHO, 1948, p. 1). This marks a shift away from defining health solely in relation to disease and reflects an acceptance of some of the other factors that influence health. It also reflects a more positive, although idealistic, approach to health. Here, health is perceived as a goal. Lupton has suggested that this overriding concern with health has reached the proportions of a

healthism   a personal, cultural and political health movement

⬅ social movement which she calls **healthism**, arguing that 'the pursuit of health has become an end in itself, rather than a means to an end' (1995, p. 70).

More recently health has been defined as a resource:

> To reach a state of complete physical, mental and social wellbeing, an individual or group must be able to identify and to realize aspirations, to satisfy needs, and to change or cope with the environment. Health is, therefore, seen as a resource for everyday life, not the objective of living. Health is a positive concept emphasizing social and personal resources, as well as physical capacities. (WHO, 1986, p. 1)

As you can see, here health is still regarded as a positive concept; however, rather than being an end in itself, it is seen as a resource for living, a means to an end.

Lay definitions of health

Although sociologists are interested in unpacking official definitions of health, in the last twenty-five years or so sociologists have become

lay definitions of health beliefs based on individual experience or folk knowledge, as opposed to 'official' or medical definitions of health

⬅ interested in understanding **lay definitions of health** and have attempted to demonstrate how an understanding of lay definitions can be useful for health professionals. This approach has been influenced by theories of social action (see chapter 1), which are concerned with the meaning that individuals give to their own experiences. Official, or medical, definitions are thought to be based

universal and generalizable knowledge knowledge assumed to be common

⬅ on **universal and generalizable knowledge** in scientific terms, whereas lay definitions are thought to be unscientific and based on individual experience. Although our own health beliefs are 'unscientific', they are essential to the way in which we make sense of health and illness, and, indeed, the very subjective nature of health has led some researchers to argue that lay definitions are the only valid measure of health. Williams and Popay (1994) suggest that lay definitions of health and illness are organized in the following way:

1   they do not mimic medical views;
2   they are logical and coherent;
3   they are biographical (based on lived experience);
4   they are culturally framed within particular systems of belief.

One of the most comprehensive studies of lay health in the UK is the Health and Lifestyles Survey (Blaxter, 1990), involving 9,000 individuals. This survey asked individuals the following questions: (1) Think of someone you know who is very healthy. Who are you thinking of ? How old are they? What makes you call them healthy? (2) At times people are healthier than at other times. What is it like when you are healthy? An analysis of responses to these questions revealed ten major lay concepts of health (see box 3.1).

Activity 3.1   **Lay 'experts'?**

It seems reasonably clear (from where we stand now) that during the latter stages of the 20th century medical practitioners have been required to be more clearly and openly accountable to lay assessment and more sensitive to patient viewpoints than had previously been the case . . . These trends are undoubtedly related to the operation of other, wider, forces that have led to a challenge on the expertise of professionals. Thus medicine – as with so many other forms of professional activity – has been confronted by something of a legitimation crisis. . . . [There has been] an increased interest in what lay people have to offer by way of knowledge of health and illness [and] there has been a tendency to argue that lay knowledge can be every bit as valuable as professional knowledge. . . . patients can have extensive knowledge of their own lives and the conditions in which they live . . . they can (and sometimes have to) turn themselves into experts in order to challenge medical hegemony. . . . [However,] for the most part, lay people are not experts . . . What is more they can often be plain wrong about the causes, course and management of common forms of disease and illness. (Prior, 2003, pp. 42–5)

(a)   Do you think that nurses are accountable to lay assessment and sensitive to patient viewpoints?

(b)   Does the concept of the 'lay expert' apply equally to all groups of patients (e.g. patients with learning disabilities or mental health problems, or children). If not, try to explain why this is the case.

(c)   How and why might the expertise of health professionals be challenged? Have you ever felt that your expertise has been challenged by patients? If so, how did this make you feel?

Box 3.1   **The Health and Lifestyles Survey: lay concepts of health**

Health as not ill
You are healthy when you do not have any symptoms of disease. This is a concept popular amongst people of all ages, but particularly older people, and is most likely to be used to describe others.

Health as absence of disease/health despite disease
A definition focusing on disease and drawing on a medical model of health, most commonly used by those who described themselves as feeling healthy despite disease.

Health as a reserve
The idea that someone is healthy due to an inborn reserve of health.

Health as behaviour
A healthy person was often defined in terms of their healthy behaviour, and the phrase was most likely to be used to describe the behaviour of others.

Health as physical fitness
The concept of fitness was most commonly referred to by men of all ages, although young men tended to stress strength and the ability to play sports. Young women rarely mentioned sports but often mentioned being (or feeling) slim.

Health as energy
Having energy, vitality and enthusiasm was seen by women and older men as important.

Health as a social relationship
This concept was particularly important to women, who saw health in terms of having good relationships with others or the ability to help other people.

Health as function
This refers to being able to carry on with everyday tasks and was often used to describe a man. It was also used to refer to older people who could get along despite advanced age.

Health as psycho-social well-being
This category often included some of the other concepts of health, such as health as energy, or health as social relationships. However, some individuals saw health purely as a state of mind.

Negative answers
A small group of respondents were not able to define being healthy. Most of these were not interested in 'healthy behaviour'.
(Adapted from Blaxter, 1990)

Lay definitions of health are variable and are, generally speaking, often dependent on factors including age, gender, disability, and so on (see part II). Activity 3.2 asks you to consider children's definitions of health.

3   Understanding models of health

Models of health offer nurses different ways of thinking about health and how they might offer care to patients. These models differ because they identify distinct causes of illness, sickness and disease and therefore offer different suggestions for the prevention of ill-health. In this section we examine the biomedical and the social models of health.

Activity 3.2   **Understanding children's perceptions of health and ill-health**

Drawing courtesy of Maria Perry, aged 9

(a)   Drawing techniques are often used as a research method when exploring children's perceptions of health and illness. What does the picture above tell us about children's views of what makes us healthy and unhealthy?

(b)   What are the implications of this for nursing children?

(c)   In what other ways could nurses encourage children to discuss their experiences of health and illness?

The biomedical model

The present system of medical knowledge within modern Western societies is commonly known as the biomedical, or medical, model. This model is characterized by several features (see box 3.2).

The biomedical model has been and, some would argue, still is dominant within modern Western health care. However, this perspective is not without its critics. Blaxter (1990), for example, argues that the medical model of health does not always focus narrowly on biomedical science and that more holistic concepts of health are also part of medical practice. Nonetheless, there are many who believe that a biomedical model is outmoded and unhelpful and that it acts as a 'strait-jacket' for thinking about nursing care (Allott and Robb, 1998; Engebretson, 2003).

In response to this, alternative models of health have emerged. The next model we consider here is the social model, which identifies the role of social factors in the production and distribution of disease.

Box 3.2   Characteristics of the biomedical model

- Health is the absence of disease, and disease is the absence of health;

- Illness can be reduced to disordered bodily functions within the individual;

- Health services treat sick and disabled people largely within specialisms (e.g. paediatrics, obstetrics, podiatry, etc.);

- Health services are remedial and curative;

- Each disease is thought to be caused by a specific (potentially identifiable) pathogen, often leading to an overreliance on pharmacological intervention;

- The production of medical knowledge via the use of 'scientific' research methods is valued over the use of qualitative research methodologies;

- Health professionals are the 'experts' with the power to diagnose disease and decide on treatment.

The social model

The social model of health has developed largely as a critique of the biomedical model. Whilst sociologists have offered various critiques of biomedicine, three characteristics are usually central (Annandale, 1998).

First, the social model assumes that health and disease are socially produced; biomedicine is reductionist because it assumes that disease is natural and located in the individual. Second, biomedicine is characterized by the 'doctrine of specific aetiology', which refers to how the biomedical model assumes a direct relationship between pathology and disease. In contrast, the social model recognizes that other factors play a role in determining who becomes sick and why. In fact, some commentators suggest that diseases should be classified by their social causes rather than by specific aetiology.

The third critique of the biomedical model relates to the belief that medicine is neutral and scientific; this is referred to as scientific neutrality. However, the social model emphasizes the way in which health care is influenced by a range of social factors. For example, a study of the treatment of patients in accident and emergency departments (Jeffery, 1979) demonstrates that certain patients – 'drunks, tramps, nutcases and self-harmers' – are not treated equally (see chapter 2).

The social model cannot tell you how to nurse patients, but it can provide you with interesting insights into the causes of disease and the way in which social factors help to shape treatment. Whilst the biomedical model focuses on the diagnosis and treatment of disease, the social model focuses more on prevention and is a useful model for nurses involved in health promotion (see also chapter 10 for a discussion of a public health model) and those interested in promoting patient empowerment and partnership.

4 Social influences on health and disease

One of the most significant contributions that medical sociologists have made has been to show how health and disease are influenced by a range of social factors. In this section, we examine the relationship between changing patterns of disease and changes within society. We then explore the way in which the process of medicalization has had a significant impact on the way we define health and disease.

medicalization the process by which aspects of everyday life enter the domain of the medical profession to become medical problems requiring diagnosis, treatment and cure

Changing patterns of disease

Various writers have suggested that modern societies have passed through three distinct types of disease patterns:

1 *Disease in pre-agricultural societies*—Evidence suggests that, before 10,000 BC, most people died from environmental and safety hazards, for example, exposure. Infectious diseases and so-called lifestyle diseases, such as heart disease and cancer, were uncommon.

2 *Disease in agricultural societies* A range of infectious diseases such as tuberculosis and cholera were the most common.

3 *Disease in the modern industrial era* By the mid-twentieth century infectious diseases were no longer a primary cause of death. Chronic and degenerative diseases, such as cancer, diabetes and cardiovascular disease, have become more common. (Fitzpatrick, 1986)

Why do you think that disease prevalence has changed? It could be argued that advances in medicine and health care provision have had a significant impact on the prevalence of certain diseases. This may be true in some instances, but sociologists would suggest that, if we examine the changing patterns of disease, we can see that they are closely related to social and economic factors. If, for example, we take the case of tuberculosis (TB), official records show that death rates began to fall quite rapidly in the first half of the nineteenth century, well before the introduction of chemotherapy treatments in the 1940s and the BCG vaccination in the 1950s, and even before the identification in 1882 of the tubercle bacillus (Department of Health, 1998). It is worth noting, however, that reported cases of TB in the UK began to rise in the early 1990s, particularly amongst migrants from Africa and the Indian subcontinent and refugees (www.doh.gov.uk).

Although the incidence of TB continues to increase in England it has decreased again in Northern Ireland, Scotland and Wales (table 3.1). This reinforces the view that social and economic factors can have a significant influence on patterns of disease.

Table 3.1 Notification rates of tuberculosis (rates per 100,000 population)

	1996	1997	1998	1999	2000	2001	2002	2003	2004	2005	2006
United Kingdom	10.7	10.9	11.3	11.4	12.1	12.2	12.2	11.7	12.1	13.4	13.2
England	11.3	11.6	12.1	12.1	13.0	13.3	13.3	12.8	13.1	14.8	14.7
Wales	5.6	6.7	5.9	7.1	6.6	4.9	4.3	4.6	6.1	5.4	5.2
Scotland	10.0	8.5	9.0	9.8	9.3	8.7	8.3	8.3	9.1	7.6	6.9
Northern Ireland	4.5	4.5	3.6	3.6	3.5	2.8	4.0	2.2	4.3	3.9	2.8

Note: UK and Scotland figures are provisional.
Source: Adapted from ONS, 2008, table 7.7, p. 146.

The medicalization of everyday life

Zola (1973, p. 261) argues that, 'if anything can be shown in some way to affect the workings of the body and to a lesser extent the mind, then it can be labelled . . . "a medical problem"'. Sociologists have shown that healthy physical processes, such as menstruation, pregnancy and the menopause, have become medicalized (see, for example, Martin, 1989; Oakley, 1984; and Watkins, 2007). Sociologists also suggest that what comes to be defined as a disease is dependent upon a range of political and economic factors. For example, Hunt (1994) and Lee (1998) point out that the construction of the menopause as an 'oestrogen-deficiency' disease developed in the 1960s and was strongly associated with the development and availability of hormone replacement therapies. Gambling (Bernhard, 2007), alcoholism (May, 2001) and sexuality (Hart and Wellings, 2002) have been similarly medicalized.

However, just as some healthy processes become medicalized, others become demedicalized. A good example of this is the demedicalization of homosexuality, which until 1973 was listed in the *Diagnostic and Statistical Manual of Mental Disorders* as a pathological psychiatric disorder. This demonstrates how the labelling of a process or behaviour as a disease is only tangentially related to a distinct physiological or psychological occurrence.

Medicalization has been widely criticized by sociologists. For example, Ivan Illich (1976) developed a theory of iatrogenesis in which he identifies three types:

iatrogenesis
'doctor-caused illness'

- *clinical iatrogenesis*: where individuals are directly harmed by medicine through treatment itself or through the ineffectiveness or the uncertainty of treatment. This also includes the actions taken by doctors to avoid litigation – for example, an increase in the caesarean section rate;

- *social iatrogenesis*: where individuals become dependent upon medicine for their understanding of natural processes and become consumers of health care;
- *structural iatrogenesis*: where the nature of society renders people unable to care for themselves and each other without recourse to medical attention and medical concepts of health. It also refers to the way that individuals strive to achieve better health.

Activity 3.3   **Medical 'problems'?**

BALDNESS	FRECKLES	UGLINESS
JET LAG	SMOKING	GAP TEETH
SHORTNESS	NAIL-BITING	BAD BREATH
SHYNESS	INSOMNIA	HAIRINESS

(a) Think about the list of 'problems' identified above. Are these medical problems?

(b) Who decides what becomes a medical problem and why?

(c) What are the implications of medicalizing such problems, for individuals, for health professionals and for society as a whole?

Routine screening, such as mammography for early signs of cancer, is an increasing part of people's normal contact with the health care system in the Western world.

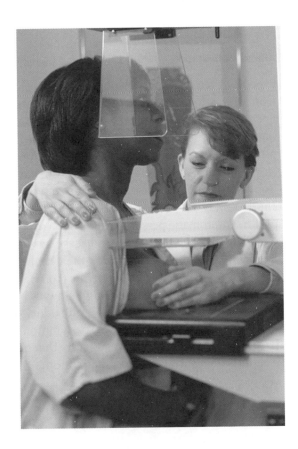

surveillance
observation of
individuals/populations

◄ The rise of health **surveillance** is becoming an increasingly normal part of everyday life for those living in the modern Western world and is another example of how people's lives have become medicalized. For example, most women will, at some time in their life, be asked when they had their last cervical smear (Howson, 1998; Bryder, 2008), and men are now under increasing surveillance for diseases such as prostate and testicular cancers.

There is a great deal of evidence to suggest that surveillance serves to create tension and anxiety (for example, see Greer, 1999; Press, Fishman and Koenig, 2000; Bryder 2008). However, some commentators have argued that the process of medicalization is not so widespread, and, despite the expectation that individuals will comply with various aspects of medicalization and surveillance, there is a great deal of 'non-compliance' in participation and treatment (Stevenson et al., 2002).

5 Experiences of illness, sickness and disease

Whilst some sociologists have focused on the social factors influencing health and disease, others are more interested in the experiences of ill-health, recognizing that responses to illness are influenced by our own experiences as much as by the biological symptoms of disease (see chapter 2 for a discussion of the role of sociology in nursing).

Illness behaviour

Everybody feels ill at some point in their lives but, as we all know from our own experiences, when we feel ill we don't always go to the doctor. Research suggests that most of the illness in society goes unreported, as health professionals get to see only a very small proportion of all illness; this is known as the clinical iceberg.

illness behaviour
actions of people when
they feel unwell

◄ Sociologists are interested in **illness behaviour** because, as Robinson argues, 'a person's readiness to consider himself, or another, ill cannot adequately be explained by reference to the severity of the symptomatic person's condition' (1971, p. 7). In other words, it would appear that the nature of disease has little relation to the likelihood of someone consulting their health practitioner. In a classic study carried out by Mechanic (1968), a wide range of factors were seen to contribute to seeking help (see box 3.3).

In this context, we can see that individuals respond not just to a symptom, but to the meaning of the symptom and the effect that it has on their lives. Zola (1973) suggests that there are triggers which lead individuals to seek medical attention:

1 *The occurrence of an interpersonal crisis*—This refers to the presence of an event of some kind which calls attention to the symptoms, forcing the individual to do something about them.

> **Box 3.3** **Factors influencing help-seeking behaviour**
>
> - The extent to which symptoms are visible and recognizable;
> - Their perceived seriousness and consequent levels of anxiety;
> - The extent to which they impact on the sufferer's life;
> - Their perceived frequency and persistence;
> - The degree to which an individual can tolerate them;
> - Knowledge about what symptoms may mean;
> - Competing needs;
> - Competing explanations for the symptoms;
> - Availability of treatment and assistance.

2   *The perceived interference with social or personal relations* The extent to which symptoms seem to interfere, at any given time, with daily life.

3   *Sanctioning* This refers to when the decision to seek medical attention lies with another person, who sanctions that decision.

4   *The perceived interference with vocational or physical activity* This usually refers to the extent to which symptoms seem to interfere with work.

5   *The temporalizing of symptomatology* The setting of external time criteria, after which treatment will be sought.

The sick role

sick role the sanctioning of illness within society

deviance behaviour considered unacceptable within a society or culture

As we have seen above, not everyone who is ill will receive treatment for their illness, but sociologists have argued that those who do will achieve the status 'sick'. The concept of the sick role was developed by the sociologist Talcott Parsons, who believed that illness is 'partly biologically and partly socially defined' (1991, p. 431). Parsons argued that ill-health was a form of deviance and disruptive to the normal functioning of society (also see chapter 1). He also suggested that the role of medicine was to ensure that only those who are truly ill are permitted to adopt the sick role. Those who claim to be sick without being truly ill are perceived as skivers and malingerers. Entering the sick role, therefore, requires that certain conditions be met; these are best understood in terms of expectations placed on the patient and on the doctor (see box 3.4).

The concept of the sick role is perceived to be a good explanation for temporary bouts of ill-health to which any of us could reasonably become susceptible, for example, influenza or a broken leg. However, there have been many criticisms of the concept of a sick role,

Box 3.4	On being sick: roles and responsibilities

The patient

- is exempted from normal social role responsibilities, e.g. going to work;

- is not responsible for his or her illness and cannot get well on his or her own – cannot, for example, just 'pull himself together';

- must want to get better; and

- must seek technically competent help and comply with treatment.

The doctor

- must act in a professional and objective manner;

- must do everything possible to help the patient recover;

- must be well trained and competent;

- must be able to examine the patient.

especially in relation to its inability to explain the experiences of specific groups, for example those with chronic illness (see chapter 7).

Stigma and disease

stigma social disgrace attached to any condition

The sociology of stigma and disease has been particularly influenced by the work of Erving Goffman (1963), who argued that stigma is a powerful discrediting label that can change, and 'spoil', the way in which the person is viewed. Goffman's work is influenced by theories of social action (see chapter 1) and the view that individuals are active agents within the social world.

Goffman argues that there are two types of condition: discrediting conditions, which are conditions that are clearly visible to others, for example eczema, psoriasis, physical impairments, or stammering; and discreditable conditions, those that are usually not visible to others, or can be easily concealed, for example epilepsy, HIV, depression, or diabetes. The attention given to people with Down's syndrome provides us with a good example of the distinction between discrediting and discreditable conditions. Generally speaking, Down's syndrome is a discrediting condition, as the facial features of the individual are distinct from those of other people, thus immediately stigmatizing that person. Media reports have highlighted cases of parents who are seeking cosmetic surgery for their children with Down's syndrome, arguing that it is the visibility of this condition which leads to stigma, rather than the condition itself. Arguably, by changing the visible aspects of Down's syndrome, parents are turning a discrediting condition into a discreditable one. The ethics of this type of surgery on children are strongly disputed by organizations such as the Down's Syndrome Association (downs-syndrome.org.uk) and others. For example, in a press release on cosmetic surgery for children with Down's syndrome, Down's Syndrome Scotland state:

> If society does not like the way a person with Down's syndrome looks, then the problem is with society – not the individual with Down's syndrome. It is up to all of us to challenge ignorance and prejudice and to make sure that children, young people and adults are included and involved in their own communities and in society generally. In this way each may reach their full potential, and focus will be on skill and ability, rather than appearance and disability. (Down's Syndrome Scotland, 1999)

AIDES is an international charitable organization that aims to tackle the stigma and discrimination of people living with HIV/AIDS.

COULD I STILL BE YOUR HEALTH CARE PROVIDER IF I WERE HIV-POSITIVE?
STOP HIV, NOT PEOPLE LIVING WITH HIV
AIDES
www.aides.org

Some conditions lead to stigma because of the moral attributes associated with a particular condition. HIV and AIDS are commonly associated with sexual promiscuity, drug use and homosexuality (Rhodes and Cusick, 2000), so individuals who are HIV-positive often experience what is known as 'enacted' stigma (Scambler, 1989; Richardson, 2009); this is the type of stigma that leads to actual discrimination. People with other types of condition may experience 'felt' stigma, which refers more to feelings of shame rather than to an actual experience of discrimination. This is often relevant to people with rectal cancer (Macdonald and Anderson, 1984), epilepsy (Scambler, 1989), prostatic problems (Pateman and Johnson, 2000) and testicular cancer (Chapple and Ziebland, 2004).

Lastly, it is worth considering the concept of 'courtesy stigma', which has been defined as a 'tendency for stigma to spread from the stigmatized individual to his close connections' (Goffman, 1963, p. 30). There is evidence, for example, that the family and carers of

---

Activity 3.4   **Autism and stigma**

The extract below presents data from a study of stigma among parents of children with high functioning autism living in the Brisbane metropolitan region of Australia. The data were collected using in-depth semi-structured interviews with fifty-three parents whose children were aged between five and twenty-six years (Gray, 2002, pp. 739–41).

'As a mother, when a child sort of acts up . . . you don't want him to do it, because it's a bit embarrassing. And you feel like it reflects on you a little bit. I mean I'm intelligent enough to know that that's not the case, but it's very difficult to take yourself away from the situation.' [mother]

'I have always taken my boys shopping, always . . . Oh it's a disaster initially. [My son] threw a jar of vegemite at an elderly old lady who smiled at him, you know . . . they look at me as though I'm a mother who obviously isn't very good at being a mother.' [mother]

'Occasionally we'd ask [some] family down and we'd have a drink or whatever, but we never got invited [back] . . . we never seem to be reciprocated. They don't say, "Well, come over". So, yes, you do feel like they've sort of judged and thought, "Give them a miss".' [father]

'We went on . . . camp and we were pretty apprehensive about going . . . We were the only ones with an autistic child and . . . he performed in front of all those people there and had to take charge. And he called me an idiot in front of all those people, and swearing started to come out, and everybody just freezes. Everybody is just embarrassed.' [mother]

(a)   What kinds of stigma are being experienced by these parents of autistic children?

(b)   Why might mothers be more likely than fathers to experience stigma?

(c)   Do you think that nurses contribute to the stigma experienced by patients and their relatives or carers? Can you think of any examples from your own practice?

(d)   What role can nurses play in enabling patients and their carers to manage stigma?

those with Alzheimer's disease often experience considerable embarrassment and shame (Werner and Heinik, 2008). Courtesy stigma is also relevant to others, including the family and friends of those with mental health problems and learning disabilities.

6   Health, holism and nursing

Sociology can provide nurses with a great deal of insight into the social factors that contribute to health and illness, but it is not surprising that some nurses and other health professionals feel that this is nothing to do with them. Although nursing is still predominantly situated within a biomedical model of health, it is widely acknowledged that contemporary nursing is also influenced by the notion of holistic care. However, the exact nature of this term is not always clear and it can be subject to numerous interpretations.

What is holistic care?

In very general terms, holistic care has been equated with the biopsychosocial model, or, as Wynne, Brand and Smith (1997, p. 471) have argued, a holistic approach is underpinned by an 'acceptance that health is determined and defined by inter-related social, psychological and biological factors'. Other commentators have defined holism in nursing as an understanding that 'the whole is greater than the sum of its parts'; this is known as whole-person holism (Kolcaba, 1997). Other definitions of holism also exist; for example, Patterson argues that holism 'implies mind, body and spirit' (1998, p. 289).

holism   an approach which seeks to move away from a biomedical model

Holistic care: rhetoric or reality?

However holism is defined, the question of whether nurses do, in fact, deliver holistic care has also been widely discussed in the literature (for example, Wynne, Brand and Smith, 1997). Whilst the provision of nursing care within a holistic framework provides an idealistic picture of the role of the nurse, it must be acknowledged that nursing work is both 'messy and contingent' (Williams, Cooke and May, 1998, p. 122). For example, a lack of resources can limit the amount of time that nurses devote to each individual patient, which interferes with the provision of holistic care. Some sociologists argue that, for the vast majority of nursing work, it is the pathological and dysfunctional body that remains the primary focus. However, it is important to consider why the concept of holistic care has become so popular within nursing. May (1992) suggests that it is a way of defining what nursing is and what nurses do, adding emotional and intellectual value to nursing work. Indeed, Radwin (1996) claims that knowing the patient is fundamental and marks expertise in nursing.

Other sociologists are more sceptical and suggest that the concept of holism is simply another way in which medicine attempts to gain control over people's lives (Armstrong, 1986). Smart is also critical of holism within nursing; she argues:

> Holism and its tool, individualized patient care, has granted us permission to peel away the layers of the onion that is patient care, but perhaps we do not always need to do so because the knowledge we thereby gain is not necessary for the care of patients, and may have costs for them as people.
> (Smart, 2005, p. 19)

However, if nurses continue to adopt a holistic model of patient care, then this clearly demonstrates the role of sociology – and the social – in understanding the social world.

Activity 3.5   **Understanding the social in holistic care**

Providing holistic care requires nurses to acknowledge social, psychological and biological factors when planning patient care. Read the case study and then answer the questions below.

Adrian is fifty-six years of age and received a C4 spinal cord lesion following a fall at home five years ago. He has incomplete quadriplegia with no mobility in his legs and only very limited mobility in his arms. He was admitted to the ward because he was suffering from persistent bladder infections and his GP believed that he was now at considerable risk of autonomic dysreflexia. He has had other similar episodes of ill-health over the last few years, although a suprapubic catheter was inserted to alleviate some bladder difficulties. When you approach him to take his observations his mood seems quite low and he is uncommunicative.

(a) Imagine that you are preparing a care plan for this patient. What social factors might you need to consider? How might you go about providing holistic care for this patient?

(b) What does holistic care mean to you?

(c) Reflect on your own practice experience. Are you always able to provide holistic care for patients? What enables you to do so? What prevents you from doing so?

Summary and Resources

Summary

- Official definitions of health have changed over time, but the most pervasive is that of health as an absence of disease.

- The biomedical model is dominant within Western health care and is characterized by the belief that illness can be reduced to the existence of a specific pathogen.

- The social model developed as a critique of the biomedical model and highlights the importance of social factors in understanding health and illness. The types of disease prevalent within any society are related to social, political and economic factors.

- There are many reasons to explain why people who feel ill do not go to the doctor, including the stigma associated with some conditions.

- Holistic care is characterized by the emphasis on the physical, social, psychological and spiritual needs of the person. Holism is widely accepted within nursing but questioned by sociologists and others.

Questions for Discussion

1 In what ways does specialization within nursing reinforce a medical model of health and illness?

2 Think about Illich's theory of iatrogenesis and consider it in relation to (a) breast enhancement and (b) sadness.

3 How far do you think that Parsons's concept of the sick role can be used to explain ill-health amongst the following groups: older people who care for ageing spouses; fat children; and people with myalgic encephalomyelitis (ME)?

4 Do you agree that a holistic approach makes nursing more emotionally and intellectually rewarding?

Further Reading

E. Annandale: *The Sociology of Health and Medicine: A Critical Introduction*. Cambridge: Polity, 1998.
This book explores issues in much more depth but may be useful once you have mastered the material presented here.

S. Nettleton: *The Sociology of Health and Illness*. 2nd edn, Cambridge: Polity, 2006.

This text will enable you to follow up on some of the themes identified within this chapter. Chapter 2 ('The social construction of medical knowledge') and chapter 3 ('Lay health beliefs, lifestyles and risk') are particularly useful.

See www.politybooks.com/sociologyfornurses for some useful online resources, additional annotated further reading and more questions for discussion.

References

Allott, M., and Robb, M. 1998: *Understanding Health and Social Care: An Introductory Reader*. London: Sage.

Annandale, E. 1998: *The Sociology of Health and Medicine: A Critical Introduction*. Cambridge: Polity.

Armstrong, D. 1986: 'The problem of the whole-person in holistic medicine'. *Holistic Medicine*, 1, 27–36.

Barbour, A. B. 1995: *Caring for Patients: A Critique of the Medical Model*. Stanford, CA: Stanford University Press.

Bernhard, B. S. 2007: 'The voices of vices: sociological perspectives on the pathological gambling entry in the Diagnostic and Statistical Manual of Mental Disorders'. *American Behavioral Scientist*, 51(1), 8–32.

Blaxter, M. 1990: *Health and Lifestyles*. London: Tavistock/Routledge.

Bryder, L. 2008: 'Debates about cervical screening: an historical overview'. *Journal of Epidemiology and Community Health*, (62)4, 284–7.

Chapple, A., and Ziebland, S. 2004: 'The role of humor for men with testicular cancer'. *Qualitative Health Research*, 14(8), 1123–39.

Department of Health 1998: *The Interdepartmental Working Group on Tuberculosis: The Prevention and Control of Tuberculosis in the United Kingdom*. London: HMSO.

Down's Syndrome Scotland 1999: 'Cosmetic surgery for children with Down's syndrome', press release; www.dsscotland.org.uk/news-and-events/press-releases/cosmetic-surgery [last accessed 20 August 2008].

Engebretson, J. 2003: 'Cultural constructions of health and illness: recent cultural changes towards a holistic approach'. *Journal of Holistic Nursing*, 21(3), 203–27.

Falk, S., Wahn, A.-K., and Lidell, E. 2007: 'Keeping the maintenance of daily life in spite of chronic heart failure: a qualitative study'. *European Journal of Cardiovascular Nursing*, 6(3), 192–9.

Fitzpatrick, R. M. 1986: 'Society and changing patterns of disease'. In D. L. Patrick and G. Scambler (eds), *Sociology as Applied to Medicine*. 2nd edn, London: Ballière Tindall, pp. 16–39.

Goffman, E. 1963: *Stigma: Notes on the Management of a Spoiled Identity*. Englewood Cliffs, NJ: Prentice-Hall.

Gray, D. E. 2002: '"Everybody just freezes. Everybody is just embarrassed": felt and enacted stigma among parents of children with high functioning autism'. *Sociology of Health & Illness*, 24(6), 734–49.

Greer, G. 1999: *The Whole Woman*. New York: Knopf.

Hart, G., and Wellings, K. 2002: 'Sexual behaviour and its medicalization: in sickness and in health'. *British Medical Journal*, April, 324, 896–900.

Howson, A. 1998: 'Embodied obligation: the female body and health surveillance'. In S. Nettleton and J. Watson (eds), *The Body in Everyday Life*. London: Routledge, pp. 218–40.

Hunt, K. 1994: 'A "cure for all ills?" Constructions of the menopause and the chequered fortunes of hormone replacement therapy'. In S. Wilkinson and C. Kitzinger (eds), *Women and Health: Feminist Perspectives*. London: Taylor & Francis, pp. 141–65.

Illich, I. 1976: *The Limits to Medicine*. London: Penguin.

Jeffery, R. 1979: 'Normal rubbish: deviant patients in casualty departments'. *Sociology of Health & Illness*, 1(1), 90–108.

Kelman, S. 1975: 'The social nature of the definition problem in health'. *International Journal of Health Services*, 5(4), 625–42.

Kolcaba, R. 1997: 'The primary holism in nursing'. *Journal of Advanced Nursing*, 25, 290–6.

Lee, C. 1998: *Women's Health: Psychological and Social Perspectives*. London: Sage.

Lupton, D. 1995: *The Imperative of Health*. London: Sage.

Macdonald, L., and Anderson, H. 1984: 'Stigma in patients with rectal cancer: a community study'. *Journal of Epidemiology and Community Health*, 38, 284–90.

Martin, E. 1989: *The Woman in the Body: A Cultural Analysis of Reproduction*. Buckingham: Open University Press.

May, C. 1992: 'Nursing work, nursing knowledge and the subjectification of the patient'. *Sociology of Health & Illness*, 14, 307–15.

May, C. 2001: 'Pathology, identity and the social construction of alcohol dependence'. *Sociology*, 35(2), 385–401.

Mechanic, D. 1968: *Medical Sociology*. New York: Free Press.

Oakley, A. 1984: *The Captured Womb: A History of the Medical Care of Pregnant Women*. Oxford: Blackwell.

ONS (Office for National Statistics) 2008 *Regional Trends 40*. London: ONS.

Parsons, T. 1991: *The Social System*. London: Routledge.

Pateman, B., and Johnson, M. 2000: 'Men's lived experiences following transurethral prostatectomy for benign prostatic hypertrophy'. *Journal of Advanced Nursing*, 31(1), 51–8.

Patterson, E. F. 1998: 'The philosophy and physics of holistic health care: spiritual healing as workable interpretation'. *Journal of Advanced Nursing*, 27, 287–93.

Press, N., Fishman, J. R., and Koenig, B. A. 2000: 'Collective fear, individualized risk: the social and cultural context of genetic testing for breast cancer'. *Nursing Ethics*, 7(3), 237–49.

Prior, L. 2003: 'Belief, knowledge and expertise: the emergence of the lay expert in medical sociology'. *Sociology of Health & Illness*, 25, silver anniversary issue.

Radwin, L. E. 1996: 'Knowing the patient: a review of research on an emerging concept'. *Journal of Advanced Nursing*, 23, 1142–6.

Rhodes, T., and Cusick, L. 2000: 'Love and intimacy in relationship risk management: HIV positive people and their sexual partners'. *Sociology of Health & Illness*, 22(1), 1–26.

Richardson, E. 2009: 'HIV/AIDS: A highly stigmatized long term condition'. In E. Denny and S. Earle (eds), *The Sociology of Long Term Conditions and Nursing Practice*. Basingstoke: Palgrave Macmillan, pp. 217–42.

Robinson, D. 1971: *The Process of Becoming Ill*. London: Routledge.

Scambler, G. 1989: *Epilepsy*. London: Routledge.

Smart, F. 2005: 'The whole truth?' *Nursing Management*, 11(9), 17–19.

Stevenson, F., Britten, N., Barry, C. A., Bradley, C. P., and Barber, N. 2002: 'Perceptions of legitimacy: the influence on medicine taking and prescribing'. *Health*, 6(1), 85–104.

Turner, B. S. 1995: *Medical Power and Social Knowledge*. 2nd edn, London: Sage.

Watkins, E. S. 2007: 'The medicalisation of male menopause in America'. *Social History of Medicine*, 20(2), 369–88.

Weatherhead, S. C., and Lawrence, C. M. 2006: 'Melanoma screening clinics: are we detecting more melanomas or reassuring the worried well?' *British Journal of Dermatology*, 154(3), 539–41.

Werner, P., and Heinik, J. 2008: 'Stigma by association and Alzheimer's disease'. *Aging & Mental Health*. 12(1), 92–9.

Williams, A., Cooke, H., and May, C. 1998: *Sociology, Nursing and Health*. Oxford: Butterworth Heinemann.

Williams, G., and Popay, J. 1994: 'Lay knowledge and the privilege of experience'. In J. Gabe, D. Kelleher and G. Williams (eds), *Challenging Medicine*. London: Routledge, pp. 118–39.

WHO 1948: Preamble to the constitution of the World Health Organization as adopted by the International Health Conference, New York, 19–22 June 1946, by the representatives of 61 states (Official Records of the World Health Organization, no. 2, p. 100) and entered into force on 7 April 1948. Geneva: World Health Organization.

WHO 1986: Ottawa Charter for Health Promotion, First International Conference, Ottawa, 21 November 1986 [who/hpr/hep/95.1]. Charter adopted at an international conference on health promotion – The Move Towards a New Public Health, November 17–21, 1986. Ottawa, Ontario: World Health Organization.

Wynne, N., Brand, S., and Smith, R. 1997: 'Incomplete holism in preregistration nurse education: the position of the biological sciences'. *Journal of Advanced Nursing*, 26, 470–4.

Zola, I. K. 1973: 'Pathways to the doctor – from person to patient'. *Social Science and Medicine*, 7, 677–89.

4 Nursing as an Occupation

Elaine Denny

Key issues in this chapter

- The origins of nursing
- Nursing and gender
- Socialization into nursing
- Nursing within the health division of labour
- Nurse education

By the end of this chapter you should be able to . . .

- understand the link between the history of nursing and its present construction;
- discuss the effects of gender stereotypes on nursing;
- identify the mechanisms by which nurses internalize the values of the occupation;
- discuss nursing's place within the health division of labour;
- understand the role played by education in the production of nurses.

---

1 Introduction

When you decided to become a nurse your decision was probably based on an idea of what you thought that nursing was. This in turn is likely to involve the work that nurses do, or nursing tasks. As you progress through your nurse education and the reality of the job begins to influence your thinking, your ideas about the role of nursing may change. You may become less certain that you really know what nursing is.

This is not surprising, as nurses and academics have debated for many years the question 'What is nursing?' Is it an art or a science? Does it possess a discrete body of knowledge? The debates continue, and to date no one has devised a universally agreed definition of nursing.

If we begin by considering nursing's origins and the influences on its development, we can begin to see why 'nursing' is such a problematic concept. The chapter will continue the theme raised in chapter 2, which highlighted the concept of a sociology of nursing, that is, it will examine the occupation of nursing and the structural influences on it, particularly gender, socialization and the division of labour.

2   The origins of nursing

Nursing in a form that would be recognizable to us today began in the nineteenth century but has been in existence since ancient times. Before the dissolution of the monasteries in England and Wales in the sixteenth century, monks would look after people in need, and the care of military casualties was until the mid-nineteenth century carried out by men.

The majority of care of the elderly, the sick, and women during and after childbirth was, however, undertaken by a variety of healers, mainly female, such as handy women and midwives, and by other women as part of their domestic role. In hospitals nurses were concerned mainly with domestic duties, and, although they had the reputation of being drunken, dishonest and promiscuous, there is evidence that many hospitals strove to employ respectable working women (Dingwall, Rafferty and Webster, 1988). More skilled roles were undertaken by male apothecaries, dressers and medical students. Within the 'madhouses' and asylums, which housed those we would today describe as having mental health problems or learning disabilities, men dominated, as control and constraint were the main duties, so a gender division of labour was apparent within institutions, based on the type of work carried out.

During the nineteenth century, as the UK industrialized and became a more urban society, care became institutionalized and medicine developed into a unified and collegiate profession. A different type of worker was needed on hospital wards to observe the patient's condition and to report it accurately, and to be trustworthy in carrying out the doctor's instructions when he was not present. Within Victorian patriarchal society it was considered that female nurses who conformed to the ideal of acquiescent and subservient femininity could carry out this role, yet would not threaten the doctor's authority as male workers might (Rafferty, 1995). Nursing has always been defined and constructed by its relationship to medicine (Denny, 2003), and changes in the medical profession acted as a catalyst for developments in nursing.

This shift in the nursing role could not have occurred without another change within Victorian society. From 1851 the census showed an excess of women over men. The middle-class woman, who was brought up to manage the domestic sphere, did not have the skills necessary to support herself financially. University education and entry into the emerging professions was barred to women until the end of the century, so the only occupations available to them were those of companion or governess.

To attract middle-class women into nursing with the aim of transforming it into a professional occupation, the hygiene and

The author's mother, a trained psychiatric nurse, c. 1944. Notice the uniform, which was adopted from the traditional general nurse uniform.

domestic elements of the nursing role were redefined as scientific (Rafferty, 1996), and training schemes modelled on medical training were introduced. Initially this was confined to the voluntary hospitals, but the ethos spread to other forms of institution (see photograph). Asylums and children's hospitals began to regard a training in general nursing as superior to a specialist training, and by the early twentieth century had made it a requirement for promotion above staff nurse level.

Nurse registration, with its separate registers for children's nurses, asylum nurses and male nurses amongst others, served to reinforce these hierarchical divisions within nursing.

The call for nurse registration was made by those who wanted to develop nursing as a profession and opposed by those who perceived nursing as a vocation, with 'character' as the primary requirement. Witz (1992) called the campaign for registration a female professional project, in that pro-registrationists were attempting to create an autonomous occupation for women, on a par with medicine, aiming for occupational closure. Although registration was introduced in 1919, nursing failed to gain autonomy or control of entry to the occupation. The General Nursing Council (GNC) set up to certify nurses was a body with few powers.

In summary, nursing evolved over the course of the nineteenth century from the female domestic role of caring, in a subservient position to medicine, to a more skilled occupation which was attempting to professionalize. A hierarchy of nursing specialisms developed, with the values originally associated with general nursing being adopted by other areas of nursing.

professional project an attempt by an occupation to become a profession, using strategies aimed at enhancing power and status

occupational closure the monopoly of work to maintain power and status over other occupational groups

3   Men in nursing

If nursing has traditionally been viewed as 'women's work', what does this mean for men who take up nursing as a career? In the past men worked mainly in areas such as psychiatry or the military, which were not associated with the feminine caring roles of female nurses. As men have moved into other areas of nursing (moves often resisted by female nurse leaders), certain suspicions have been raised about their motives. Evans (1997) states that, within patriarchal society, men in nursing, although in a minority, are given a special and privileged status. They gain power disproportionate to their numbers and dominate in elite specialisms and administrative positions, which are considered more reflective of masculine values.

In the UK men constitute around 10 per cent of the nursing workforce (a percentage that has remained more or less unchanged over the past twenty years) yet hold over 40 per cent of senior management and education posts (Miers, 2000). Williams (1994) argues that men view nursing differently from women and move into management as a way of reinforcing their masculinity. She further states that as well as advantage, men encounter discriminatory treatment based on gender stereotypes, and she has summed up the stereotype of male nurses as lazy, on the glass escalator, or gay. Evans (2002) adds that the stereotype of male nurses as gay is compounded by the stereotype of gay men as deviant and sexually predatory. This is particularly difficult when men are working with vulnerable groups such as children or people with learning disabilities, and in intimate areas of care that involve touch.

In a qualitative study of male nurses and touch, Hardy, North and Perkins (2008, p. 88) argue that, although touch is a problematic area of care for all nurses, it is 'even more challenging for male nurses because of discourses that have feminized touch and sexualised men's touch'. This confirms earlier work by Evans, who states that, 'Unlike women's touch which is considered a natural extension of women's traditional caregiver role, men's touch is surrounded by suspicion that implies that men nurses' motives for touching are not care oriented, but sexual in nature' (Evans, 2002, p. 446). Men may therefore gravitate to areas that require less intimate touching of patients, and in so doing avoid having to confront the stereotypes. Hardy, North and Perkins also suggest that this is inadequately addressed within nurse education, which leaves men vulnerable when dealing with issues of touch. Inoue, Chapman and Wynaden (2006)

What obstacles to effective nursing practice might there be for men as a result of traditional views of nursing as 'women's work'?

agree that male nurses are not adequately prepared to deal with intimate work and use coping strategies that are learned on the job rather than taught during their education.

The view of nursing as a female occupation has proved problematic for men entering the profession, as stereotypes of masculine and feminine qualities can lead to the motivation of men in nursing being questioned. On the other hand those same stereotypes can lead to men experiencing advantage in recruitment and promotion.

4   Socialization into nursing

The first time you went on placement and someone called you 'nurse' it probably felt rather strange; you may even have felt like an impostor. By the end of your education you will feel quite comfortable with the term, not only because you will have more knowledge and be confident in carrying out the work, but also because you will have internalized the values and attitudes of nursing. The way that this occurs has been demonstrated by two sociological studies.

Davis described the way in which, over the course of training, students are socialized into nursing and states that the socialization of student nurses is 'the process by which the student passes from identification with a "lay" to a "professional" culture' (Davis, 1975, p. 116). He argues that the socialization process comprises six stages during which the nurse passes from 'lay innocence', when his or her imagery of nursing is that shaped by previous perceptions, to 'stable internalization', where the self-image of the student is that of a professional nurse.

Melia (1987) studied student nurses' experiences of education and training and found that a division existed between the way in which nursing was represented in college and the way it was practised on the wards. This is often referred to as the 'theory–practice gap', examples of which were given in chapter 2. Students learned to manage this tension by adopting strategies which allowed them to fit in on the wards. Melia identifies five categories by which students achieve this (see box 4.1).

In describing the way in which student nurses internalize the values of nursing and begin to identify themselves as members of the profession, Davis and Melia show how this is not just the result of increasing nursing knowledge but also a social process in which the student learns the shared norms of nursing. More recent work conducted since the status of student nurses became supernumerary has shown that similar problems still exist for student nurses. In her observational study Wakefield (2000) found that students are now seen as external to the ward environment and are categorized as 'visitors' rather than 'belonging' to the hospital. Students themselves have problems in getting practice in skills, as health care assistants (HCAs) now receive extra training and carry out more tasks than previously, taking over what always used to be regarded as a student nurse's role. Wakefield argues that this has led to a change in power relations, with students being treated as subordinate by HCAs.

Box 4.1   **Strategies adopted by student nurses**

- 'Learning the rules' is concerned with the way in which students pass as workers to the satisfaction of permanent workers on the ward.

- 'Getting the work done' describes how nursing work is organized and achieved on hospital wards. Clarke (1978) found that student nurses feel they are judged by their success in 'learning the ropes' and 'getting through the work', in other words by how soon they can function effectively within the ward routine.

- Student nurses have to achieve the above within the constraints of the dual role of the third category, 'learning and working', although the situation has changed somewhat with student nurses achieving supernumerary status.

- 'Just passing through' reflects on the student's transient status, with the consequent relearning of the first and second categories on each new placement.

- Another consequence of the transient experience is the fifth category of 'nursing in the dark', where students find that they are not always given the information about patients that the permanent staff possess.

Source: Adapted from Melia (1987).

Activity 4.1   **Socialization into nursing**

(Melia's study was carried out before nursing moved into higher education and nurses became supernumerary.)
Think about a placement that you have done.

(a)   How well does each of Melia's categories apply to your experience?

(b)   Do different types of placement (e.g. hospital, community, group home) have different rules and different ways of 'getting the work done'?

(c)   From your placements, can you identify with Walker's findings about students not always having the opportunity to develop skills?

(d)   Discuss your experience with someone from a different branch of nursing.

5 Nursing within the health division of labour

Profession and professionalization

Although the image of nursing as women's work persists, and 90 per cent of the nursing workforce is female, the position of nursing within the health division of labour today is more complex than that described above. In order to examine nursing's place within the health division of labour, it is useful to review the concept of profession as it has traditionally been defined within sociology, and to consider whether we need a new way of looking at occupations in order to explain the development of nursing practice.

Sociological definitions have tended to view professions as particular types of occupation which possess specific traits or attributes that distinguish them and which give them a higher status within society. Typically these include public service, an ethical code, and some form of training in higher education (see, for example, Millerson, 1964). This functionalist approach is criticized as being ahistorical, that is, it does not question how or why these occupations were able to achieve these attributes and become dominant in an area of work. Nor does it take a critical approach towards the motives for professional development, but stresses the important role professions play within society, the altruistic role of medicine being a prime example.

Freidson (1970), adopting a neo-Weberian stance (see chapter 1), defines a profession as possessing certain characteristics (see box 4.2).

So a profession has a large amount of control over its working practices. The power that professions possess within Western societies has enabled them to lay claim to areas of work, and to dominate and constrain subordinate occupations within the same sphere. This is social closure (Parkin, 1979), and can be used to explain the actions of both dominant and subservient occupations. Exclusionary tactics include the use of entry qualifications, legislation or other means to restrict access to the occupation, and demarcation describes the placing of boundaries around the work of a subordinate occupation. For example, the medical profession fought against the introduction of nurse prescribing for several years, as it would erode the monopoly power it enjoyed.

Subordinate occupations may attempt to adopt the same values and characteristics as the dominant one – what are known as inclusionary tactics. Expanded roles in nursing, where nurses take on tasks traditionally undertaken by doctors, may be defined as inclusionary strategies. Subordinate occupations may also use exclusionary tactics in order to maintain boundaries between themselves and occupations that they consider subordinate, for example the division between the roles of qualified nurses and HCAs. The latter are restricted in the tasks they may carry out, with some roles being reserved for qualified nurses.

social closure the means by which one social group maintains power and status in society by closing entry to other groups. In occupational closure, control of entry into the occupation and monopoly over an area of work are the means usually adopted

expanded roles roles that include activities formerly carried out within other occupations, which expands the range of tasks to be carried out

Box 4.2   Characteristics of a profession

- Specialist knowledge gained through higher education and qualifications.

- Monopoly over certain tasks and procedures.

- Autonomy – control of working conditions and entry into the profession.

- Possession of an ethical code, or code of conduct.

Source: Freidson (1970).

Activity 4.2   Nurse staffing and patient outcomes

In a study of thirty hospital trusts in England which looked at the relationship between nurse staffing levels and patient outcomes, Rafferty et al.

> found a large and consistent effect of nurse staffing on mortality outcomes in surgical patients as well as on nurse job outcomes and nurse ratings of quality of care. Hospitals in which nurses cared for the fewest patients each had significantly lower surgical mortality and FTR [failure to rescue] rates compared to those in which nurses cared for the greatest number of patients each. . . .
>
> In addition to better outcomes for patients, hospitals with higher nurse staffing levels had significantly lower rates of nurse burnout and dissatisfaction. The nurses in the hospitals with the heaviest patient loads were 71% more likely to experience high burnout and job dissatisfaction than hospitals with the most favourable nurse staffing. . . .
>
> Our findings that hospitals with more favourable nurse staffing show the best outcomes for patients and nurses provide the kind of research evidence called for by the UK Healthcare Commission in its report on ward staffing (Healthcare Commission, 2005). The findings suggest that quality of care and nurse retention would improve if staffing levels across the NHS were brought more into line with those in the best-staffed hospitals in this study.

Source: Rafferty, Clarke and Coles et al., 2007, pp. 175–82.

The following questions can be completed with reference to placements that you have already done, but you can also think about them on future placements. Discuss your findings with colleagues who have had placements in different clinical areas.

1   How many nurses are on duty at different times of the day and night? Do different types of clinical area and different NHS trusts have different staffing levels?

2   How many of the nurses are qualified and how many are health care assistants?

3   Which nurses appear to experience burnout, and which have a high level of job satisfaction?

4   Apart from the effect on patient mortality and nurse burnout, what other benefits do you think will come from the improved staffing levels called for in this research?

If medicine is viewed as the archetypal profession within the health care system, nursing has been described as a semi-profession (Etzioni, 1969) because of its perceived limited knowledge base and lack of autonomy. This concept is somewhat deterministic as it implies that there is no opportunity for nursing to develop professionally. In order to counter such definitions of nursing, some feminist writers (notably Davies, 1995; Witz, 1992) have criticized traditional notions of profession for emphasizing power and an esoteric knowledge base which separates the practitioner from the client. Davies (1995) argues that this form of power, which relies on denying knowledge to others, is a very masculinist interpretation of profession. Within this model nursing can never be accepted as a profession, as it seeks to share expertise and to encourage empowerment and participation by patients and families through strategies such as negotiated care. Davies advocates a new model of

An important part of the health care worker's role is to seek to share expertise and encourage patient empowerment.

professionalism in which partnership and reflective practice constitute the basis of professional expertise, and where nursing roles and values are acknowledged and given credibility. This is

enhanced roles roles that allow nurses to use their expert knowledge to make autonomous decisions

consistent with the notion of **enhanced roles** in nursing, in which the carative elements of health care are viewed as part of the specialist skills of nursing and as an area of autonomous nursing practice.

Many of the enhanced and expanded roles within nursing, and other health occupations, have been as a result of changes in the NHS, particularly the reduction in junior doctors' working hours and new consultant and GP contracts. The increasing prominence of long-term illness has encouraged the development of community matrons, who provide leadership in the care and management of this group (see also chapter 12). Nurses, particularly in the community, are now trained to prescribe medicines, either independently or as supplementary prescribers. These roles have facilitated changing relationships within the health care team as more nurses work as independent practitioners in all branches. One new area of work (as opposed to existing tasks being undertaken by a different occupational group) has been in telemedicine. NHS Direct is a nurse-led telephone triage, advice and helpline service introduced in 1998. The nurses are based in call centres and are trained to give advice to callers using computer software that guides their questioning and assists assessment of the urgency of the problem. From this, appropriate advice can be offered. Snooks et al. (2007) state that, although it is increasingly used in developed countries, telemedicine is a break with traditional hands-on nursing. In their study on the views of nurses working for NHS Direct Wales and nurses working more traditionally, they found that working in telemedicine offered nurses opportunity to develop new skills and practice. However, the new experience of remoteness from the patient was a source of stress for nurses working for NHS Direct. Interestingly, this study finds that both groups of nurses use the idea of 'real nursing' in order to rationalize their support for or opposition to telemedicine. Nurses not working for NHS Direct also questioned the cost effectiveness of the service and the ability of more marginalized groups in society to access it.

Elitism in nursing

elite a small group that has power and influence by virtue of its social position

The idea of an **elite** in nursing would seem to be paradoxical, as nurses are not viewed as a powerful group (Mowforth, 1999). They are often marginalized when decisions are made, which in theory should preclude them from holding power. However, both horizontal and vertical elites exist within nursing.

Vertical elitism exists between nurses of different grades. The higher the position within the organization, the greater is the prestige. In nursing, status is gained by moving away from clinical work with patients/clients into management or education. So, in order to gain promotion, nurses must cease to do the work they came into nursing for. What Davies (1995) has called the polo mint problem is created – a hole caused by a skills shortage at the bedside and in clinical teaching – as experienced nurses no longer undertake this work. As Daykin and Clarke (2000) demonstrate, this has raised questions about the relationship of nursing to basic health care, with nurses in their study demonstrating ambivalence to the changing role of the nurse. Many nurses expressed concern at the perceived threat to their claim to a distinct contribution to health care if HCAs carry out much of the bedside care, albeit in a subservient position. At the same time they recognized the reality of workplace imperatives, most crucially the shortage of qualified nurses to carry out care (see also chapter 2 for a longer discussion of this research).

Horizontal elitism is influenced by the medical model and the value this places on science and technology. Medicine, along with other professions, uses its possession of expert knowledge to maintain its high status. The gap between the knowledge of the doctor and that of the patient creates a mystique about medical knowledge. This is said to depersonalize, or deny the experience of, the patient, privileging the scientific over other forms of knowledge. It is those within nursing who are seen to have some insight into this scientific knowledge, such as those in intensive therapy units (ITU), special care baby units or accident and emergency departments (A & E), who are perceived as elite by themselves and by the public. Each nursing discipline has its elite roles, but those within the high-technology areas associated with adult and children's nursing have the highest status within wider society.

New technologies which require extra monitoring and interpretation are associated with clean as opposed to dirty work. Wolf (1996) has argued that those who perform dirty work are soiled by association. Being involved with bodily functions has little status, and Clarke (1999) states that many nurses believe that an increase in nursing status is not compatible with these tasks. So care of the elderly or chronically ill does not carry the same prestige as more high-technology specialisms, even though it could be argued that the art of nursing (the skills that make nursing unique) is more apparent in the former. Nursing work associated with caring is seen as 'natural' and therefore not requiring intellect or education (Miers, 1999). Nurses within highly technologized areas do carry out 'dirty work', such as continence care; however, they are characterized not by this, but by their work with the technology.

Within mental health nursing, status is aligned to the clean work of psychotherapy with short-term patients, rather than to what is often regarded as the menial work of care of long-term patients (Godin, 2003).

The concept of expanded roles within nursing, such as nurse prescribing or acting as a surgeon's assistant, adds status by taking nurses further away from the caring role and towards cure, which is a feature of clinical medicine. This removes the nurse from the 'dirty work' of nursing and into the 'clean' world of medicine. A consideration of the roles that nurses have taken on shows most to be fairly routine, repetitive tasks, which doctors themselves do not find as rewarding as other parts of their job. However, they do give some nurses the opportunity to work more autonomously as part of multi-disciplinary teams. Paradoxically these new roles also bring nursing further under the control of medicine, as the medical profession defines the terms of nursing involvement and circumscribes and supervises the work that the nurse takes over (Denny, 2003). This can be demonstrated by the changes that have taken place within mental health nursing, where Brimblecombe (2005) argues that a shift to community care from the 1970s provided a catalyst for a new interest in greater professional autonomy and status amongst mental health nurses. This resulted in greater independence for nursing, being outside of the direct influence of psychiatry, and taking direct referrals from GPs. This move, however, also led mental health nurses away from a focus on severe mental illness, and it was the return to working more with this client group that reinforced the link between mental health nurses and psychiatry, with the latter continuing to exert influence over the former both at a policy-making and a clinical level (ibid.).

Activity 4.3　　　**Elitism in nursing**

Make a list of nursing tasks or roles within your branch that are generally considered to be high-status, and another list of low-status tasks and roles.

(a)　What do you think makes them high- or low-status?
(b)　Who usually carries out the high- and low-status work?
(c)　Discuss your lists with someone from another branch of nursing. Are there similarities and differences in the lists?

Working with doctors

Earlier in the chapter we considered the nineteenth-century image of doctors as powerful and nurses as obedient and subservient. This emanated from the relative position of men and women in Victorian society, which is now obsolete. Relationships are less monolithic; for example, mental health nurses tend to see their role as complementary to that of psychiatrists, and learning disability nurses view themselves as the expert workers in an area where the closure of institutions has seen the decline of the medical specialist (Denny, 2003).

Porter (1999) summarizes research that has looked at the doctor–nurse relationship. The first to consider this issue was Stein (1967), who viewed matters as more complex than the traditional power relationship and described the situation as a game. Doctors are trained in a manner that creates certainty (in diagnosis, and in treatment), and for nurses to question or comment on their decisions would undermine this. Stein showed how nurses often had more knowledge of patients and their treatments than doctors who rotated through the specialisms, but they would never openly contradict them. Instead the nurse would put forward suggestions which the doctor could present as his or her own idea. The sub-servient nurse would not risk disagreement with the more powerful doctor. As Stein (1967, p. 699) states: 'The nurse is to be bold, have initiative, and be responsible for making significant recommendations, while at the same time she must appear passive. This must be done in such a manner so as to make her recommendations appear to be initiated by the physician.' For example, nurses often complete forms for diagnostic tests for a doctor to sign, or tell the doctor that a patient cannot sleep and suggest that a particular drug has helped in the past. The doctor then makes the decision to do the test or to prescribe the drug as if it was his or her decision. The notion of the doctor–nurse game as a process of negotiation is taken up in chapter 15.

More recently other writers have reviewed the doctor–nurse game and found that it has evolved as roles have developed, and Stein, Watts and Howell noted in 1990 that in many hospital settings nurses were challenging medical decisions.

Hughes (1988) found that, given the right circumstances, nurses have the power to contribute to decision-making. These can relate to the turnover of medical staff, the degree of post-registration nurse training, or the closeness of the working relationship. It most often occurs in areas such as accident and emergency departments or ITU. However, structural power relationships mean that doctors can always overrule nurses if they wish.

Porter (1999) also states that nurses themselves have the authority to identify and solve problems. Nurses have formally sanctioned decision-making processes that are independent of medical power. Central to this is the concept of the nursing process and care planning, which is nurse-led and outside the control of medicine.

Porter (1995) found that in different circumstances all of these processes are involved. He argues that the above relationships still apply and are played out differently according to the specific circumstances of the clinical area, and were more apparent within informal decision-making processes than in formal ones. He found that, in areas where most nurses had specialist qualifications, such as accident and emergency departments, they were more likely to have some autonomy and be involved in decision-making, although this was still constrained by professional boundaries. Expanding roles within nursing are likely to make these relationships more complex, as some nurses gain in autonomy but others gain skills that bring them more under the control of medicine. Much of the research that considers the relationship between nursing and medicine has taken place in specialist departments such as ITU/ICU, and Carmel, in his ethnographic study of an ICU, argues that occupational boundaries (particularly between doctors and nurses) are blurred in these specialist areas, and nurses have become incorporated into an 'ICU project' (Carmel, 2006, 174), whereas organizational boundaries between ITU and the rest of the hospital are reinforced, with ITU being perceived as different from general wards.

Prowse and Allen (2002) also focused on the context of relationships, and in her study of nurses' accounts of their day-to-day interactions with doctors in a post-anaesthetic recovery unit (PACU) found that they adapted their interactional style according to context. Many features of the doctor–nurse game were displayed during routine interactions, but during critical incidents nurses were able to display their knowledge and expertise, act assertively and focus purely on patient outcome. Like Porter's and Carmel's work, this study is set in a clinical area where nurses normally have additional training and develop expertise. In their research conducted in the less specialized world of a general medical and a surgical ward, Snelgrove and Hughes (2002) found that, while teamwork was valued by both doctors and nurses, for nurses the 'team' was a collegiate entity while doctors viewed a team as consisting of a leader and the led. The multi-disciplinary teams (MDT) in this study made decisions that were peripheral to core medical decisions, with doctors feeling that diagnosis and the planning of treatment were outside of its remit. The MDT supports the professionalizing strategy of nursing, yet Snelgrove and Hughes argue that nurses' statements about shared decision-making were not supported by credible examples, most being related to discharge planning and social aspects of care. Many of the doctors in the study did not view nurses as equal partners, and both doctors and nurses recognized the continuing power of medical hierarchies.

These studies support Wicks's (1998) findings that structural factors, such as power relationships, may be overcome by individual agency in certain circumstances, most usually when nurses have expertise derived from experience and specialist education.

This section has examined nursing's place within the health division of labour. It has pointed to a changing power relationship between medicine and nursing as nursing develops, and also to the complex situation within nursing specialisms brought about by the expansion of nursing roles and the greater autonomy achieved by some nurses.

Activity 4.4   **Relationship with doctors**

The following are examples of interactions between nurses and doctors taken from Porter's (1995) observational research on nursing's relationship with medicine.

A

Doctor: Everything OK?

Nurse: [The patient's] pain isn't well controlled.

Doctor: Yes, I think he could do with another 2 ml per hour of morphine.

Nurse: Fine.

B

Doctor: Could you take Mrs _____'s morphine pump down please? She's been on it long enough now.

Nurse: I don't think she's ready for that yet. We've been trying to reduce it today, but every time we do you can see the pain breaking through.

Doctor: If you can try and reduce it over the next 24 hours, we'll think about it again tomorrow.

C

Nurse: Did I tell you that we stopped his morphine at midnight?

Doctor: No, I don't think so.

Nurse: He was too doped.

Doctor: That's grand. We'll keep it down unless he gets sore again.

(a)   Which of the categories below do you think that each example falls into?
  The doctor–nurse game
  Nurses contributing to decision-making

(b)   Think about a situation where you have witnessed an interaction between a nurse and a doctor. Who did most of the talking? Who made the decisions? Who carried them out?

6 Nurse education

One of the factors that has facilitated changing roles within nursing has been the shift from an apprentice style of training to an education system based on a university model. This can be explained as an inclusionary strategy, based on traditional professional training, and Witz (1994) describes the model of nurse education introduced by Project 2000 (P2K) as a credentialist tactic, giving nurses greater control over the educational curriculum and entry onto nursing courses. Despite this, these moves have not been uncritically accepted. Meerabeau (2001, p. 431), in her review of the literature on the debate over pre-registration nursing, points to critics within the press who denounced the need for a degree programme, frequently citing the pollution involved in nursing work (referred to above as dirty work), 'bedpans and bottoms', and what are classified as 'basic tasks' as justification for their argument.

Miers (2002) points to cultural factors inhibiting the entry of nursing into higher education. Attitudes within higher education concerning the status of practice-based professions, particularly care professions, have seen many nursing departments viewed as less than academic. Within nursing there exists an anti-intellectualism, where nursing research is viewed as an 'ivory tower', removed from the real work of nursing. So nurses themselves are often hostile to diplomas and degrees in nursing, and have used sanctions against those who expressed individuality and questioned or challenged existing practices. Miers argues that this has been a consequence of an education system where practical caring courses more often undertaken by students from lower social classes have the lowest status in the educational hierarchy. The anti-intellectualism within nursing may be viewed as a defensive reaction against a culture that values abstract thinking more highly than practical activity.

Nurses with degrees have been particularly affected by this anti-intellectualism, as was discussed by Green and Earle in chapter 2. Meerabeau (2001) also argues that nursing has remained a marginal subject in higher education. Unlike other university courses it is not funded by the Department of Education and Skills, but is commissioned by strategic health authorities, to whose expressed needs universities respond when developing curricula.

Davies et al. (2000) state that there was an expectation that changes in nurse education introduced by P2K would result in those with diplomas receiving faster promotion and making more effective managers than those who were traditionally trained. From a random sample of nurses entered on the UKCC register between 1992 and 1995, both P2K and traditionally trained, it was found that there was no significant difference in the type of nurse recruited by employers or in career grade. However, P2K nurses felt more prepared to work in rehabilitation, ITU or terminal care and were more willing to work in primary care. Degree nurses considered themselves able to work in management, research and education. Traditionally trained nurses felt more prepared to work in learning disability, paediatrics and mental health, and this group were most likely to be considering leaving nursing. The study was carried out with nurses who had been qualified between one and four years, and so was a restricted sample.

In summary, nursing has shifted from an apprenticeship model of training to become an academic professional education. This has not been uncritically accepted, either by the higher-education sector or by nurses themselves.

Activity 4.5   **No angels**

Read the extract from an article 'Why nurses are no angels' by a junior doctor, published in *The Independent* newspaper on 18 July 2006, and then answer the questions below.

> It is an open secret that the standard of nursing in British hospitals is poor, at least in the inner cities. . . . I have worked with many excellent nurses: people who take pride in their work, who value the business of caring, and who are expert in the ward management of patients in their specialty. Mainly they are nurses of the old school who have declined the move into hospital management. Safety, cleanliness, comfort and dignity are the basics of proper patient care, and if they are not attended to then the medicine means, and can achieve, nothing.
>
> Sadly, excellent nurses who choose to stay working on the ward are the exception rather than the rule. In my daily working life I encounter far too many unmotivated, off-hand people who seem to be unable to differentiate between life-threatening scenarios and simple patient requests, who vanish whenever a patient is incontinent, who spend their days bleeping the doctor with every little thing and then writing 'Dr informed' in the notes, before going to tea, satisfied that their problem is now safely my problem. Worse, if the problem appears to be routine rather than life-threatening, even after a lengthy conversation I can never be confident of it, and have taken to getting them to put the patient on the phone instead.

(a)   Critically evaluate this extract. What are the main points being made? Do you agree or disagree with what has been written about modern nurses?

(b)   What do you think are the main tasks of nursing care in your branch?

(c)   Do you think that a nurse with a degree will not want to carry out those tasks?

(d)   Why do you think that nursing has been the target of press criticism over the past few years?

Summary and Resources

Summary

- The present occupation of nursing developed from the domestic role of women in caring for the sick in institutions and the community.

- The idea of nursing as 'women's work' has led to advantages for men in nursing, as they are deemed to possess qualities required for leadership, but they may also be treated with suspicion, particularly when working with vulnerable groups.

- Nurses have attempted social closure strategies in order to raise the status of nursing and to lay claim to a distinct contribution to health care.

- Although nursing has traditionally been constrained in its development by a powerful medical profession, recent nursing developments have made occupational relationships more complex.

- Nurse education has shifted from an apprenticeship model of nursing training in health care institutions to become an academic professional education, with the award of degrees and diplomas.

Questions for Discussion

1 Historically nursing was considered as 'women's work' because of the association between women and caring work. Does this have any relevance for nursing today? Do men and women have different expectations from a career in nursing?

2 'In all branches of nursing status is gained by moving away from direct care, creating the "polo mint problem" ' (Davies, 1995). What can nurses do to raise the value of caring roles within society?

3 Debates continue over whether the move of nurse education into higher education better prepares nurses for present and future roles than the old apprenticeship training. What are the benefits to nursing of a combination of an academic education and learning in practice?

Further Reading

C. Hart: *Nurses and Politics*. Basingstoke: Palgrave, 2004. This volume provides a historical and contemporary analysis of the issues facing nursing. Although nurses are the largest single occupational group in health care, this is one of the few texts that considers how issues such as private finance initiatives, foundation trusts, and devolution affect them.

S. Proctor: *Caring for Health*. Basingstoke: Palgrave, 2000.
Caring is a fundamental part of nursing and yet has become
increasingly marginalized. This volume uses nursing and sociological
knowledge to examine the role of caring and the link between caring
and health.

R. Simpson: *Men in Caring Occupations*. Basingstoke: Palgrave, 2009.
This book considers how men in caring jobs manage gender and
identity in feminized occupations. Part 1 draws on theoretical
concepts, while part 2 uses specific occupational settings (including
two chapters on nursing) to explore the experience of men in these
roles.

G. Wilkinson and M. Miers (eds): *Power and Nursing Practice*.
Basingstoke: Palgrave, 1999.
This edited text examines sociological concepts of power, and applies
them to nursing work. It is particularly useful in that separate
chapters explore power issues for each branch of nursing.

**For more useful learning resources on nursing as an occupation,
see www.politybooks.com/sociologyfornurses.**

References

Brimblecombe, N. R. 2005: 'The changing relationship between
mental health nurses and psychiatrists in the United Kingdom'.
Journal of Advanced Nursing, 49(4), 344–53.

Carmel, S. 2006: 'Boundaries obscured and boundaries reinforced:
incorporation as a strategy of occupational enhancement for
intensive care'. *Sociology of Health & Illness*, 28(2), 154–77.

Clarke, J. 1999: 'The diminishing role of nurses in hands on care'.
Nursing Times, 95(27), 48–9.

Clarke, M. 1978: 'Getting through the work'. In R. Dingwall and
J. Macintosh (eds), *Readings in the Sociology of Nursing*. Edinburgh:
Churchill Livingstone, pp. 67–86.

Davies, C. 1995: *Gender and the Professional Predicament in Nursing*.
Buckingham: Open University Press.

Davies, C., Stillwell, J., Wilson, R., Carlisle, C., and Luker, K. 2000:
'Did Project 2000 training change recruitment patterns or career
expectations?' *Nurse Education Today*, 20, 408–17.

Davis, F. 1975: 'Professional socialisation as subjective experience:
the process of doctrinal conversion among student nurses'. In
C. Cox and A. Meade (eds), *The Sociology of Medical Practice*.
London: Collier-Macmillan, pp. 116–31.

Daykin, N., and Clarke, B. 2000: '"They'll still get the bodily care."
Discourse of care and relationships between nurses and health
care assistants in the NHS'. *Sociology of Health & Illness*, 22(3),
349–63.

Denny, E. 2003: 'The class context of nursing'. In M. Miers (ed.), *Class, Inequalities and Nursing Practice*. Basingstoke: Palgrave, pp. 77–97.

Dingwall, R., Rafferty, A. M., and Webster, C. 1988: *An Introduction to the Social History of Medicine*. London: Routledge.

Etzioni, A. 1969: *The Semi-Professions and their Organization*. New York: Free Press.

Evans, J. A. 1997: 'Men in nursing: issues of gender segregation and hidden advantage'. *Journal of Advanced Nursing*, 26, 226–31.

Evans, J. A. 2002: 'Cautious caregivers: gender stereotypes and the sexualisation of men nurses' touch'. *Journal of Advanced Nursing*, 40(4), 441–8.

Freidson, E. 1970: *The Profession of Medicine: A Study in the Sociology of Applied Knowledge*. New York: Dodd Mead.

Godin, P. 2003: 'Class inequalities in mental health nursing'. In M. Miers (ed.), *Class, Inequalities and Nursing Practice*. Basingstoke: Palgrave, pp. 125–43.

Hardy T., North N., and Perkins, R. 2008: 'Sexualizing men's touch: male nurses and the use of intimate touch in nursing'. *Research and Theory for Nursing Practice*, 22(2), 88–102.

Healthcare Commission 2005: *Ward Staffing*. London: Commission for Healthcare Audit and Inspection.

Hughes, D. 1988: 'When nurse knows best: some aspects of nurse/doctor interaction in a casualty department'. *Sociology of Health & Illness*, 10(1), 1–22.

Inoue, M., Chapman, R., and Wynaden, D. 2006: 'Male nurses' experience of providing intimate care for women clients'. *Journal of Advanced Nursing*, 55(5), 559–67.

Meerabeau, E. 2001: 'Back to the bedpans: the debates over preregistration nursing education in England'. *Journal of Advanced Nursing*, 34(4), 427–35.

Melia, K. 1987: *Learning and Working: The Occupational Socialisation of Nurses*. London: Tavistock.

Miers, M. 1999: 'Nursing teams and hierarchies: nurses working with nurses'. In G. Wilkinson and M. Miers (eds), *Power and Nursing Practice*. Basingstoke: Palgrave, pp. 64–79.

Miers, M. 2000: *Gender Issues and Nursing Practice*. Basingstoke: Macmillan.

Miers, M. 2002: 'Nurse education in higher education: understanding cultural barriers to progress'. *Nurse Education Today*, 22(21), 2–9.

Millerson, G. L. 1964: *The Qualifying Association*. London: Routledge & Kegan Paul.

Mowforth, G. 1999: 'Elitism in nursing'. In G. Wilkinson and M. Miers (eds), *Power and Nursing Practice*. Basingstoke: Palgrave, pp. 51–63.

Parkin, F. 1979: *Marxism and Class Theory: A Bourgeois Critique*. London: Tavistock.

Porter, S. 1995: *Nursing's Relationship with Medicine*. Aldershot: Avebury.

Porter, S. 1999: 'Working with doctors'. In G. Wilkinson and M. Miers (eds), *Power and Nursing Practice*. Basingstoke: Palgrave, pp. 97–110.

Prowse, M., and Allen, D. 2002: Routine and emergency in the PACU: the shifting context of nurse–doctor interaction. In D. Allen and D. Hughes (eds), *Nursing and the Division of Labour in Healthcare*. Basingstoke: Palgrave, pp. 75–98.

Rafferty, A. M. 1995: 'The anomaly of autonomy: space and status in early nursing reform'. *International History of Nursing Journal*, 1, 43–56.

Rafferty, A. M. 1996: *The Politics of Nursing Knowledge*. London: Routledge.

Rafferty, A. M., Clarke S. P., Coles, J., et al. 2007: 'Outcomes of variation in hospital nurse staffing in English hospitals: cross-sectional analysis of survey data and discharge records'. *International Journal of Nursing Studies*, 44(2), 175–82.

Snelgrove, S., and Hughes, D. 2002: 'Perceptions of teamwork in acute medical wards'. In D. Allen and D. Hughes (eds), *Nursing and the Division of Labour in Healthcare*. Basingstoke: Palgrave, pp. 53–74.

Snooks, H.A., Williams, A.M., Griffiths, L. J., et al. 2007: 'Real nursing? The development of telenursing'. *Journal of Advanced Nursing*, 61(6), 631–40.

Stein, L. 1967: 'The doctor/nurse game'. *Archives of General Psychiatry*, 16, 699–703.

Stein, L., Watts, D. T., and Howell, T. 1990: 'The doctor–nurse game revisited'. *New England Journal of Medicine*, 322(8), 546–9.

Wakefield, A. 2000: 'Tensions experienced by student nurses in a changed NHS culture'. *Nurse Education Today*, 20, 571–8.

Wicks, D. 1998: *Nurses and Doctors at Work*. Buckingham: Open University Press.

Williams, C. 1994: 'Nurses' voices – men in nursing: Lazy? On the glass escalator? Or gay?' Paper presented at the British Sociological Association Annual Conference, Preston.

Witz, A. 1992: *Professions and Patriarchy*. London: Routledge.

Witz, A. 1994: 'The challenge of nursing'. In J. Gabe, D. Kelleher and G. Williams (eds), *Challenging Medicine*. London: Sage, pp. 23–45.

Wolf, Z. R. 1996: 'Bowel management and nursing's hidden work'. *Nursing Times*, 92(21), 26–8.

Part II

Inequalities and Diversities in Health and Health Care

It is important to be aware of diversity amongst patient/client groups and the impact of this on health and health care. This part examines health inequality and diversity, focusing specifically on gender, age, disability, class, and race and ethnicity. It also considers health as a global issue.

In chapter 5, 'Gender', the emphasis is on the significance of sex and gender for health and illness. The chapter provides a definition of sex and gender and a historical overview of some key gendered concerns, emphasizing how 'gender issues' do not relate just to women and girls, but also to men and boys. Whilst it is often the case than 'men get sick and women die', the picture is much more complex than this, and this chapter unpacks some of the key issues. The concepts of masculinity and femininity are explored and the question 'What makes women and men sick?' is addressed. The chapter concludes by arguing that, just as it affects perceptions of what makes women and men sick, sexism also affects service provision. You are encouraged to think about how gender and sexism influence the treatment and care you offer to patients.

Chapter 6, 'Age and Ageing', suggests that, whilst we may think about 'ageing' solely in relation to older people, the study of age and ageing is relevant to all nurses. Nurses work with patients of all ages, and assumptions are made about health care in relation to age. Drawing on a life-course perspective, this chapter challenges some of these assumptions and explores the social construction of ageing. It explores definitions of 'age' and examines the changing structure of the population. You will be introduced to both traditional and more contemporary theories of ageing and will examine the impact of ageism on health. The chapter encourages you to explore your own stereotypes about 'age', to reflect on anti-ageist policies and to consider how these might affect your nursing practice.

Diversity and inequality in relation to disability are dealt with in chapter 7, 'Chronic Illness and Disability'. The classification and definition of disability and impairment are considered, and you are introduced to some of the sociological theorizing on disability. The chapter discusses the social model, which has been very influential within sociological thinking on disability; the social model makes a distinction between 'impairment' and 'disability' and suggests that disability is socially constructed. The chapter also considers the health challenge of the increase in chronic (or long-term) illness and brings sociology of the body into the debate, in particular with a focus on chronic pain.

In chapter 8, 'Social Class and Health', we explain the traditional sociological concept of class and discuss the more contemporary measurement of socio-economic differences. The chapter maps the history of the relationship between class and health and considers the widening gap in inequalities between the richest and poorest. It then turns to a discussion of the evidence relating to class inequalities in health. Some of the policies used to tackle health inequalities in the twenty-first century are discussed and the explanations for such inequalities are evaluated. Chapter 8 encourages you to investigate and understand the significance of class and health for nursing practice.

Chapter 9, 'Race and Ethnicity', draws the distinction between the concepts of 'race' and 'ethnicity'. Although ethnicity relates to both individual identity and structural or cultural differences, this chapter highlights that it is important for nurses to recognize the considerable individual and social diversity within and between ethnic groups. It provides a brief history of immigration in Britain, which now boasts over 4.5 million people who describe themselves as belonging to a minority ethnic group. The relationship between ethnicity and health and health care is examined, and there is some discussion of the methodological issues involved in measuring the relationship between health and ethnicity. This chapter encourages you to reflect on the implications of ethnic diversity for nursing practice.

Chapter 10, 'Global Health', is an additional chapter for this edition which demonstrates the growing recognition of health as an issue that has repercussions beyond national borders. Greater migration and easy travel have meant that health can no longer be viewed parochially, and this has an impact on the experience of (ill-) health and the delivery of health care. Global patterns of disease are changing, and in some ways are becoming more similar, although great inequalities remain between low and high income countries. These issues impact on nursing care, as more nurses migrate in order to find work or to gain experience, or for altruistic reasons. The chapter discusses why the resulting movement of nurses has been described as both a 'brain drain' and a 'brain gain'.

All of the chapters within this section share certain features. First, each explores the significance of definition and classification, demonstrating not just how this has changed over time, but also how the definition of difference and diversity can affect treatment and care. Second, they share methodological concerns and highlight the fact that we cannot separate what we know to be true from the way in which that 'truth' has emerged. Although there is consensus on the existence of inequalities in health, there is considerable debate on the extent and nature of these inequalities and how they should be measured. Finally, all of the chapters within this section encourage you to reflect on the way in which diversity affects your practice and how inequalities in health may influence treatment and care.

5 Gender

Gayle Letherby

Key issues in this chapter

- Definitional and historical issues
- The significance of sex and gender in relation to health and illness
- The gendered experience of health care
- The relationship between gender and other 'measures' of stratification

By the end of this chapter you should be able to . . .

- explain how historical definitions and expectations of men and women affect contemporary definitions and experiences;
- explain how historical views on the relationship between gender and health affect contemporary views and experiences;
- understand the significance of sex and gender for patterns of health and illness;
- explain the relationship between gender roles, masculinity and femininity, and health and illness;
- recognize the need to take a gendered perspective, whilst acknowledging that other differences are also relevant.

---

1 Introduction

This chapter begins with some definitions. When considering issues of gender in relation to health and illness (or to family life, work and leisure, education, crime – in fact, in relation to anything) it is important to understand what gender means. Gender does not (as some people mistakenly think) refer only to the experiences and perspectives of women but to the significance of similarities and differences between female and male experiences. It is also important to remember that gender is a concept distinct from the concept of sex: **sex** is a term referring to biological differences between men and women and **gender** a term referring to cultural differences (Oakley, 1972). Gender, then, refers to culturally prescribed expectations of women and men and differs over time and place. Thus, gender is not a fixed aspect of our identity, but is fluid, negotiated on a daily basis and something that we 'do' as well as 'have' (also see Marchbank and Letherby, 2007).

sex the biological differences between males and females

gender cultural differences between males and females

In this chapter the relationship between sex and gender, and health, illness and caring is considered. The chapter is divided into four main sections, which focus on historical definitions and contemporary concerns, challenging myths, the relationship between gender and caring, and diversity and difference. This is followed by a brief summary of the main issues.

2   Historical definitions and contemporary concerns

The sixteenth and seventeenth centuries were particularly significant in their effect on understandings of gender and health in the Western world. The scientific knowledge which emerged at this time was argued to be objective knowledge. As Gunew (1990) and Wajcman (1991) note, historically and to date (see Ahmed, 2004), men are believed to be capable of objectivity and women are not.

The dominant message then was that women were not just different from men but physically, psychologically, emotionally and socially inferior to men (Doyal, 1995; Letherby, 2003) and characterized as 'sensitive, intuitive, incapable of objectivity and emotional detachment and . . . immersed in the business of making and maintaining personal relationships' (Oakley, 1981, p. 38). Thus, women were considered naturally weak and easy to exploit, and their psychological characteristics implied subordination, for example, submission, passivity and dependency. From this perspective women are more like children than adults, in that they are immature, weak and helpless (Oakley, 1981; Evans, 1997). If women adopt these characteristics they are considered well adjusted

hysteria   the term was first coined by Hippocrates and is derived from the Greek word *hystera*, or uterus. The theory of female hysteria gained popularity in the works of Sigmund Freud in the early twentieth century and then by Jean-Martin Charcot, a French neurologist

emotion work   the regulation, management and care of one's own and others' feelings and emotions

(Oakley, 1981), but being considered well adjusted clearly comes with a price; in the eighteenth and nineteenth centuries defining women as weak justified their exclusion from the world of work and education.

However, although women have historically been constructed as weak and prone to **hysteria**, they have always performed large amounts of physical labour both in the home and outside of it, and on top of this have been, and still are, held responsible for the dominant share of domestic and **emotion work** (Frith and Kitzinger, 1998; Marchbank and Letherby, 2007) (see chapter 2). Despite this, the image of women as inferior is still significant in defining

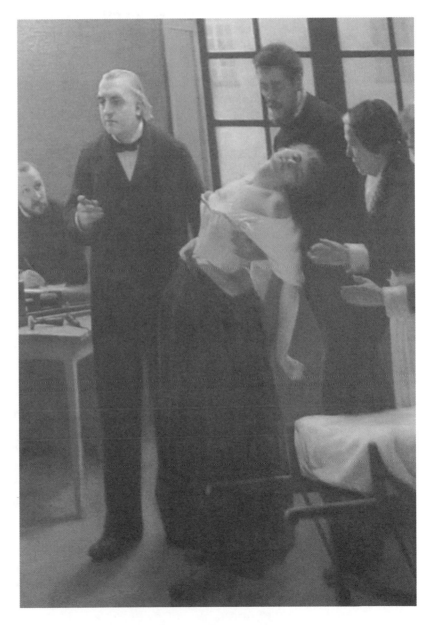

The nineteenth-century neurologist Jean-Martin Charcot was one of the key proponents of the theory of hysteria.

women's lives (for example, Coppock, Haydon and Richter, 1995; and Doyal, 1995).

All of this has implications for women in terms of their health and of general perceptions of women as healthy or not. In the nineteenth century, middle-class women were thought to be particularly weak and susceptible to illness: menstruation was thought to be an 'indisposition' or illness which sapped women's energy, making it necessary for them to rest; childbirth was termed 'confinement', and a long period of bed rest was thought to be necessary after the birth of a baby; and the menopause was considered a disease which marked the beginning of senility (Webb, 1986).

Oddly, working-class women were not seen as being susceptible to the same problems. They were considered to be physically stronger, emotionally less sensitive, and well able to work fourteen hours a day outside of the home and still be able to 'cook, clean and service their husbands, and bear children without such suffering' (Webb, 1986, p. 6). Furthermore, working-class women were seen as potentially polluting through their work in the kitchen, the nursery and the brothel (Abbott et al., 2005). The harshest reading of this is that working-class women were not viewed as women at all, and the most generous that, whereas middle-class women were 'sickly', working-class women were 'sickening'.

Current lay and medical definitions of the gendered significance of health seem to continue the sexist view of women as 'sickly'. When asked to think of someone they consider to be healthy, both men and women are more likely to choose a man (Blaxter, 1990). Psychologists and clinicians are more likely to define women's than men's health problems as psychological, and definitions of mental health are often related to traditional notions of **masculinity and femininity**: healthy men are thought to be independent, logical and adventurous and healthy women less aggressive, more emotional and easily hurt (Webb, 1986; Miers, 2000; Ahmed, 2004; Marchbank and Letherby, 2007).

masculinity and femininity the ways in which men and women are expected to behave, think and feel

Evidence from research also suggests that women make more use of health services and appear to feel less healthy than men (Annandale and Clark, 1996). However, in some interpretations of data where comparisons are made between males and females, the health status of men is glossed over or informed by simplistic, stereotypical approaches (Miers, 2000; Watson, 2000). This construction of women's health as poor has consequences for men too, in that there is an implicit assumption that men's health is 'good'. The result of this is that men's poor health remains invisible and differences between men are not considered (Annandale and Clark, 1996; Watson, 2000; Featherstone, Rivett and Scourfield, 2007).

The seeking of professional help for both physical and mental health needs is gendered, and it is well known that men are

Activity 5.1   Gendered definitions: the case of hysteria

> The word hysteria is usually used to describe a woman
> as though she were simply behaving according to
> expectations . . . Hysteria now refers to a specific
> psychoneurosis that may affect anyone, male or female. In
> popular usage it is a state of excessive fear or other emotion
> in individuals or masses of people, but in this sense men –
> whether individually or in groups – are seldom said to be
> hysterical. After a series of rapes at a large college in 1974,
> news stories repeatedly described a 'mood of hysteria' among
> women students on the campus. The description, according
> to the dean of women, was totally false. 'The mood of the
> women is one of concern and anger,' she told reporters.
> 'When men feel concern and anger, it is called concern and
> anger, never hysteria.' (Mills, 1991, p. 127)

(a)   Can you think of some more examples of women being described
       as hysterical?
(b)   Do you think that the association of hysteria with womanhood
       affects the ways we popularly define women's and men's, and
       girls' and boys', mental health and well-being? If so, what are the
       implications for the treatment and care of women and men with
       mental health problems?

generally less likely to seek professional help than women
(Featherstone, Rivett and Scourfield, 2007). However, stressing
men's reluctance to access medical care can support the problematic
view that the health and well-being of men and children is the
responsibility of women:

> They [women] are seen as responsible for bringing up
> healthy children and maintaining the health of their men for
> the nation. Health visitors, social workers and other
> professional state employees 'police' the family to ensure that
> women are carrying out their task adequately. (Abbott et al.,
> 2005, p. 196)

It is also important to note that, for some illnesses, there is little
gender difference in help-seeking (Galdas, Cheater and Marshall,
2005; Featherstone, Rivett and Scourfield, 2007).

So, historically and to date, lay and medical perceptions of the
relationship between sex, gender, health and illness are based
on sexist assumptions of what women and men are and should
be like.

Activity 5.2   **Gender and socialization: learning to be different**

Learning to care

(a) Why are women still expected to be mainly responsible for the care of children – in the home and the nursery, the school and the hospital? How does our childhood socialization perpetuate this view?

(b) Can you think of examples from your own childhood where gender stereotypes were reinforced?

(c) What are the positives and negatives of encouraging more men to care for children (within the family and through their work)?

3 Challenging myths: masculinity, femininity and health and illness

The phrase 'women get sick and men die', which historically has been central to research findings in the area of gender inequalities in health, still holds some truth, but it oversimplifies the complex relationship between gender and health. Abbott and her colleagues (2005) note that a gendered pattern is found in all societies with women, on average, living longer than men. However, there are social class differences between women within societies, and the male–female gap in life expectancy varies significantly between countries – for example, Russia has the largest male–female gap in life expectancy, whereas in some countries in South East Asia and parts of sub-Saharan and West Africa the gap is much smaller or even virtually eliminated. As health service use increases with age in societies where women do live longer, not surprisingly they have higher consultation rates over a lifetime, especially when we take into account the visits related to menstruation, pregnancy, childbirth, post-natal care and menopause. Furthermore, women appear to find it easier and more socially acceptable to discuss their own health, and there may also be important psychosocial factors such as how men and women evaluate symptoms (Watson, 2000; Featherstone, Rivett and Scourfield, 2007).

The main causes of lower life expectancy for men lie in higher death rates from coronary heart disease, lung cancer and chronic obstructive airways disease, accidents, homicides, suicides and AIDS (Miers, 2000). Men are more likely to die of occupationally related illnesses, men engage in more physical risk-taking than women, and accidents and homicides have always been a feature of masculine rather than feminine experience (Featherstone, Rivett and Scourfield, 2007). Cigarette smoking has, hitherto, been a major cause of death among men (although in the 1990s male and female smoking rates in the UK began to even out) and men drink more than women (although this is changing too, and gender is not the only signifier of differential substance use). For example, King and McKeown (2003) report high levels of alcohol and substance misuse among (especially young) lesbian, bisexual and gay (LBG) people and link this to the importance of pubs and clubs in LBG social life.

The poorer aspects of men's health are often associated with stereotypical male gender roles: trying to live up to a macho image and lifestyle which is itself dangerous to health. From this perspective, much ill-health among men is a consequence of lifestyle, which nurses and other health professionals can address in their role as health educators. However, the challenge to change male behaviour and resist stereotypical masculinity is problematic because it presumes that masculinity is a unitary construct and that all men benefit equally from being male in a patriarchal society (Featherstone, Rivett and Scourfield, 2007; Dolan, 2007).

In common with stereotypical views, just as men's 'dangerous lives' are thought to be detrimental to their health, women's mental and physical weaknesses are thought to be of major significance to women's ill-health. Statistics suggest that about twice as many women as men suffer from a mental disorder. However, yet again, in reality things are more complex, as there are distinctive gender patterns associated with different mental phenomena. For example, anorexia nervosa is a predominantly female condition, and women report anxiety, phobias and depression more often than men, while substance-use disorders and personality disorders and suicide are more common among men (Featherstone, Rivett and Scourfield, 2007). However, as with physical ill-health, not all men and not all women are the same, and the labelling of an illness or a condition as 'women's' or 'men's business' is often inaccurate and has serious medical, social and emotional consequences.

Men are sometimes reluctant to seek health advice. This health promotion campaign, fronted by the professional footballer David James, highlights awareness of testicular cancer.

Activity 5.3 **Reproductive health**

Very little information is available on the risks and benefits of various forms of contraception for women with disabilities.

Only certain types of disabilities interfere with fertility in women.

Some believe that eugenics and general perceptions of women with disabilities as asexual are responsible for the high rate of hysterectomy in younger women with disabilities.

Women with disabilities may not receive the same amount of sexuality and reproductive health information from the same sources, as non-disabled women. . . .

Minority status and sexual orientation both have disproportionately negative impacts on women with disabilities.
(*Improving the Health and Wellness of Women with Disabilities: A Symposium to Establish a Research Agenda June 2003*)

Go to the 'Improving the Health and Wellness of Women with Disabilities' webpage (http://www.crowdbcm.net). What other information can you find – on this site and others – about the reproductive and other health needs of women (and men) with disabilities, including learning disabilities?

Overall, then, the expectations of both men and women and their roles and responsibilities have consequences for health. As noted earlier, despite enduring stereotypical views of women as weak and helpless, work, both paid and unpaid, is a significant aspect of women's lives. However, most research into the relationship between paid work and ill-health has focused on male-dominated occupations. It is widely believed that female jobs are neither physically hazardous nor stressful, but research demonstrates otherwise (for example, Hochschild, [1983] 2003; Doyal, 1995; Morgan, Brandth and Kvande, 2005). On your next placement, it is worth considering the extent to which you find nursing work hazardous or stressful. The sexist bias in occupational health research is further extended by traditional assumptions of women's weaknesses, for example: 'Researchers have been concerned for some time to determine whether or not menstruation interferes with women's capacity to work. They have been much less interested in how women's work affects their experiences of menstruation' (Doyal, 1995, p. 169). The hazards of domestic work are even more hidden, although we know that being a 'good' wife and mother can make women sick. Evidence suggests that women prioritize the needs of other family members, allocating them more resources and caring for them to the detriment of their own health – not least because, as argued earlier, this is expected of them (for example, Doyal, 1995; Abbott et al. 2005).

Furthermore, many women and children live in danger of ill-health, even death, as the result of men's emotional, psychological, sexual and physical violence (Stanko, 1990; Letherby et al., 2008). Both Kelly's (1988) and Daly and Wilson's (1988) careful examination of homicide reveal men's use of violence to control their female partners across industrial and non-industrial societies. While they argue that the killing of women is relatively rare, the use of violence is not. While men's violence to women is usually characterized as 'losing control' or flying into a 'blind rage', all the evidence suggests that both battered women and the men who batter tell the same story, that men's behaviour is used as a means of control. On the other hand, although men do experience violent attacks by women, this constitutes the smallest proportion of assaults on men, and men are much more likely to be victims of physical and sexual violence from other men (Newburn and Stanko, 1994; Marchbank, 2008).

Overall, then, although differences between male and female patterns of health and illness do have some basis in biology (for example, the protective effects of oestrogen in pre-menopausal women), these patterns are more complicated than biology alone. As noted in chapter 3, whilst sociologists accept the significance of biology, they look for social explanations of health and illness that do not rely on sexist stereotypes of 'male' and 'female' illnesses and problems.

4   Gender and caring

Just as sexism affects the dominant views on what makes men and women sick, so it affects the treatment and care individuals receive. With reference to waiting lists, there is evidence that women are disproportionately affected in particular areas – for example, family-planning services have been significantly reduced in many parts of the UK – and their longer life expectancy means that older women are more likely than older men to be affected by the withdrawal of continuing-care beds. Domestic responsibilities, lack of transport and cultural or linguistic barriers may also affect women more (Doyal, 1998).

It has long been argued that diseases and illnesses that proportionately affect men in greater numbers receive more resources than those that more often affect women. More recently it has been suggested that it is not only that 'men's diseases' are taken more seriously but male patients are too. For example, in the US, men on dialysis are significantly more likely than women with the same symptoms to obtain a kidney transplant and men with cardiac symptoms are more likely than women to be given diagnostic catheterization. The continuing failure to include women in sufficient numbers either in epidemiological research or in clinical trials has also made it difficult to investigate gender differences or to assess the overall significance of gender in the delivery of effective care (Doyal, 1998; Lockyer, 2009).

paternalism/paternalistic the sexist treatment of women

In 1986 Webb suggested that paternalism, sexism and stereotyping formed the hallmark of much health care. For example, the cultural emphasis on breasts as objects of male sexual interest and male sexual pleasure is significant within treatment for breast cancer (Wilkinson and Kitzinger, 1994) and in relation to breast augmentation (Conrad and Jacobson, 2003), and women often report feeling infantilized during consultations relating to various aspects of reproduction (for example, see Earle and Letherby, 2003).

When dissatisfaction with treatment is an issue, complaining can be difficult. Patients who resist may be labelled a nuisance and become unpopular with medical staff (for example, see Denny's (2009) discussion of 'heartsink patients'), which could in turn affect their experience of treatment. The 'gratitude factor' (Coyle, 1999) has also been identified as a barrier to patients complaining or expressing dissatisfaction. Given assumptions of and socialization into 'appropriate' feminine behaviour, it would be easy to think that women are more likely to find it difficult to resist and complain than men. However, it is important not to view patients – male or female – as passive victims. Research suggests that both patients and doctors attempt to control and direct the consultation along their own desired line in order to persuade the other of their preferred solution (Annandale and Hunt, 2000), and research on lay people's use of the internet suggests that the information discovered is sometimes used

Activity 5.4   ## Improving on biology/challenging nature?

Read the extract from the news story below (you may like to access the full version on the internet) and answer the following questions.

There's been a surprising explosion in vanity surgery for men . . .
From Botox to liposuction, nose jobs to breast implants. The domain of cosmetic surgery is often associated with vain women . . . [but] a growing number of men are willing to pay thousands of pounds to improve what God, genetics or exercise couldn't! . . . Steve King, editor of Men's Health magazine, explains this barrage of images of 'perfection' has resulted in a rush of men desperate to go under the knife . . . 'I hate to say it,' says Steve, 'but women are putting pressure on men. They want us to look like the guy from the Calvin Klein advert.'

. . .

Facial MOT
Mike Wood is a car dealer from Stockport. He's been around the block a few times and feels his face needs an MOT. Mike decided to have Botox and restylane to iron-out his wrinkles. Mike says, 'I'm a bit of a sucker for the ladies. I'm not getting any younger so maybe I'll be able to go for a younger girl.'

(BBC, 2003)

(a)   What gender stereotypes are supported *and* challenged by this extract?

(b)   When is cosmetic surgery a physical/mental health care issue and when is it 'vanity'? Is this different for men and for women?

(c)   Should gender reassignment (sex change) surgery, bariatric (weight loss) surgery, surgery for Down's syndrome children to make eyes look more 'normal' and tongues less protruding, and skin whitening for black and Asian people be funded by the NHS? Would the sex of the person concerned affect your decision?

(d)   Find some more surgery news stories and reflect on the significance of gendered stereotypes, roles and responsibilities to the decisions and experiences of all those involved.

to understand and sometimes question medical decisions (Broom, 2005; Foroushani, 2008).

The response to sexism in health care has a history of at least thirty-five years. A number of books with the aim of informing women about their own bodies and their own health hit the bookstores in the 1970s (perhaps the most well known being *Our Bodies Ourselves*, first published by the Boston Women's Health Book Collective in 1973). These were written by women and were grounded in women's experiences. However, as Hockey (1997) notes, these early texts were relevant mostly for white middle-class audiences, and it was not until the 1980s that books aimed at black, lesbian, working-class and older women began to appear. There are fewer books even today specifically concerned with men's health, although during the 1990s men's health was an increasing concern within the media, with reports on increasing stress and incidences of cancer, declining fertility and reluctance to visit the doctor (Watson, 2000). In turn, all of this has led to further debate on the state of men's health and what to do about it. Attempts in the UK to encourage men to pay more attention to their health have included the production of a men's health manual modelled on the car manuals produced by Haynes (and the reference to a 'facial MOT' in activity 5.4 perhaps demonstrates a different use of the analogy of the man's body as a car).

With their emphasis on empowerment, many of the personal health texts stress the fact that individuals should take control of their

The Haynes 'owner's manual' for men's health

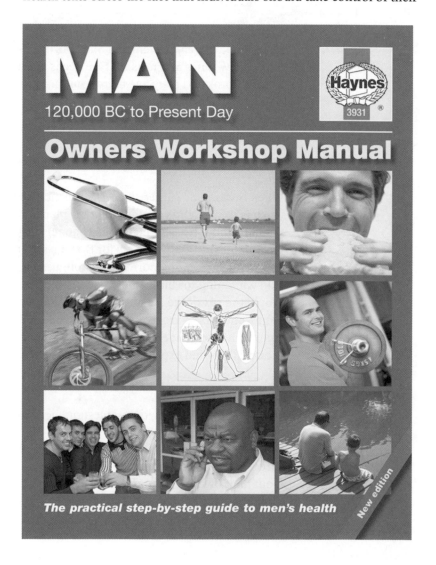

own bodies and minds and be active rather than passive. Empowerment from this perspective, then, often suggests resistance to the dominant medical model and supports 'alternative' health care. Yet there is a problem here, as the dominant message from many alternative health care self-help books and tapes is that we become ill because of unhealthy attitudes and that we can cure ourselves.

Activity 5.5

Gender, health and media

The following extract is taken from a popular UK women's magazine, *Take a Break* (9 October 2003, p. 23):

> Everyone knows that men and women are different. Everyone, it seems, but the people who make and test our medicines. For the best part of 50 years, the drugs industry has assumed that despite our distinctively different external features, men and women are pretty much the same on the inside. But that's a dangerous assumption to make. Vivienne Parry carried out research into the way that drugs work for One Man's Medicine, a programme broadcast by BBC Radio 4. She says: 'Out of ten recent recalls in the US, four have been related solely to adverse effects in women. But given that men and women differ fundamentally in almost every system of their bodies, it shouldn't be a surprise that they have such different responses to drugs. Many are well known.' She says that women:

- come out of anaesthesia faster than men
- have a greater response to some painkillers
- have more side effects with antihistamines, antibiotics, antidepressants and steroids.
- And drugs which prevent fatal alterations to the heartbeat in men can cause them in women.

(a) Consider some of the implications of these findings for women's and men's health.

(b) What are the implications of popular magazines reporting regularly on health issues?

(c) Find some other examples of women's and men's magazines that have articles on health. Can you identify any differences in the articles aimed at men from those aimed at women?

One of the most important attractions of complementary and alternative medicines (CAM) is that they offer the possibility of 'stepping out of the victim role'. However, Wilkinson and Kitzinger (1994) argue that this deflects attention from the state's failure to provide health services for all society's members. Furthermore, the medical profession's authority as the arbiter of 'truth' in health care creates barriers for the professionalization of CAM groups (Kelner et al., 2004) and for general public perceptions of CAMs. Wilkinson and Kitzinger (1994), by contrast, recognizing the problems inherent in both traditional and alternative health care provisions, note that a **feminist** analysis of health and illness begins by acknowledging that women (and some men) are victims of a patriarchal world which perpetuates gendered inequalities in health. Feminists advocate campaigns and community action to change current medical, social and political attitudes (e.g. Wilkinson and Kitzinger, 1994; Lorber and Moore, 2002). Theories of social structure are relevant here in that the structure of society is seen to perpetuate gendered inequalities in health (see also chapter 1).

feminist relating to the ◄ political theory and practice that challenges the oppression of women

Obviously, it is not only women who are disempowered by the health service. Male members of economically and ethnically marginalized or disadvantaged groups are likely to find it hard too. Such groups are increasingly being brought within the policy gaze (Watson, 2000; Featherstone, Rivett and Scourfield, 2007). In addition there remains the problem in unequal help-seeking practices (between men and women) with heterosexual middle-aged men (Watson, 2000) and both younger and older men (Featherstone, Rivett and Scourfield, 2007) being identified as less visible groups in practice.

5   Diversity and difference

As Di Stephano (1990, p. 78) argues, gender is significant and functions as 'a difference that makes a difference' to our lives. However, when we do consider differences between men and women we need to remember that 'Much of what it is to be human and live in societies is the same for men and women' (Carpenter, 2000, p. 48). Also, as you will become aware from the other chapters in this part of the book, gender is not the only 'difference' that we need to take seriously. Differences of age, class, sexuality, ethnicity, and physical and learning disability are also relevant to our experience of health, illness and health care.

Taking ethnicity as an example, we know that 'race' adversely affects black women's and men's experiences in relation to health (and, indeed, all other areas of social life). Yet 'race' is not a coherent category, and the lives of those usually classified together under the label 'black' can be very different. Thus, culture, class, religion, nationality, sexuality, age, and so on, in addition to gender, can all have an impact on women's and men's lives, and it is necessary to challenge the homogeneity of experience previously ascribed to women by virtue of being 'black'. For example, as Douglas (1998) notes, the health status of black and ethnic-minority women in the

UK reflects the interaction between their experiences of race, gender, class and culture (see also chapter 9). So health and well-being are determined in these groups of women by a complex mixture of social and psychological influences and biological and genetic factors. Ethnic-minority women are not a homogeneous group with uniform needs: 'They may be South Asian, Asian, Chinese, Vietnamese, African or African-Caribbean. They may have been born in the UK, may have migrated recently and may be refugees. They may have disabilities, be older, be lesbian . . . ' (Douglas, 1998, p. 70). Further, as Maynard (1994) points out, individuals do not have to be black to experience racism, as attention to the historical and contemporary experience of Jewish and Irish people demonstrates.

The issue of HIV/AIDS not only demonstrates further the need to consider gender in connection with other differences but also indicates the political complexity of health inequalites and responses to these:

> professionals and volunteers in the HIV field worked hard in the late 1980s and early 1990s to get across the message that anyone could contract HIV through unsafe practices and that it was unprotected sex or shared needles that posed risks rather than so-called 'high risk groups'. This was a conscious attempt at an anti-discriminatory strategy and was understandable in the context of homophobic discourse of gay men being to blame for HIV/AIDS. However, activists such as Gay Men Fighting AIDS set out to challenge this consensus among those working in care and prevention on the basis that by far the greatest number of people getting ill and dying were in fact gay men. (Featherstone, Rivett and Scourfield, 2007, p. 122)

Thus, as the examples in this section indicate, in addition to taking gender seriously, other aspects of difference should be taken equally seriously, remembering to consider when and how gender intersects and overlaps with other aspects of difference.

Summary and Resources

Summary

- The historical definition of women as weaker – both physically and emotionally – affects contemporary definitions, and when asked to think of a healthy person most people choose a man.

- The view that men die but women are more likely to get sick simplifies the complex relationship between gender and health. Women's and men's roles and responsibilities do have consequences for health, so patterns of health and illness relate to more than biological differences. Having said this, it is important not to rely on sexist stereotypes of 'male' and 'female' illnesses and problems and to remember that gender is a fluid and not a fixed category.

- Dominant views on what makes men and women sick also affect the treatment and care individuals receive, and there is some evidence to suggest that 'men's diseases' and male patients are taken more seriously. However, both men and women are able to challenge and resist medical dominance.

- It is clear that gender is significant to the health and well-being of men and women, and boys and girls, but it is also important to consider how gender intersects with other aspects of difference, such as age, class, sexuality, ethnicity, and physical and learning dis/ability.

Questions for Discussion

1 Why and how is gender significant when we consider issues of health and illness?

2 Why and how is gender significant when we consider the care of the sick? To what extent have you been aware of this significance during your placements?

3 Why is it important to consider the relationship between gender and other aspects of difference and diversity when considering health and illness and the care of the sick?

Further Reading

E. Annandale and K. Hunt (eds): *Gender Inequalities in Health*. Buckingham: Open University Press, 2000; J. M. Ussher (ed.): *Women's Health: Contemporary International Perspectives*. Leicester: British Psychological Society, 2000; J. Watson: *Male Bodies: Health, Culture and Identity*. Buckingham: Open University Press, 2000: J. Lorber and L. J. Moore: *Gender and the Social Construction of Illness*. 2nd edn, New York: AltaMira Press, 2002;

B. Featherstone, M. Rivett and J. Scourfield: *Working with Men in Health and Social Care.* London: Sage, 2007.
For gender-specific books, have a look at one of the above. A useful book that focuses on both male and female experience is the text by Annandale and Hunt, which not only provides detailed insight into gender differences but considers the relationship between sex and gender and other differences. Thus, attention is given to (amongst other things) social class, age and cross-cultural issues.

S. Earle and G. Letherby (eds): *Gender, Identity and Reproduction: Social Perspectives.* Basingstoke: Palgrave, 2003.
Difference and diversity are also a key theme within this text, as are agency and resistance in relation to health care.

J. Marchbank and G. Letherby: *Introduction to Gender: Social Science Perspectives.* Harlow: Pearson Longman, 2007.
Useful as a general introduction to the study of gender.

M. Miers: *Gender Issues and Nursing Practice.* Basingstoke: Macmillan, 2000.
This provides a very useful discussion of the relationship between gender and nursing practices.

References

Abbott, P., Wallace. C., and Tyler, M. 2005: *An Introduction to Sociology: Feminist perspectives.* London: Routledge.

Ahmed, S. 2004: *The Cultural Politics of Emotion.* London: Routledge.

Annandale, E., and Clark, J. 1996: 'What is gender? Feminist theory and the sociology of human reproduction'. *Sociology of Health & Illness.* 18(1). 17–44.

Annandale, E., and Hunt, K. (eds) 2000: *Gender Inequalities in Health.* Buckingham: Open University Press.

BBC 2003: 'Cosmetic surgery for men', Inside Out, 6 January; www. bbc.co.uk/insideout/northwest/series2/cosmetic_surgery_men_ vanity_botox_restylane.shtml [last accessed 12 November 2008].

Blaxter, M. 1990: *Health and Lifestyles.* London: Tavistock/Routledge.

Boston Women's Health Book Collective [1973] 1998: *Our Bodies Ourselves.* 25th anniversary edn, New York: Touchstone.

Broom, A. 2005: 'Virtually he@lthy: the impact of internet use on disease experience and the doctor–patient relationship'. *Qualitative Health Research,* 15(3), 325–45.

Carpenter, M. 2000: 'Reinforcing the pillars: rethinking gender, social divisions and health'. In E. Annandale and K. Hunt (eds), *Gender Inequalities and Health,* Buckingham: Open University Press, p. 36–63.

Conrad, P., and Jacobson, T. J. 2003: '"Enhancing" biology: cosmetic surgery and breast augmentation'. In S. J. Williams, L. Birke and G. Bendelow (eds), *Debating Biology: Sociological Reflections on Health, Medicine and Society.* London: Routledge, pp. 223–34.

Coppock, V., Haydon, D., and Richter, I. 1995: *The Illusions of 'Post-Feminism': New Women, Old Myths*. London: Taylor & Francis.

Coyle, J. 1999: 'Exploring the meaning of "dissatisfaction" with health care: the importance of "personal identity threat"'. *Sociology of Health & Illness*, 21(1), 95–123.

Daly, M., and Wilson, M. 1988: *Homicide: Foundations of Human Behaviour*. New York: Aldine de Gruyter.

Denny, E. 2009: 'Heartsink patients and intractable conditions'. In E. Denny and S. Earle (eds), *The Sociology of Long Term Conditions and Nursing Practice*. Basingstoke: Palgrave Macmillan.

Di Stephano, C. 1990: 'Dilemmas of difference: feminism, modernity and postmodernism'. In L. Nicholson (ed.), *Feminism/Postmodernism*, London: Routledge, pp. 63–82.

Dolan, A. 2007: '"Good luck to them if they can get it": exploring working class men's understandings and experiences of income inequality and material standards'. *Sociology of Health & Illness*, 29(5), 711–29.

Douglas, J. 1998: 'Meeting the health needs of women from black and minority ethnic communities'. In L. Doyal (ed.), *Women and Health Care Services*. Buckingham: Open University Press, pp. 69–82.

Doyal, L. 1995: *What Makes Women Sick: Gender and the Political Economy of Health*. Basingstoke: Macmillan.

Doyal, L. (ed.) 1998: *Women and Health Services: An Agenda for Change*. Buckingham: Open University Press.

Earle, S. and Letherby, G. (eds) 2003: *Gender, Identity and Reproduction: Social Perspectives*. Basingstoke: Palgrave.

Evans, M. 1997: *Introducing Contemporary Feminist Thought*. Cambridge: Polity.

Featherstone, B., Rivett, M., and Scourfield, J. 2007: *Working with Men in Health and Social Care*. London: Sage.

Foroushani, P. S. 2008: 'The internet: a place for different voices in health and medicine? A case study of attention deficit hyperactivity disorder'. *Mental Health Review Journal*, 13(1), 33–40.

Frith, H., and Kitzinger, C. 1998: '"Emotion work" as a participant resource: a feminist analysis of young women's talk-in-interaction'. *Sociology*, 32(2), 299–320.

Galdas, P. M., Cheater, F., and Marshall, P. 2005: 'Men and help-seeking behaviour: literature review'. *Journal of Advanced Nursing*, 49(6), 616–23.

Gunew, S. (ed.) 1990: *Feminist Knowledge: Critique and Construct*. London: Routledge.

Hockey, J. 1997: 'Women and health'. In D. Richardson and V. Robinson (eds), *Introducing Women's Studies*. 2nd edn, London: Macmillan, pp. 250–71.

Hochschild, A. R. [1983] 2003: *The Managed Heart: Commercialization of Human Feeling*. 20th anniversary edn, Berkeley: University of California Press.

Kelly, L. 1988: *Surviving Sexual Violence*. Cambridge: Polity.

Kelner, M., Wellman, B., Boon, H., and Welsh, S. 2004: 'Responses of established healthcare to the professionalisation of complementary and alternative medicine in Ontario'. *Social Science and Medicine*, 59(5), 915–30.

King, M., and McKeown, E. 2003: *Mental Health and Social Wellbeing of Gay Men, Lesbians and Bisexuals in England and Wales*. London: Mind.

Letherby, G. 2003. *Feminist Research in Theory and Practice*. Buckingham: Open University Press.

Letherby, G., Williams, K., Birch, P., and Cain, M. (eds) 2008: *Sex as Crime*. Cullompton, Devon: Willan.

Lockyer, L. 2009: 'Coronary heart disease: moving from acute to long term accounts'. In E. Denny and S. Earle (eds), *The Sociology of Long Term Conditions and Nursing Practice*. Basingstoke: Palgrave Macmillan.

Lorber, J., and Moore, L. J. 2002: *Gender and the Social Construction of Illness*. 2nd edn, New York: AltaMira Press.

Marchbank, J. 2008: 'War and sex crime'. In G. Letherby, K. Williams, P. Birch and M. Cain (eds), *Sex as Crime*. Cullompton, Devon: Willan.

Marchbank, J., and Letherby, G. 2007: *Introduction to Gender: Social Science Perspectives*. Harlow: Pearson Longman.

Maynard, M. 1994: '"Race", gender and the concept of "difference" in feminist thought'. In H. Afshar and M. Maynard (eds), *The Dynamics of 'Race' and Gender: Some Feminist Interventions*. London: Taylor & Francis, pp. 9–25.

Miers, M. 2000: *Gender Issues and Nursing Practices*. Basingstoke: Macmillan.

Mills, J. 1991: *Womanwords*. London: Virago.

Morgan, D., Brandth, B., and Kvande, E. 2005: *Gender, Bodies and Work*. Aldershot: Ashgate.

Newburn, T., and Stanko, E. A. 1994: 'When men are victims: the failure of victimology'. In T. Newburn and E. A. Stanko (eds), *Just Boys Doing Business? Men, Masculinities and Crime*. London: Routledge, pp. 153–65.

Oakley, A. 1972: *Sex, Gender and Society*. London: Temple Smith.

Oakley, A. 1981: *Subject Women*. Oxford: Martin Robinson.

Stanko, E. A. 1990: *Everyday Violence: How Women and Men Experience Sexual and Physical Danger*. London: Pandora.

Wajcman, J. 1991: *Feminism Confronts Technology*. Cambridge: Polity.

Watson, J. 2000: *Male Bodies: Health, Culture and Identity*. Buckingham: Open University Press.

Webb, C. 1986: *Feminist Practice in Women's Health Care*. Chichester: John Wiley.

Wilkinson, S. and Kitzinger, C. 1994: 'Towards a feminist approach to breast cancer'. In S. Wilkinson and C. Kitzinger (eds), *Women and Health: Feminist Perspectives*. London: Taylor & Francis, pp. 124–40.

6 Age and Ageing

Pat Chambers

Key issues in this chapter

- The relevance of 'age' and 'ageing' to all nurses
- Defining age
- The social construction of age
- Theoretical perspectives of age and ageing
- Ageism, diversity, discrimination and best nursing practice

By the end of this chapter you should be able to . . .

- explore your own stereotypes of 'age';
- consider ways in which 'age' is structured in contemporary Western societies;
- consider the impact of 'ageism' on nursing practice;
- develop your own guidelines for anti-ageist practice;
- reconsider the relevance of 'age' for nurses.

1 Introduction

It is a truism to say that nurses work with patients of all ages, from pre-natal to very old. Indeed, pathways within nursing programmes are often delineated by 'age' either explicitly or implicitly. However, 'age' is often assumed to be 'neutral', an undeniable 'fact' on which we all agree. Sociologists often refer to this as making use of taken-for-granted knowledge. Surely 'age' is simply a useful way of summarizing the number of years we have been alive, and is manifested and celebrated via ceremonies such as birthdays and symbols such as birthday cards and presents. And yet, as this chapter seeks to demonstrate, chronological age is only one aspect of 'age'.

Birthdays are often important occasions. But chronological age is only one aspect of 'age'.

social gerontology the critical study of ageing

Rather, as the study of **social gerontology** demonstrates, the way in which 'age' is constructed and understood in any society is extremely complex and has implications for practice. The image of working with older people created by well-worn phrases such as 'no previous experience needed' only serves to reinforce the 'age' hierarchy.

The first part of this chapter seeks to challenge some of these assumptions. A discussion follows of the way in which the age structure of societies is changing and how this has given rise to what might be described as a **moral panic** amongst policy makers and some professional groups.

moral panic media-inspired overreaction to a certain group or to a type of behaviour that is taken as a sign of impending social disorder

life-course perspective a view of a person's whole life, taken in order to comprehend better their present experiences and beliefs

Sociological theories of ageing and their relevance to 'age' across the life course will be explored, and a **life-course perspective** on 'age' that draws on current social gerontological thinking will be developed. In the final section of the chapter, we will consider the potential impact of 'ageism' on nursing practice. An opportunity will be provided to develop personal guidelines for anti-ageist practice in nursing.

2   Definitions of age

Activity 6.1

What is 'age'?

Individually list five characteristics which you associate with the following age groups: 65+; 18–64; 12–17; 0–11.

Compare your answers with a colleague's and note similarities and differences in your lists. Are there differences between the ways in which you characterize the different age groups?

If yes, why do you think this is? Do you think there would be further differences if you were to consider the issue of learning disability in relation to these age groups?

Sociologists have found that more positive characteristics are often noted for under-65s than for over-65s. 'Growth and development', 'good health' and 'happiness', for example, are more likely to be listed as characteristics of the under-65s, whereas 'decline', 'ill-health' and 'loneliness' are likely to be listed for the over-65s. The Centre for Confidence and Well-being (n.d.) reports stereotypes of old people as being needy, unhappy, senile, inactive, unable to learn new things, and less useful than their younger counterparts.

Each of these stereotypes has been refuted by research findings and yet they persist, even in nursing practice (Bernard, 1998), as will be explored later in this chapter.

Given that 'age' is clearly more than the sum total of a person's birthdays, we must beware of making assumptions or engaging with stereotypes based purely on chronology. Kirkwood (1999) concurs and argues that, although physiology, linked to chronology, is popularly (and sometimes professionally) assumed to be the most important component in defining 'age', it is only one among many. For example, evidence suggests that we do not all 'age' physiologically at the same rate: social, economic and cultural factors have a profound effect on this process (Fennell, Phillipson and Evers, 1989). Poverty, low educational attainment, poor diet, unhealthy social behaviours, such as smoking, and low levels of exercise all contribute to our physiological status.

Let us consider two phenomena which emerged during the twentieth century and their relationship to the changes in economics and social policy during that time in order to understand the way in which society conceptualizes and organizes, sometimes through social policy, an age grouping to meet its perceived values, ideas or

Does this conform
to your stereotype
of older people?

needs. First, the 'pensioner', a term which did not exist in the earlier part of the last century but one which is now applied collectively to all those who, on reaching 'retirement age', are forced to retire from employment in order to create jobs for younger members of society. For some this is a sentence to living on a vastly reduced income, whereas for others it is a time of choice and opportunity. However, this is fluid and dependent on the demographics and economy of a society, and retirement age in the UK is set to rise to sixty-six years in 2024, sixty-seven years in 2034, and sixty-eight years in 2044 for both sexes (Department for Work and Pensions, 2006). Second, the 'teenager', a term applied to those between the ages of thirteen and eighteen. Although originally conceived in the 1950s as a descriptor for the years between childhood and adulthood, a time of rebellion against adult values, and certainly during the 1960s encompassing young workers with disposable incomes, the term 'teenager' is now increasingly synonymous with extended full-time education and economic dependency on parents or the state.

History – that is, the period of time in which we live – and the cultural values of the society at that time in relation to normality and difference also have a place in the construction of 'age'. Let us consider this briefly in relation first to childhood and then to adulthood.

Childhood

Interestingly, one dictionary definition of 'child' offers a physiological explanation: 'young human being below the age of puberty' (*Concise Oxford Dictionary*, 1996). Such a definition, however, takes no account of more complex ideas of 'age'. Social history accounts (see, for example, Pinchbeck and Hewitt, 1973) remind us that childhood, like old age, has been constructed and defined differently across history and cultures. In nineteenth-century Britain, child labour was the norm (it remains so within some cultures), with education and health care available only for the privileged few; indeed, what we would now consider to be 'childhood' was a relatively short period prior to adulthood. 'Extended' childhood and state provision for children – financial support, education, health care – are all products of the post-war welfare state, and reflect specific 'historical' values towards an 'age group'. The emergence of the child as 'dependent' on adults until achieving adult status was a phenomenon of the twentieth century, a process which Lee (2001, p. xiii) describes as 'child human becomings' moving through to 'adult human beings', with 'adulthood' as the desired state of stability and completion that constituted arrival at the 'journey's end' (ibid., p. 7). He goes on to argue that this image of the 'journey's end' has been crucial in maintaining the authority that adults have had over children and the right and duty to make decisions for them (ibid., p. 9). The international conferment of rights on 'children' in the United Nations Convention on the Rights of the Child (1989) has begun to shift this relationship, and at the beginning of the twenty-first century the status of children as beings in their own right ('child human beings') is emerging. Childhood, then, although it has always existed, has been, and will continue to be, redefined and restructured (see Hockey, 1993). Our understanding of what constitutes the 'age of childhood' is both culturally and historically bound and is in a state of continual flux. An example of this is the right of children to consent to medical procedures and treatment, which used to be entirely a matter for parents. Young people between the ages of sixteen and eighteen years can now provide their own consent, and even younger children may do so if they are deemed 'Gillick competent' – that is, they 'can demonstrate sufficient maturity and intelligence to understand the nature and implications of the proposed treatment, including the risks and alternative courses of action' (Wheeler, 2006, p. 807).

Adulthood

Let us now turn to 'adulthood', using a dictionary definition again as our starting point: 'adult: mature, grown-up; a person who has reached the age of majority' (Concise Oxford Dictionary, 1996). A definition such as this one is, however, static and takes no account of the way in which adulthood, like childhood and old age, has been subject to redefinition and restructure. Even the term 'age of majority' is fluid and dependent on social policy and law. In the nineteenth century, 'adulthood', when construed in policy terms, encompassed what we now perceive to be adolescence and old age, although it must be acknowledged that chronologically 'old age' differed from today. Boys and girls born in 1901 could expect to live only to forty-five and forty-nine years respectively. Data from the Office of National Statistics tell us that these figures have changed dramatically in the course of one hundred years: boys born in 2004–6 can expect to live for seventy-seven years and girls for eighty-one years.

Activity 6.2

Meet the Browns

Read the following case study about the Brown family.

John and Katie Brown are in their early forties and have two children, Mark (fifteen) and Rachel (ten). They live in a London suburb, although John spends a lot of time working abroad as a computer consultant. Katie works as a teacher in a nearby primary school, and during term time Rachel is cared for after school by John's parents, David and June, who are retired and live nearby. Mark also goes to his grandparents after school, particularly if he is hungry!

Mark is studying for GCSEs and is doing well at school, but struggles with maths and often needs his mother's help with his homework. Rachel is very keen on gymnastics, and when her father is at home he spends weekends taking her to competitions. Katie says it is the only time she ever gets to herself.

David's mother, Joyce, lives nearer to London in a warden-controlled flat. She is becoming frail and sometimes forgetful but is fiercely independent. She receives visits from one of the family at least twice a week, and Mark will sometimes stay with her if he wants to go to see a band in the city.

David and June find it difficult to manage on their pension, and John pays the tax and insurance on their car in order for them to get around and to be able to visit Joyce and to do her shopping.

For each member of this family:

(a)   What do you think the needs are for their particular stage in life?
(b)   How is each one dependent on the others and for what?

Think of your own family structure. How do the different generations help and support each other?

---

3   The changing age structure of the population

Just as childhood and middle age have been redefined and restructured historically, so, too, has old age. In the 1980s fears about the ageing of the population, sometimes described as the 'greying' of the population, both contributed to and were a part of the negative stereotyping of older people, and have reinforced our notions of age structures. **Demography** can tell us the age structure of a particular population at a particular point in time. For example, in the UK numbers of over-sixties have increased by 8.3 per cent over the last twenty years; more recently, the proportion of over-sixties in England and Wales increased from 20.7 per cent in the 1991 census (ONS, 1991) to 20.9 per cent in the 2001 census (ONS, 2001). By contrast, children under sixteen made up 20 per cent of the population in 2001 compared with 23 per cent in 1961. The fastest growing age group in the population is eighty years and over, which constitutes 4.5 per cent (2,749,507) of the total population. This is an increase of over 1.1 million between 1981 and 2007 (1,572,160 to 2,749,507), from 2.8 per cent to 4.5 per cent (National Statistics, 2008). Conversely, in 2004 there were 11.6 million people aged under sixteen in the United Kingdom, a decline of 2.6 million since 1971, and 9.6 million people aged over sixty-five, an increase of 2.2 million. Projections suggest that the proportion of the population who are children will continue to fall to around 18 per cent of the total by 2011. Figure 6.1 shows that by 2014 there will be more people over sixty-five than under sixteen, and by 2025 there will be 1.6 million more people over the age of sixty-five than people under sixteen.

Why is the population ageing? The age structure is dependent on three variables: fertility, mortality and migration. Let us focus on the first two.

demography   the study of populations

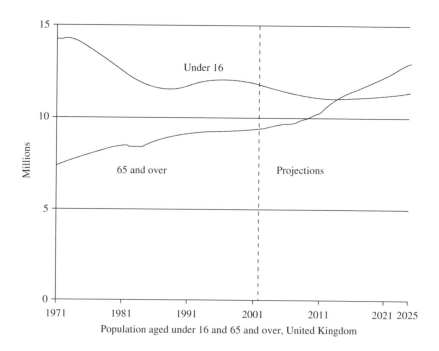

Figure 6.1 Age structure of the population

Population aged under 16 and 65 and over, United Kingdom

Fertility and mortality

Before the end of the nineteenth century, fertility rates were high but life expectancy was low. High rates of infant mortality, epidemics and infections, poor working conditions, and deaths in childbirth meant that those who survived to old age were in the minority. At the beginning of the twenty-first century in the UK, as elsewhere, fertility rates had decreased as a result of education, access to contraception, government policies, and so on. At the same time, we have seen improved mortality rates as a result of the massive public health measures undertaken in the nineteenth and twentieth centuries. At a local level, migration can accelerate the greying of the population, by either an exodus (for employment) or an influx (for retirement) of one age group. This changing demography has caused alarm in some quarters: in the last part of the twentieth century, 'old age' became the source of a moral panic, and the ensuing debate only served to reinforce the ageist structure of British society. Rather than old age being celebrated and the prospect of a longer life span and a potentially fitter old age being welcomed, the ageing of the population was thought instead to be burdensome, and claims were made that younger adults would have to work for longer and pay higher taxes in order to support 'hordes' of frail, dependent older people. Gerontologists (such as Phillipson, 1998) have challenged this perspective, pointing to the diversity of the ageing population, which includes older adults who contribute to the overall economy as volunteers and as family carers (of children and other adults), as well as those who continue in paid employment beyond the 'state' retirement age. Like all other 'age groups', old age is certainly not a homogeneous state; some older people will find themselves in need of more health and social care services than others, but for most older people 'old age' itself is not problematic.

4   Theories of ageing

Traditional theories

structured ageing   the
social construction of
ageing

Traditional theories of human development and decline have also served to reinforce age difference and contribute to notions of structured ageing. Until the 1980s old age was theorized as a life stage, separate from childhood and adulthood. Cumming and Henry (1961) put forward a theory – disengagement theory – which suggested that, in their sixties, older people 'disengage' from society: they do this willingly and with the approval of successive generations who benefit via the enhanced employment opportunities which then become available. By contrast, activity theorists argued that the only way to resist disengagement was to maintain a 'middle age' lifestyle (Fennell, Phillipson and Evers, 1989). Disengagement theory has been challenged as a convenient rationale for supporting the exclusion of older people from public life and activity theory as taking no account of diversity. Critics argued that, although many older people do withdraw from the public sphere, there is little evidence to suggest that they do so voluntarily; rather, ageist policies and practices (low retirement income and dependency-creating services) restrict their capacity to remain active citizens.

Contemporary theories

Contemporary theories have sought to challenge such rigid, and uncritical, perspectives on ageing, highlighting societal, rather than individual, responsibility for structuring ageing. First, the political economy perspective highlights the impact of an individual's location within the social and economic structure, during the earlier part of their life course, on their financial status, their social location and the life choices available in old age (Phillipson, 1998). This perspective, in particular, acknowledges the way in which advantages and disadvantages accrued earlier in the life course impact on an individual in old age. An example of this is the way in which many older women find themselves with reduced access to financial resources in later life as a result of working in part-time, low-paid and low-status employment or a lifetime's financial dependence on a spouse (Arber and Ginn, 1991). A political economy perspective on ageing also points to increasing polarity of the ageing experience, ranging from the social exclusion of those older people living in areas of extreme economic deprivation (Scharf et al., 2002) to those 'young-at-heart', fit and wealthy older people who are the new 'niche' markets of the tourism and travel industry (Warnes et al., 1999; Ylanne-McEwen, 1999).

Second, social gerontologists are increasingly acknowledging the importance of the subjective experience of ageing, as encapsulated in biographical studies, and the impact of this on ageing identities (Chambers, 2005; Ray, 2007). This cannot be understood in isolation from historical location or political economy. Ruth and Oberg (1996, p. 171), for example, in a quest to understand the experience of old age for Finns from the generation of 'the Wars and the Depression', argue that knowledge based solely on current circumstances is inadequate: 'Ageing must be seen as a continuation of an integrated process, starting with an earlier life, where the life lived gives meaning to old age.' In chapter 1 we argued that sociology is multi-paradigmatic; thus experiences of ageing must be understood from the perspective of social structure as well as that of social action.

Age throughout the life course is characterized by and perhaps best understood in terms of 'diversity' of gender, ethnicity, social class, disability, geographical location, and so on. Talking about 'age groups' is useful only as a marker, a shorthand term to describe those people who share a chronological age, and to provide some information relating to physiology. We would do better to try to understand an individual's experience of the life course, wherever she or he happens to be located at a particular point in time.

Activity 6.3   **Biography and ageing**

(a) Note down the major events or 'milestones' in your own life so far, in relation to your early years, family, relationships, school, work, and so on.

(b) Interview a person who is much older than you, but the same gender, about the major milestones in their life. Note the differences and similarities.

(c) What does this exercise tell you about individual (personal) and collective (cohort, sharing the same historical time) ageing and the way in which 'age', at different points in the life course, has been differentially structured over time? How might this understanding help you in your nursing practice?

---

5 Ageism

ageism discrimination on the basis of age

According to Bytheway (1995), **ageism** exists throughout the life course. For example, a survey on ageism in 2003 found that, in some industries, particularly those 'young' areas such as information technology or the media, workers were 'too old' at thirty-five (Dilley, 2003). One in ten of the workers who told researchers they had been victims of ageism were between thirty-five and forty years old and 3 percent of those who felt their employers were discriminating against them for being too old were under thirty-five. By contrast, according to a report by the Department for Work and Pensions' Age Positive team (Department for Work and Pensions, 2001), school leavers and graduates feel themselves to be less favoured than older workers doing similar jobs. Anecdotal evidence pointed to ageism working against young employees, who felt they had unfairly missed out on job vacancies, promotions and pay rises. Some young people felt they were stereotyped as being unreliable. The report suggested that, while those in their teens and twenties felt they were less discriminated against than workers in their fifties, sixties and beyond, they were nonetheless concerned.

It would seem therefore that stereotypes of all ages abound in the world of employment. However, the term 'ageism' is usually used in relation to later life and is rooted in the 'social construction' of ageing highlighted earlier. According to Bytheway and Johnson (1990, pp. 25–6):

> Ageism is a set of beliefs originating in the biological variation between people and relating to the ageing process. It is in the actions of corporate bodies, what is said and done by their representatives, and the resulting views that are held by ordinary ageing people that ageism is made manifest.

Bytheway (1995) goes on to say:

> Ageism generates and reinforces a fear and denigration of the ageing process, and the stereotyping assumptions regarding competence and need for protection. In particular ageism *legitimates* the use of chronological age to mark out classes of people who are systematically denied resources and opportunities that others enjoy, and who suffer the consequences of such denigration – ranging from well-meaning patronage to unambiguous vilification.

Ageism therefore is not simply a matter of personal prejudice but has its roots in the way society is organized and, unlike many other 'isms', will potentially be experienced by us all to some degree. It is manifested in the following ways:

- marginalization;
- the use of dismissive and demeaning language;
- humour and mockery;
- physical, sexual, emotional and financial abuse;
- economic disadvantage;
- restricted opportunities or life chances.

As a result of living in an ageist society, many older people internalize ageist views, become ageist towards their peers, and try to distance themselves from other 'old people'. Furthermore, ageing women in particular feel coerced into 'passing' for middle aged via strategies such as colouring their hair, dressing in 'younger' clothes and, more recently, cosmetic surgery. However, they have to tread a fine line if they are not to be accused of being 'mutton dressed as lamb': it is not easy being an older woman in an ageist and sexist world!

According to Thompson (1995), ageism occurs on a number of fronts, among them personal (individual experience), cultural (language, images, media), and structural (differential access to services and opportunities). He goes on to demonstrate that the impact of ageism on health and social care practice with older people includes dehumanization, ageist language, elder abuse, infantilization (treating older people as if they were children), denial of citizenship, welfarism, and medicalization. Unlike some other forms of discrimination, ageism is only illegal in the workplace, and ageism in healthcare has been widely reported in the media (BBC News Online, 2000, 2007,

Activity 6.4   ### Nurses and ageism

Read the following extract (or, better, the whole article – see References) and answer the questions below.

> There is now a certain amount of evidence to support the contention that ageism is not only rife amongst the population at large, but also amongst many of those who care for older people in a professional capacity. Given that many of these professionals are women caring for other women . . . this should at the very least give us serious cause for concern. . . . Negative attitudes though are merely one facet of that particular form of social oppression which we now recognise as 'ageism'. One feature of the operation of ageism is that it can generate and reinforce a fear and denigration of the process of ageing. Nurses, like everyone else, work and live against this societal backdrop and are therefore not totally immune to the impact of these pressures on their own practice. Perhaps more worrying though is the evidence that many professionals, nurses included, in actual fact hold more ageist attitudes than do the population at large. . . . [Previous] research showed that nurses responded quite differently according to whether their patients were male or female: women patients were far more likely to be depersonalised; the nurses knew a lot less about them than they did about their male patients; they were cared for in quite different ways; and they tended to be labelled as more 'difficult' than the men culprits. . . . there are various reasons for these observed differences in professional attitudes and behaviours. First, there is a suggestion that looking after men was less problematic for female nurses because this was more closely related to what many of them did anyway. . . . Second, the men too tended to be 'in role' and were much more accepting of being looked after. In other words, being a patient was often simply an extension of their conventional relationship to women in their families. Third, . . . for many of the older women, who had themselves been experts in caring work, for their own families in their own homes – being in a situation of dependency on other women was extremely difficult . . . many of the nurses actually found caring for older women threatening . . . both groups see themselves as 'expert carers' and this can set up tensions. [And they were daily confronted with images of what they themselves might become in the future, and so would operate strategies which enabled them to distance themselves to a degree from their female patients.] (Bernard, 1998)

(a)   To what does the author attribute nurses' ageism?

(b)   What can you learn from this about guiding your own practice?

2008). In addition, a small body of literature has highlighted evidence of ageism within nursing practice (Bernard, 1998; Koch and Webb, 1996). However, in 2002 the Labour government made a commitment to root out ageism in health and social care services and Standard One of the National Service Framework for Older People (Department of Health, 2001) states that health services will be provided, regardless of age, on the basis of clinical need alone.

6 Anti-ageist practice

In working with older people we must recognize that our starting point is one of disadvantage and discrimination rather than equality. According to Hughes (1997), **anti-ageist practice** embodies the following three values:

anti-ageist practice
health and social care
practice which does not
discriminate on the basis
of age

personhood: ascribes to all people of all ages the authenticity and worth of being alive and of having lived;
citizenship: relationship between the individual and society and how that relationship is defined; emphasizes rights of individual and reciprocal responsibilities of individual and society; validates membership of society; and is different from 'consumer';
celebration: age to be celebrated as an achievement and as a period to be valued in its own right.

Although specifically addressing 'old age', these values should underpin practice with all age groups. Furthermore, such practice should be underpinned by the key principles set out in box 6.1.

Box 6.1

The principles of anti-ageist practice

Empowerment: ensuring that the person has or acquires control over their own life and all that goes with power and control (freedom, autonomy, dignity and feelings of self-worth)

Participation: meaningful sharing and involvement

Choice: important means of personal validation as well as a right in terms of personhood and citizenship

Integration: into mainstream of life at every level

Normalization: making available whatever is necessary to enable all people to live in the same way, with the same quality of life as other people in society

---

Anti-ageist practice, then, requires that we do not discriminate on the basis of 'age'. This means, for example, that we do not assume that the early years of life are a period of development and the later years a period of decline. Nor do we assume that the 'voice' of a child is less important, or less believable, than that of an adult. Rather, for all those for whom we care, we should seek to maximize quality of life and build in potential development, regardless of age. This idea will now be explored further in relation to three areas of practice: conceptualizing and responding to falls; understanding the patient's subjective experience; and working with grief and loss.

Employment – be it paid or voluntary – can be a very important factor in empowering and increasing the participation of older people in society.

Falls and our response to them

First, let us consider the way in which we 'conceptualize' and respond to falls. Young children regularly fall over when they are learning to walk. The common response is to encourage the child to get back on its feet and try again. Imagine, then, another scenario, this time with an older person. She has already fallen a couple of times and has been deemed by family and professionals to be 'at risk of falling'. Nonetheless, the older person wishes to maintain her independence. However, in going to the toilet, a very private sphere of life and one in which she does not wish for support, she falls, and is told off for taking risks. Why the difference? According to Kingston (1998), falls are socially constructed on the basis of age, and risk-assessment tools are a manifestation of such a construction. Older people are not allowed to take risks, and, if they do, they are chastised and considered to be 'reckless' and 'selfish'. Young children who fall, by contrast, are considered to be 'bold'. It would seem that 'age' is the determining factor.

An anti-ageist approach to practice ensures that a nurse using a risk-assessment tool with an older person does not use it mechanistically but rather takes into account the key values of 'personhood', 'citizenship' and 'celebration' discussed above.

Patients' subjective experiences

Increasingly, the literature on childhood, learning disability, mental ill-health and old age points to the importance of subjective experiences: 'how it feels' from the inside (patients' perspective) rather than 'how it is' from the outside (professionals' perspective). Fundamental to this approach is 'personhood' and listening to the 'voice' of patients rather than jumping to 'age-based assumptions'. Lee (2001) reminds us that, until fairly recently, children's voices were silent. Even today, although the failings of individual adults and adult institutions are acknowledged, there is still a tension between the need for children to speak and the traditional view that only adults are worth listening to (ibid., p. 91). He goes on to stress the importance of recognizing that policies and practices devised for children have often rested on assumptions that children are vulnerable 'becomings', 'investments to be cultivated and protected' (ibid., p. 100). Anti-ageist practice challenges this, and enables the nurse to work in partnership with the child or young adult and to value the patient's subjective experience – that is, 'what it feels like'. One way of accomplishing this is through the use of 'life story' books, in which the patient is encouraged to share their understanding of their illness in pictures or words, or both, in the context of personal autobiography. This is particularly helpful with children with chronic illness or learning disability, and can enable the nurse to gain an 'insider' perspective that can provide a useful counterbalance to so-called objective, often age-based, accounts of illness.

Depression, grief and loss

Finally, let us consider the way in which anti-ageist practice can be used in relation to depression, grief and loss in work with older people and young children. Old age is commonly construed as 'a time of loss', and it therefore follows that depression in old age is an automatic consequence of the ageing process and does not need to be treated. The reality is that many older people adjust perfectly well to loss; after all, they expect to experience loss at that point in their life (Chambers, 2000, 2002, 2005). However, they may need support and acknowledgement of their loss and must be allowed the time and space to give expression to their feelings. Some older people will suffer from depression; it may or may not be associated with loss, but without treatment they may not recover. Nurses who follow anti-ageist practices will be vigilant and will not assume that depression is an automatic consequence of the ageing process. Instead, they will seek appropriate interventions to enable the older person to return to maximum health (see, for example, Department of Health, 2001, Standard 7). Nor will they ignore the older person who needs time and space to grieve in order to adjust to loss.

In a similar vein, the social construction of 'early childhood' often militates against the needs of very young children who experience loss being adequately addressed. Nurses who have an understanding of, and follow, anti-ageist practice are well placed to support children who are bereaved.

Activity 6.5	**Anti-ageist practice**

Anti-ageist practice

Using the guidelines offered by Hughes (1997), and with reference to one of the three values listed in section 6, draw up a list of your own dos and don'ts for anti-ageist practice in relation to working with one of the following groups:

(a) children;
(b) young adults with learning difficulties;
(c) adults with mental ill-health;
(d) older people.

There is now general agreement, resulting primarily from the pioneering work of Stroebe et al. (1996), that the bereaved person, young or old, has to confront both the loss and the changes that result from that loss; this has come to be known as the dual-orientation approach, that is, to both loss and restoration.

Summary and Resources

Summary

- 'Age' is a complex process and state of being which is more than the sum total of birthdays a person has notched up. In addition to chronology, it encompasses physiology, psychology, law, social policy, culture and sociology.

- A society constructs its own meanings of 'childhood', 'adulthood' and 'old age', and these are constantly changing according to the social and economic needs of that society.

- Stereotypical assumptions are made on the basis of age, and nurses are no more or less immune to such ageist assumptions than other members of society.

- A life-course perspective, rather than an 'age-based' perspective, is advocated.

- An understanding of ageism and anti-ageist practice is essential for nurses in all branches of nursing.

Questions for Discussion

1 What, in relation to 'age', informed your choice of nursing route? Consider the values and attitudes underpinning this choice.

2 How can an understanding of the social construction of 'age' inform best practice? Discuss this in relation to your chosen branch of nursing.

3 Look at the way in which birthday cards and road signs depict different ages. What do you notice? What does it tell us about the way age is constructed in contemporary British society?

4 Why might the next generation of older people – 'the baby boomers' – challenge notions of ageism?

Further Reading

P. Chambers, G. Allan, C. Phillipson and M. Ray: *Family Practices in Later Life*. Bristol: Policy Press, 2009.
This challenges a stereotypical, 'welfare' view of older people's roles and relationships with their families. A variety of family relationships are explored and new perspectives presented.

M. Bernard and T. Scharf (eds): *Critical Perspectives on Ageing Societies*. Bristol: Policy Press, 2007.

This edited text reviews the way the field of gerontology has developed over a quarter of a century and discusses some of the ethical and practical problems of researching in this area.

A. Bowling: *Ageing Well: Quality of Life in Old Age.* Buckingham: Open University Press, 2005.
As well as health, this book considers those issues, such as home and neighbourhood and income, that impact on health and well-being. It draws on relevant literature, survey data and interviews with older people.

P. Chambers: *Older Widows and the Lifecourse: Multiple Narratives of Hidden Lives.* Abingdon: Ashgate, 2005.
Based on literature and qualitative research, this book challenges some of the dominant thinking on widowhood as a time of decline and loneliness to reveal a multiplicity of experience. It portrays widowhood as being embedded in the life course, which then influences the way it is experienced.

A. James and A. L. James: *Constructing childhood.* Basingstoke: Palgrave, 2004.
This looks at the way in which childhood is constructed and the tensions between media representations and the vision of childhood in the law and social policy. Case studies include health and the family.

N. Lee: *Childhood and Society: Growing up in an Age of Uncertainty.* Buckingham: Open University Press, 2001.
From a sociological perspective, Nick Lee examines what it means to be a child and critically evaluates the way in which our understanding of 'childhood' is ever changing.

You will find other useful sources on the website at www.politybooks.com/sociologyfornurses.

References

Arber, S., and Ginn, J. 1991: *Gender and Later Life.* London: Sage.
Bernard, M. 1998: 'Backs to the future? Reflections on women, ageing and nursing'. *Journal of Advanced Nursing,* 27, 633–40.
BBC News Online 2000: 'Call for enquiry into NHS "ageism"', 9 February; http://news.bbc.co.uk/I/hi/health/635688.stm.
BBC News Online 2007: 'Doctors "deny elderly treatments"', 14 February; http://news.bbc.co.uk/I/hi/health/6357627.stm.
BBC News Online 2008: 'NHS age discrimination "common"', 27 January; http://news.bbc.co.uk/I/hi/health/7850881.stm.
Bytheway, B. 1995: *Ageism.* Buckingham: Open University Press.
Bytheway, B., and Johnson, J. 1990: 'On defining ageism'. *Critical Social Policy,* 27, 27–9.

Centre for Confidence and Well-Being (n.d.): The detrimental influence of negative stereotypes; www.centreforconfidence.co.uk/projects.php?p=cGlkPTk5 [last accessed 1 December 2008].

Chambers, P. 2000: 'Widowhood in later life'. In M. Bernard, J. Phillips, L. Machin and V. Davies (eds), *Women Ageing: Changing Identities, Challenging Myths*. London: Routledge, pp. 127–47.

Chambers, P. 2002: 'The life stories of older widows: situating later life widowhood within the life course'. In C. Horrocks, K. Milnes, B. Roberts and D. Robinson (eds), *Narrative, Memory and Life Transitions*. Huddersfield: Huddersfield University Press, pp. 23–41.

Chambers, P. 2005: *Older Widows and the Lifecourse: Multiple Narratives of Hidden Lives*. Abingdon: Ashgate

Concise Oxford Dictionary 1996: London: Oxford University Press.

Cumming, E. and Henry, W. E. 1961: *Growing Old: The Process of Disengagement*. New York: Basic Books.

Department for Work and Pensions 2001: *Ageism: Attitudes and Experiences of Young People*. Nottingham: DWP.

Department for Work and Pensions 2006: *Security in Retirement: Towards a New Pensions System*; www.dwp.gov.uk [last accessed 1 December 2008].

Department of Health 2001: *National Service Framework for Older People*. London: HMSO.

Dilley, R. 2003: *Ageism hits generation X?* 10 June; http://news.bbc.co.uk/1/hi/uk/2975754.stm [last accessed 3 December 2008].

Fennell, G., Phillipson, C., and Evers, H. (eds) 1989: *The Sociology of Old Age*. Milton Keynes: Open University Press.

Hockey, J. 1993: 'Constructing personhood: changing categories of the child'. In J. Hockey and A. James (eds), *Growing Up and Growing Old*, London: Sage, pp. 45–72.

Hughes, B. 1997: *Older People and Community Care*. Buckingham: Open University Press.

Kingston, P. 1998: 'Older people and falls: a randomised control trial of health visitor intervention: a study of 108 older women who attended an accident and emergency department after a fall'. PhD thesis, Keele University.

Kirkwood, T. 1999: *Time of our Lives: The Science of Human Ageing*. London: Weidenfeld & Nicolson.

Koch, T., and Webb, C. 1996: 'The biomedical construction of ageing: implications for nursing care of older people'. *Journal of Advanced Nursing*, 23, 954–9.

Lee, N. 2001: *Childhood and Society*. Buckingham: Open University Press.

National Statistics 2008: www.statistics.gov.uk [last accessed 1 December 2008].

ONS (Office for National Statistics) 1991: Census, etc., www.statistics.gov.uk.

ONS (Office for National Statistics) 2001: The Census in England and Wales. www.statistics.gov.uk/census2001 [last accessed 4 December 2008].

Phillipson, C. 1998: *Reconstructing Old Age*. London: Sage.

Pinchbeck, I., and Hewitt, M. 1973: *Children in English Society*. 2 vols, London: Routledge & Kegan Paul.

Ray, M. 2007: 'Redressing the balance? The participation of older people in research'. In M. Bernard and T. Scharf (eds), *Critical Perspectives on Ageing Societies*. Bristol: Policy Press.

Ruth, J.-E., and Oberg, P. 1996: 'Ways of life: old age in a life history perspective'. In J. E. Birren et al. (eds), *Explorations in Adult Development*. New York: Springer, pp. 167–86.

Scharf, T., Phillipson, C., Smith, A. E., and Kingston, P. 2002: *Growing Older in Socially Deprived Areas: Social Exclusion in Later Life*. London: Help the Aged.

Stroebe, M., Gergen, M., Gergen, K., and Stroebe, W. 1996: 'Broken hearts or broken bonds'. In D. Klass, P. R. Silverman and S. L. Nickman (eds), *Continuing Bonds: New Understandings of Grief*. Washington, DC, and London: Taylor & Francis, pp. 31–44.

Thompson, N. 1995: *Age and Dignity*. Aldershot: Arena.

United Nations Convention on the Rights of the Child 1989: www.unicef.org.

Warnes, A. M., King, R., Williams, A. M., and Patterson, G. 1999: 'The well-being of British expatriate retirees in southern Europe'. *Ageing and Society*, 19(6), 717–40.

Wheeler R. 2006: 'Gillick or Fraser? A plea for consistency over competence in children'. *British Medical Journal*, 332, 807.

Ylanne-McEwen, V. 1999: 'Young at heart: discourses of age identity in travel agency interaction'. *Ageing and Society*, 19(4), 417–40.

7 Chronic Illness and Disability

Nick Watson and Elaine Denny

Key issues in this chapter

- Definitions of disability
- Sociological theories of disability and chronic illness
- The social model of disability, barriers and discrimination
- Sociology of the body
- Disability, chronic illness and the role of nurses

By the end of this chapter you should be able to . . .

- understand differences between definitions and classifications of disability;
- explore different sociological theories of disability and chronic illness;
- recognize the role of the disability movement and the significance of the social model of disability;
- discuss disabling barriers;
- explore the experience of long-term illness;
- examine the role of nursing in relationship to removing disabling barriers.

---

1 Introduction

It is estimated that there are around 500 million disabled people worldwide, the largest number of whom are to be found in the majority world. There is, moreover, a higher prevalence of disabled people in wealthier nations relative to population. Advances in medical science and medical interventions which

majority world also referred to as the 'developing world'

prolong life, coupled with demographic changes in the age of the population, suggest that these numbers will increase in the future (also see chapter 10). These same factors mean that more people are surviving illnesses that would have proved fatal a generation ago, but many are left with chronic ill-health. For example, cancer was once considered inevitably fatal, but many cancer patients are now being controlled with therapy and medication for many years. The implications of these factors in terms of social and economic policy will be far-reaching, and new demands are being placed on the health professionals who care for those with long-term illness and disability.

This chapter introduces you to sociological perspectives on disability and long-term (or chronic) illness. It begins with a discussion of the classification and definition of disability and explores different models of disability. It also focuses on disabling barriers and encourages you to think about what nurses can do to dismantle these. The chapter then moves on to consider the growing importance both of long-term illness as a major challenge for twenty-first-century health care systems, and of nurses in managing this challenge. Although for clarity the issues of disability and long-term illness are treated separately, it is acknowledged that people with long-term illness constitute a large proportion of those living with disability.

Activity 7.1   **Representation of disability and long-term illness in soap operas**

Think about how people with disability or long-term illness are represented in popular soap operas.

(a) How many people with disability or long-term illness are portrayed in soap operas?

(b) What are the main impairment and illness groups covered?

(c) How is disability and long-term illness handled as an issue in soap operas?

(d) What does this tell us about how disability and the chronically ill are perceived in popular culture?

---

2   Disability

The meaning of disability and the personal consequences for individual lives of being disabled have changed considerably in the last forty years. Before the 1970s the majority of disabled people, in most of the Western world at least, would have been found in large, isolated residential establishments. Job opportunities for many were restricted to special 'training centres' or sheltered employment with an emphasis on work as rehabilitation. These centres typically offered poor training, little opportunity for advancement and low wage levels. Disabled children were segregated from their non-disabled peers and, under the guise of rehabilitation, denied access to a full curriculum while spending much of their time in physiotherapy. This in turn served to deny them future opportunities. Disabled people were also denied sexual rights, the right to form relationships, reproductive rights and the right to lead independent lives. Whilst these conditions still exist for many disabled people, increasing numbers have been able to access mainstream employment and mainstream schooling, live independently in the community, form relationships and have children. The fact that some can do it suggests that all should be able to do it and that they are held back by social, economic and political factors rather than their impairment.

discrimination may occur as the consequence of prejudice which disadvantages certain social groups

Further evidence for the **discrimination** experienced by disabled people is provided by an overview of disability in Scotland by Riddell and Banks (2001) (see box 7.1).

The classification and definition of disability

The traditional way to view disablement is to see it simply as a medical problem. Disability, in this approach, and the problems faced by disabled people arise as a result of impairment. For example, people would say, 'She is disabled because she has epilepsy' (Thomas, 1999). This is called the medical or individual model of disability. It is the basis for most current social policy aimed at resolving the problems faced by disabled people, and it is also the approach that lies at the centre of much medical treatment aimed at disabled people. It is the basis of the World Health Organization's *The International Classification of Impairments, Disabilities and Handicaps* (ICIDH) (WHO, 1980). Put simply, this approach suggests that impairments are the result of a biological or psychological abnormality, that disabilities are the resulting restrictions in activity, and that handicaps are the disadvantages faced by disabled people that arise as a result of impairments or disabilities. Impairment is therefore seen as the cause of the disadvantages faced by disabled people.

However, many disabled activists and organizations of disabled people have been very critical of the WHO's model. The individual disabled person becomes the centre of attention and the focus is on changing the individual, usually through the modification of their impairment. Emphasis is placed on cure and rehabilitative medical intervention. Through this reification of impairment, control over the

Box 7.1   Disability and discrimination

- Disabled people are less likely to be in employment than non-disabled people, and the unemployment rate for disabled people is almost double that for non-disabled people.

- Disabled people are around eight times as likely as non-disabled people to be out of work and claiming benefits.

- Disabled people are twice as likely as non-disabled people to have no qualifications.

- Disabled people have difficulty in finding suitable housing and are less likely to be owner-occupiers than non-disabled people.

- There are approximately 20,000 households in Scotland where a household member uses a wheelchair, but only 5,000 dwellings of full wheelchair standard.

- Only 12 per cent of buses in operation in Scotland have a lowered floor and over 50 per cent of bus providers do not intend to operate low-floor buses in the next three years.

- In Scotland in 2000 disabled people were more likely to be living in poverty than the rest of the population. Thirty-three per cent of households have an income of less than £6,000 per annum compared with 26 per cent of households without a disabled person. Only 6 per cent of households with a disabled person have an income of more than £20,000, in contrast to 24 per cent without a disabled person.

Source: Riddell and Banks, 2001.

lives of disabled people moves to the medical profession. The medical 'expert' defines what it is that an individual needs, how these needs should be met and how the negative consequences of an individual's disability can be minimized (Barnes, Mercer and Shakespeare, 1999). Autonomy is removed and the picture of a disabled person as one who is a victim of their impairment emerges, what Oliver (1990, p. 1) has called 'the personal tragedy theory of disability'. In addition, as Barnes and his colleagues (1999) point out, the medical model, by linking impairment with disability, presents the environment as 'neutral' and stable. The possibility of changing environments and thus removing barriers is ignored. These authors also suggest that in the medical model the onus is on the individual to adapt, to adopt coping strategies and to limit their own hopes and ambitions.

These criticisms of the ICIDH have led the WHO to produce what is termed the *International Classification of Functioning and Disability* (ICF) (WHO, 1997, 2002). In this model, disability arises through the interaction between the health condition (the disease or the disorder) and contextual factors, such as environmental factors (which are external to the individual and include disabling attitudes and architectural barriers) and personal factors (such as the individual's gender, age and social background). There are three levels of human functioning in this model: at the level of the body or body part, of the whole person, and of the whole person in a social context. Disability arises when there are problems at one or more of these levels. The definitions of the components of the ICF are given in box 7.2.

Whilst this model removes the causal link between impairment and disablement and allows for a socio-medical analysis, much emphasis is still placed on health classified within a medical domain, and its approach is still individualistic (Hurst, 2000). It is also expert-led; that is, health service professionals are, through this model, able to judge and make decisions about the quality of life of people who are disabled (Pfeiffer, 2000).

This, however, is the domain in which much mainstream medical sociology operates when it writes about disability. It ignores, in the main, the socio-political aspects to life as a disabled person, focusing instead on the impacts that an impairment can have on an individual.

Box 7.2 **International Classification of Functioning and Disability**

Part 1 Functioning and disability
Body functions   The physiological functions of body systems (including psychological functions)

Impairments   Problems in body function or structure such as a significant deviation or loss

Activity   The execution of a task or action by an individual

Participation   Involvement in a life situation

Activity limitations   Difficulties an individual may have in executing activities

Participation restrictions   Problems an individual may experience in involvement in life situations

Part 2 Contextual factors
Environmental factors   The physical, social and attitudinal environment in which people live their lives

---

Disability and the 'sick role'

As discussed in chapter 3, the sick role was first proposed by the American sociologist Talcott Parsons (also see the discussion of functionalism in chapter 1). According to Parsons, illness results in physical disability or incapacity, which acts to prevent an individual from fulfilling his or her role in society. People who have an impairment or illness are seen as involuntarily deviant, but, regardless of the involuntary nature of the condition, they must fulfil certain roles if they are to escape censure from society. They must try to get well and put themselves in the hands of their doctor or other medical professional, fulfilling their sick role. By doing this they are absolved from societal obligations and culpability for their condition is removed (Parsons, 1951). However, when it is applied to disabled people there are problems with Parsons's analysis. For many people with stable impairments such as cerebral palsy, the impairment can cease to be a medical problem. Albrecht (1993) points out that impairments which are short-lived lend themselves better to Parsons's sick role, whilst those which are chronic, and from which recovery is unlikely, do not allow a return to the full pre-illness role; thus, Parsons's analysis is unworkable. This applies whatever the impairment, be it physical, sensory, intellectual or mental. So it could be argued that a discussion of the sick role has no place in a chapter on the sociology of disability!

involuntarily deviant
enacting the unwilled transgression of prescribed norms

3   The social model of disability

In the late 1960s and the 1970s disabled people throughout the world began to organize, to challenge their isolation and to demand equal rights. In doing so they also challenged the individual medical model of disability. Organizations such as the Union of the Physically Impaired Against Segregation (UPIAS) in the United Kingdom, the Independent Living Movement in America and the Handicappenförbundens Centralkommitté in Sweden all called for an alternative approach to disability. The UPIAS document *The Fundamental Principles of Disability*, published in 1976, laid the foundations for what Oliver later called the social model of disability. Oliver, in his influential monograph *The Politics of Disablement* (1990), gives a clear description of the social model. His work is materialist, in that he emphasizes the role of social structures and political, economic and environmental factors as the cause of disability (see chapter 1 for an introduction to materialist approaches within sociology). These are factors beyond the control of the individual, and Oliver argues that it is society which disables people with impairment by its failure to include them. He further argues that disability is a consequence of the individualizing nature of capitalism and also, importantly, the rise of medicalization in everyday life. Through increased control he contends that medicine determined who, for example, was able to work, who had the right to go to school, who could get married and who could have children. Medicine created the notion of 'able-bodiedness' against which normality could be judged, and it is this ideology that permeates society and impacts on the way that disabled people are treated.

Consider this picture of a paralympics event: does it make sense to think of 'able-bodied' and 'disabled bodies', or just bodies performing amazing feats in different ways?

The rejection of any link between impairment and disability, in contrast to the view of the ICIDH above, has been adopted by the majority of organizations of disabled people throughout the world. Disabled People International has adopted the definition of disability shown in box 7.3.

The disabled writer Jenny Morris eloquently explains the difference between impairment and disability:

> An inability to walk is an impairment, whereas an inability to enter a building because the entrance is up a flight of stairs is a disability. An inability to speak is an impairment but an inability to communicate because appropriate technical aids are not made available is a disability. An inability to move one's body is an impairment but an inability to get out of bed because appropriate physical help is not available is a disability. (1993, p. x)

Box 7.3   **The social model of disability**

Impairment   The functional limitation within the individual caused by physical, mental or sensory impairment

Disability   The loss or limitation of opportunities to take part in the normal life of the community on an equal level with others owing to physical and social barriers

---

The social model moves the attention from an individual's impairment to the external environment in which they are situated and the obstacles imposed on disabled people, thus drawing predominantly on sociological theories of social structure (see chapter 1). Disablement has nothing to do with an individual's impairment, but is the result of social oppression (Oliver, 1996). Implicit in this approach to disability, in contrast to that of the ICF, is the idea that disabled people are the best experts on their own lives.

This political shift in the definition of disability has led to an upsurge in the consciousness of disabled people, the formation of new self-organized groups, and campaigns for anti-discrimination legislation and independent living. The Disability Discrimination Act (1995) arose as a consequence of the adoption of the social

Alison Lapper is an English artist who was born without arms and is the subject of the sculpture *Alison Lapper Pregnant*, shown here, which was on display in Trafalgar Square until late 2007. Art has been used as a powerful medium to move people to reconsider their impressions of disability.

Activity 7.2   **Impairment groups**

(a)   Think about the various impairment groups: people with learning difficulties, people with mental health problems, people with visual impairments, people with hearing impairments, people with mobility impairments, people with breathing problems.
Make a list of the main problems and barriers these groups face in their day-to-day lives.

(b)   Which of these problems are due to barriers and which are due to their impairment?

(c)   Is the social model of disability equally applicable to all these groups?

model by organizations of disabled people. New techniques, such as direct action, and new forms of cultural expression, such as disability arts, have accompanied new ways of identifying and organizing.

What are the barriers?

barriers   barriers which
prevent disabled people
from participating fully
within society

The barriers that disabled people face can be divided into two broad categories: those arising from discrimination and those arising from prejudice. Discriminatory **barriers** include those that physically exclude disabled people, such as stairs rather than lifts, the absence of disabled toilets, heavy doors, poor lighting or high counters. These barriers also include those of a more structural nature. For example, Barnes, Mercer and Shakespeare (1999) document how educational attainment for the many disabled children who are educated in segregated schools is below that of their non-disabled peers and they experience a narrower curriculum. Consequently they leave school with fewer academic skills and qualifications than their peers, which limits their opportunities in later life. Employment, as the same authors show, is another area where disabled people face exclusion. In the UK the unemployment rate for disabled people in 1995 was nearly three times that of non-disabled people. Similarly, a poll in the USA found the employment rate for people with disabilities was 57 per cent, compared to 63.9 per cent for non-disabled people. Among those with severe disabilities, the employment rate is about 30 per cent (US Census Bureau, 2002). Furthermore, the majority of jobs open to disabled people tend to be low-paid, low-skilled jobs. Disabled men earn about a quarter less than their non-disabled counterparts. Structural discrimination also exists in housing, in the provision of public transport, and in welfare and other social services. Oliver and Barnes (1998) argue that the systemic nature of the inequalities faced by disabled people has not been addressed by social policy initiatives, which, they suggest, have tended to focus on the individual as the problem rather than address any social and economic causes. At best these policy initiatives will simply fail to solve the problem they seek to address, at worst they will add to the difficulties faced by disabled people – as, for example, in the case of special education.

prejudice   the negative
feelings of an individual
towards a particular
social group

Prejudice also presents barriers to the full participation in society of disabled people. Disabled people are subjected to stares, are made the centre of unwanted attention, are denied anonymity as they go about their day-to-day lives and are patronized (Morris, 1991). Disabled people have an identity imposed upon them. It does not matter what they do, what their job is or what they say, what is important in the eyes of many is the fact that they are disabled. As a consequence non-disabled people feel free to make comments about their physical condition and deny them the respect they would accord to others (Watson, 2003).

Lois Keith (2001), in her analysis of disability in classic fiction for girls, provides a graphic description of how society's attitudes about disability and disabled people are produced. Books such as *Heidi* or *The Secret Garden* portray disabled characters as suffering and unhappy. By the end of the books they are all miraculously cured and running about. Similarly, Barnes (1992), in his exploration of disabled imagery in the media, shows how disabled people are presented as pitiable and pathetic, as objects of violence, as sinister and evil, as 'super cripples', as objects of ridicule, as their own worst and only enemy, as burdens, as sexually abnormal, as being incapable of participating fully in community life or of being normal.

When such identities are foisted on disabled people, these can not only, as Morris (1991) argues, impact on the way that people think about themselves, they also constrain opportunities for disabled people. For example, Davis, Watson and Cunningham-Burley (2000) illustrate how the closed minds of some people working with severely disabled children limit not only their expectations of the child, but also what the child is willing to do. They show how, through employing what they term reflexivity when working with the children – that is, self-analysis and political awareness – they encourage the children to show much more ability and to be more willing to co-operate and communicate. They argue that the key to meeting the challenge of working with these children is to examine your own feelings and prejudices and how these impact on practice. The problems, they suggest, lie not with the child, but with the way that the child is treated. It is worth thinking about this in relation to your own practice.

How might a disabled child's self-identity be affected by being treated as though they are fully dependent upon the help of others?

Activity 7.3   **Disability and charity**

This activity asks you to consider the representation of disabled people within society.

1   Go to the websites of various charities and organizations of and for disabled people, for example:
Scope (www.scope.org.uk/);
Capability (www.capability-scotland.org.uk/);
People First (www.peoplefirst.org.uk);
Spinal Injuries Association (www.spinal.co.uk/);
Multiple Sclerosis Society (www.mssociety.org.uk/);
Christopher Reeve Paralysis Foundation (www.apacure.com/);
Children in Need (www.bbc.co.uk/pudsey/index.shtml).

(a)   What models of disability are these various organizations using?
(b)   Why are these models being used and what message do these groups send out about disability?

2   Go to the websites of charities concerned with long-term illness, for example, Cancerbackup, MS society, Asthma UK, Diabetes UK.

(a)   What do they offer to people with the diseases?
(b)   What is their main focus – e.g. information giving or research funding?
(c)   What do they want to achieve for people living with the condition?

4 Critiques of the social model of disability – sociology of the body

While the social model has provided an invaluable model for explaining disability, it is not without its critics, from within the ranks of disabled people as well as without. Some of their critiques focus on the body, a relatively new concept for sociological investigation, which, as chapter 1 has explained, has been traditionally concerned with structural concepts. For many sociologists the body was considered the preserve of anthropology, and the impaired body lay within the exclusive expertise of the medical profession (Hughes and Patterson, 1997). Structural perspectives in sociology reinforced the Cartesian mind–body dualism, that is, the idea that the mind and the body are separate, and that one does not influence the working of the other. The 1990s, however, saw a move away from such ideas, with a realization that our body impacts on, and is influenced by, social structure (Nettleton and Watson, 1998). This coincided with technological developments in medicine and sports science, for example, which made viewing and manipulating the body possible to a greater extent than ever before. Antenatal screening, organ transplantation, and athletes using exercise and diet to reach peak physical performance are all examples of how bodies are the object of scrutiny.

Let us consider the way in which we view our bodies. Three hundred years ago women's bodies were seen as attractive if they had plenty of flesh, especially around the breasts and hips. A thin woman in those times might well have felt inadequate and dissatisfied with her body. Today the opposite is true, and many women strive for a thin body with little extra flesh. It is those who are deemed overweight and those who cannot achieve the perceived ideal who are more likely to be unhappy with their bodies. Increasing consumerism and rejection of imperfection has seen a recent rise in the scope and amount of plastic surgery carried out – attempts to manipulate the body to conform to ideas of perfection. So social structure influences the way we view our bodies. However, this cannot be divorced from biological processes such as ageing, which impact on how we construct ideas of the body.

Turning to the social model of disability, Hughes and Patterson (1997) argue that the social model has focused entirely on disability (social discrimination) while leaving impairment (the body) within the realm of medical science. It rejects the part played by physical impairment in disability, thereby acknowledging the dualism. Williams and Busby (2000) add that the social model has ignored bodily change and decay.

Although not denying the crucial importance of structural oppression, some writers argue for impairment to be included within a sociology of disability. Living in constant pain, for example, may impact on a person's ability to engage in 'normal' activity as much as discrimination. Similarly, Crow (1997, p. 71) calls for a recognition of the implications of impairment: 'What this renewed social model of disability does is broaden and strengthen the current social model, taking it beyond grand theory and into real life.' In other words, both the interpretive sociology of the body and structural oppression have a part to play in explaining the realities of life for those living with disability.

5 Exploring disability through individual accounts of chronic illness

In two of the most influential reviews of the sociological literature on chronic illness and impairment, Michael Bury (1991, 1997) has identified three main themes which have emerged within a body of literature that has been strongly influenced by sociological theories of social action (see chapter 1).

First, *biographical disruption* (Bury, 1982, 1991, 1997) is a term used to explain the impact that a chronic condition can have on an individual's expectations and achievements. The presence of a chronic condition and its effect on activity and independence, Bury contends, disrupt that person's life, altering their life situation and social relationships (1997, p. 124). However, this changes over time.

At the onset of the condition, it is the *consequences* and *significance* of the condition that are paramount. That is, it is the impact that it has on a person's everyday roles and relationships and the symbolic and cultural meanings which surround different sorts of illnesses and impairments. Over time, biographical disruption can be overcome through individuals constructing explanations for their conditions and establishing their legitimacy.

symbolic and cultural meanings   the way in which concepts and ideas are expressed through culture

legitimacy   is achieved when an individual acknowledges that their lifestyle has changed as a consequence of acquiring a chronic condition and incorporates these changes into social interactions

The impact of treatment on everyday life refers to the way in which individuals come 'to grips with treatment regimes and medical interventions, and with the bureaucracies from which they emanate' (Bury, 1997, p. 126). It involves the person gaining an understanding of the official diagnosis and labelling, searching for information on their condition, making sense of this and incorporating it into their restructured social world. As discussed in chapter 3 (see, in particular, activity 3.1), people living with chronic illness are increasingly regarded as 'lay experts' on their own health and health care needs.

Adaptation and management of illness and disability describes how individuals cope with an impairment, how they develop a strategy and a style to achieve 'the best quality of life possible' (Bury, 1997, p. 129). It is the way that individuals achieve a 'normal' life, despite the presence of an impairment. The term *coping*, as Bury (1991, 1997) acknowledges, implies a moral framework against which an individual's ability to manage is judged. Despite claims by Bury and others that the notion of 'coping' is not judgemental, the very nature of the approach implies that there is something wrong with the individual in the first place. Disabled people or people with a chronic condition are presented as essentially different from their non-disabled peers in that they have lost their sense of worth because of the presence of impairment. You may have seen people on your placements who are described as 'coping well' or 'not coping' with their illness or disability, and have noticed the expectation from health professionals that they will learn to 'cope'.

The *strategies* that disabled people assume form the second element of the adaptation process (Bury, 1991, 1997). These refer to actions or practices people adopt in the face of chronic illness or impairment rather than to meanings or attitudes. Through successful actions the individual learns how to maintain hope and a sense of the future.

Whilst this approach has provided useful avenues of research within sociology, the analysis does raise a number of issues. Bury and others have allowed an exploration of the consequences of being a disabled person in practical situations. The position of disabled people is taken seriously and credence is given to their views. However, despite the acknowledgement of conditions of inequality, powerlessness and violence (see, for example, Bury, 1997), they are rarely placed at the centre of the research or analysis (Williams, 1996). Even in work that claims to incorporate or acknowledge wider social issues, the focus is still very much on the individual. This work, by focusing on the impact of treatment and care, presents an image of disabled people as being in need of care. It also fails to analyse how people who are born with an impairment perceive that impairment and the impact it has on their lives.

Simon Williams (1996) writes about the ups and downs of chronic illness, but seems to ignore such matters in daily life. We all face change throughout our lives (leaving school, ending a relationship, having children, and so on) which challenge our sense of worth and identity and result in biographical disruption. Yet these are seen as normal and are rarely used as defining characteristics of an individual. Disability or impairment is presented as a *master status*, one that limits an individual's ability to access social roles, so that they are reduced to adopting a range of subsidiary roles (Gerhardt, 1989).

For these reasons, and others, the disabled people's movement has not endorsed this approach to disability.

6   Sociological perspectives on long-term illness

Whereas biographical disruption has been criticized as a way of explaining disability, it has been very influential in the sociological analysis of long-term illness. For example, in their study of widespread pain, Richardson, Ong and Sim (2006) suggest the need to add perceptions of life stage and life expectancy to the concept of biographical disruption in order to obtain a fuller social and biographical context.

Although, as stated earlier, long-term illness is often the cause of disability, there are crucial differences in the experience of each that affect the way in which we need to view them. When discussing sociology of the body, the importance of pain and reduced mobility for many people living with long-term illness was identified as a crucial part of the experience. Yet for many disabled people who do not have a physical illness this may not be an issue, and such individuals would not even consider themselves as ill or unhealthy. Similarly, those with a long-term illness may actually want and seek out the medical control of their condition that those within the disability movement reject.

So both structural and interpretive perspectives play a part in sociological accounts of long-term illness, and indeed much of the interpretive work on long-term illness has arisen out of personal interest (e.g. Jobling, 1988). Interpretive perspectives seek to understand the impact that living with a chronic illness has on the person and their family and carers. This work has been criticized as reinforcing a medical model, as many studies focus on specific diseases, but it does highlight the day-to-day experience of people's lives and the effects of living with a long-term illness. This is in sharp contrast to the perspectives of health practitioners whose views have dominated policy and practice. Chapters 11 and 14 demonstrate how these patient experiences are now much more influential in shaping health and social care policy. Indeed, the use of the term 'long-term illness' as opposed to 'disease' reflects sociology's interest in these experiences as opposed to a paternalistic medical model in which credibility is given to diagnosis and treatment.

Sociological work on 'lived experience' often uses narrative methods to discover what it is like to live with a particular illness over many years and the impact it has on one's life. The use of such methods allows the participant to impart the issues that are important to them, and gives voice to their interpretation of their condition and their life.

Hydén (1997) suggests that the relationship between narrator, narrative, and illness can give rise to at least three types of illness narrative. In the first type, illness *as* narrative, illness is articulated and expressed through narrative. The illness, the narrator and the narrative may be combined in the same person. This encompasses the person's story regarding the occurrence of the illness and the way in which it is accommodated into the totality of that person's life. Thus it is possible to integrate symptoms and consequences of illness into a new being. The second type, narrative *about* illness, is primarily about the illness rather than the person, and constructs and conveys knowledge and ideas about illness. Health professionals use narratives about illness to gain information on a patient's illness, to reach a diagnosis and to formulate acceptable treatment regimes. Hydén's third type, narrative *as* illness, reflects instances when the inability to narrate or to articulate is a crucial aspect of illness, as in the case of aphasia associated with a stroke.

Charnaz (2000) has argued that the primacy of acute illness in Western health care systems permeates thinking about long-term illness and influences policy and practice. She goes on to say that people with long-term illness lose the taken-for-granted continuity of their previous life. Others have also pointed out the uncertainties posed by the diagnosis of a disease for which there is no cure. Williams sums this up as '*diagnostic* uncertainty, *symptomatic* uncertainty and *trajectory* uncertainty' (2003, p. 97, original emphasis). Studies also point to what Robinson (1988) has called the medical merry-go-round of people consulting various health specialists trying to achieve a diagnosis or some kind of meaning or explanation for what is happening to them, and finding a treatment for the cause of their illness.

The Western health care system has traditionally focused on the diagnosis and cure of problems, often through the use of drugs. What limits might this narrow vision of 'illness' as an 'abnormal' state have in relation to those who live with disability or chronic illness?

One area where the interpretive research on patient experience is frequently explored within a structural framework is the growing sociological work on chronic pain. Pain is generally accepted within the health field as a bio-psychological phenomenon, but for sociologists it is an individual, embodied experience that needs to be understood within a structural analysis, for example gender and culture. Bendelow (2000) states that, although experimental research demonstrates a lower pain threshold in women, her study on beliefs and perceptions of pain found that women are perceived as being more able to cope with pain. The consequence is that women's pain is not taken as seriously as men's. Her respondents also felt that men would take longer to admit to pain or to seek treatment, but that when they did they would receive more attention and be taken more seriously. Bendelow argues that 'Being a gendered body in a hierarchical organized gender-differentiated world must have an impact on the ways in which different forms of pain are experienced and expressed' (ibid., p. 132) (see also chapter 5). Im (2006), in her study of white cancer patients' perceptions of pain, also found gender to be an issue raised by participants. The women all perceived gender differences in the experience of pain, with most feeling that they were treated differently because of their gender, whereas none among the small sample of men mentioned this. The sample also felt that predominant values within their culture influenced their experience of pain.

Activity 7.4   **Pain and the sick role**

Read the following case study and discuss the questions below with your colleagues.

Stan is a 56-year-old man who has chronic back pain following an injury, but no cause has been found for this. He has been unable to work for five years.

'When I first had the injury I thought the pain would go and that I would get back to work. I couldn't accept that I would not work again, and so I did not claim benefits. I lived on my savings after my sick pay ran out, rather than admit that this would be permanent.

The problem with a condition like back pain is that it can't be seen, not like a broken leg or something. People don't understand that you can look normal but still be disabled. For instance when I go to the supermarket and park in a disabled parking bay, and then walk round without a stick or anything you can see people looking at you and thinking you are a fraud.

People do get fed up with you after a while when you don't get better, and can't do things. They are sympathetic at first but as time goes on friends and even family start to wonder whether you are putting it on, and not helping yourself. Being in pain is lonely.

Even health professionals don't understand. They see you for a few minutes at an appointment, they don't see what it is like day in day out. They see the part that's in pain, not the whole person. When I see the doctor he doesn't want to talk about anything other than my back.'

(a)   How helpful do you think that the sick role is in explaining Stan's life?

(b)   How can Stan be seen as having a stigmatized condition?

(c)   What can nurses do to understand and help people like Stan with unexplained illness?

---

7   Implications for nursing

Nursing, and much of nursing research, has tended to focus on the experience of having a chronic condition and on the individual aspects of disability. Emphasis has been on how disabled people and those living with long-term illness manage the effects of their impairment. Whilst this research is valuable, it has tended, in the main, to ignore the socio-political elements of disability. This has meant that the focus of nursing care has attempted to change individual disabled people rather than to change the environment in which disabled people live. This, it could be argued, has served to reinforce the notion of difference between disabled and non-disabled people. However, this is perhaps inevitable given that nursing is aimed at individual care. Nursing care does not, normally, extend to campaigning for social change. Also, individual disabled people want to be treated as such; they want individual care and they want that care to be based on evidence so as to ensure that the best care possible is provided. They also want health professionals to understand the impact that living with a disability or long-term illness has on their day-to-day lives, to have their interpretation of their experience accepted as valid. This means that nurses do need to know and understand what it means to an individual who acquires an impairment, or how an individual with an impairment, lives his or her life. They also need to be a source of knowledge and provide disabled people with information about the everyday management of their impairment.

However, this does not mean that nurses should eschew the socio-political approach to disability. There are elements of the social model that they could, and indeed should, incorporate into their practice. As well as ensuring the physical accessibility of their premises, nurses should start by examining their own practices and procedures, rather than assuming that it is only and always the disabled person who is the problem. For example, when dealing with people with a learning difficulty who exhibit what is termed 'challenging behaviour', the question should be asked 'Whose challenging behaviour, the nurse's or the patient's?' Unless such an approach is taken, nurses run the risk of constructing and reinforcing difference.

Activity 7.5	**Working with disabled people and those with long-term illness**

(a) What do you think are the most important issues for nurses working with disabled people and the long-term sick?

(b) Should you concentrate on providing them with information about how to manage their impairment or should you examine how you can help them overcome the barriers that they meet?

(c) Is the latter activity too political for nurses? Should nursing concentrate only on medical issues?

agents   individuals who ◄ have the capacity to act outside of (structural) constraints

Nurses should treat disabled people as **agents** who are capable of expressing views and having preferences, and they should try to meet these preferences wherever possible. They need to accept that a person who lives with a long-term illness day to day may have a different interpretation of that illness and possess different priorities from health professionals. These issues can raise some difficult concerns. For example, do people with learning difficulties who do not want to take medication have a right not to do so, regardless of the consequences? Or do the nurse and those who care for that person have a duty to ensure that the person takes medication, regardless of that individual's wishes? Should a person with undiagnosed and intractable pain receive the same attention and resources as someone with a medically diagnosed condition for which treatment can be offered? These and similar issues need to be addressed when dealing with disabled and chronically ill people, and if this is to be done successfully it is essential that the problem is located in the right place. Impairment is not the problem; the problem is the way that people with impairment are treated.

Summary and Resources

Summary

- Disabled people experience discrimination throughout their lives. For example, they are denied equal access to the built environment, to educational opportunities, to transport and to housing.

- The traditional sociological approach to disability focuses on the experience and impact of impairment on an individual. It argues that having an impairment can cause *biographical disruption*.

- The social model of disability argues that disability arises as the consequence of the way that society is organized. There is no link between impairment and disablement.

- The social model of disability states that, to improve the life chances of disabled people, we should focus on changing society rather than changing the individual.

- Critiques of the social model argue that the experience of impairment can also be disabling, and that this has been downplayed.

- Nursing, in the main, focuses on changing the individual rather than on changing society.

Questions for Discussion

1. Disabled people are more likely to experience unemployment, low pay, prejudice and discrimination. What effect do you think that these experiences may have on health?

2. How can nurses provide individual care and yet still adopt the social model of disability within their practice?

3. On your next placement, make a list of all the barriers you find to providing the best care for people with impairments.

Further Reading

E. Denny and S. Earle (eds): *The Sociology of Long Term Conditions and Nursing Practice*. Basingstoke: Palgrave Macmillan, 2009. This book is written specifically for nurses and takes a sociological perspective on long-term illness. The first part considers theory, policy and research, while part 2 focuses on some of the specific diseases and conditions that are prevalent in society today.

H. Thomas: *Sociologies of Disability and Illness*. Basingstoke: Palgrave, 2007.

Thomas provides an analysis of the competing and conflicting perspectives on disability and chronic illness. The book explores the debates between interpretive and structuralist approaches within sociology, and looks at disability studies from historical traditions to recent shifts in theoretical positions.

D. G. Race: *Learning Disability: A Social Approach*. London: Routledge, 2002.
This book combines academic knowledge with real-life experience, and some of the contributors have learning disabilities. It critiques some of the widely used models with the field such as 'normalization'.

M. Priestley: *Disability: A Life Course Approach*. Cambridge: Polity, 2003.
This book explores important issues and debates in disability studies and examines how disability is experienced across the life course. It contains sections on birthrights, childhood, youth, adulthood, old age and dying. There are case studies throughout illustrating key issues, together with suggestions for discussion.

For additional further reading, questions and online resources go to www.politybooks.com/sociologyfornurses.

References

Albrecht, G. 1993: *The Disability Business*. London: Sage.

Barnes, C. 1992: *Disabling Imagery and the Media*. Halifax: British Council of Organisations of Disabled People and Ryburn Publishing; www.leeds.ac.uk/disability-studies/archiveuk/Barnes/disabling%20imagery.pdf.

Barnes, C., Mercer, G., and Shakespeare, T. 1999: *Exploring Disability: A Sociological Introduction*. Cambridge: Polity.

Bendelow, G. 2000: *Pain and Gender*. Harlow: Prentice-Hall.

Bury, M. 1982: 'Chronic illness as biographical disruption'. *Sociology of Health & Illness*, 4, 167–82.

Bury, M. 1991: 'The sociology of chronic illness: a review of research and prospects'. *Sociology of Health & Illness*, 13, 451–68.

Bury, M. 1997: *Health and Illness in a Changing Society*. London: Routledge.

Charnaz, K. 2000: 'Experiencing chronic illness'. In G. L. Albrecht, R. Fitzpatrick and S. C. Scrimshaw (eds), *The Handbook of Social Studies in Health and Medicine*. London: Sage, pp. 277–92.

Crow, L. 1997: 'Including all of our lives: renewing the social model of disability'. In C. Barnes and G. Mercer (eds), *Exploring the Divide: Illness and Disability*. Leeds: Disability Press, pp. 55–73.

Davis, J., Watson, N., and Cunningham-Burley, S. 2000: 'Learning the lives of disabled children: developing a reflexive approach'. In

CHRONIC ILLNESS AND DISABILITY   159

P. Christensen and A. James (eds), *Research with Children: Perspectives and Practices*. London: Falmer, pp. 201–24.

Gerhardt, U. 1989: *Ideas about Illness: An Intellectual and Political History of Medical Sociology*. Basingstoke: Macmillan.

Hughes, B., and Patterson, K. 1997: 'The social model of disability and the disappearing body: towards a sociology of impairment'. *Disability and Society*, 12(3), 325–40.

Hurst, R. 2000: 'To revise or not to revise'. *Disability and Society*, 15(7), 1083–8.

Hydén, L. C. 1997: 'Illness and narrative'. *Sociology of Health & Illness*, 19(1), 48–69.

Im, E.-O. 2006: 'White cancer patients' perceptions of gender and ethnic differences in pain experiences'. *Cancer Nursing*, 29(6), 441–50.

Jobling, R. 1988: 'The experience of psoriasis under treatment'. In R. Anderson and M. Bury (eds), *Living with Chronic Illness: The Experience of Patients and their Families*. London: Unwin Hyman, pp. 225–44.

Keith, L. 2001: *Take up thy Bed and Walk: Death, Disability and Cure in Classic Fiction for Girls*. London: Women's Press.

Morris, J. 1991: *Pride against Prejudice*. London: Women's Press.

Morris, J. 1993: *Independent Lives? Community Care and Disabled People*. London: Macmillan.

Nettleton, S., and Watson, J. 1998: 'The body in everyday life: an introduction'. In S. Nettleton and J. Watson (eds), *The Body in Everyday Life*. London: Routledge, pp. 1–23.

Oliver, M. 1990: *The Politics of Disablement*. Basingstoke: Macmillan.

Oliver, M. 1996: *Understanding Disability: From Theory to Practice*. Basingstoke: Macmillan.

Oliver, M., and Barnes, C. 1998. *Disabled People and Social Policy from Exclusion to Inclusion*. London: Longman.

Parsons, T. 1951: *The Social System*. New York: Free Press.

Pfeiffer, D. 2000: 'The devils are in the details: the ICIDH-2 and the disability movement'. *Disability and Society*, 15(7), 1079–82.

Richardson, J. C., Ong, B. N., and Sim, J. 2006: 'Is chronic widespread pain biographically disruptive?' *Social Science and Medicine*, 63, 1573–85.

Riddell, S., and Banks, P. 2001: *Disability in Scotland: A Baseline Study*. Glasgow: Disability Rights Commission Scotland Office.

Robinson, I. 1988: *Multiple Sclerosis*. London: Routledge.

Thomas, C. 1999: *Female Forms: Experiencing and Understanding Disability*. Buckingham: Open University Press.

UPIAS (Union of Physically Impaired Against Segregation) 1976: *The Fundamental Principles of Disability*. London: UPIAS.

US Census Bureau 2002: *Facts for Features*, CB02–FF.11, 12 July. Washington, DC; www.census.gov.

Watson, N. 2003: 'Daily denials: the routinisation of oppression and resistance'. In S. Riddell and N. Watson (eds), *Disability, Culture and Identity*. London: Pearson Education, pp. 34–52.

Williams, S. 1996: 'The vicissitudes of embodiment across the chronic illness trajectory'. *Body and Society*, 2(2), 23–47.

Williams, S. J. 2003: *Medicine and the Body*. London: Sage.

Williams, G., and Busby, H. 2000: 'The politics of disabled bodies'. In S. J. Williams, J. Gabe and M. Calnan (eds), *Health, Medicine and Society*. London: Routledge.

WHO (World Health Organization) 1980: *The International Classification of Impairments, Disabilities and Handicaps (ICIDH)*. Geneva: WHO.

WHO (World Health Organization) 1997: *The International Classification of Impairments, Activities and Participation (ICIDH-2)*. Geneva: WHO.

WHO (World Health Organization) 2002: *Towards a Common Language for Functioning, Disability and Health*. Geneva: WHO.

Social Class

Terry O'Donnell

Key issues in this chapter

- A historical overview of the relationship between class and health
- Class and the measurement of socio-economic difference
- The extent and causes of health inequalities
- The policies adopted to tackle health inequalities
- Contemporary nursing, class and health

By the end of this chapter you should be able to . . .

- map the history of the relationship between class and health;
- explain the concepts of class and understand the measurement of socio-economic difference;
- discuss the evidence relating to class inequalities in health;
- explore some of the policies used to tackle health inequalities;
- understand the significance of class and health for nursing practice.

1 Introduction

Low incomes, poor environments and social deprivation are all associated both with earlier death and with poorer health at all ages during life. The association between ill-health and material deprivation was first made in the early nineteenth century. During the last two decades of the twentieth century,

Box 8.1   **Health inequality in Britain**

- Half of all lone-parent families are on low incomes, compared with one in five couples with children. Two-fifths of all the children in low-income households are in lone-parent households.[*]

- Life expectancy at birth for a boy is about five years less in the two lowest social classes than in the two highest, at seventy and seventy-five years respectively.[*]

- Babies whose parents are manual workers are more likely to have a low birth weight than those from non-manual backgrounds: 8 per cent compared with 6.5 per cent.[*]

- Infant deaths are still 50 per cent more common among those from manual backgrounds than among those from non-manual backgrounds.[*]

- Children from manual households are more likely to suffer from chronic sickness than children from non-manual households.[*]

- Children from manual households are more likely to suffer from tooth decay than children from non-manual households.[*]

- Each of the main disease groups shows a wide health gap among men, with those in the highest two social classes experiencing lower mortality than men in the lowest two.[*]

- In both sexes, the prevalence of and mortality from cardiovascular disease increased as household income decreased.[**]

- Mortality from all major causes has been found to be consistently higher than average among unemployed men; unemployed women have higher mortality from coronary heart disease and suicide.[**]

- Two-fifths of all adults aged forty-five to sixty-four on below-average incomes have a limiting longstanding illness or disability, twice the rate for those on average incomes and three times the rate for those on high incomes.[*]

(*Sources*: [*]www.poverty.org.uk; [**]DH, 2004)

the gaps between both the incomes and the health of the richest and poorest in our society actually widened (Acheson, 1998). Box 8.1 outlines some of the key health inequalities in Britain today.

In over two centuries of gathering hard evidence showing that disease and death are related to deprivation and disadvantage, we have often encountered political dispute about the validity of the research findings, how they should be interpreted and whether, and how, governments should act to improve the people's health. It is only since the very end of the twentieth century that we have had concerted efforts by a British government both to tackle health inequalities and to do so using strategies clearly informed by the full range of research findings, rather than just selecting those findings that it found acceptable.

This chapter begins with a brief historical overview of the relationship between class and health. It will explore the sociological concept of 'class' and discuss the ways in which socio-economic difference has been measured. Drawing on current research evidence, it will examine the extent and the causes of health inequalities and review some of the policies adopted to tackle these. Lastly, this chapter will explore how class and health inequalities are relevant to contemporary nursing practice.

2   Modernization, class and health

modern describes a kind of society that began in eighteenth-century Europe, in which scientific knowledge, technology, progress and individualism are highly valued

class the major form of social stratification in modern societies

As the nineteenth century opened, Britain was already on an increasingly fast track towards becoming a new kind of social formation – a **modern** society in which wealth was increasingly created through industrial manufacture. The population of England and Wales doubled, from 9 million to 18 million, between 1801 and 1851, by which time more than half of these people lived in towns and cities (Mathias, 1983). It is during this early period of modernization and industrial growth that the term and concept of **class** came to a greater extent into common usage.

Class

'Working class' came to describe the masses who depended on working for either a capitalist or a member of the aristocracy. Very long hours were worked for wages that were often inadequate to meet even the most basic necessities of rent and food. The aristocracy were the main landowners, although some also invested in the new industry, and were considered to be the upper class. The capitalists owned the new forms, or means, of industrial production, including factories, workshops, raw materials and transport; they were considered to be middle class. This class also encompassed owners of shops, farmers and the members of the growing professions, such as doctors, lawyers, accountants and clergymen.

The earliest theoretical account of this new class society was provided by Marx – a structural theorist – in 1848, and the relationship between what he called the bourgeoisie and the proletariat is discussed in chapter 1.

Health

The main causes of death in the nineteenth century were infectious diseases such as respiratory tuberculosis, typhoid and cholera. For much of this century, it was believed that these diseases were caused by bad air coming from the filth generated by both living and working conditions. This polluted air was called miasma and its presence was detected by bad smells.

A growing number of studies showed that the killer diseases infected the working class in greater numbers, and killed them more often, than the middle and upper classes. The studies varied in their explanations of why this was so and what should be done. Chadwick's report (1842), the *Inquiry into the Sanitary Condition of the Labouring Population of Great Britain*, was the result of a national statistical survey that showed:

- mortality rates were highest for the poorest;
- urban dwellers were more adversely affected than those living in rural areas;
- the poorer classes lived in the most unsanitary areas.

Chadwick, who believed in miasma theory, argued for schemes to dispose safely of the filth he believed to be an inevitable consequence of modernization. Most social reformers at this time focused only on the environmental impact of the Industrial Revolution and sought to improve the physical condition of homes and workplaces.

Engels, a close collaborator of Marx, took a different perspective. His study of working-class life and death, mainly in the Manchester area, was published as *The Condition of the Working Class in England* in 1845 and used several sources, including official reports from the registrar-general for England and Wales, to document working-class mortality. He observed appalling living and working conditions and argued that they were the result of actions by the propertied classes. Engels argued that the propertied classes failed to deal with the pollution they caused in their workplaces, imposed hazardous working conditions for which they paid very low wages, and provided poor housing that lacked appropriate basic services and for which they charged high rents. Furthermore, Engels maintained that these actions, driven by profit, were directly responsible for the patterns of disease and early death in the working class and that they amounted to what he termed 'social murder'.

It was not until the last two decades of the nineteenth century that the full extent and causes of poverty were fully explored. Charles Booth (Fried and Elman, 1971) and Seebohm Rowntree (1902) showed that poverty was caused mainly by incomes below subsistence levels, either from low wages or from inadequate provision for when people could not work. They also showed that poverty undermined individual efforts to struggle for respectability, health and well-being.

Nonetheless, governments tended more heavily towards the view that poverty was caused by the personal shortcomings of poor people and how they chose to live.

3   Understanding class

social stratification
the division of society into levels that form a hierarchy with the most powerful at the top

By the early twentieth century, it was evident that, far from polarizing into just two classes, as Marx predicted, we had moved instead to a complex of groups ranked in relation to ideas about their social and economic differences; this is also known as **social stratification**. Both the working class and the middle class contained subgroups reflecting significant differences in relation to such matters as size and security of income, housing circumstances, schooling experiences and perceived social prestige. Weber (1958) (see also chapter 1) provided a theoretical basis for understanding this growing complexity by distinguishing between class situation and status situation. Like Marx, he viewed a person's class situation as determined by her or his position in the markets for capital and labour. Those owning property, such as shares and land, are placed on the capital side of the main economic divide, whilst the possession of more, or less, valued skills or educational credentials puts the majority on the labour side of the main economic divide. According to Weber, we also have a status situation that groups us with similar others according to the social value placed on our styles of life, which includes our tastes, our social networks and our consumption practices, both for goods, such as cars, and for services, such as education. Weber took the view that our life chances are shaped not only by our class situation, but also by our status situation, which has an important impact on our well-being.

Various schemes of social and occupational classification, described below, have been developed to try to allocate us to a place in these socio-economic hierarchies.

Social and occupational classifications

Rose and Pevalin (2001) identify two major traditions of socio-economic classification in Britain. The dominant one, in terms of its use in the analysis of official data, especially in relation to life, health and death, comes from successive generations of government statisticians. In 1911 this tradition produced the Registrar-General's Social Classification (RGSC), which was modified in 1921 and in 1980 and renamed in 1990 (see box 8.2). The other tradition was formed by British sociology as it analysed the various expressions of class identity, and changes in the British class structure, from 1945 onwards.

Contemporary sociological analysis of class

The early compilers of the RGSC believed that society consisted of a definite social hierarchy that ranked people according to their inherited and innate abilities. These beliefs about social structure have increasingly limited its validity as a measure of socio-economic difference for sociologists today. Sociology is interested in the relations between the classes, and has developed sociological classifications to study social mobility, in particular. In doing so, it has identified many limitations of the RGSC. Concern about these limitations, combined with the impact of ongoing class analysis within sociology, led in 1994 to a thorough review of the RGSC and its replacement by a new scheme, the National Statistics Socio-economic Classification (NS-SEC), from 2001 (see box 8.3).

Box 8.2   **Registrar-general's social class based on occupation**

Class	Description of occupations
I	Professional: accountants, doctors, lawyers
II	Managerial and technical/intermediate: managers, senior technicians, school teachers, police officers, nurses
IIIN	Skilled non-manual: clerks, secretaries, waiters, shop assistants
IIIM	Skilled manual: HGV and PSV drivers, fitters, electricians
IV	Partly skilled: warehouse workers, machine tool operators
V	Unskilled: labourers (e.g. building, roads, tunnels construction), cleaners

Important notes

- People are assigned to a class on the basis of what they state as their occupation.

- Each job is assigned to a specific class, but if, within an occupation, persons are supervisors or managers, they are placed in a higher class than the others holding that job.

- People in the armed forces are treated separately and put in an additional group: Occupied – other.

- People known to be employed, but who have provided inadequate details, are also placed in Occupied – other.

- People who say they have never worked or who give no information are put in an additional group: 'Unoccupied'.

The NS-SEC classification was developed from the Goldthorpe schema (Goldthorpe, 1980, 1997) produced by sociologists in the 1980s and revised in the 1990s. This separates employers (who buy and direct the work of others) and the self-employed (who work for themselves) from employees, who account for up to 90 per cent of the economically active population. Employees clearly have only the fact that they work for someone else in common. They otherwise differ with regard to:

- stability of their job and income;
- size of that income;
- prospects for advancement and promotion;
- pension provisions and other indirect elements of remuneration;
- specialized knowledge and expertise and how these are valued;
- relative importance of educational qualifications compared with competences acquired in organizations;
- authority over others;
- personal autonomy and control over their job.

Box 8.3	National Statistics Socio-Economic Classification (NS-SEC)

1 Higher managerial and professional occupations

   1.1 Large employers and higher managerial occupations: health service managers, company directors

   1.2 Higher professional occupations: doctors, teachers, social workers, university lecturers

2 Lower managerial and professional occupations: nurses and midwives, journalists, police officers, laboratory technicians

3 Intermediate occupations: dental nurses, secretaries

4 Small employers and own account workers: publicans, farmers, restaurateurs

5 Lower supervisory and technical occupations: train drivers, plumbers, electricians

6 Semi-routine occupations: hairdressers, shop assistants, security guards

7 Routine occupations: waiters, cleaners, labourers, couriers

8 Never worked and long-term unemployed

By seeking to take account of these crucial lines of difference, the NS-SEC reflects contemporary socio-economic differences in the labour market and work situations. It may be useful to identify the class position of nurses and to consider some of the differences identified above.

The research discussed below also shows that these differential experiences of employment markets and job characteristics influence our experiences of health and disease, both directly and indirectly.

The Black Report

The value of the RGSC scheme for identifying and tracking health differentials is most clearly shown in the *Inequalities in Health Report* (Black et al., 1980), commissioned by a Labour government and published in 1980. It is popularly known as the Black Report and gives a detailed analysis of official statistics showing that a clear gradient of inequality runs all the way from the richest to the poorest (Townsend, Davidson and Whitehead, 1988). Those in Class V had worse health and died sooner, and in greater numbers, from the major causes of death – heart disease, cancers and strokes – than those in Class IV, and so on in a straight line up to those in Class I, who had the lowest death rates, the longest life expectancy, and the best health. Death from skin cancer was the only clear exception to this pattern. The health gap between Classes I and II combined and Classes IV and V combined widened between 1948 and the mid-1970s. The gap was particularly wide for infant death (under one year) and child death (under fifteen years).

■Activity 8.1   **Obesity and social class**

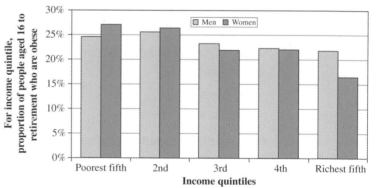

Source: Health Survey for England, DH; the data is the average for 2004 to 2006; England; updated June 2008

(a)   What social classification is being used in this chart and how does obesity vary by social class?

(b)   Explain how food poverty contributes to obesity.

(c)   Are there other factors that might help to explain the connections between obesity and social class?

(d)   What role can nurses play in reducing obesity and alleviating food poverty?

Box 8.4   **The Black Report 1980: explaining the findings**

Artefact explanation
The difference between classes was unintentionally enlarged by
the techniques used to measure class and the methods of
managing the statistics.
Evaluation   There are some technical problems, but the findings
are likely to be real. The Longitudinal Study and the Whitehall
Studies subsequently endorsed the reality of widespread health
inequalities.

Social selection explanation
People's class is determined by their health, not the other way
round. It is all part of a natural pattern whereby the least able
occupy the least demanding and rewarding jobs.
Evaluation   Only an insignificant amount of downward mobility
is caused by illness. A range of subsequent studies point to a
complex interaction between individual biology, psychosocial
stresses and material disadvantage that accumulates across the
life course.

Behavioural/cultural explanation
Poor health is caused by individual behaviours within personally
chosen lifestyles. Middle-class culture tends to embrace health-
enhancing behaviours whilst working-class culture seems to value
health-detracting behaviours, such as smoking and unhealthy
dietary choices.
Evaluation   Individual health-detracting behaviours are involved
and feature more heavily amongst working-class people. However,
they were produced in an impoverished socio-economic
environment that renders daily life a constant struggle to make
ends meet. The behaviours should be understood as coping
mechanisms and as efforts to obtain some pleasure and
enjoyment within generally adverse circumstances. However,
some health-detracting behaviours are not only more common in
the lower RGSC and NS-SEC classes, but also do more damage to
them. For example, Whitehall II showed smokers in the highest
civil service job grades had less heart disease and longer life
expectancy than smokers in the lowest messenger grades.

Materialist/structuralist explanation
Poor health and earlier death are dimensions of marked socio-
economic inequalities in society as a whole. In particular, they stem
from low and insecure incomes, unemployment and unstable
employment, poor working conditions, and poor housing in
materially and culturally under-resourced neighbourhoods.

Evaluation   The Black Report identified this as the dominant explanation. The Acheson Report, drawing on data from the 1990s, validated this analysis. There is no serious, empirical basis for questioning its central thesis that tackling health inequalities means tackling social inequalities. This perspective has informed wide-ranging government policy since 1999.

Middle-class people are more likely to engage in health-enhancing behaviours such as yoga.

Activity 8.2   Mental disorders in childhood and social class

Table 8.1 The prevalence of mental health problems amongst five- to fifteen-year-olds by family social class

	| Family social class							
	I	II	IIIN	IIIM	IV	V	Never worked	All
Percentage of children								
Emotional disorders	1.8	3.4	5.3	4.5	5.5	5.8	8.4	4.3
Conduct disorders	2.5	3.4	6.1	5.0	7.8	10.1	15.5	4.3
Any disorder	5.2	7.0	11.6	9.4	12.4	14.5	21.1	9.5

Source: Adapted from London Health Observatory, 2005, table 1.

  (a)   How much more likely are children in unskilled families (V) to have a mental disorder than children in professional families (I)?

  (b)   How much more likely than the national average are children in families where the head of the household has never worked to have a mental disorder?

  (c)   What factors do we need to take into account when trying to explain these patterns, and how do these factors influence nursing practice?

The Black Report concluded that Britain's health inequalities were determined by inequalities in the distribution of wealth, power and status. The report evaluated four possible approaches to explaining its findings (see box 8.4) but was neither welcomed, nor implemented, even partially, by the Conservative government to which it reported in 1980.

4 Tackling health inequalities in the twenty-first century

The 1990s ended with a combination of research developments and governmental commitment to act on research evidence that offers real prospects of achieving some reductions in health inequalities by the end of the first decade of the new century. These key developments are outlined in box 8.5.

The Acheson Report observes that average mortality has fallen in the last fifty years, but that unacceptable health inequalities still exist, and in some instances have widened. Indeed, some populations in the UK still have the same levels of early death as the national average during the 1950s. Acheson supports the view that health inequalities are a dimension of wider social inequalities. These shape

---

Activity 8.3   **The health gap**

In the preface to *Tackling Health Inequalities: 2007 Status Report on the Programme for Action* (DH, 2007), Michael Marmot wrote:

> This report shows a very welcome improvement in life expectancy for all social groups but no narrowing of the gap. In 1995–97, life expectancy in the most deprived areas (the spearhead group) was 72.7 years for men and 78.3 years for women. Few observers would have predicted that this worst off group would have life expectancy of 75.3 (men) and 80.0 (women) in 2004–6. There was, however, a similar improvement in England as a whole.
>
> So, too, with infant mortality. Babies born to families in the 'routine and manual' social groups have the same infant mortality rate in the latest figures, 5.6 per 1000 live births, as the average seven years earlier – a welcome improvement. But, the average rate improved and the gap did not narrow.

(a)   What do these figures tell us about life expectancy?
(b)   What do you think can account for the continuing health gap?
(c)   Why do you think nurses should know about these inequalities?

neighbourhood and community environments as well as patterns of work, and they influence individual lives from conception onwards.

Contemporary explanations of health inequalities

Research begun in the 1990s is developing our knowledge of the pathways that link the bodies of individuals to their life experiences, including their material resources, and how these are all shaped by the social structure (see also chapter 1). It is through these complex, connected mechanisms that the less affluent, especially the poor, become sicker, at an earlier age, than the more affluent. Bartley (2004) gives a detailed account of the psychosocial explanation, the life-course explanation (introduced in chapter 6) and the neo-materialist explanation, and discusses how these can inform each other and thus provide the potential for deepening our understanding.

Psychosocial explanation   Contemporary ways and conditions of life produce social stresses that affect social classes unevenly, and members of these groups have uneven access to material and personal resources to manage these stresses. Such stresses do not affect only mental well-being. They also affect the body through the cardiovascular, endocrine and immune systems. Siegrist et al. (1990) argue that *socio-emotional distress* occurs when a high workload is matched with job insecurity, poor promotion prospects and low control. They suggest such effort–reward imbalance at work predicts heart disease and its precursors, such as raised blood pressure and high fibrinogen levels. Psychoneuroendocrine and psychoneuroimmune mechanisms may thus contribute to diseases such as cancers and, especially, heart disease. Additionally, negative experience of hard-to-manage stress – for example, ever increasing debt – often induces harmful coping mechanisms such as smoking, high levels of alcohol consumption, and unhealthy eating patterns. Ability to change these health-damaging behaviours is restricted by access to important resources of money, time and supportive outlets such as gyms, health clubs and community networks. Kaplan et al. (1996) argue that high levels of psychosocial stress not only reflect exposure to antisocial behaviour, violent crime and reduced social cohesion, but also help to produce and maintain patterns of reduced social participation. However, these stresses occur in poor neighbourhoods. They are *ecological* experiences, which means they characterize places rather than individuals.

social cohesion   a sense of belonging to wider society

Lynch et al. (2000) use an airline travel metaphor to illustrate the shortcomings of the psychosocial explanation. They point out that first-class passengers on long-haul flights have more space, better food and seats that recline into beds, and so tend to arrive relatively refreshed. Economy-class passengers lack these advantages and are inclined to arrive feeling a bit rough. The problem is more likely to be

Manual work, such as mining, can be harmful to health.

Box 8.5	**Key developments on health inequalities, 1990s–present**

- Wilkinson (1996) analysed mortality and morbidity data from several countries and found that the widest gaps in health inequalities were to be found in those countries that had the widest gaps in incomes.

- The Office for National Statistics published a *Health Inequalities Decennial Supplement* in 1997 containing evidence-based accounts of health and mortality in children, unemployment and mortality, illness and health behaviours in adults and data from the Longitudinal Study (Drever and Whitehead, 1997).

- The *Independent Inquiry into Inequalities in Health* (Acheson, 1998) concluded that, although overall mortality had fallen over the past fifty years, unacceptable inequalities still existed.

- In July 1999 a new public health strategy, *Saving Lives: Our Healthier Nation*, was published which accepted the recommendations of the Acheson Report and identified some immediate strategies to reduce health inequalities, for example Health Action Zones (HAZs) and Healthy Living Centres (DH, 1999).

- In 2002 the *Cross-Cutting Review* identified a long-term strategy to reduce health inequalities involving all areas of government and calculated its costs (HM Treasury and DH, 2002).

- In 2003 the government published *Tackling Health Inequalities: A Programme for Action*, which was a three-year plan to lay the foundations for achieving various challenging targets for reducing health disadvantage in key areas such as infant mortality and deaths from heart disease, cancers and suicide by 2010 (DH, 2003).

- In 2008 *Tackling Health Inequalities: Progress and Next Steps* (DH, 2008) reported that many of these targets have been met, and beyond 2010 the goal is to focus on wider inequalities that are the root of health inequalities. The key areas are investing in early years and parenting; using work to improve health and well-being; promoting equality; developing mental health services further; and co-ordinating action – both nationally and locally.

that they could not sleep in cramped conditions than that knowledge of the better provisions in first class kept them awake.

Nurses and other health care professionals can contribute to projects in deprived areas that aim to empower communities as well as to address some of the direct effects of poverty. Such projects involve the members of the community as decision-makers and include setting up credit unions and food co-operatives that provide access to cheaper, healthy foods, training people to run health and fitness courses in their neighbourhoods, and providing free community transport to social events as well as to clinics and hospitals. In addition, nurses and their colleagues can avoid contributing to disempowerment by ensuring that service users from all communities across the life span are fully informed, active participants rather than passive recipients.

Life-course explanation   The health effects of adverse socio-economic circumstances accumulate from conception, through childhood and adolescence, to adulthood and life in later years. Early work by Barker et al. (1989) led to the concept of *foetal programming*, which argues that poor maternal nutrition and the generally poor health associated with living in poverty affect the developing baby during pregnancy. Material and social disadvantage for adults are thus reflected in the lower birth weight and poor health of their children – for example, in higher levels of asthma. Bartley et al. (1994) found that **longitudinal** study data showed low birth weight itself predicted socio-economic disadvantage through childhood and adolescence. Additionally, poor socio-economic conditions in childhood have been shown to have an independent effect on both adult health and adult socio-economic status. Indeed, the highest health risks have been found in those who both grow up, and remain, in disadvantaged material circumstances (van de Mheen, Stronks and Mackenbach, 1998).

Health problems in adult life do not result in downward mobility, but poor health in childhood and youth, combined with poor socio-economic circumstances, can produce a downward spiral. Health care

longitudinal describes a research study that follows the same group of people over time

is delivered at specific points in time. However, the life-course perspective asks those working in health care to recognize that illness and health-damaging behaviours occur in social contexts in people who are living their lives in good or poor circumstances, and with varying degrees of control over their lifestyles. Nurses are especially well placed to take account of the whole person with an ongoing life story and to challenge **victim blaming** within their practice. Victim blaming oversimplifies the pathways through which major diseases such as coronary heart disease, diabetes and cancers occur in particular individuals and may lead to low self-esteem, which can further detract from health.

victim blaming considering people to be individually responsible for their own ill-health

Neo-materialist explanation   Adverse socio-economic and psychosocial environments and the risky exposures and experiences associated with them are the material productions of social formations. These social formations have historically produced an unequal distribution of personal income and wealth, which, in turn, shapes unequal access to the infrastructure of markets for food, transport, housing, health care, education and lifestyle consumption. In Britain, for example, the poorest tenth of the population receives around 1.5 per cent of the country's total income, the second poorest tenth around 4 per cent. More than 3 million children live in households whose income is less than 60 per cent of the average (**median**) income. By contrast, the richest 10 per cent of the population receive 30 per cent of total income, and the second richest tenth 15 per cent (Palmer, MacInnes and Kenway, 2007). It is these structured inequalities that produce **social exclusion** and low levels of **social capital**.

median   the midpoint; so the median income is the point at which half of all incomes lie above, and half below

social exclusion   the impact of poverty and low income on involvement in mainstream social life

social capital community spirit, social cohesion, social networks, social trust, shared values and civic participation

Researchers working within this explanatory approach warn against putting too much emphasis on social cohesion, social participation and self-esteem, so that the consequences of inequality become the focus of attention rather than the need for structural change (Lynch et al., 2000). They point out that losing sight of the unequal social structure whilst working on what socially excluded and materially deprived communities can do for themselves may be a subtle form of victim blaming. From a neo-materialist perspective, it is income inequality together with inequitable distribution of public resources such as health services, schooling and social welfare provisions that produce health inequalities. These wider inequalities are themselves produced by economic and political processes operating at a macro-level and as such require major social interventions to create effective change. Professional organizations, such as the Royal College of Nursing and the British Medical Association, recognize the importance of the neo-materialist perspective, study evidence in its support, and debate the impact of economic structures on health. All individual members of such organizations may follow and participate in these activities.

Activity 8.4   **Learning disability and economic disadvantage**

A study based in three day centres in Northern Ireland by McConkey and Mezza (2001) looked at the views of both care workers and people with learning disabilities about possibilities for, types of, and benefits from paid employment. Some of their key findings are outlined below.

Experience of work or training for work

- 42 per cent of the 275 day centre attendees had previously had an unpaid job or done work experience.

- 33 per cent had previously had a vocational training placement provided by a voluntary organization.

- 17 per cent had previously had some other placement set up by a day centre.

- 25 per cent were currently doing a specific job in a day centre.

- 22 per cent were currently on a further education college course.

- Only 1.5 per cent (four people) had ever had paid employment.

Aspirations of people with learning difficulties

- Significantly more people who had done two or more placements wanted a paid job compared with those who had no, or limited, work experience.

- Twice as many people who were on an FE course, or had been in the last year, wanted a paid job compared with those who had not been to college.

- Those who wanted a paid job were significantly younger than those who didn't.

- Overall, eighty-five of the day centre attendees said they wanted a paid job.

Key workers' perceptions about suitability of clients for paid employment

- Staff rated 38 per cent of those who wanted a job as being capable of doing one and 29 per cent as unlikely to cope; they were unsure about the prospects of the rest.

- Staff preferred the chances of those whom they rated as above average in self-care skills, those who had been on three or more work experiences, and those who had above average skills in reading, writing, and time- and money-management skills.

- Staff thought the main obstacles to clients holding down jobs were poor concentration, poor communication skills and understanding, and lack of motivation.

- Staff also identified instances where they thought parents might be a negative force in their adult child's work prospects.

(a) In what ways might current patterns of attendance at day centres be unhelpful for clients' prospects of holding down paid work?

(b) Consider the roles that work-derived income and social contacts from work might play in relation to both the well-being and the socio-economic position of people with learning disabilities. You might want to think about this for both those living with their parents and those living in supported independent settings. You may also find it helpful to think about applying the concepts of social exclusion and social capital to your analysis.

Health care and the inverse care law

The inverse care law is a phrase first used by Julian Tudor Hart to describe how those who have most need of NHS services actually obtain them later, and in smaller amounts, whilst those who have less need use more, and often better, health services (Hart, 1971). Hart did not carry out a systematic review of evidence but rather observed his working environment as a GP and coined the phrase to make a political point. However, subsequent research has shown the description of an inverse pattern within health care to be largely accurate. Gainsbury (2008) reports that budgets allocated to GPs to pay for drugs and hospital care for their patients show that the wealthiest tenth of the population are, on average, more than 2 per cent overfunded while the poorest tenth are 2 per cent underfunded.

For example, a detailed review by Dixon et al. (2003) has shown that hip replacements are 20 per cent less frequent among lower socio-economic groups, despite around 30 per cent higher need, and that a one-point move down a seven-point deprivation scale resulted in GPs spending 3.4 per cent less time with the individual concerned. The review shows that these inequities result from two sorts of disadvantage: those that make access to services difficult, such as lack of transport and available time away from work, and those that make consultations less productive, such as patients being less assertive about demanding information, participation in treatment decisions, and appropriate referrals for further treatment. Nurses have an important role to play in helping to restore patients' 'voice' by listening and by encouraging more talk and self-expression. They may also act as mediators and advocates for patients in encounters with other health care professionals.

Older people living in poverty and isolation are at greater risk of ill-health. They often struggle to make their needs known, even though they are often in the greatest need of support.

Activity 8.5

Living on the Seacole

The Seacole estate was built in the late 1960s on the outer edges of a medium-sized town in the Midlands. The estate has a population of 7,000 living in low-rise houses, maisonettes and a few blocks of flats of three to six storeys. The jobless rate in Seacole is above the national average and the jobs done by those residents in work tend to be low-paid, putting household incomes below the national average. There is a fairly dilapidated shopping centre with one small independent supermarket and two other food stores. The nearest large supermarket is about 4 miles from the estate.

Most of the Seacole children go to one of the two primary schools on the estate and then to a very large secondary school that also draws from some neighbouring estates. Parents seem to be fairly happy with their children's primary schooling. Whilst it is still usually quite difficult to get parent participation in the school's governing body, attendance at parents' evenings has increased in the last couple of years and some parents have occasionally helped out during the school day. The secondary school, however, does not enjoy a good reputation with either parents or its students. Neither does it perform well in relation to national figures on educational attainment or attendance. There are currently six teacher vacancies that the school is finding difficult to fill. Residents complain about a growing pattern of mostly eleven- to fifteen-year-olds 'hanging out' in some specific locations. The young people are held to be at best noisy and at worst aggressive and threatening in their behaviour towards those living nearby. The young people themselves complain about a complete absence of social venues or activities for them locally and the lack of affordable transport into town. Studies have shown that Seacole residents have a high reportage level when asked if they have been victims of crime in the last three years. A small number of those under sixteen – mainly boys – have persistent offender records, usually for crimes committed on or near the estate.

(a) Describe what you would expect the broad patterns of ill-health to be in Seacole and say why you think this is the case.

(b) Identify some government projects and initiatives to do with supporting families and engaging communities that might be helpful in tackling the social inequalities that exist in Seacole.

(c) Explain how the concepts of social exclusion and social capital might be useful in understanding the social difficulties outlined above.

(d) How can nursing contribute to tackling these social inequalities?

Summary and Resources

Summary

- Class, socio-economic differences and health inequalities have been a persistent feature of modern societies.

- Health inequalities are produced through complex pathways, but good explanations take account both of how life experiences are socially produced and of how they have an impact inside our bodies.

- Nurses, individually and as a profession, can contribute to tackling health inequalities at many levels; this involves tackling wider social inequalities.

- Effective policies to reduce health inequalities need to be informed by research.

Questions for Discussion

1   'Beer, fags and chips – that's the size of the problem.' What kind of explanation of health inequalities does this view reflect? See the explanations identified in the Black Report (box 8.4). Which of these explanations do you find most convincing? Which of these explanations do you think are most widely accepted amongst nurses? What implications might this have for practice?

2   'In our society the attainment of adult status is marked by employment, moving into your own home, entering relationships and marriage. Yet our services for adults have barely begun to address these issues for the bulk of the people who use them' (McConkey, 2001, p. 371). McConkey is referring to service users who have learning disabilities. Do you agree or disagree with his view? What bearing do the areas he mentions have on well-being and health for people with learning disabilities? How can nurses contribute to enhancing not only the health of such people but also their experience of life changes?

3   The life-course perspective shows how health disadvantage accumulates through life from before conception through to later years. Can nursing intervention across the life course help to make a difference? How can the education and training of nurses enable them to develop an awareness of inequalities and an 'inequalities imagination'? Can anything be done by nurses who subscribe to neo-materialist explanations of health inequalities?

Further Reading

H. Graham: *Unequal Lives: Health and Socioeconomic Inequalities*. Maidenhead: McGraw-Hill, 2007.
Graham is one of the most respected writers in the field of inequality and health, and this book looks at contemporary evidence on the persistence of inequality and the ways in which we can understand it.

C. Pantazis, D. Gordon and R. Levitas: *Poverty and Social Exclusion in Britain*. Bristol: Policy Press, 2006.
This book reports on the most comprehensive survey of poverty and social exclusion to be undertaken in Britain. It contains chapters on mental health, children, youth, single mothers and pensioners.

S. E. Curtis: *Health Inequality: Geographical Perspectives*. London: Sage, 2004.
This volume considers health and well-being, as well as disease, from a geographical perspective, which is not widely used within health care. It shows how space and location can advantage or disadvantage the health of individuals and communities.

M. Bartley: *Health Inequality: An Introduction to Theories, Concepts and Methods*. Cambridge: Polity, 2004.
This is a detailed exploration of research methods and findings on health inequality at the beginning of the twenty-first century. It is a difficult, but thorough, account and will be useful to those who wish to probe further.

H. Sutherland, T. Sefton and D. Piachaud: *Poverty in Britain: The Impact of Government Policy since 1997*. York: Joseph Rowntree Foundation, 2003.
This review examines many sources of evidence in its assessment of government policies aimed at reducing inequalities.

To explore some of these issues in more depth, go to www.politybooks.com/sociologyfornurses, where you will find further useful resources.

References

Acheson, D. 1998: *Independent Inquiry into Inequalities in Health: Report* [Acheson Report]. London: HMSO; www.archive.official-documents.co.uk/document/doh/ih/ih.htm [last accessed 29 November 2008].

Barker, D. J. P., Martyn, C. N., Osmond, C., Hales, C. N., and Fall, C. H. D. 1989: 'Growth in utero, blood pressure in childhood and adult life, and mortality from cardiovascular disease'. *British Medical Journal*, 298, 564–7.

Bartley, M. 2004: *Health Inequality: An Introduction to Theories, Concepts and Methods*. Cambridge: Polity.

Bartley, M., Power, C., Blane, D., Smith, G. D., and Shipley, M. 1994: 'Birth weight and later socio-economic disadvantage: evidence from the 1958 British cohort study'. *British Medical Journal*, 309, 1475–8.

Black, D., et al. 1980: *Inequalities in Health: Report of a Research Working Group* [Black Report]. London: Department of Health and Social Security.

Chadwick, E. 1842: *Inquiry into the Sanitary Conditions of the Labouring Population of Great Britain*. London: W. Clowes.

DH (Department of Health) 1999: *Saving Lives: Our Healthier Nation*. London: HMSO.

DH 2003: *Tackling Health Inequalities: A Programme for Action*. London: HMSO; www.dh.gov.uk/en/Publicationsandstatistics/ Publications/PublicationsPolicyAndGuidance/DH_4008268 [last accessed 29 November 2008].

DH 2004: *Health Survey for England 2003*. London: HMSO; www.dh.gov.uk/en/Publicationsandstatistics/Publications/ PublicationsStatistics/DH_4098712 [last accessed 29 November 2008].

DH 2007: *Tackling Health Inequalities: 2007 Status Report on the Programme for Action*. London: HMSO; www.dh.gov.uk/en/ Publicationsandstatistics/Publications/DH_083471 [last accessed 29 November 2008].

DH 2008: *Tackling Health Inequalities: Progress and Next Steps*. London: HMSO; www.dh.gov.uk/en/Publicationsandstatistics/ Publications/PublicationsPolicyAndGuidance/DH_085307 [last accessed 29 November 2008].

Dixon, A., Le Grand, J., Henderson, J., Murray, R., and Poteliakhoff, E. 2003: 'Is the NHS equitable? A review of the evidence'. *LSE Health and Social Care Discussion Paper*, 11. London: London School of Economics.

Drever, F., and Whitehead, M. 1997: *Health Inequalities Decennial Supplement 15*. London: HMSO.

Engels, F. [1845] 1999: *The Condition of the Working Class in England*, ed. D. McLellan. Oxford: Oxford University Press, 1999.

Fried, A., and Elman, R. M. (eds) 1971: *Charles Booth's London*. Harmondsworth: Penguin.

Gainsbury, S. 2008: 'Health inequalities: wealthiest overfunded as poor lose out'. *Health Service Journal*, 30 October.

Goldthorpe, J. H. 1980: *Social Mobility and Class Structure in Modern Britain*. Oxford: Clarendon Press.

Goldthorpe, J. H. 1997: 'The "Goldthorpe" class schema: some observations on conceptual and operational issues in relation to the ESRC review of governmental and social classifications'. In D. Rose and K. O'Reilly (eds), *Constructing Classes: Towards a New Social Classification for the UK*. Swindon: ESRC and ONS, pp. 40–8.

Hart, J. T. 1971: 'The inverse care law'. *The Lancet*, 1, 405–12.

HM Treasury and DH 2002: *Tackling Health Inequalities: Summary of the Cross-Cutting Review*, No. 29854, London: HMSO; www.hm-treasury.gov.uk/d/exec_sum_tacklinghealth.txt [last accessed 29 November 2008].

Kaplan, G. A., Pamuk, E., Lynch, J. W., Cohen, R. D., and Balfour, J. L. 1996: 'Income inequality and mortality in the United States: analysis of mortality and potential pathways'. *British Medical Journal*, 312, 999–1003.

London Health Observatory 2005: 'Prevalence of mental health problems amongst children and young people aged 5-to-15 years'. www.lho.org.uk/viewResource.aspx?id=9338 [last accessed 28 November 2008].

Lynch, J. W., Smith, G. D., Kaplan, G. A., and House, J. S. 2000: 'Income inequality and mortality: importance to health of individual income, psychosocial environment, or material conditions'. *British Medical Journal*, 320, 1200–4.

McConkey, R. 2001: 'Book reviews'. *Journal of Learning Disabilities*, 5(4), 369–74.

McConkey, R., and Mezza, F. 2001: 'Employment aspirations of people with learning disabilities attending day centres'. *Journal of Learning Disabilities*, 5(4), 309–18.

Mathias, P. 1983: *The First Industrial Nation: An Economic History of Britain 1700–1914*. London: Routledge.

Palmer, G., MacInnes T., and Kenway, P. 2007: *Monitoring Poverty and Social Exclusion 2007*. York: Joseph Rowntree Foundation; www.poverty.org.uk/reports/mpse%202007.pdf [last accessed 29 November 2008].

Rose, D., and Pevalin, D. J. 2001: *The National Statistics Socio-Economic Classification: Unifying Official and Sociological Approaches to the Conceptualisation and Measurement of Social Class*, ISER Working Papers 2001–4. Colchester: University of Essex.

Rowntree, B. S. 1902: *Poverty: A Study of Town Life*. London: Macmillan.

Siegrist, J., Peter, R., Junge, A., Cremer, P., and Seidel, D. 1990: 'Low status control, high effort at work and ischemic heart disease: prospective evidence from blue-collar men'. *Social Science and Medicine*, 31(10), 1127–34.

Townsend, P., Davidson, N., and Whitehead, M. 1988: *Inequalities in Health: The Black Report and the Health Divide*. Harmondsworth: Penguin.

van de Mheen, H., Stronks, K., and Mackenbach, J. P. 1998: 'A lifecourse perspective on socio-economic inequalities in health: the influence of childhood socio-economic conditions and selection processes'. *Sociology of Health & Illness*, 20(5), 754–77.

Weber, M. 1958: *The Protestant Ethic and the Spirit of Capitalism*. New York: Charles Scribner's Sons.

Wilkinson, R. 1996: *Unhealthy Societies: The Afflictions of Inequality*. London: Routledge.

9 Race and Ethnicity

Lorraine Culley and Simon Dyson

Key issues in this chapter

- Concepts of race and ethnicity
- Ethnic differences in health status
- Ethnicity and health care services
- Cultural competence and reflexive practice

By the end of this chapter you should be able to . . .

- distinguish between concepts of 'race' and ethnicity;
- describe ethnic differences in health status and understand possible explanations for these;
- understand the significance of culturally appropriate health care services;
- critically assess the relevance of cultural competence and reflexive practice.

---

1 Introduction

According to the 2001 census (ONS, 2003), approximately 7.9 per cent of the population of the United Kingdom (4.6 million people) describe themselves as belonging to a minority ethnic group; by 2007 that had increased to around 10 per cent. Indians are the largest minority group, followed by people of Pakistani origin, black Caribbeans, black Africans and Bangladeshis. An increasing number of people describe themselves as having mixed ethnic origins (15 per cent of the minority ethnic population). More recently, in areas of the country, mainly cities, where minority ethnic groups will make up a higher proportion of the population than white British, the concept of 'majority-minority' has been mooted. For example, the charity the Barrow Cadbury Trust has predicted that within the next twenty years no single ethnic group will have a majority in Birmingham (Dorling and Thomas, 2007), and Herbert (2007) has reported that Leicester is set to become the first city where white people will be in a minority. So the demographic make-up of the United Kingdom is set to change, and ethnic pluralism in various forms will be the norm in some towns and cities.

This chapter begins with a brief discussion of the concepts of race and ethnicity within sociology and an exploration of ethnic differences in health status in the UK. A number of different explanations for the ethnic patterning of health are evaluated.

The chapter goes on to raise a number of issues relating to the use of health care services by minority ethnic communities and argues that health care practitioners need to ensure that they are working in ways which respond positively to cultural diversity. It concludes by suggesting that nurses should strive to provide culturally appropriate care at an individual level and that this needs to be supported by institutional policies and practices which demonstrate a clear commitment to meeting the needs of religious and cultural minorities as service users and as employees.

2   Concepts of race and ethnicity

race a biological distinction between different groups of people, determined by genetic make-up

The terms race and ethnicity are widely used, but their meaning is the subject of considerable controversy and a good deal of confusion. Scientists have rejected the idea of the existence of distinct biological races within the human species, since there is considerable genetic or physical variation within so-called races and a great deal of genetic overlap between them (Mulholland and Dyson, 2001). Scientists have also challenged fundamentally the idea that there is a direct link between biology and behaviour. Nevertheless, ideas about racial differences continue to be very influential, since many people behave 'as if' races existed and use such ideas to justify racist behaviour. Even

racism an ideology or practice which is predicated on a belief in the existence of a hierarchy of 'races', based on inherited biological characteristics, and which promotes the social exclusion of people by virtue of their being members of different racial groups

though races do not exist, racism is a reality. This can be defined as a set of ideas, actions and structures which operate to promote the exclusion of people by virtue of their being deemed members of different racial groups (Goldberg, 1993). Some sociologists retain the term race, but put it in inverted commas ('race') to denote that, as a social rather than a biological phenomenon, it can still have a major impact on life chances.

ethnicity a socially constructed difference used to refer to people who see themselves as having a common ancestry, often linked to a geographical territory, and perhaps sharing a language, religion and other social customs

The concept of ethnicity is preferred by many sociologists; this refers to socially constructed difference. Although there is no universally accepted definition of ethnicity, the concept is generally used in sociology to refer to people with a common ancestry, usually linked to a particular geographical territory, and perhaps sharing a language, religion and other social customs (Fenton, 1999). The relative importance of these will differ between individuals, and ethnicity should not be viewed as something static or inflexible (Karlsen and Nazroo, 2006). We should not assume that, because a person accepts a particular ethnic label, it is possible to produce a list of characteristics which would apply to all who might identify themselves in this way. It is also important that ethnicity is not confused with nationality, which is a specific legal citizenship status (e.g. British).

Ethnicity can be said to refer to issues of both structure and identity. For example, the health of minority ethnic groups is heavily influenced by structural factors such as social disadvantage and poverty. At the same time, ethnicity as identity refers to the ways in which people identify with cultural traditions that provide both meaning and boundaries between groups (Karlsen and Nazroo, 2000). It may be worth reviewing the distinctions between theories of social structure and social action presented in chapter 1. Such traditions might contribute to health variations in a number of different ways, through, for example, influencing health-related behaviours such as smoking and drinking alcohol. There is, however, a tendency to 'pathologize' minority ethnic groups in terms of seeing them as representing deviant cultures or adopting lifestyles which give rise to health problems. Before we look at some of the ethnic differences in health status, let us explore ethnicity in the context of identity.

Activity 9.1   **Exploring identity**

(a) How would you describe your identity? Think of four or five ways in which you could describe yourself.

(b) How would you define your ethnic identity? What aspects of your identity are important in this definition?

(c) If a patient was described to you as 'Asian', would this be relevant to the care you provide?

Think about the following:

(d) Which identities are more important to you?

(e) How would you describe your sense of belonging?

(f) How might others categorize you?

Individuals have multiple identities, and children from ethnic minority backgrounds may behave very differently when at home with the family and when at school with children from other ethnic and cultural backgrounds.

We *all* have ethnicity, but are not defined solely by it. Individuals have multiple identities – as man or woman, young or older person, nurse, midwife, student, husband, mother, daughter, Pakistani or Irish. Different aspects of your identity might be important in different contexts. Even within our sense of ethnic identity, different aspects of this may be more or less significant in any given context. This is sometimes referred to as 'situational ethnicity'. By this is meant that, as the individual moves through daily life, what is important in ethnic identity can change according to variations in the situations and the audiences encountered. Our behaviour is heavily influenced by cultural norms, but we should think of these as flexible guidelines rather than rules that rigidly determine our behaviour (Ahmad, 1996). It is important to bear in mind that ethnic identities are subject to change and redefinition; cultures are constantly changing and evolving as they interact with each other, and so they cannot be easily captured in a cultural checklist. Attempts to do this may lead to harmful stereotyping.

Although there is a tendency to define members of minority ethnic communities primarily by their ethnic identity, it is important to note that minority ethnic groups are not homogeneous. There are divisions of social class, age and gender, for example, which may be very important for health and health care. There is also considerable diversity *between* groups commonly defined as minority ethnic groups (Modood et al., 1997). The category 'Asian', for example, though commonly used, masks an enormous diversity of ethnic identities and tells us very little about family origins, language, religion or diet. A 'British Asian' person may have family origins in India, Pakistan or Bangladesh. Their first language may be English, Gujarati, Urdu, Punjabi, Sylheti, Bengali or one of several others. They may be Hindu, Muslim, Sikh, Christian, Jain or of no faith. They may be vegetarian or meat eaters. Diversity within and between ethnic groups extends to all aspects of life, including family and household structure, education, housing, employment and, indeed, health status, as we now go on to consider.

3 Ethnic differences in health status

The health statuses of minority ethnic groups in the UK appear to be worse than the health status of the white majority population. However, health experiences are not *caused* by ethnicity. Ethnicity, as a socially constructed category, draws our attention to particular types of discrepancies, but it does not in itself tell us the *mechanisms* by which people are rendered less healthy.

Methodological problems

There are two broad ways of measuring inequalities in ethnic health – mortality (who dies prematurely) and morbidity (who gets ill) – but both measures have problems. First, mortality rates tend to concentrate on older generations and thereby primarily on immigrants, rather than on the younger generations, the majority of whom are British-born. Second, use of mortality rates tends to understate inequalities. This is because the occupation listed on the death certificate of migrants may be the highest occupational level achieved (perhaps teacher in country of origin) rather than their occupation in Britain (perhaps unskilled factory worker) owing to downward occupational mobility at the time of migration. Third, mortality rates are compiled by country of birth rather than ethnicity (Aspinall, 2006), which does not identify differences in life chances *between* groups within that country. In addition around half of the minority ethnic population of Britain is British-born.

Attempts to measure morbidity may be based on survey questions that ask for self-reported health. However, these surveys rely upon the respondent understanding symptoms, seeking health services, remembering symptoms and/or health service utilization and being willing to report any of this to an interviewer. If different ethnic groups report health differently in any systematic way then this causes problems for analysis. There are also problems with the quality and completeness of ethnic coding in administrative and routine data, for example by NHS trusts and primary care trusts (Aspinall, 2006). We must bear these limitations in mind when interpreting data on inequalities in ethnic health. It is important not to read morbidity and mortality data as evidence of an 'ethnic' effect, as the figures are not controlled for socio-economic status. 'Ethnicity' never causes health status in and of itself, but the identification of an apparent 'ethnic effect' after controlling for other relevant factors can help us to sharpen our ideas about possible causal mechanisms.

Infant mortality in minority ethnic groups

The infant mortality rate (IMR) is defined as the number of deaths under one year, and it is usually measured as the number of deaths per 1,000 live births. It is a good indicator of the overall health of a society (Department of Health, 2007) and is therefore a useful way of assessing the relative health of different community groups. In 2005, for the first time, the Office of National Statistics produced a breakdown of the IMR by ethnicity. While overall rates in the UK are falling, there is still wide variation between ethnic groups. Moreover, where a mother was born in Pakistan or the Caribbean, the IMR was higher than for that ethnic community as a whole (ibid., 2007). Deaths of Caribbean babies are concentrated in the first month of life, whereas the rate remained high throughout the first year for Pakistani babies. Overall, minority ethnic groups accounted for 11 per cent of live births, but 17 per cent of infant deaths. However, as table 9.1 demonstrates, this figure conceals wide variation.

Table 9.1 Infant mortality rate (IMR) by ethnic group babies born in 2005

Ethnicity	IMR per 1000 live births
All	5.0
Bangladeshi*	4.2
Indian*	5.8
Pakistani*	9.6
African**	6.0
Caribbean**	9.8
White British	4.5
White other	4.3
All other	5.4
Not stated	5.1

Notes: * Asian/Asian British; ** black/black British.
Source: ONS, 2008.

Activity 9.2	Interpreting mortality data

Examine table 9.1 and answer the following questions.

(a) What does table 9.1 tell you about infant mortality amongst minority ethnic groups?

(b) How might you account for the differences between groups?

(c) What factors other than ethnicity would you need to take into account when interpreting these data?

Patterns of morbidity in minority ethnic groups

Although relying on reported health, table 9.2, like table 9.1, does have the advantage of being based on ethnic classification directly rather than on country of birth.

The overall inequality in self-reported health for 'ethnic minorities' as a whole masks considerable variation between groups. Those of Caribbean and especially those of Pakistani/ Bangladeshi descent have higher levels of self-reported ill-health, whilst those of Indian and Chinese origin have levels at or below the white group. On the one hand, the raised level for those of overall 'South Asian' descent underplays the very high levels of reported ill-health for Pakistanis/Bangladeshis; on the other hand, it also hides the similar levels of reported morbidity between whites and Indians. Gypsy travellers have poorer health status than that of comparable subjects matched by age and sex, a situation exacerbated by poor access to services (Papadopoulos and Lay, 2006; see also chapter 10).

South Asians are often said to have worse heart health than whites, but this appears to be made up of very high rates amongst those of Pakistani/Bangladeshi descent (especially the younger age groups), whilst levels of heart health in Indians appear to be equal to those in whites. Caribbeans report similar levels of heart health as whites, and Chinese better heart health than whites.

Overall, whether the measurement is mortality or morbidity, the health of minority ethnic groups is generally worse, though there are important counter-trends in terms of both ethnic categories (Indians) and disease categories (cancers and respiratory diseases). We now turn to a review of some of the explanations that have been offered for these differences in the health of ethnic groups.

Table 9.2 Ratio of respondents reporting various conditions by self-defined ethnic group, 2004

	Self- reported bad/very bad health	Reported ischaemic heart disease or stroke	Obesity (measured by waist circumference)	Reported hypertension	Reported type 2 diabetes
General population	1	1	1	1	1
Caribbean men	1.37	0.85	0.66	1.37	2.37
Caribbean women	1.90	1.10	1.42	1.58	3.16
Indian men	1.45	1.18	0.70	1.15	3.17
Indian women	1.39	1.24	1.15	0.91	2.95
Pakistani men	2.33	2.12	1.23	0.98	3.27
Pakistani women	3.54	1.77	1.77	1.01	6.25
Chinese men	0.75	0.52	0.28	0.78	1.44
Chinese women	0.55	0.64	1.00	1.12	2.06

Source: Sproston and Mindell, 2006.

4   Explaining ethnic patterns in health status

There are several competing and complementary theories that have been offered as a possible explanation of the patterns of health among minority ethnic groups. Following activity 9.3, we briefly consider some of these factors and discuss the mechanisms whereby social status may impact on health status.

Activity 9.3	**Explaining health inequalities**
	Examine table 9.2 and consider what possible explanations there might be for the patterns of ethnic inequalities in health which are represented.

Genetic factors

Although scientists reject the concept of distinct races, this does not mean completely rejecting genetic factors as possible explanations of health variations between ethnic groups. At the same time, we need to beware of focusing too much on conditions in which genetic factors play a large contributory part, such as sickle cell disease, at the expense of conditions that affect all ethnic groups, such as heart disease, hypertension or diabetes. To the extent that conditions such as heart disease have any genetic component, such components may be *associated with but not caused by* the racialized identities with which social groups are labelled.

Migration

There appear to be higher levels of ill-health among migrants than among the population as a whole (Nazroo, 2006). However, the evidence does not suggest such levels of ill-health are caused by the processes of migration or by 'carry-over' of previous poor health (since the overall health of migrants is at least as good as that of British-born ethnic minorities of the same age). It does suggest that relatively healthy individuals migrate to work in poorly paid occupations in deprived environments, which is compounded by racism, so that there is a relative decline in their health over time. The evidence from Nazroo (2006) is also consistent with the socio-economic explanation that emphasizes the direct migration to conditions of poverty, poor environment and racial harassment (Taylor, 2006). This argument is further strengthened by the work of Williams (1993), who suggests that an extended length of time in Britain increases the level of poor health amongst migrants.

Racism

Racism may be said to affect health adversely in three ways. First, through *racism in health service provision and delivery*. This may be individual racism or **institutional racism.** Legitimate health needs may be undermined by a racist discourse employed by powerful health service gatekeepers (Ahmad and Bradby, 2008). Second, there is the *indirect effect of racism* (past or present) in areas of social life in which life chances are known to be linked to health. This would include immigration laws, the implementation of the social security system, and racism in housing, employment and education (see chapter 16 for discussion of racism and housing). And third, there are *the possible direct effects of racism* on health, such as the effect of racism in creating internalized anger and in raising blood pressure. Racism is an indirect cause of overall ethnic differences in health and can be a significant immediate cause, for example, in the case of a racially motivated physical assault.

institutional racism occurs when institutional policies, procedures and practices intentionally or unintentionally give rise to discriminatory outcomes and reproduce disadvantage

Access to services

Ethnic patterns in the use of health services are important in their own right as an index of the quality of service provision, but may also affect health status. There are various possible explanations for different patterns in utilizing health services. In terms of factors influencing clients seeking services, these include the health beliefs and knowledge of the population – that is, their knowledge of and attitudes towards health services and what is termed social structure (see chapter 1 for further discussion of this). In terms of the provision of services there is the overall distribution of health care resources, racism in service delivery and quality of care.

Nazroo (1997) has suggested that, broadly speaking, minority ethnic groups consult GPs as often as whites but have less equal access to hospital and community nursing care. Parents of children with sickle cell disease or thalassaemia found that ethnic minority status compounded problems of access to services experienced by other parents of children with chronic illness (Atkin, Ahmad and Anionmu, 2000). A more detailed discussion can be found in Smaje (1995a), Smaje and Le Grand (1997) and Nazroo (1997).

Materialist explanations

There are strong positive associations between socio-economic status and health status in the general population (see chapter 8). Minority ethnic groups are, in general, associated with lower socio-economic status, and therefore would be expected to have poorer overall health on those grounds. For example, whereas the percentage of children living in a household receiving less than 60 per cent of the national

median income in 2005–6 was 19 per cent for white British, it was
33 per cent for black or black British and 44 per cent for Asian or Asian
British (Dunnell, 2008). However, controlling for socio-economic
status does not itself greatly diminish the relationship between
ethnicity and health (Smaje, 1995b). It seems that what are required in
order to assess the interaction of ethnicity and material factors in
patterning health are more specific and direct measures of material
deprivation.

Nazroo (1997) provides survey evidence of ethnic variations
within given levels of income, rates of unemployment and types of
housing tenure. He develops a standard-of-living index based on
accommodation (amount of overcrowding), access to amenities (such
as indoor toilet) and access to consumer durables (such as a refrig-
erator). He finds that, for reported ill-health, this standard-of-living
index reduces differences between ethnic groups very significantly in a
manner which traditional controls for socio-economic status (class or
housing tenure) do not. Furthermore, even the standard of living
index is a relatively crude measure of deprivation, the implication being
that more sophisticated and/or more direct measures of material
inequalities may account for the majority of apparent differences in
reported ill-health between different ethnic groups.

In summary, it seems that material deprivation, when measured
relatively directly rather than by weak analytical concepts such as class,
accounts for much of the variation in the reported health status of
different ethnic groups. But accepting the general strong association
does not necessarily tell us about the precise mechanisms at work.

Culture

culture   a shared set of
values, perceptions and
assumptions based on
shared history, language
or other learned
experiences

Attempts to understand health inequalities as a product of cultural
differences have been very problematic. They tend to draw upon a very
rigid view of culture, which is seen to determine behaviour in a very
direct way. This can lead to health education campaigns which
perceive minority ethnic communities as dangerous to their own
health. An example of this is what Ahmad and Bradby (2008, p. 7)
have called 'a recent fascination' concerning sanguinity (that is,
marriage between blood relatives) as an explanation of physical
disability and other ill-effects. Cousin marriage is a favoured family
pattern in many parts of the world, and was fairly common in Britain
until the last century. In relation to Pakistani parents in particular it is
blamed by health professionals for a variety of ills, 'irrespective of
known mechanisms of causation, and often without clinicians
confirming whether or not parents are in fact blood relatives'.

The emphasis on cultural difference ignores the extent of
similarities between different ethnic groups. Cultures are not static,
but are continually changing and evolving. Culture is a product of
gender, class and other power relations as much as of ethnicity, to

It is important to consider cultural factors that may have an effect on health. For example, in Rastafarian culture the smoking of cannabis is part of spiritual worship.

which it is too often reduced. Finally, culture may be a source of nurturing and strength.

Mediating material factors and culture: social standing

Material factors are strongly associated with health status, but we understand little of the *mechanisms* by which this association may be effected. Wilkinson (1996) argues that material factors are mediated in a number of ways in affecting health, including the health of minority ethnic groups. These mediators include *social cohesion* (material inequality weakens social cohesion generally and leads to a poorer quality of life and greater levels of psychosocial stress for all of us); *social support* (which may have a health-protecting effect); and *social status in a hierarchy* (those at the bottom of a hierarchy being more likely to suffer chronic psychological stress).

5   Ethnicity and health care services

There is some evidence of the differential use of primary and secondary health care services among different ethnic groups, although some of this is contradictory, with examples of both under- and overutilization (Smaje and Le Grand, 1997). Carrying out research on this issue is difficult owing to the inadequacy of ethnic data collection in the NHS and the complexity of the relationship between health needs, demand for health care and supply of health services.

Activity 9.4

Ethnic differences in health service utilization: palliative care

Gunaratnam (2007) reports that people from minority ethnic groups face complex barriers to palliative care services. When they do access palliative care they do not benefit fully from the holistic care approach. Consider the possible explanations for this. Try to categorize reasons into the possible ethnic differences in need for services, demand for services and supply factors.

(a) Are there features of the minority ethnic population which mean that they are likely to have a lower need for cancer services?

(b) What might affect the demand for palliative care services from minority ethnic populations?

(c) Might there be differences in access to services for minority ethnic communities (supply factors)?

(For a detailed discussion of these issues, see Smaje and Field, 1997.)

What the example of palliative care services demonstrates is the complex relationship between need, demand and supply. As Smaje and Field (1997) have argued, while there is less 'need' for palliative care services within most minority ethnic groups, primarily because of the younger age structure of the minority ethnic population, the apparently lower levels of utilization probably stem from a range of additional factors, including differences in patterns of informal care in some minority communities and ethnocentrism or perhaps racism in the provision of services.

A lack of culturally appropriate services may seriously disadvantage some service users. This is a problem identified not just in palliative care, but across a range of service provision in children's health (Cooper, Smaje and Arber, 1998), disability and social services (Ahmad, 2000), mental health (Bhugra and Bahl, 1999), health promotion (Douglas, 1995), maternity services (Bowler, 1993), care of the elderly (Pharoah, 1995) and social services provision (Ahmad and Atkin, 1996). As Henley and Schott (1999) have argued, the health care needs of minority ethnic groups are broadly the same as those of white people. If people do not use services, it is more likely to be because there is inadequate information about what services are available and how to use them or because they are provided in a way which is not culturally appropriate. It could also be the case that people have had negative experiences of using services in the past and that there are language barriers and poor general communication.

Different cultures may take different approaches to health and holistic well-being. Culturally inappropriate advice may mean that certain users fail to gain any benefit from the assistance health care professionals may be trying to offer.

Ethnicity and mental health

The issue of ethnicity and mental health is one surrounded by controversy, so that it is very difficult to attempt an adequate summary in the space available here. We have already indicated the many problems of inadequate data which exist in relation to ethnicity and physical illness. In the case of mental illness this is further compounded, as the very definition of what constitutes mental illness is itself contested. There is evidence of differential rates of admission to psychiatric hospitals for some minority ethnic groups and some conditions, but interpreting the significance of this is difficult and contentious. For example, there are suggestions that an apparent ethnic difference may in fact reflect the fact that cross-cultural misunderstanding may lead to inadequate diagnosis. There is also evidence of differential treatment once a diagnosis is made, but again adequately explaining these differences poses serious problems. An analysis of this issue is beyond the scope of this chapter, and the reader is referred to the discussion of ethnicity and mental illness by Iley and Nazroo (2001).

This section has argued that there are many potential barriers to service access across all sectors of care which relate to wider structural and resource issues beyond the immediate control of

individual practitioners. There remains, however, a need for all
health professionals to ensure that they are working in a non-
discriminatory way and responding appropriately to cultural
diversity. It is not possible here to review in detail the many ways
in which culture and experience may influence beliefs about health
and illness or health behaviour (see Henley and Schott, 1999).
Rather, the next section briefly indicates how nurses in all branches
can prepare themselves to respond in a culturally competent way to
a multi-ethnic society.

6   Cultural competence and reflective practice

Several research studies have suggested that health care providers
across a range of services may sometimes portray negative
attitudes to minority ethnic clients and patients and that the
quality of care received may be compromised (Atkin, Ahmad and
Anionmu, 2000). Users report both satisfaction with services and
a range of negative experiences (Bhakta, Katbamna and Parker,
2000). Many of the latter relate to problems of communication
and the failure to respond adequately to cultural and religious needs
(Culley, 2001). Evidence shows that good communication is
essential to improving health outcomes, yet poor communication
is a common source of complaints about treatment across a
range of services. Effective inter-cultural communication requires a
set of skills and competencies which need to be learned and
practised alongside clinical skills. For example, it is necessary
to develop the capacity to respond to diversity in an open and
reflexive manner, recognizing and respecting difference and paying
attention to possible cultural factors (ethnicity, age, sex, education,
etc.) which may influence communication (Chamba and Ahmad,
2000).

   Communication is not reducible to language alone (Robinson,
1998). Nevertheless, language barriers are significant for some
users. Poor communication is likely to lead to worsening health
outcomes, and, in the case of mental health problems especially,
the lack of a common language can lead to misdiagnosis and
ineffective and harmful treatment (Bradby, 2001). Although most
British-born patients speak good English, those who have migrated
are less likely to be fluent, though this will depend on age, length
of time and age of arrival as well as general level of education and
opportunities in Britain. Nurses need to familiarize themselves
with the special skills needed to communicate across a language
barrier. Working with interpreters, for example, requires training
if the communication is to be well managed. Unfortunately, there
are often situations in which interpreters are not available. While

this is clearly fraught with problems, there are ways of reducing potential harm to patients, although you should always have a professional interpreter for important conversations. For example, you should maintain a sympathetic and unhurried manner and a reassuring tone of voice (avoid total silences); simplify your English and speak slowly and clearly (but do not shout); demonstrate things rather than simply relying on the written word and always check that the person understands what you are saying. Ensure that you keep good notes so that questions do not have to be repeated by different professionals (see Henley and Schott, 1999).

There are many checklists which act as guides to different religious and ethnic groups. Although useful in some contexts, they are open to misuse, leading both to a failure to determine individual needs and to stereotyping (Culley, 2000). People cannot be neatly divided into cultural groups and their behaviour predicted. The checklist approach ignores the enormous range of differences that exist within an ethnic group.

The key to providing culturally appropriate care at the individual level is to follow the advice of Henley and Schott (1999, p. 76): 'The only person who can tell you what will or will not be right for them is the patient. If we really want to find out, we have to ask.' This is not always easy, and there is a skill to asking effective and sensitive questions and in responding positively and respectfully to people who might express values and wishes very different from our own. However, a commitment to patient-centred care means reflecting on our own assumptions and values, considering possible variations in people's needs and wishes, and identifying the implications of these for our day-to-day practice (Papadopoulos, 2006).

Providing good individual care in any branch of nursing is about good communication; this requires enabling patients to explain their needs and wishes. At the same time, consulting and listening are equally important at the organizational and policy level. Although the above discussion has focused on elements of individual care, institutional processes are equally important in determining the adequacy of service provision to minority ethnic communities (Gerrish, Husband and Mackenzie, 1996). Individual practitioners must be supported by effective policies, adequate resources and well-informed managers and educators if the needs of religious and cultural minorities are to be met. Improving the quality of care means listening to users, for individual nurses and for health care planners and managers. Without the active and meaningful involvement of minority ethnic service users, it is highly likely that provision will continue to be reflective of the needs of white, middle-class patients and families.

Activity 9.5

Access to services

Read the following case study and then discuss the questions that follow.

Karen is a student nurse on placement in an accident and emergency department of an inner-city hospital. On a busy evening shift casualties from a car crash on the ring road have been admitted, and an ambulance has just brought in a suspected myocardial infarction.

Sitting in the waiting room is a Pakistani family who seem to have been waiting for some hours. Karen takes them into an examination room. The mother sits down with a small boy on her lap, while the father and an older child stand. Karen asks the parents what is wrong, and the older child says that the young boy has been ill for some days. When giving a history the older child answers the questions, and when she discovers how old the boy is Karen thinks that he looks young for his age and she suspects that he is developmentally delayed. However, it is hard to find out much about the family, as the older child does not know some of the details and the parents do not speak very much English. Karen is not sure if the older child is translating her questions accurately.

Unsure how to deal with the situation, Karen finds a staff nurse who tells her, 'We are busy enough with serious cases here; we don't have time to go searching for an interpreter. Anyway, they should have gone to their GP. It is probably some congenital problem that is not an emergency.'

(a) What problems of access to health care is the family experiencing?
(b) What assumptions about the family are being made?
(c) How can health services become more culturally competent?

Summary and Resources

Summary

- The concepts of race and ethnicity are contested in sociological theory but are highly relevant for an understanding of contemporary health care.

- There are ethnic differences in patterns of morbidity and mortality in Britain which may be explained by a combination of social and economic factors.

- There is a growing body of evidence which suggests that health services are not always adequately meeting the needs of minority ethnic groups.

- Nurses and other health professionals need to work towards overcoming potential barriers to effective care and develop the skills for working with diverse communities.

Questions for Discussion

1 In relation to your area of practice, consider the implications for health care if, because of a language barrier, patients and relatives cannot discuss symptoms and prognoses, ask questions or raise anxieties.

2 Consider the possible influence of religion on people's lives and in relation to your own area of practice; discuss how religious beliefs might affect attitudes towards illness and treatment.

3 Describe the ways in which health professionals in your area of practice can access the views of service users from minority ethnic communities.

4 Working with colleagues, devise a vision of what equal access and equal provision in your area of practice would look like and consider what changes may be required, both individually and institutionally, to achieve this.

Further Reading

R. Papadopoulos (ed.): *Transcultural Health and Social Care: Development of Culturally Competent Practitioners*. Edinburgh: Churchill Livingstone, 2006.
This covers a broad range of issues and practices which are important for the development of services that are culturally competent. It looks at individual conditions and at cultural groups in order to explore the issues. It has a very readable style.

R. Bhopal: *Ethnicity, Race and Health in Multi-Cultural Societies.*
Oxford: Oxford University Press, 2007.
This book takes an integrated approach towards discussing the
concepts of 'race' and 'ethnicity' in order to explain the challenge
to practitioners of providing appropriate health care to culturally
diverse populations. It contains a number of exercises, a glossary,
and links to websites that make it an accessible text.

P. Radcliffe: *'Race', Ethnicity and Difference: Imagining*
the Inclusive Society. Maidenhead: Open University
Press, 2004.
This examines many of the issues facing contemporary
societies, such as housing, education and policing. It also
considers marginalized groups, for example, refugees and
asylum seekers.

References

Ahmad, W. I. U. 1996: 'The trouble with culture'. In D. Kelleher and
    S. Hillier (eds), *Researching Cultural Differences in Health*. London:
    Routledge, pp. 190–219.
Ahmad, W. I. U. (ed.) 2000: *Ethnicity, Disability, and Chronic Illness*.
    Buckingham: Open University Press.
Ahmad, W., and Atkin, K. (eds) 1996: *'Race' and Community Care*.
    Buckingham: Open University Press.
Ahmad, W. I. U. and Bradby, H. 2008: 'Locating ethnicity and health'.
    In W. I. U. Ahmad and H. Bradby (eds), *Ethnicity, Health and Health*
    Care: Understanding Diversity, Tackling Disadvantage. Oxford:
    Blackwell, pp. 1–15.
Aspinall, P. J. 2006: 'Secondary analysis of administrative, routine
    and research data sources: lessons from the UK'. In J. Y. Nazroo
    (ed.), *Health and Social Research in Multiethnic Societies*. London:
    Routledge, pp. 165–95.
Atkin, K., Ahmad, W. I. U., and Anionmu, E. N. 2000: 'Service support
    for families caring for a child with a sickle cell disorder or beta
    thalassaemia major: parents' perspectives'. In W. I. U. Ahmad
    (ed.), *Ethnicity, Disability, and Chronic Illness*. Buckingham: Open
    University Press, pp. 103–22.
Bhakta, P., Katbamna, S., and Parker, G. 2000: 'South Asian carers'
    experiences of primary health care teams'. In W. I. U. Ahmad
    (ed.), *Ethnicity, Disability, and Chronic Illness*. Buckingham: Open
    University Press, pp. 123–38.
Bhugra, D., and Bahl, V. (eds) 1999: *Ethnicity: An Agenda for Mental*
    Health. London: Gaskell.
Bowler, I. 1993: '"They're not the same as us": midwives' stereotypes
    of South Asian descent maternity patients'. *Sociology of Health &*
    Illness, 15(2), 457–70.

Bradby, H. 2001: 'Communication, interpretation and translation'. In L. Culley and S. Dyson (eds), *Ethnicity and Nursing Practice*. London: Palgrave, pp. 129–48.

Chamba, R. and Ahmad, W. I. U. 2000: 'Language, communication and information: the needs of parents caring for a severely disabled child'. In W. I. U. Ahmad (ed.), *Ethnicity, Disability, and Chronic Illness*. Buckingham: Open University Press, pp. 85–102.

Cooper, H., Smaje, C., and Arber, S. 1998: 'Use of health services by children and young people according to ethnicity and social class: secondary analysis of a national survey'. *British Medical Journal*, 317, 1047–51.

Culley, L. 2000: 'Working with diversity: beyond the factfile'. In C. Davies, L. Finlay and A. Bullman (eds), *Changing Practice in Health and Social Care*. London: Sage/Open University Press, pp. 131–42.

Culley, L. 2001: 'Nursing, culture and competence'. In L. Culley and S. Dyson (eds), *Ethnicity and Nursing Practice*. London: Palgrave, pp. 109–27.

Department of Health 2007: *Review of the Health Inequalities Infant Mortality PSA Target*. London: HMSO; www.dh.gov.uk/en/ Publicationsandstatistics/Publications/PublicationsPolicyAnd Guidance/DH_065544 [last accessed 12 December 2008].

Dorling, D., and Thomas, B. 2007: *A Short Report on Plurality and the Cities of Britain*. www.bctrust.org.uk/pdf/short_report_on_ plurality.pdf [last accessed 3 December 2008].

Douglas, J. 1995: 'Developing anti-racist health promotion strategies'. In R. Bunton, S. Nettleton and R. Burrows (eds), *The Sociology of Health Promotion*. London: Routledge, pp. 70–7.

Dunnell, K. 2008: *Diversity and Different Experiences within the UK*. National Statistician's Annual Article on Society. www.statistics. gov.uk/articles/nojournal/NSA_article.pdf [last accessed 4 December 2008].

Fenton, S. 1999: *Ethnicity: Racism, Class and Culture*. London: Macmillan.

Gerrish, K., Husband, C., and Mackenzie, J. 1996: *Nursing for a Multi-Ethnic Society*. Buckingham: Open University Press.

Goldberg, D. 1993: *Racist Culture*. Oxford: Blackwell.

Gunaratnam, Y. 2007: *Improving the Quality of Palliative Care*. London: Race Equality Foundation.

Henley, A., and Schott, J. 1999: *Culture, Religion and Patient Care in a Multi-Ethnic Society*. London: Age Concern.

Herbert, I. 2007: 'Leicester to be first city where white people are minority'. *The Independent*, 11 September.

Iley, K., and Nazroo, J. 2001: 'Ethnic inequalities in mental health'. In L. Culley and S. Dyson (eds), *Ethnicity and Nursing Practice*. London: Palgrave, pp. 67–89.

Karlsen, S., and Nazroo, J. 2000: 'Identity and structure: rethinking ethnic inequalities in health'. In H. Graham (ed.), *Understanding Health Inequalities*. Buckingham: Open University Press, pp. 38–57.

Karlsen, S., and Nazroo, J. Y. 2006: 'Defining and measuring ethnicity and "race": theoretical and conceptual issues for health and social care research'. In J. Y. Nazroo (ed.), *Health and Social Research in Multiethnic Societies*. London: Routledge, pp. 20–38.

Modood, T., Berthoud, R., Lakey, J., Nazroo, J., Smith, P., Virdee, S., and Beishon, S. 1997: *Ethnic Minorities in Britain: Diversity and Disadvantage*. London: Policy Studies Institute.

Mullholland, J., and Dyson, S. 2001: 'Sociological theories of "race" and ethnicity'. In L. Culley and S. Dyson (eds), *Ethnicity and Nursing Practice*. London: Palgrave, pp. 17–37.

Nazroo, J. Y. 1997: 'Health and health services'. In T. Modood, R. Berthoud, J. Lakey, J. Nazroo, P. Smith, S. Virdee and S. Beishon, *Ethnic Minorities in Britain: Diversity and Disadvantage*. London: Policy Studies Institute, pp. 224–58.

Nazroo, J. Y. 2006: 'Demography of multicultural Britain'. In J. Y. Nazroo (ed.), *Health and Social Research in Multiethnic Societies*. London: Routledge, pp. 1–19.

ONS (Office for National Statistics) 2003: *Ethnicity: Population Size*. www.statistics.gov.uk/cci/nugget.asp?id=273 [last accessed 15 December 2008].

ONS (Office for National Statistics) 2008: *Large Differences in Infant Mortality by Ethnic Group*. www.statistics.gov.uk/pdfdir/imetho608.pdf [last accessed 11 December 2008].

Papadopoulos, I. 2006: 'The Papadopoulos, Tilki and Taylor model of developing cultural competence'. In I. Papadopoulos (ed.), *Transcultural Health and Social Care*. Edinburgh: Churchill Livingstone, pp. 7–24.

Papadopoulos, I., and Lay, M. 2006: 'Culturally competent health promotion for minority ethnic groups, refugees, gypsy travellers and new age travellers in the UK'. In I. Papadopoulos (ed.), *Transcultural Health and Social Care*. Edinburgh: Churchill Livingstone, pp. 175–200.

Pharoah, C. 1995: *Primary Health Care for Elderly People from Black & Minority Ethnic Communities*. London: HMSO.

Robinson, L. 1998: *'Race', Communication and the Caring Professions*. Buckingham: Open University Press.

Smaje, C. 1995a: *Health, 'Race' and Ethnicity: Making Sense of the Evidence*. London: King's Fund.

Smaje, C. 1995b: 'Ethnic residential concentration and health: evidence for a beneficial effect?' *Policy and Politics*, 23(3), 251–69.

Smaje, C., and Field, D. 1997: 'Absent minorities? Ethnicity and the use of palliative care services'. In D. Field, J. Hockey and N. Small (eds), *Death, Gender and Ethnicity*. London: Routledge, pp. 166–86.

Smaje, C., and Le Grand, J. 1997: 'Ethnicity, equity and the use of health services in the British NHS'. *Social Science and Medicine*, 45, 485–96.

Sproston, K., and Mindell, J. (eds) 2006: *Health Survey for England 2004*, Vol. 1: *The Health of Minority Ethnic Groups*. London: Information Centre for Health and Social Care; www.ic.nhs.uk/webfiles/publications/healthsurvey2004ethnicfull/HealthSurveyforEnglandVol1_210406_PDF.pdf.

Taylor, G. 2006: 'Migrants and refugees'. In I. Papadopoulos (ed.), *Transcultural Health and Social Care*. Edinburgh: Churchill Livingstone, pp. 45–64.

Wilkinson, R. G. 1996: *Unhealthy Societies: The Afflictions of Inequality*. London: Routledge.

Williams, R. 1993: 'Health and length of residence among South Asians in Glasgow: a study controlling for age'. *Journal of Public Health Medicine*, 15(1), 52–60.

Global Health

Sarah Earle

> **Key issues in this chapter**
> - Global patterns of health and disease
> - Globalization, nursing and health
> - Patient care and nursing work in a global context
> - Nursing and migration
>
> **By the end of this chapter you should be able to . . .**
> - explain general patterns of health and disease across the world;
> - define and understand the concept of globalization as it applies to health and nursing;
> - describe how migration can change the nature of nursing work;
> - discuss the significance of the global context for the nursing workforce.

1 Introduction

Every day, individuals make choices that influence their own health and that of those around them. Individual choices can have far-reaching consequences, but these choices are shaped, influenced and sometimes even determined by local, national and international events. Sociology is significant because it can throw light on the relationship between the individual and the wider society. In recent years, events such as the SARS crisis, the 9/11 terrorist attacks, the impact of global warming and the financial crisis of 2008 demonstrate the global consequences of individual actions and the impact of global events on individual health and well-being. This chapter is organized into four sections. The first section begins by outlining global patterns of health and disease, and the second section defines and explores globalization and considers the impact of this for health and well-being. Next, the role of migration in nursing work is considered, first, by exploring the needs of patients and the challenges of migration for nursing practice. The final section examines the phenomenon of international nurse migration within the context of a global health workforce crisis.

Diseases such as SARS and swine flu can affect people around the whole world.

2 Global patterns of health and disease

child mortality   child death under the age of five

Globally, health is improving. Over the last fifty years, global life expectancy has increased by twenty years and child mortality (which is an excellent indicator of a nation's present and future health) has decreased by approximately 7 million (WHO, 2003). However, good health is not shared by all and is not equally distributed. For example, according to the World Health Organization (WHO, 2005), more than half of all child deaths across the world occur in just six countries (China, the Democratic Republic of the Congo, Ethiopia, India, Nigeria and Pakistan). Children, especially those under the age of five, are particularly at risk from inequalities in health, facing the acute dangers of birth injury, infectious diseases, malnutrition and pollution. Maternal health and child health are strongly intertwined, and the need for improved reproductive and sexual health across the world is widely recognized. Box 10.1 tells you more about global health inequalities.

Box 10.1   Global health inequalities

- About 4 million children die each year before the age of one month and an additional 3.3 million are stillborn. Of all these child deaths, 99 per cent occur in low- and middle-income countries.

- Approximately one-quarter of all children in developing countries are underweight and at risk of the longer term effects of undernourishment.

- More than 500,000 women in developing countries die each year in childbirth or of complications from pregnancy.

- In low- and middle-income countries, 30 per cent of all deaths occur between the ages of fifteen and fifty-nine, compared with 15 per cent in high-income countries.

- Virtually all deaths from communicable diseases, maternal and perinatal conditions, and nutritional deficiencies occur in low- and middle-income countries.

- In sub-Saharan Africa, two-thirds of all deaths can be attributed to communicable diseases (including HIV/AIDS), perinatal conditions and nutritional deficiencies; these causes were responsible for one-third of all deaths in South Asia.

(*Sources:* Lopez, Begg and Bos, 2006; UNDESA, 2008)

More recently, the global burden of neuropsychiatric disorders, which had previously been largely ignored, has come to the attention of policy-makers. Whilst mortality is undoubtedly an important measure of health and disease, it is accepted that disability and ill-health caused by disease and injury can play a really important role in determining the overall health of populations across the world (for example, see table 10.1).

Globally, neuropsychiatric conditions are the most important cause of disability, affecting both men and women equally. Depression is the leading cause of disability for men and women, but women have higher burdens from anxiety disorders, migraine and dementia. In contrast, the global burden for alcohol and drug use disorders is six times higher for men than for women. Children who survive malnutrition, infectious diseases and other childhood threats are also likely to suffer from physical and learning disabilities into adult life. For example, children who have survived cerebral malaria can experience severe anaemia and neurological complications that can irreversibly impair cognitive function (Global Health Council, n.d.).

Table 10.1 Disability adjusted life years for neuropsychiatric conditions for men, 2001

	Cause	Europe and Central Asia region (thousands)									Sub-Saharan African region (thousands)								
		0–4	5–14	15–29	30–44	45–59	60–69	70–79	80+	Total	0–4	5–14	15–29	30–44	45–59	60–69	70–79	80+	Total
1	Unipolar depressive disorders	—	306	426	334	169	46	8	1	291	0	170	488	446	316	110	27	4	1,561
2	Bipolar affective disorder	—	48	524	41	1	0	—	—	615	—	17	279	36	1	0	0	0	334
3	Schizophrenia	—	28	492	34	2	0	0	0	556	0	76	277	20	6	4	2	0	386
4	Epilepsy	107	145	228	155	89	36	12	4	777	9	24	56	60	38	11	4	1	202
5	Alcohol use disorders	—	10	274	197	97	15	6	1	600	2	14	620	561	294	56	10	1	1,557
6	Alzheimer's and other dementias	29	9	6	5	16	36	65	30	197	13	7	10	12	37	99	199	97	474
7	Parkinson's disease	0	0	—	5	15	15	15	4	54	1	1	1	8	21	33	23	4	93
8	Multiple sclerosis	—	4	13	9	1	0	0	0	29	0	3	16	21	14	4	2	0	60
9	Drug use disorders	—	11	472	165	49	2	0	0	699	1	5	188	154	73	8	1	0	430
10	Post-traumatic stress disorder	—	4	35	14	8	0	0	0	61	0	0	25	17	10	0	0	0	52
11	Obsessive-compulsive disorder	—	59	145	32	14	3	0	0	254	—	29	73	62	11	2	4	0	181
12	Panic disorder	—	11	155	2	5	1	0	0	174	—	5	100	1	6	1	1	0	114
13	Insomnia (primary)	—	1	58	41	23	10	3	0	136	—	7	2	24	28	24	13	1	99
14	Migraine	18	42	21	10	0	0	0	0	92	4	62	50	10	1	0	0	0	128

Source: Adapted from Mathers, Lopez and Murray, 2006, tables 3C.3 and 3C.7, pp. 194, 218.

Activity 10.1   The global burden of disease

Study the information provided in table 10.2 and then answer the questions below.

Table 10.2 Deaths and burden of disease by cause: low- and middle-income countries and high-income countries (number in 1,000s per cent)

Selected cause group	Low- and middle-income		High-income	
I Communicable diseases, maternal and perinatal conditions, and nutritional deficiencies	Deaths	DALYs[1]	Deaths	DALYs
Diarrhoeal diseases	1,777 (3.7)	58,697 (4.2)	6 (<.1)	444 (0.3)
HIV/AIDS	2,552 (5.3)	70,796 (5.1)	22 (0.3)	665 (0.4)
Lower respiratory infections	3,408 (7.0)	83,606 (6.0)	345 (4.4)	2,314 (1.6)
Measles	762 (1.6)	23,091 (1.7)	1 (<.1)	23 (<.1)
Tuberculosis	1,590 (3.3)	35,874 (2.6)	16 (0.2)	219 (0.1)
II Non-communicable conditions				
Chronic obstructive pulmonary disease	2,378 (4.9)	33,453 (2.4)	297 (3.8)	5,282 (3.5)
Cirrhosis of the liver	654 (1.4)	13,633 (1.0)	118 (1.5)	2,146 (1.4)
Diabetes mellitus	757 (1.6)	15,804 (1.1)	202 (2.6)	4,192 (2.8)
Ischaemic heart disease	5,699 (11.8)	71,882 (5.2)	1,364 (17.3)	12,390 (8.3)
Stomach cancers	696 (1.4)	9,616 (0.7)	146 (1.9)	1,628 (1.1)
Unipolar depressive disorders	10 (<.1)	43,427 (3.1)	3 (<.1)	8,408 (5.6)
Vision disorders, age-related	0 (0.0)	15,364 (1.1)	0 (0.0)	1,525 (1.0)
III Injuries				
Falls	316 (0.7)	13,582 (1.0)	71 (0.9)	1,459 (1.0)
Road traffic accidents	1,069 (2.2)	32,017 (2.3)	121 (1.5)	3,045 (2.0)

Note: [1] Disability adjusted life year
Source: Adapted from: Lopez et al., 2006, p. 8, table 1.1.

(a)   Describe the main differences in global patterns of disease between low- and middle-income countries compared with high-income countries.

(b)   What is the leading cause of death in low- and middle-income countries?

(c)   What is the leading cause of death in high-income countries?

(d)   What does table 10.2 tell you about the comparative global burden of non-fatal illnesses?

The measurement of global patterns of disease and mortality is not an easy task. Data are drawn from a variety of sources which are not always comparable. For example, death registration systems are not universally implemented and, even when implemented, are not always complete. Cause of death is also not always recorded accurately and, for deaths from causes such as HIV/AIDS, malaria and tuberculosis (TB), **epidemiological** estimates are used (Mathers, Lopez and Murray, 2006). However, in general, people living in developing countries have shorter life expectancies than those in developed countries and tend to live a higher proportion of their lives in poorer health.

epidemiological referring to epidemiology, the branch of medicine that studies the causes, distribution, and control of disease in populations

Demographic changes in the world's population also have a profound impact on the global burden of disease and on patterns of health and illness; two global demographic changes are particularly significant.

First, the world population has increased exponentially since the beginning of the twentieth century, and it continues to rise. In 2008 the world population was approximately 6.7 billion (IPC, 2008), and it is expected to continue to rise to over 9 billion by 2050, with population growth at its highest in developing countries (UNDESA, 2007). However, the countries with the largest populations are also often the ones with the fewest resources available to support this growth.

Second, the population is also ageing. A report on world population ageing, published by the United Nations Department of Economic and Social Affairs (UNDESA, 2007), has shown that the **ageing population** is an unprecedented process without parallel in the history of humanity (see box 10.2).

ageing population a population ages when an increase in the proportion of older people is coupled with a reduction in the proportion of children and persons of working age

Demographic changes across the world can have enormous consequences on health and well-being and can place different and competing demands on health care services. Good health is not enjoyed equally by all, and there are considerable inequalities in health across the globe. The next section in this chapter further examines global change by exploring the concept and process of globalization.

Box 10.2	Global population ageing

- Globally, the number of older people in the population is expected to exceed the number of children for the first time in 2047. In developed countries, the number of older people exceeded the number of children in 1998.

- Population ageing affects nearly all the countries of the world.

- Population ageing results mainly from reductions in fertility. Fertility is unlikely to increase substantially to reverse this trend.

- Population ageing has major consequences for all aspects of human life. At an economic level it affects economic growth, savings, investment, consumption, labour markets, pensions and taxation. In the social sphere it affects family composition and living arrangements, housing demand, migration trends, epidemiology, and the demand for health and social care services.

Source: UNDESA, 2007.

3   Globalization, nursing and health

Globalization is an economic, cultural, technological and political process involving the movement of people, goods, services, cultures, technologies and ideas across international borders

Globalization is much discussed and debated. It has been described as a concept, a process, a project and even a revolution. However it is described or defined, though, it is associated with some of the most important changes in the late twentieth and early twenty-first centuries, and it cannot be ignored (Scriven, 2005).

Globalization means that people all over the world are becoming interconnected in unprecedented ways, spreading messages and ideas right around the globe.

Attempting to critically theorize the concept of globalization, Kellner argues:

> the key to understanding globalization is theorising it as at once a product of technological revolution and the global restructuring of capitalism in which economic, technological, political, and cultural features are intertwined. From this perspective, one should avoid both technological and economic determinism and all one-sided optics of globalization in favour of a view that theorises globalization as a highly complex, contradictory, and thus ambiguous set of institutions and social relations, as well as one involving flows of goods, services, ideas, technologies, cultural forms, and people. (Kellner, 2002, p. 285)

In a nutshell, globalization refers to the expansion of capitalism and is an economic phenomenon (Geertz, 1998). However, as

Kellner suggests, globalization is also much more than this. For example, changes in information and communications technologies (ICTs) are also part of globalization. Mobile phones and the increasing availability of broadband internet facilitate commerce and communication across international borders in a way never seen before.

There is considerable debate between globalization scholars, including sociologists, as to the nature of globalization, how and why it has come about and even if it really exists! (for example, see Castells, 1996). Leaving that debate aside, there is also extensive discussion as to whether globalization is a force for good or a negative influence on society. Many sociologists believe that globalization is 'Janus-faced' (Guillén, 2001); that is, they believe that globalization is simultaneously positive and negative. Pro-globalization groups (for example, the International Policy Network or World Growth) argue that free trade, in the form of goods, services, ideas and technologies, creates global wealth which, in turn, creates peaceful, prosperous and healthy societies. In contrast, anti-globalization groups (such as Consumers International or Friends of the Earth International) argue that free trade is not fair trade and that globalization destroys traditional cultures, communities and local economies, leading to poverty and inequalities in health.

Referring specifically to the impact of globalization on health, McMichael and Beaglehole (2000) describe it as a 'mixed blessing'. On the one hand they highlight how rapid economic growth and the availability of new technologies have led to a welcome global increase in life expectancy and, indeed, dramatically enhanced health and well being for some. Whereas, on the other, they suggest that globalization – including the flow of goods, services, ideas, technologies, cultural forms and people – poses a serious health risk across the world (McMichael and Beaglehole, 2000, 2003) (see box 10.3).

The 2007 World Health Report (WHO, 2007), which focused on global public health security, noted some of these concerns and stated:

> Today's highly mobile, interdependent and interconnected world provides myriad opportunities for the rapid spread of infectious diseases, and radionuclear and toxic threats. . . . Infectious diseases are now spreading geographically much faster than at any time in history. It is estimated that 2.1 billion airline passengers travelled in 2006; an outbreak or epidemic in any one part of the world is only a few hours away from becoming an imminent threat somewhere else. (WHO, 2007, p. 6)

The UK government strategy *Health is Global* (Department of Health, 2008) is the first cross-government strategy to tackle the issues connected to global health. This strategy outlines a set of principles and actions on which the UK government will focus between 2008 and 2013 to improve the health of people across the world, including

Box 10.3   **Globalization and potential health risks**

Globalization results in:

- marginalization and poverty, which develop and maintain higher morbidity and mortality rates;

- global environmental degradation, such as the spread of invasive species, the dispersal of organic pollutants and atmospheric changes;

- increased power of global capital, together with fragmentation of labour markets, leading to lower standards of occupational health and safety;

- the expansion of the international drug trade;

- the expansion of trafficking in people;

- increased international travel, leading to the faster spread of toxins and infectious diseases;

- increased refugee populations and rapid population growth, leading to greater chance of ethnic and civil conflict;

- increased consumerism and the global marketing of harmful commodities, such as tobacco.

Sources: Yach and Bettcher, 1998, p. 737; McMichael and Beaglehole, 2003, p. 12.

Box 10.4   **UK global health strategy: five areas for action**

1   Better global health security

2   Stronger, fairer and safer systems to deliver health

3   More effective international health organizations

4   Stronger, freer and fairer trade for better health

5   Strengthening the way we develop and use evidence to improve policy and practice (Department of Health, 2008, p. 18)

---

those living in the UK. *Health is Global* outlines five specific areas for action (see box 10.4) and commits billions of pounds to the project of global health security.

So far, this chapter has demonstrated that globalization is a process with far-reaching consequences for the health of people and populations. The next section focuses on one aspect of this, the movement of people across international borders, and the consequences of this for nursing work and patient care.

4 Patient care and nursing work in a global context

People leave their homes for a multitude of reasons, sometimes crossing international borders in order to do so. The newspapers, radio and wider media are full of examples of both 'natural' and so-called unnatural disasters, such as earthquake, flood, war and famine, which can cause people to leave their homes. The next section in this chapter focuses specifically on the international migration of nurses, but here the focus is on the needs of patients and nursing work.

Activity 10.2 **The mass movement of people across the globe**

(a) Drawing on your own personal or professional experiences, or on knowledge gained from the media, give at least three examples of the mass movement of people from one region to another.

(b) Discuss with a colleague why you think this movement occurred.

---

refugee a person fleeing from persecution in their country of nationality for reasons of race, religion, nationality, membership of a particular social group or political opinion

asylum seeker a person who has left their own country, possibly because of war or human rights abuses, and has applied for recognition as a refugee and is awaiting a decision on their application

It is not possible to provide a general statement on the health status of migrant groups because there are many reasons why people migrate. Some people may be described as economic migrants, and their health needs may not be dissimilar to those of the general population of the country they enter, although this is not always the case. The needs and experiences of refugees and asylum seekers are, however, quite different and relatively well documented. For example, in a review of primary health care services in the UK, Feldman (2006) notes that refugees and asylum seekers often have difficulties in accessing health services and find it hard to register with a general practitioner. Language barriers can be problematic, and chronic physical and mental health needs often go unmet. From the point of view of health care providers, caring for patients who cannot speak English and present with multiple, often complex, medical and social problems can be extremely time-consuming. Feldman (ibid., p. 811) argues that, to benefit fully from the health care system, refugees and asylum seekers need:

- access to primary care with full permanent registration;
- information about health services;
- appropriate and comprehensive health assessments, including mental and physical health;
- adequate access to translation, interpreting and advocacy services in appropriate languages;
- adequate and appropriate responses to mental health problems;

- access to specialist services for survivors of torture and organized violence;
- advice and information on health promotion.

Refugees and asylum seekers often travel great distances and come into contact with health care systems that may be alien to them. What changes might this pose, and how can they be overcome?

Activity 10.3   Meeting the needs of asylum seekers and refugees

Read the extract, which draws on the findings of a research project designed to explore whether HIV/AIDS services in Leeds are meeting the needs of asylum seekers and refugees, and then answer the questions below.

With increasing numbers of asylum seekers attending clinics . . . the department has had to make changes. . . . Materials are now available for staff to assist them in informing patients for whom English is not their first language. Training has been undertaken . . . and is necessary to ensure that staff are aware of difficulties that asylum seekers face. For example, issues such as housing or immigration may have greater importance in their lives than HIV status. Training has helped staff to empathize with these difficulties, but language and time constraints may mean that asylum seekers do not receive a service that meets their needs as well as it does for permanent residents. Cultural issues relating to time keeping of appointments have caused difficulties, so a designated member of staff at LCSH (Leeds Centre for Sexual Health) now co-ordinates the patient, doctor and interpreter for appointments. Interpreting services were very important at LCSH and HAT (the Health Access Team) for accessing care . . .

A lack of understanding of how the NHS works and differences in healthcare provision in different countries mean that patients frequently arrive with multiple, complex needs and the expectation that LCSH will be able to sort everything out. HAT aims to see all asylum seekers within 1 week of arrival in Leeds and encourages access to primary health care. This is not always achieved and LCSH has implemented strategies to help asylum seekers register with a general practitioner. Services at HAT are geared specifically for asylum seekers, so they are used to using interpreters to overcome patient difficulties, for example enabling access to mainstream services. During observations of consultations at HAT, it was apparent that there was no specialist service for referral of patients who had been victims of torture . . .

Barnardo's Castle Project provides support that is culturally and socially aware, sensitive to the needs of their clients. They feel that it can be difficult for white people to access this client group and that, in such a difficult situation, African clients find it easier to develop trust with people who understand their culture. Although it was stressed that all individuals differ in their needs, the peer support group is one of the most appreciated services. Emergency cash payments to people who would otherwise be destitute are also highly valued. One difficulty for asylum seekers and HIV services is the issue of confidentiality; two-thirds of those diagnosed will not access the service in case they meet a family member or someone they know. One-to-one meetings can be arranged in a private room or elsewhere in Leeds if clients are anxious about this . . .

The project worker for CASAC (Community Access and Support Against Crime) is female. She found that male asylum seekers were often embarrassed talking about sexual activity to a woman, but having a male translator has helped.

Source: Allan and Clarke, 2005, pp. 309–10.

(a)   The findings of this project highlight the way in which service providers have adapted services to meet the needs of asylum seekers and refugees. Why might this client group find it difficult to access services?

(b)   Drawing on the case study above, make a list of the innovations implemented to help meet the needs of asylum seekers and refugees.

(c)   Do you feel enabled to meet the needs of asylum seekers and migrant workers? If so, how? If not, why not?

Other groups also find it difficult to access health care services. Travellers, for example, are often not registered with a GP, and they experience quite marked inequalities in health, suffering from high levels of morbidity and premature death (Van Cleemput and Parry,

2001). Innovative solutions are often necessary to help ensure that these 'hard to reach' groups are able to access appropriate health care services.

Activity 10.4	Health care services for 'hard to reach' groups

Read the case study and then answer the questions below. It reports on the evaluation of a primary care service in Norwich designed to meet the needs of 'hard to reach' groups.

When the only GP in Norwich willing to see homeless people announced his retirement in early 2002, and the night shelter where he had held his clinics closed down, the local health care provider (Norwich Primary Care Trust (PCT)) could not find another health practitioner to take on this service. The provision of primary care to homeless people had completely broken down and needed to be comprehensively reinvented. At the same time a single health visitor was struggling to reach the traveller community, and the trust was informed that Norwich would become a distribution centre for asylum seekers and refugees in the near future . . . Finally, a women's refuge approached the trust because many of their clients had difficulty in becoming registered with local GPs. For all these groups the provision of primary care was unsatisfactory, and the local view was that the needs of all these 'hard-to-reach' groups could not be met using conventional approaches. A decision was therefore made to set up specific services which could have a more flexible approach.

In the UK, attempts to improve the health situation of these groups are frequently focused at only one needy population at any one time. Rather than create several services with distinct but frequently overlapping approaches, Norwich PCT aspired to reduce local inequalities in health by establishing one combined service. 'CityReach' (CR) opened in May 2002 as a primary care service for these 'hard-to-reach' groups. Four GPs, eight nurse practitioners, a health visitor and five other health professionals . . . aim to provide care for their patients in easily accessible places, including shelters for the homeless, a women's refuge and travellers' sites. Provision for asylum seekers and refugees is integrated into mainstream GP surgeries, with the CR professionals supporting the GPs and surgery staff. Sex workers are approached using a specifically designed mobile unit.

Source: Pfeil and Howe, 2004, pp. 185–6.

(a)   Why do you think that the client groups outlined in the case study are defined as 'hard to reach'?

(b)   The extract above indicates that the health care services for asylum seekers and refugees were mainstreamed (integrated into regular service provision). Why do you think this is the case? What are your views on the mainstreaming of services for hard-to-reach groups? Should all services be mainstreamed?

(c)   Thinking of your own professional experiences, what role can nurses play in meeting the health needs of hard-to-reach groups?

5 Nursing work: a global view

Globally, there is a health workforce crisis (WHO, 2006). That is, there is a serious shortage of health care workers across the world, and this is seen as a crucial factor in the achievement of health and development goals, such as the United Nations Millennium Development Goals (see box 10.5). Overall, there is a critical shortage of nurses, midwives and doctors, equivalent to 2.4 billion workers worldwide. According the *World Health Report 2006* (ibid.) there are fifty-seven countries (mostly in Africa, Asia and South America) that face a particularly acute crisis. There is considerable inequity between countries, with those that have the greatest need for quality health care experiencing the greatest threat to their workforce. There is also inequity between urban populations – where there are sometimes high concentrations of health workers – and rural populations, where there is often scarcity at unsafe levels, especially in the least developed countries. Organizations such as the Global Health Workforce

Alliance, which is an alliance hosted and administered by the World Health Organization, work in partnership with governments, civil society, finance institutions, international agencies, professional associations and others to identify and implement solutions to the global health workforce crisis.

Box 10.5	United Nations Millennium Development Goals
1	Eradicate extreme poverty and hunger
2	Achieve universal primary education
3	Promote gender equality and empower women
4	Reduce child mortality
5	Improve maternal health
6	Combat HIV/AIDS, malaria and other diseases
7	Ensure environmental sustainability
8	Develop a global partnership for development

Source: UNDP, 2008.

The global health workforce is large and diverse. It consists of a range of individuals employed in a variety of occupations, working with individuals, groups and communities at local, regional, national and international levels. In all countries, a well-educated and flexible health workforce is essential to the delivery of health care services, as well as to the performance of health systems in more general terms. Beaglehole and Bonita (2001) argue that most governments have neglected public health workforce development and that in some developing countries the situation is especially acute.

In a globalized world the migration of people across borders is not uncommon. Nurse migration happens for a variety of reasons; economists describe this as the 'push' and the 'pull'. Push factors might include low wages, job insecurity, poor prospects and discrimination. Among pull factors are higher salaries, safe work environments, job security and better training and education opportunities.

push factors refer to conditions or circumstances that encourage nurses to leave their country

pull factors refer to conditions in the destination country which attract movement into that country

Whilst low-income countries often rely on NGOs for health service delivery, high-income countries such as the UK, the United States, New Zealand and Australia often recruit nurses from other countries; indeed, industrialized countries such as these have a long history of welcoming health care workers from overseas. However, when nurses and other health care workers migrate from poorer to richer economies, this instability can have a very negative impact on the health care workforce and, in turn, on health and health care provision. A recent review suggests that mass migration can have a negative impact on nurse education (Hancock, 2008) and that migrant nurses are socially devalued (Allan, Tschudin and Horton, 2008). 'NHS bosses have been accused of adding to a developing world "skills drain" in nursing', reported the UK national news (BBC, 2000). Writing specifically about African countries, other commentators (Sanders et al., 2003) suggest that the 'brain drain' from Africa to the developed world is one of the most serious problems facing African countries. Furthermore, they argue that high levels of expatriation means that health care workers who stay have increased workloads, which leads to low productivity, poorer service delivery and, thus, the conditions that push further migration.

However, the movement of health workers can have advantages for all concerned, and what is seen as a 'brain drain' can actually become a 'brain gain'. For example, recipient countries are helped to resolve worker shortages or skill-mix gaps. Migrants, who migrate for many different reasons, often learn new skills and – if they return home – bring back with them a wealth of experience, skills and expertise. Additionally, remittances (money sent back home by migrants) is thought to reduce poverty in their country of origin. Some countries, such as the Philippines, have traditionally seen large numbers of nurses migrating to work in other parts of the world (see box 10.6), but the Philippine Overseas Employment Administration has developed an incentive programme, including tax-free shopping, subsidized business loans and scholarships, to encourage migrants to return home (WHO, 2006). In an article reported in the *Nursing Times*, one British nurse acknowledges her gain in having worked with migrant nurses during her career:

> I feel very privileged to work with such compassionate and knowledgeable people, and to be given the chance to learn about life and attitudes in different parts of the world. Without foreign nurses, some of our hospitals would not be able to cope with the demands made on them, and people would not receive the care they need. The burden on existing nurses such as myself would be intolerable, and any joy or satisfaction from nursing would disappear under an increasing mountain of work. (Crampton, 2003, p. 13)

National policies and incentive programmes which encourage the return of emigrant workers are beneficial. However, given the huge global crisis, organizations such as the World Health Organization suggest that global solidarity is needed to resolve

Box 10.6

Providing nurses for the world? The Philippines

An estimated 150,000 Filipino nurses – 85 per cent of employed Filipino nurses – work abroad. The combination of degree-prepared nurses, mostly with a good standard of English, and a Filipino Government-approved programme of producing nurses for export, has resulted in thousands of nurses working overseas. Remittance income from nurses is a major source of hard currency for developing countries and has been a major motivator for the Philippines to train nurses for overseas.

Research in 1993 estimated that Filipinos working abroad sent home more than US$800 million in remittance income. The exodus of nurses from the Philippines prompted a warning from the Philippine Nurses' Association in 2003 that if the exodus continued, it would prompt a serious public health crisis by 2006. There are an estimated 30,000 nursing vacancies in the Philippines and government agencies and the Department of Health have noted that inexperienced health workers were the ones remaining in the Philippines.

Source: O'Connor, 2005.

this problem. In particular, the WHO (2006) argues that three specific actions should be taken to respond to the global health workforce crisis:

1   *catalysing knowledge and learning* to include the pooling of experience and expertise to help countries tap into the best talent and practices, among them identification and support for priority research issues;
2   *striking cooperative agreements* to protect the health and safety of global migrants, relief workers and volunteers, the adoption of ethical recruitment practices, and a willingness to commit human resources to assist in humanitarian emergencies;
3   *responding to workforce crises* in the poorest developing countries to include both the immediate and long-term financing of the health care workforce.

The UK government strategy-*Health is Global* (Department of Health, 2008) also recognizes that action needs to be taken to ensure that the global shortage of health care workers is addressed. The strategy promises up to £6 billion for the development of health systems and services, especially in low- to middle-income countries and effective development assistance to low-income countries to help them train and retain staff.

Activity 10.5   Globalization, migration and nursing work

Read the case study and then answer the questions below.

Fatima Ansari* . . . is a trim, well-dressed woman in her mid-thirties with dark eyes that communicate calm and strength. She was born in the Middle East, member of an ethnic community representing only 7 percent of the national population. Life was difficult but she grew up in a happy home, sheltered by her immediate and extended family. Ansari dreamed of being a nurse, but making the wish a reality was a continuing challenge. Women were expected to marry young, care for their husbands, and immediately build families. In spite of the powerful social pressures, Ansari persevered and with the support of her parents finished nursing school. What a momentous occasion, the day she received her diploma! It came with the promise of a wonderful future.

   In her first job Ansari faced what would become an insurmountable obstacle. The fact that she belonged to an ethnic minority made her the butt of intolerable discrimination. In the eleven years Ansari worked as a nurse in her home country, she was never given a permanent position and was daily victimized by the harmful and unfair practices of her colleagues and employers. Eager to pursue her nursing education, she made countless unsuccessful attempts to enrol in continuing education courses and advanced university programs. Despite her qualifications and willingness to learn, she was consistently refused admittance. Earning very little money and only offered sporadic temporary work contracts, she often had to work more than one job to make ends meet. Despite all her efforts, a permanent position, professional fulfilment, and career advancement became an illusion. Every day she felt more insecure and unsafe . . .

   Ansari knew that in her country there was a serious nursing shortage. Seeing the desperate need for nurses made her job insecurities and poor working conditions that much more stressful and difficult to bear. Given no hope for a better future in her home country, Ansari finally decided to join her sister and brother in Sweden.

*This is a pseudonym.

Source: Kingma, 2006, pp. 9–10.

(a)   Why did Ansari become a nurse migrant?
(b)   Can you think of other reasons why nurses might migrate to work in another country? Make a list of these.
(c)   What are the benefits of nurse migration and what are the costs?

Summary and Resources

Summary

- Globally health is improving. However, there is considerable disparity in health and disease across different parts of the world.

- Globalization can be defined in different ways and can be described as 'Janus-faced'.

- The global health workforce crisis poses a serious threat to the achievement of health and well-being for all.

- International nurse migration is influenced by both 'push' and 'pull' factors and has been described as both a 'brain drain' and a 'brain gain'.

Questions for Discussion

1 Define globalization and describe the impact of globalization on health.

2 Why is an understanding of the global context important for nurses and nursing work?

3 Would you migrate to work as a nurse in another country? What sort of 'push' and 'pull' factors would influence your decision?

Further Reading

M. Kingma: *Nurses on the Move: Migration and the Global Health Care Economy*. London: ILR Press, 2006.
This is a really comprehensive book which explores the social, economic and political context of international nurse migration. It draws on poignant interviews with nurse migrants and offers an excellent insight into the 'real face' of nurse migration.

M. MacLachlan: *Culture and Health: A Critical Perspective Towards Global Health*. 2nd edn, Oxford: Wiley Blackwell, 2006.
This is a much more challenging text but one that you might want to pick up if you decide to pursue a project or dissertation on the subject of global health. The book begins with the premise that most nurses and other health care professionals practise in a multicultural society and should, therefore, seek to understand the relationship between culture, health and health care.

L. Ray: *Globalization and Everyday Life*. London: Routledge, 2006.
This provides a more detailed yet accessible sociological introduction to globalization, with a focus on understanding the process of

globalization and the way that it is created and sustained by the everyday actions of individuals.

More questions, web resources and annotated further reading can be found at www.politybooks.com/sociologyfornurses.

References

Allan, C. L., and Clarke, J. 2005: 'Are HIV/AIDS services in Leeds, UK, able to meet the needs of asylum seekers?'. *Public Health*, 119, 305–11.

Allan, H., Tschudin, V., and Horton, K. 2008: 'The devaluation of nursing: a position statement'. *Nursing Ethics*, 15(4), 549–56.

BBC 2000: 'UK "fuelling global nurse shortage"'. 21 December; http://news.bbc.co.uk/1/hi/health/1082120.stm [last accessed 5 September 2008].

Beaglehole, R., and Bonita, R. 2001: 'Challenges for public health in the global context – prevention and surveillance'. *Scandinavian Journal of Public Health*, 29, 81–3.

Castells, M. 1996: *The Rise of the Network Society*. Oxford: Blackwell.

Crampton, J. 2003: 'Foreign nurses are highly valued members of the NHS'. *Nursing Times*, 99(18), 13.

Department of Health 2008: *Health is Global: A UK Government Strategy 2008–13*. London: HMSO.

Feldman, R. 2006: 'Primary health care for refugees and asylum seekers: a review of the literature and a framework for services'. *Public Health*, 120(9), 809–16.

Geertz, C. 1998: 'The world in pieces: culture and politics at the end of the century'. *Focaal: Tijdschrift voor Antropologie*, 32, 91–117.

Global Health Council n.d.: *Child development in developing countries*; www.globalhealth.org/child_health/impact/ [last accessed 11 November 2008].

Guillén, M. 2001: 'Is globalisation civilising, destructive or feeble? A critique of five key debates in the social science literature'. *Annual Review of Sociology*, 27, pp. 235–60.

Hancock, P. K. 2008: 'Nurse migration: the effects on nursing education'. *International Nursing Review*, 55(3), 258–64.

IPC 2008: US Census Bureau, Population Division; www.census.gov/ipc/www/ [last accessed 14 October 2008].

Kellner, D. 2002: 'Theorizing globalization'. *Sociological Theory*, 20(3), 285–305.

Kingma, M. 2006: *Nurses on the Move: Migration and the Global Health Care Economy*. London: ILR Press.

Lopez, A. D., Begg, S., and Bos, E. 2006: 'Demographic and epidemiological characteristics of major regions, 1990–2001'. In A. D. Lopez, C. D. Mathers, M. Ezzati, D. T. Jamison and C. J. L. Murray (eds), *Global Burden of Disease and Risk Factors*. Washington, DC, and New York: World Bank/Oxford University Press.

Lopez, A. D., Mathers, C. D., Ezzati, M., Jamison, D. T., and Murray, C. J. L. 2006: 'Measuring the global burden of disease and risk factors, 1990–2001'. In A. D. Lopez, C. D. Mathers, M. Ezzati, D. T. Jamison and C. J. L. Murray (eds), *Global Burden of Disease and Risk Factors*. Washington, DC, and New York: World Bank/Oxford University Press.

McMichael, A. J., and Beaglehole, R. 2000. 'The changing global context of public health'. *The Lancet*, 356(9228), 495–9.

McMichael, A. J., and Beaglehole, R. 2003: 'The global context for public health'. In R. Beaglehole (ed.), *Global Public Health: A New Era*. Oxford: Oxford University Press.

Mathers, C. D., Lopez, A. D., and Murray, C. J. L. 2006: 'The burden of disease and mortality by condition: data, methods, and results for 2001'. In A. D. Lopez, C. D. Mathers, M. Ezzati, D. T. Jamison and C. J. L. Murray (eds), *Global Burden of Disease and Risk Factors*. Washington, DC, and New York: World Bank/Oxford University Press.

O'Connor, T. 2005: 'The Philippines – providing nurses for the world'. *Kai Tiaki: Nursing New Zealand*, May; http://findarticles.com/p/articles/mi_hb4839/is_/ai_n29183078 (last accessed 15 October 2008].

Pfeil, M., and Howe, A. 2004: 'Ensuring primary care reaches the "hard to reach"'. *Quality in Primary Care*, 12(3), 185–90.

Sanders, D., Dovlo, D., Wilma, M., and Lehmann, U. 2003: 'Public health in Africa'. In R. Beaglehole (ed.), *Global Public Health: A New Era*. Oxford: Oxford University Press.

Scriven, A. 2005: 'Promoting health: a global context and rationale'. In A. Scriven and S. Garman (eds), *Promoting Health: Global Perspectives*. Basingstoke: Palgrave.

UNDESA, 2007: *World Population Ageing*. New York: United Nations.

UNDESA, 2008: *The Millennium Development Goals Report*. New York: United Nations.

UNDP, 2008: *Millennium Development Goals*. www.undp.org/mdg/basics.shtml [last accessed 15 October 2008].

Van Cleemput, P., and Parry, G. 2001: 'Health status of gypsy travellers'. *Journal of Public Health Medicine*, 23, 129–34.

WHO (World Health Organization), 2003: *The World Health Report: Shaping the Future*. Geneva: WHO.

WHO, 2005: *World Health Report 2005: Make Every Mother and Child Count*. Geneva: WHO.

WHO, 2006: *World Health Report 2006: Working Together for Health*. Geneva: WHO.

WHO, 2007: *World Health Report 2007. A Safer Future: Global Public Health Security in the 21st Century*. Geneva: WHO.

Yach, D., and Bettcher, D. 1998. 'The globalization of public health, I: Threats and opportunities'. *American Journal of Public Health*, 88(5), 735–8.

Part III

Where Does Care Take Place?

There are often both implicit and explicit assumptions that nursing work is located primarily within the hospital. Historically, and to date, the organization and funding of health care has constructed and maintained this myth. It is further reinforced by the media, with its focus on the more acute and 'sexy' side of health care work – the popular medical dramas *Casualty* and *Holby City* are illustrative of this.

Of course, nurses work in a variety of places – in the community, in people's homes and in schools, as well as in hospitals and other institutions. However, nurses are not the only ones who provide care for those who are ill. Much of it is provided by a range of health workers, including families and, particularly, women. The three chapters in this section focus on the care provided within and by families, the community and institutions.

Chapter 11, 'The Family, Health and Caring', focuses on the contribution made by the family both to health and well-being and to ill-health. It begins by unpacking 'common-sense' views of the nuclear family, demonstrating the diversity that exists within family life. It then introduces some key sociological perspectives on the family. This chapter considers the role of the family in maintaining health, focusing on the care and caring work carried out both within and by family members, and concludes by exploring the ways in which families can cause ill-health, for example, via domestic violence or the burden of caring for the chronically ill.

In chapter 12, 'Primary Care in the Community', various definitions of primary care are explored. The chapter then considers the history of general practice and its role within health care. A policy overview and a brief history of the development of primary care are also given, and a major focus is the changing nature of health care professionals in primary care as commissioners of services. This has resulted in a shift away from the hospital as the major locus of health care to 'care closer to home'. This chapter concludes by encouraging you to reflect on the role of nurses within primary health care teams.

In 'Hospitals and Institutions' (chapter 13) a sociological critique of 'institutions' is given, focusing on the process of institutionalization. Different types of institution are considered and a brief historical overview is given; the development of the general hospital, the asylum and the children's hospital is discussed. This chapter examines the shift to community care and explores the role of residential care homes, nursing homes and hospices and the consequent change to the structure and the role of hospitals. You are encouraged to recognize the importance of institutions in providing care, the different types of institutional care that exist, and the problems that arise through institutionalization.

All of the chapters within this section encourage you to reflect on what we mean by 'caring', who cares, and where care takes place.

11 The Family, Health and Caring

Geraldine Brown and Corinne Wilson

Key issues in this chapter

- The concept of 'the family'
- Sociological perspectives on the family
- Health and the family
- The family and caring

By the end of this chapter you should be able to . . .

- understand the nuclear family and family diversity;
- discuss the sociological perspectives on the family;
- explore the link between family life, health, illness and caring;
- recognize the need to challenge common-sense ideas around the family.

1 Introduction

This chapter considers the relationships between the family, health, illness and caring. It begins by exploring some of the debates around families and then moves on to highlight a few of the relevant issues when considering the impact of the family on health, illness and caring. The aim of the chapter is to draw your attention to the fact that sick people are often part of a family and that families can play an important role in patient care. However, families also hold the potential to make people sick!

In recent times, there has been an ideological shift in thinking about the family and health. In particular, there has been a conscious move away from all-encompassing, state-provided health care to an emphasis on self-care and care by families. It appears that the family has a greater role in health care than ever before, but what are the consequences of this shift? How are families coping with this increased pressure to care for sick, frail or disabled family members and maintain the health of the nation? Arguably, with the growth in unemployment, poverty and the number of one-parent families, and the greater involvement of women in paid work, the ability of the family to take on an even bigger role in health care is in question. The family has an increasingly major role in health care; however, before considering this, it is important to ask the question, What is 'the family'?

Activity 11.1   **Defining the Family**

It is useful, before you even begin to read further in this chapter, to start thinking about how you would define the family.

(a)   Write down what immediately comes to mind when you think about the family.

(b)   Who are the members of your family?

(c)   How important are the people you have identified as members of your family in your everyday life?

---

2   The concept of 'the family'

Most of us are born into families and spend, whether we choose to do so or not, most of our childhood and teenage years within that family (Bernades, 1997, p. 1).

Look at what you have written down for activity 11.1. What it is important to recognize is that definitions of the family change and that 'the family' can mean different things to different people, according to their personal circumstances and life experiences. Writing about the challenges of diversity when working with families, Doane and Varcoe note:

> At times we find ourselves in situations where we are working with families who come from backgrounds, religious faiths, or life situations different from our own. As nurses we provide care to people and/or families whose values we do not share and who we may see making choices different than those we would make. We may find ourselves in relation with families where members harm one another or where it is difficult to connect because some family members are absent. (Doane and Varcoe, 2006, pp. 7–8)

Common sense and 'the family'

There is a common-sense understanding of what we mean when we talk of 'the family', but common-sense understandings mask the complexities of family life (see chapters 1 and 2 for further discussion of 'common-sense' understandings). This masking perpetuates and maintains images of supposedly normal families and the naturalness of roles ascribed to individual family members. It prevents us from understanding the impact on family life of differences such as gender, class, ethnicity, racism, sexuality, and so on. Thinking about the family sociologically enables us to unpick these overarching common-sense understandings. Sociological explanations challenge common-sense assumptions and understandings and allow us to recognize that society, today, throughout history and across cultures, encompasses a diversity of family forms. It also enables us to question the 'natural' roles assumed by individual family members – for example, women's innate ability to care. With specific reference to the purpose of this chapter, understanding the diversity of family life is important; as Bond and Bond (1994) argue, the family is the context within which health is maintained and where illness occurs and is resolved.

For health professionals who are moving beyond common-sense understandings, recognizing the complexities of family life is important when providing a more holistic approach to health care.

3   Sociological perspectives on the family

The 'universal' nuclear family

An important starting point is to recognize that families are social, not natural, phenomena; therefore, they change over time and are influenced by social, economic and political developments. However, in Western societies there has existed a powerful assumption of a universal family form. The concept of 'the family' has rested on the image of a **nuclear family** consisting of a husband, wife and their dependent children, living together and connected by mutual affection, care and support (Scott, Treas and Richards, 2004). This family type has been powerful and influential and exists as a standard of how sexual, emotional and parental responsibility should be structured. There now exists an enormous body of work that contains many different explanations pertinent to the existence, the functions and the role of 'the family' in society, some of which are considered below.

nuclear family   the nuclear family comprises merely parents (or a parent) and their dependent child(ren)

Functionalist perspectives on the family

One of the most prominent and influential sociological attempts to explain the existence of the family was put forward by Talcott

Parsons (1955) (see also chapter 1). Parsons's theory was prominent in the 1950s and 1960s and was based on research carried out with American middle-class families. From Parsons's perspective, it is argued that families exist because of the functions they perform and, consequently, have evolved over time because of the role they play in helping us meet the social and economic demands of society. However, what is crucial in the functionalist analysis is the notion of the evolution of the nuclear family. These small **kin groups** have evolved to fit the needs of an industrial economy. Before the rise of industrialization, Parsons suggests, there existed large kin groups that performed a variety of functions vital to the group's survival. The smaller kin group – the nuclear family – emerged from the fact that the family was no longer required to perform many of the functions that were necessary before industrialization, for example, economic, education, health and welfare functions. The functions were increasingly shifting away from the family to become the responsibility of the newly developing state institutions, such as education and health care. It is these smaller kin groups that Parsons argues were better able than large kin groups to perform the specialized functions essential to the maintenance of society.

kin groups   the social relationships and lineage groups bound together through a system of well-defined customs, rights and obligations; kin relationships may either derive from descent or be established through affinity

An extended kin group

The nuclear family consists of a breadwinner/husband and a homemaker/wife and dependent children. There is a clear distinction between the roles of the wife/mother and the husband/father. The husband/father role is to provide economically for his family. The wife/mother role is concerned principally with looking after the well-being of the husband and children. In the functionalist account, these roles arose out of the biological differences between women and men and primarily out of women's reproductive capability. For example, Parsons (1955) argues that the two most important functions performed by the nuclear family are the socialization of children and the provision of psychological support for adults. According to Cheal (2002), functionalism is a theoretical approach that emphasizes the positive benefits of families; that is, the socialization of children enables them to grow into valuable, productive, law-abiding members of society.

Critiques of functionalist perspectives

Functionalist accounts, such as that of Parsons, have not been without their critics. The assertion made by Parsons that industrialization brought about a decrease in family size has been challenged. Research undertaken by Laslett (1972), for example, demonstrates that household size remained fairly constant and that, before industrialization, the nuclear family was predominant. He suggests that it was the most common family form from the Middle Ages, and this appears to have been the norm even in the most rural of families. There is also the suggestion that geographical mobility was a common occurrence in pre-industrial society; for example, children were often sent away to go into domestic service or take up apprenticeships. This challenges Parsons's notion that the nuclear family evolved to fit the needs of an industrial society. With regard to

extended family
a family group consisting of three or more generations of relatives living either within the same household or in close proximity

◄ the **extended family** or wider kin networks, Laslett points out that, owing to high mortality rates, very few children were likely to have parents alive when they got married, again challenging the idea that the nuclear family evolved from larger kin groupings. Laslett argues that the pre-industrial nuclear family was able to adapt relatively easily to industrialization.

In contemporary Western societies, the maintenance of health and well-being is sometimes not believed to be a vital function of the modern nuclear family. In Britain, the National Health Service (NHS) dominates the provision of health care, yet, despite this, we know that the health services do not act alone. For example, when we are ill, our contact with the NHS is often limited to making a brief visit to the doctor's surgery. Indeed, there are few of us requiring long-term specialist hospital care. The tending of those who are ill and recovering from illness and the care of the long-term sick and disabled is, on the whole, done by families and, in particular, women. There is an implicit recognition that, without this informal care, medical institutions would not be able to cope. Furthermore, with policy developments within the health arena, for example community care and its underlying principles, it is possible to argue that this function has never been lost, and the assumption remains that care will be provided by the family (see chapter 12 for further discussion of non-institutional care). It is also important to note that the duty on the family to care is imposed not just on the nuclear family but on all families, and particularly on all wives, mothers and daughters.

Feminist perspectives on the family

Not all sociologists have described the family in a positive light.
Feminist accounts have recognized the implications of the nuclear
family for all women's lives (see also chapter 5). The separation of the
home from the workplace that emerged in the nineteenth century has
implications for all women and their role within families. The legacy
of nineteenth-century domestic ideology and the image of the 'angel
in the home' (Hall, 1982, p. 18) impact upon women's roles today.
Victorian middle-class ideology (see chapter 1 for a definition of
ideology) identified mothers and wives who went out to work as
endangering the whole of society. Engels ([1845] 1999), for example,
wrote that the wife's employment would not dissolve the family
entirely but turn it upside down. If the wife supports the family and
the husband sits at home and looks after the children and performs
domestic tasks, the result will be the unsexing of the sexes. Engels
goes on to argue that men would be left without their masculinity and
women without their 'true' femininity (see chapter 5 for a definition
of these terms). What is evident here is the linking of masculinity to
paid work and femininity to domestic labour and childcare. It is
important to note the similarities with functionalist allocation of
gender-specific roles, where the emphasis is on the 'naturalness' of
women's role as rooted in her biology.

When talking about families, Engels was not referring to all family
forms but to a specific family form, the nuclear family, and his
thoughts reflected those held by many middle-class commentators
of the time. These sentiments were reinforced through legislation,
for example the Factory Acts of the 1840s, which limited children's
and women's employment. This further reinforced the notion of
women's role and encouraged their economic dependence upon the
husband/father (Barrett and McIntosh, 1991).

At the end of the nineteenth century, with the recognition in
political circles that the working-class male child was a national
asset, the health and welfare of children became entrenched in state
practices. Connections were made, not to structural inequalities, but
to immoral mothers who neglected their children by going out to
work. The responsibility for the health of children and, implicitly,
the future health of the nation was placed firmly in women's hands.
It became increasingly clear that women's role within the family was
to care not just for dependent children but also for her husband.

By the twentieth century normal family life had come to be defined
by the breadwinning husband and the domesticated wife. Women's
role was firmly located within the private sphere and women were
responsible for caring for the family in health and, usually, in
sickness. The role of men was located within the public sphere, as
the economic provider responsible for financial stability and the
material well-being of the family. These gender-specific roles have

material   relating to
economic factors

implications when we consider issues relating to family life, health, illness and caring.

The traditional nuclear family

Feminist critics of the family have highlighted how male breadwinning and the accompanying family wage ideology has prohibited, and continues to prohibit, women from gaining equal access to paid work. The dependence of women and children on a male breadwinner creates a damaging power imbalance within the family. These inequalities are maintained by the state through social and economic policies that assume families contain a male breadwinner and a woman who is responsible for childcare and domestic work (Budig, 2004). As Jackson (1997, p. 328) argues, 'family ties are ties of economic co-operation of support and dependency, but also inequality and exploitation'.

The representation of the family as heterosexual (whereby the only sexual relations to be sanctioned were those between husband and wife for the purpose of reproduction), class-specific (the family form of the new middle classes) and gender-specific (with its particular division of labour) has had far-reaching consequences. While this ideal may not have been the reality for many poor working-class families in the twentieth century, it was pervasive at that time, and while it is not the reality for a great many people today, its legacy lives on (Weeks, Heaphy and Donovan, 2004).

Activity 11.2   **The legacy of the nuclear family**

(a)   How important do you think the legacy of the nuclear family is today?

(b)   Can you think of any examples of how the ideology of the nuclear family impacts on everyday life?

(c)   How might the legacy of the nuclear family affect patient care?

Diversity and family form

This ideal becomes problematic when one takes into consideration the diversity of family life that exists in the UK today. The 2001 census gives us an indication of this diversity. The census statistics show there were 21,660,475 households in England and Wales and that 30 per cent of these were one-person households. Almost half of the one-person households were one-pensioner-only households and three-quarters of these (2,366,000) were occupied by a woman living alone (ONS, 2001). So it is evident that a large number of people do not live in a nuclear family.

The issue here is that, if welfare, and in particular health policy, rests on the implicit assumption that maintaining health and caring are important functions of the family, and 'the family' is viewed in the context of the nuclear family, then we need to consider the implications for all those people who do not live in this type of family and do not have access to the resources the family provides.

It is acknowledged that health care comes from a variety of sources, for example the state, private markets, volunteers, family and friends; however, the care provided by family and friends is recognized to be the most fundamental (Graham, 1999). In what is now a landmark document, the Griffiths Report states, 'Families, friends and other local people provide the majority of care in response to needs that they are uniquely well placed to identify and respond to. . . . The proposals take as their starting point that this is how it should be' (Griffiths, 1988, p. 5). So it is clear that, while in the UK we do have state-provided health care in the form of the National Health Service, state-provided health care cannot exist without the large amount of caring work carried out in and by the family. We could suggest that it is important to draw on informal sources of caring, and indeed

Activity 11.3   Diversity, the family and health

The following extract is taken from an article published in *The Guardian* as part of a series on 'the world in 2020'. Read the extract and then answer the questions below.

> . . . all are agreed that by 2020 it will be very hard to talk of a 'typical family', such will be the variety of shapes and types of families.
>
> The most marked characteristic of families since the 1960s has been that the traditional conception of the British family has disintegrated. The married couple with 2.4 children is disappearing. The sequence of life events – marriage, sex and children – has been radically reordered. Marriage rarely comes first and increasingly does not happen at all. Over the past 30 years, levels of cohabitation have trebled, the number of babies born outside marriage has quintupled, and the number of single-parent families has trebled.
>
> The most dramatic change, however, has been to the 'happy ever after' bit in the picture of family life. In the past 30 years, the rate of divorce has doubled; and half of all children now experience their parents' divorce before they are 16.
>
> All four trends – cohabitation, divorce, births outside marriage and single parents – are likely to be even more pronounced by 2020. . . . There will be dozens of different types of co-parenting arrangements, with combinations of stepfamilies, or adults with children from previous relationships entering long-term relationships with others in the same position but choosing not to live together.
> . . .
>
> One of the most dramatic social changes of the past 30 years has been in women's patterns of employment. In the UK the proportion of women in full-time employment has trebled in the past 30 years and maternal employment has leapt from 57% to 65% during the 1990s. . . . The norm in families now is for one male full-time worker and one female part-time. By 2020, more women will be the primary breadwinner . . .
> (Bunting, 2007)

(a) Consider the implications for future health care provision by the family.

(b) What significance might this have for nurses (in their professional *and* personal lives)?

families can be a vital source of support to some people. But, as will be demonstrated, these normative assumptions can have serious consequences for individuals caring and being cared for within the family. Relying on the family to provide an informal network of care can be problematic. It is important not to assume that all families have the propensity to provide informal care.

4   The family, health and caring

Families play an important role in caring for sick, frail and disabled people. As mentioned previously, most of us have minimal contact with formal health institutions, and when we are ill the majority of our care takes place within the family. It is estimated that there are 6 million **carers** in the UK and that one in ten adults is a carer, saving the public purse an estimated £87 billion (Princess Royal Trust for Carers, 2008). Caring for others can often be very demanding and time-consuming. While it may involve the normal daily tasks we associate with caring for the well, these often need to be performed more frequently. In addition, although family carers do not constitute a homogeneous group and there are clear generational and cultural differences, amongst others, there are some general characteristics that can be identified amongst carers, for example:

carers people who, without payment, provide help and support a partner, child, relative, friend or neighbour

- high levels of stress, depressed mood and sleep disturbance;
- reduced earnings and poverty;
- employment difficulties;
- poor health and difficulty in accessing health care for themselves;
- feelings of isolation;
- inadequate housing;
- marital breakdown. (Department of Health, 2008)

It is estimated that one in ten adults in the UK is a carer, often of a family relative. Being a carer can take a toll on one's own health, and the needs of carers are sometimes overlooked.

Caring for others often becomes the responsibility of female family members, as this role can be perceived as an extension of the normal caring that women perform within the family; and this holds true across all ethnic groups (Department of Health, 2008). Some of the factors identified above may affect women adversely to a greater extent than other family members. While most illnesses may be considered minor and requiring a relatively short period of care, caring for people who are frail, chronically ill or disabled may be a long-term commitment that can have a significant impact on family life. Families often take on this role because there is a lack of appropriate services for those with complex health care needs.

To illustrate the point we are making here, it will be useful to consider the effect of childhood asthma on families. Statistics suggest that one in eleven children in the UK has asthma (Asthma UK, n.d.) and that the prevalence of asthma is increasing in most countries, especially amongst children (GINA, 2007). Research carried out among families with children suffering from asthma and other respiratory conditions (Fiese, 2008; Marchant et al., 2008) identifies the multiple impact such conditions have on family life, demonstrating how the health status of one family member can adversely affect both the material and emotional well-being of all family members. For example:

- parents often take less well-paid jobs closer to home to be nearer their children;
- emergency care can mean a loss of earnings owing to time off work;
- one-off costs (e.g. new bedding) and regular costs (e.g. hospital visits) can be a financial drain;
- asthma attacks can cause disrupted sleep for all family members, leading to tiredness, irritability and lack of concentration.

Caring is often perceived to be both a natural means of demonstrating love and support and something that is carried out unstintingly. However, while families can offer a significant amount of support in times of ill-health, the burden of caring for a family member or being cared for by the family can exacerbate existing illness or make other family members sick.

Writing about terminal illness, Jocham et al. (2006) suggest that the whole family should be the focus of care and recommend that nurses should be aware and adjust their practice to take account of the disruptive effects of illness on family functioning. Arguably, such a focus is applicable not only to families caring for someone with a terminal illness but to all families with caring responsibilities.

In recognition of the important role of carers to families, communities and society, the Westminster government has announced a carers' strategy for England and Wales which is underpinned by £255 million. The vision set out in this strategy is summarized in box 11.1.

Box 11.1	A vision for valuing and supporting carers

- Carers will be respected as expert care partners and will have access to the integrated and personalized services they need to support them in their caring role.

- Carers will be able to have a life of their own alongside their caring role.

- Carers will be supported so that they are not forced into financial hardship by their caring role.

- Carers will be supported to stay mentally and physically well and treated with dignity.

- Children and young people will be protected from inappropriate caring and have the support they need to learn, develop and thrive, to enjoy positive childhoods and to achieve against all the *Every Child Matters* outcomes.

Source: Department of Health, 2008, p. 1.

Over the past 40 years there has been an increasing amount of literature highlighting what has been called the 'hidden side' of family life. This literature has put the family under scrutiny and uncovers the risks many women, and children, face every day; there is also now a growing body of work that focuses on violence perpetrated against men. What is increasingly evident is that sociology, together with other disciplines, has been instrumental in challenging the dominant ideology that portrays family life as nurturing and harmonious. Giddens (1989) claims that home is, in fact, the most dangerous place in modern society.

domestic violence
includes physical violence as well as psychological, emotional, sexual and economic abuse. It can be perpetrated within intimate relationships as well as by other family members and can include forced marriage, genital mutilation and honour killings

If we look first at **domestic violence**, it estimated that one in four women will experience this at some point in their lives. Domestic violence features in at least one in every four divorces, and two women in England and Wales die each week at the hand of their current or former partner (Refuge, 2008). In 2001, in a speech given to the Women's Aid Federation in England, the minister for women, Sally Morgan, said that 'a man who is capable of violence towards his wife or partner is also capable of violence towards his children'.

There is a wealth of research on the effects of domestic violence on women's health and some research on its impact upon the health of children in the family. For example, a study exploring the effect of domestic violence on children under five shows that such children can suffer from emotional, physical and behavioural problems, including speech and language difficulties, regression and post-traumatic stress (Refuge, 2005).

A report on the role of health professionals in tackling domestic violence (Taket, 2004) highlighted the importance of making routine enquiries, pointing out the advantages of this as:

- giving all women basic information about the unacceptability of domestic violence in all its forms;
- giving all women information that will be relevant, not just to them, but to their friends, family members and neighbours;

Activity 11.4

Domestic violence: the role of nurses

Read the case study and then consider the questions below.

Lakshmi is twenty-seven and lives in the West Midlands with her husband of seven years; she works in a call centre. They have two children, a daughter aged four and a son aged six. When her son reached his second birthday, Lakshmi became very worried about his behaviour but her husband told her 'it was nothing'. Lakshmi wanted to take him to the doctor but her husband wouldn't allow this. When her son started school, teachers began to express concern, and he was soon referred to an educational psychologist. After some time, and after consultation with other specialists, her son was diagnosed with autism. Lakshmi told her husband but he did not believe that there was anything 'wrong' with his son. He told Lakshmi not to tell anyone about their son's condition, especially members of their family.

Lakshmi felt that she needed to tell members of her own family and spoke to her mother and sister. When she mentioned to her husband that she had done this he became really angry. He beat her unconscious, breaking her arm in two places, fracturing her cheekbone and burning her with a cigarette. While Lakshmi was hospitalized with these injuries, he told both their families that she was a liar and that she was frequently aggressive and had tried to kill him. Both families disowned her. Later that week, when Lakshmi was beginning to recover from some of her injuries, her brother-in-law was overheard by a nurse on the hospital ward threatening to kill her after she was discharged.

(a) Define domestic violence and explain how and why Lakshmi was subjected to domestic violence.

(b) Imagine that you are the nurse who overheard Lakshmi's brother-in-law threatening to kill her. What would you do? Explain your reasons.

(c) More generally, think about the role that you can play in the prevention of domestic violence and its consequences (in a personal and professional capacity). Make a list of these.

- helping to reduce the stigma of abuse and the taboo nature of domestic violence;
- giving a clear message to women that they are not alone, that abuse is unacceptable, and that there are services available to help them.

As most physical abuse occurs in the privacy of the family home it often remains invisible. It is suggested that most physical assaults on children are not reported as crimes, and parents who perpetrate these assaults are not defined as abusive. However, what is important to note is that when children are killed it is usually by their parents. Cheal (2002) suggests abusive parents kill children of all ages, but those at greatest risk are very young children who are more likely to die when they are exposed to severe physical abuse. Accurate figures on abuse as a cause of death in children are very difficult to come by, but the implication for children's physical health and emotional well-being cannot be overstated.

It is important when thinking about abuse within the family that we recognize that this is not always perpetrated by men against

---

Activity 11.5   **Families can harm your health**

In 2007 the National Centre for Social Research, together with researchers at King's College, London, produced a report on behalf of the charity Comic Relief and the Department of Health which focused on the prevalence of abuse and neglect of older people. Table 11.1 shows some of the findings of this research. The commentary that follows shows the reaction to this report by the charity Carers UK, an organization which campaigns for the rights of carers.

Examine table 11.1 and read the commentary, then answer the questions below.

Table 11.1 The mistreatment of older people (percentages)

Relationship of perpetrator	Type of mistreatment[a]				
	Neglect	Financial	Interpersonal[b]	Any abuse (excl. neglect)	Any mistreatment
Partner	70	13	57	40	51
Other family	58	54	37	43	49
Close friend	3	2	6	5	5
Care worker	14	31	–	12	13

Notes: [a] Respondents were able to give more than one answer.
[b] Interpersonal abuse included psychological, physical and sexual abuse.
Source: Adapted from O'Keefe et al., 2007, table 4.1, p. 59.

Carers UK reaction to elder abuse report, 14 June 2007

> Commenting on the UK Study of Abuse and Neglect, Imelda Redmond, Chief Executive of Carers UK said: 'This is the first in-depth study of elder abuse that has been undertaken and it challenges some of the prejudices that people have that domestic abuse stops when someone gets older.'

This survey shows, quite clearly, that it continues into older age. This is wholly unacceptable and needs to be urgently tackled. We welcome the measures being announced today by Ministers, such as the registers of abuse.

The research highlights some shocking facts such as the level of sexual abuse. It also raises critical questions about the nature of relationships between the older person and their abuser. For example, if the person carrying out the abuse is supposed to be caring for them, what agreement do they have about caring?

Is the abuser withholding support to make the older person suffer on purpose or are they simply not able to provide the level of care and support that the older person wants them to? For example they may not be able to visit as often as the older person would like. Whilst systematic abuse needs to be firmly and swiftly dealt with, we must also recognize that in some cases there is a mismatch between expectations and the support that can actually be provided.

This research is helpful because it challenges prejudices. We also need more research to unpick some of these more complicated questions to look at the real risks of abuse and we need urgent action to tackle persistent abuse for people of all ages, including older people.

(a)   To what extent do you think that the family can make you sick?

(b)   What do you think might be some of the methodological problems encountered when researching abuse of older people or other vulnerable groups (it might be useful to re-read parts of chapter 1)?

(c)   To what extent is the home the most dangerous place in modern society?

(d)   Can nurses make a contribution to making the family a safer place?

women or by parents against their children; it can also take the form of women abusing men or a child abusing a parent, and can occur within same-sex relationships or between siblings (Bernardes, 1997).

Families play an enormous role in providing care for others, but families can also harm your health.

Summary and Resources

Summary

- The ideology underpinning the nuclear family is still pervasive, but the reality today is that many of us live in families that bear little resemblance to this model.

- The ideology of the nuclear family has played an important role in informing the organization and delivery of health care in Britain. Nurses should be sensitive to this and avoid stereotyping families according to this ideology.

- Families are pivotal to the maintenance of health, but at the same time are facing a growing responsibility to care for sick, frail and disabled people; this can place an increasing pressure on family members of which nurses should be aware.

- Some family members, particularly women, are perceived to be 'naturally' more inclined to caring and nurturing roles, with the majority of the health task role being deemed their responsibility.

- Whilst families can be of vital support for many individuals, there are also occasions when families can affect health negatively, and it is important to recognize that not everyone's experience of family life is positive.

Questions for Discussion

1 Is it important for health professionals to challenge common-sense (or traditional) ideas about 'the family'? How may they do this?

2 Why and how do families play an important role in maintaining health?

3 Why is it important to consider the diversity of family life in nursing work?

Further Reading

E. Dermot: *Intimate Fatherhood: A Sociological Analysis*. London: Routledge, 2008.
A really interesting book which focuses on contemporary fatherhood and men's parenting behaviour, allowing you to explore this aspect of family life in more depth.

C. Gatrell: *Hard Labour: The Sociology of Parenthood, Family Life and Career*. Buckingham: Open University Press, 2002.
An innovative book exploring fatherhood, motherhood and family life.

H. Graham: *Women, Health and Family*. Brighton: Wheatsheaf, 1984. A classic text that considers the relationship between women's role in the family and health.

Also see www.politybooks.com/sociologyfornurses for additional useful resources.

References

Asthma UK n.d.: www.asthma.org.uk [last accessed 13 November 2008].

Barrett, M., and McIntosh, M. 1991: *The Anti-Social Family*. London: Verso.

Bernardes, J. 1997: *Family Studies: An Introduction*. London: Routledge.

Bond, J., and Bond, S. 1994: *Sociology and Health Care: An Introduction for Nurses and other Healthcare Professionals*. 2nd edn, Amsterdam: Elsevier.

Budig, M. 2004: 'Feminism and the family'. In J. Scott, J. Treas and M. Richards (eds), *The Blackwell Companion to the Sociology of Families*. Oxford: Blackwell, pp. 416–34.

Bunting, M. 2007: 'Family Fortunes.' *The Guardian*, 25 September; www.guardian.co.uk/world/2004/sep/25/2020.madeleinebunting [last accessed 13 November 2008].

Carers UK 2007: 'Carers UK reaction to elder abuse report', 14 June; www.carersuk.org/Newsandcampaigns/News/1181828209 [last accessed 13 November 2008].

Cheal, D. 2002: *Sociology of Family Life*. Basingstoke: Palgrave.

Department of Health, 2008: *Carers at the Heart of the 21st-Century Families and Communities: 'A Caring System on your Side. A Life of your Own'*. London: HMSO.

Doane, G. H., and Varcoe, C. 2006: 'The "hard spots" of family nursing – connecting across difference and diversity'. *Journal of Family Nursing*, 12(1), 7–21.

Engels, F. [1845] 1999: *The Condition of the Working Class in England in 1844*, ed. D. McLellan. Oxford: Oxford University Press.

Fiese, B. H. 2008: 'Breathing life into family processes: introduction to the special issue on families and asthma'. *Family Processes*, 47(1), 1–5.

Giddens, A. 1989: *Sociology*. Cambridge: Polity.

GINA (Global Initiative for Asthma) 2007: *Global Strategy for Asthma Management and Prevention*. www.ginasthma.org [last accessed 13 November 2008].

Graham, H. 1999: 'The informal sector of welfare: a crisis in caring?' In G. Allen (ed.), *The Sociology of the Family*. Oxford: Blackwell, pp. 283–300.

Griffiths, R. 1988: *Community Care: Agenda for Action: A Report to the Secretary of State for Social Services*. London: HMSO.

Hall, C. 1982: 'The home turned upside down? The working-class family in cotton textiles 1780–1850'. In E. Whitelegg, M. Arnott, V. Beechey, L. Birke, S. Himmelweit, D. Leonard, S. Ruehl and M. A. Speakman (eds), *The Changing Experience of Women*. Oxford: Martin Robertson, pp. 17–30.

Jackson, S. 1997: 'Women, marriage and family relationships'. In V. Robinson and D. Richardson (eds), *Introducing Women's Studies*, Basingstoke: Macmillan, pp. 323–49.

Jocham, H. R., Dassen, T., Widdershoven, G., et al. 2006: 'Quality of life in palliative care cancer patients: a literature review'. *Journal of Clinical Nursing*, 15(9), 1188–95.

Laslett, P. 1972: 'Mean household size in England since the sixteenth century'. In P. Laslett and R. Wall (eds), *Household and Family in Past Time*. Cambridge: Cambridge University Press, pp. 125–58.

Marchant, J. M., Newcombe, P. A., Juniper, E. F., et al. 2008: 'What is the burden of chronic cough for families?' CHEST, 134(2), 303–9.

O'Keefe, M., Hills, A., Doyle, M., McCreadie, C., Scholes, S., Constantine, R., Tinker, A., Manthorpe, J., Biggs, S., and Erens, B. 2007: *UK Study of Elder Abuse and Neglect of Older People: Prevalence Survey Report*. London: National Centre for Social Research/King's College.

ONS (Office for National Statistics) 2001: Census 2001 information; www.statistics.gov.uk/StatBase/Product.asp?vlnk=9343 [last accessed 13 November 2008].

Parsons, T. 1955: *Family Socialization and Interaction Process*. Glencoe, IL: Free Press.

Princess Royal Trust for Carers 2008: *Key facts about carers*. London: Princess Royal Trust for Carers; www.carers.org/articles/ information-for-press,2822,CA.html [last accessed 13 November 2008].

Refuge 2005: *Refuge Assessment and Intervention for Pre-School Children Exposed to Domestic Violence, August 2005*. London: Refuge; www.refuge.org.uk/cms_content_refuge/attachments/ Effects%20of%20domestic%20violence%20on%20pre-school% 20children.pdf [last accessed 13 November 2008].

Refuge 2008: *Domestic Violence: The Facts*. www.refuge.org.uk/ page_11-2_12-162_13-175_.htm [last accessed 13 November 2008].

Scott, J., Treas, J. and Richards, M. (eds) 2004: *The Blackwell Companion to the Sociology of Families*. Oxford: Blackwell.

Taket, A. 2004: *Tackling Domestic Violence: The Role of Health Professionals*. Development and practice report 32. London: Home Office.

Weeks, J., Heaphy, B. and Donovan, C. 2004: 'The lesbian and gay family'. In J. Scott, J. Treas and M. Richards (eds), *The Blackwell Companion to the Sociology of Families*. Oxford: Blackwell, pp. 340–55.

12 Primary Care in the Community

Mike Filby

Key issues in this chapter

- Defining primary care
- The role of general practice
- Policy developments within primary care
- Nursing, primary and community care

At the end of this chapter you should be able to . . .

- explore different definitions of primary care;
- understand the history of general practice and the role it plays within the modern health service;
- discuss policy developments within primary care;
- recognize the position of nursing in primary and community services.

1 Introduction

In a recent formal meeting, primary care was described as 'a mystery'. As the individual who made this comment was a primary care manager with more than twenty-five years' experience in community nursing, this was a little surprising. It did also beg the question as to what newly qualified or student nurses can be expected to make of primary care if this is the view of an experienced practitioner!

This chapter seeks to make sense of the mystery of primary care. It begins with a brief discussion of the organization of primary care and the way in which this has changed over time and then considers the role of general practice, reflecting on its history and the part it plays within modern health care. In the next section, attention is given to some of the key policy

developments within primary care, and the chapter concludes
with a discussion of the role of nurses in primary care and
community service provision.

2   The 'mystery' of primary care

Sociologically speaking, the dynamic of change is driven by the
dilemmas of a publicly funded, universal health service, as the state –
which is responsible for the management of the service – strives to
balance a number of competing forces in the context of economic
constraints. In addition, governments of the day have a distinct
preference to retain sufficient popularity to be re-elected, and so also
drive this dynamic for change!

In a classic text, the German sociologist Claus Offe (Offe, 1984)
has described this as the contradiction of the welfare state. His point
is that, while the state is compelled to support such systems, its
inability to do so effectively undermines its legitimacy. Be that as it
may, it can certainly be agreed that universal health systems, free at
the point of delivery, such as the NHS, exhibit recurring dilemmas.
These are reflected in a permanent process of policy and health
service puzzle-solving and organizational swings of centralization
and decentralization, autonomy and control. The only certainty in all
this is that the shelf life of such organizational and policy solutions is
limited; while particular policies are important and require attention,
sociologically it is as important to appreciate the overall constraints
of the system which generate a permanent imperative of reform. This
is not to say, however, that nothing changes or that, indeed, in a very
unsociological phrase, things do not get better. They do, and there
have been tangible improvements in many services and patient
experiences over the past few years. However, as discussed in more
detail below, one of the key features or constraints of the primary care
system is the nature and economic form of doctoring outside of
hospitals that is general practice. 'Dealing' with general practice has
been central to policy dilemmas in the NHS.

The early part of the decade saw the establishment of **primary care
trusts** (PCTs) as a principal organizational expression of a 'primary
care-led NHS'. PCTs have substantial resources to commission and
provide a wide range of health care services to citizens in the
community. Following merger rounds, PCTs are substantial
organizations, but they were also required to separate their
'commissioning' and 'provider' arms by the end of 2008. Following
the Darzi (DH, 2008b) proposals, services will be contracted to
independent organizations, including 'social enterprises'. This
reflects a preoccupation in the last decade or so with 'contestability'
in the system as a proxy for competition.

primary care trusts
are primary care
organizations within the
NHS. They were first
created in 2000 to
commission, provide and
develop primary care
services in a geographical
area and were established
across the whole of
England by April 2002,
replacing primary care
groups. Following the
Darzi review (DH, 2008a),
PCTs were encouraged to
adopt a different form of
name, removing the
reference to 'primary
care' and replacing it
with, for example,
(Placename) NHS Trust

payment by results replaced the block contract method of commissioning hospital services by PCTs with an activity-based system with a set of nationally applicable tariffs for different types of procedures. These were initially based on the actual average cost of procedures. PbR is intended therefore to provide incentives to greater efficiency by reducing costs below the tariff; to increase output, as this leads to more revenue; and to improve quality of care as both price competition is eliminated and patient choice mechanisms establish quality as the competitive advantage

National Service Frameworks were introduced in 1998 in an attempt to improve the quality and consistency of care in a number of priority clinical areas. NSFs typically comprise a set of service standards, implementation guidance and performance measures which are intended to apply nationally

PCTs also commission services from acute hospital trusts for their populations according to a 'payment by results' (PbR) system introduced in 2003; in 2008, 80 per cent of the NHS budget was channelled through PCTs. This reflects a further important feature of primary care which has also become a focus for levering changes in other parts of the system – in the case of PbR, to drive increases in productivity (reducing costs) and quality (through patient choice 'choose and book') in hospitals. PCTs also have obligations to local population health improvement and the implementation of National Service Frameworks (NSF) and other central government yardsticks.

The changing landscape of primary care will continue to offer opportunities for nurses. Nurse-led services are an increasing feature of out-of-hospital care, including the management of long-term conditions, where experienced community nurses are the key caseworkers co-ordinating medical and nursing support to improve life quality and lessen hospital (re)admissions (Hewison and Cox, 2009). In some cases of high health need, nurses have also taken over practices, employing GPs and other staff (Houghton, 2002). Aspects of the Darzi proposals present further opportunities for nursing in the design and delivery of primary and community services (and these are discussed below). The developments in the role of the 'hospital' (chapter 13) and the policy emphasis on the provision of health care 'closer to home' provide the context for an increasing range, specialization and challenge in patient-centred, nurse-led services.

Innovation in primary care: the effects on nursing

Nurses have also played a key role in extending access to primary care in the community. Although various means of providing for urgent out-of-hours care have developed following the withdrawal of this service in the 2003 GP contract, nurse-led services such as NHS Direct and walk-in centres (WiC) have been an important innovation. Initial hopes that such centres would impact on unnecessary attendances at A&E, for example, were overly optimistic. There is evidence of some substitution, but the norm is for new general health care services simply to amplify demand.

Nevertheless, in many areas WiCs have met an expressed demand for non-bookable, extended opening hours, nurse-led primary care. Nurses, then, have demonstrated the capacity to lead user-responsive services in the community, and this trend is likely to increase.

However, at the other end of the continuum, many nurses, and practice nurses in particular, find their professional aspirations and development possibilities restricted, their employment conditions poor, and work experience infused with traditional gender expectations and power relations (for a further discussion of gender relations, see chapter 5). A National Audit Office report on the new GP contract (NAO, 2008) noted that significant numbers of practice staff, including nurses, did not have contracts of employment.

A walk-in health
care centre

A central reality of primary care is that small, male-dominated businesses remain at the heart of service delivery.

These are two faces of primary care. They reflect the problem of variability in provision and quality which has been high on the government's modernization agenda for primary care, as represented in the National Plan, which noted that 'The development of primary care services is the key to the modernization of the NHS' (DH, 2000, p. 79) but that there was a 'huge gap between the best and the rest in the NHS' (ibid., p. 27). Almost a decade later, however, there remains considerable variability in term of both access and the quality of patient experience in primary care between different PCT populations (Healthcare Commission, 2008).

In the discussion which follows, attention will be drawn to the meaning of primary care, the critical role of general practice in the structuring of primary care, the more recent development of primary care policy and the link with community care. The chapter concludes with some critical speculation on the position and politics of nursing in primary care.

3   What is 'primary' about primary care?

'Primary' care is not a natural given of reality, rather the outcome of the interaction of different ways of speaking about health and health care – that is to say, a discourse. For example, starting with the Conservative government's White Paper *Primary Care: Delivering the Future* (DH, 1996), official policy discourse became more prominent and served to expand the notion of primary care. Indeed, 'primary care' – as opposed to primary health care, or even primary medical care – symbolized a move towards a more inclusive meaning of the term, albeit one that stopped short of including social care.

Peckham and Exworthy (2003) provide a very good account of how definitions of primary care have reflected ideas about levels of care, activities, functions and geographical provision and how these interact with ideologies of health and health care. They draw attention to the fact that the notion of primary care originated in the Dawson Report, published in 1920 (Dawson, 1920), to refer to a 'level' of care in an ascending hierarchy of specialism. This is reflected in the 'point of first contact'.

Activity 12.1	**Health priorities in primary care**
	Use an internet search engine, such as Google, to locate the websites of your local and one other PCT. Identify similarities and differences in the health priorities and issues presented by the two organizations.

A home visit: primary health care being delivered in a patient's home

An enormous range of services is now being provided by primary care organizations (PCOs) and, as we have noted, these will likely both expand and become more specialized with the 'care closer to home' agenda. The organizing rationale, for example, in managing chronic illness in the community or services for older people is centred on providing care and support for patients at home. Many such people have entered secondary care directly as an acute emergency and are being referred back for some package of ongoing and often complex care. The historical emphasis on 'first contact' as the defining feature of primary care also owes something to the specific British context of the NHS where access to specialist services required referral from a GP. However, in other countries individuals have more freedom, albeit related to economic resources, to seek care directly from a specialist. Residents of inner cities in Britain, which are not overprovided with health care services, frequently use their local hospital accident and emergency department as their point of first and preferred contact. So, does this make the A&E department a primary care service? From the user's point of view it is; providers tend to differ. Indeed, bizarrely perhaps, it has been mooted that GP practices should be fined when patients in their list use A & E services 'inappropriately'.

This example demonstrates the differing definitions of primary care by patients and health care practitioners. As Williams (2000) has shown, while health care professionals in the field have few difficulties in subscribing to the value and values of primary care, their occupational histories and cultures mean that they often accent these in different ways. District nurses are more likely to see primary care as bringing health care near to where people live, whereas GPs and practice nurses are prone to emphasize the provision of a range of services under one (practice) roof, and this is related very much to what they actually do as primary care practitioners.

Activity 12.2 **Primary care meanings**

During your practice placements, make a mental note of spontaneous references to primary care among professionals and patients.

(a) Try to identify similarities and differences in the working meanings that different role holders reflect.

(b) Exchange informal notes with your peers from your own and other branches of nursing; are there any systematic differences, and does it matter if there are?

An increasing emphasis in health policy concerns the role of PCOs in the improvement of the nation's health and the imperative to work in partnership with agencies across a spectrum of public services in achieving this (also see chapter 14). Indeed it has become increasingly recognized that many of the key factors impacting on population health are outwith the control of primary care trusts.

From the above discussion it could be argued that the concept of primary care has possibly outlived its usefulness.

4   General practice

Primary care has moved into the policy spotlight in recent years, but the role of the peculiar institution of general practice is critical to an understanding of primary care and, indeed, community services in Britain. It is not simply that general practice is 'part of a complex web of primary care services' (Audit Commission, 2002, p. 12), but that general practice has a determining impact on the shape and texture of this sector of health care, and indeed on the structure of primary care nursing. As the Audit Commission report notes, for many people primary care and general practice are one and the same thing. This represents something of a triumph for a branch of doctoring which for most of its history remained in the shadow of more prestigious varieties of hospital-centred medicine. While general practice has evolved, it persists in its historically recognizable form. The introduction in 2003 of a new contract for GPs which attempted to relate elements of payment to performance and quality and the encouragement by the government to new providers in primary care seem more rather than less likely to undermine the historical leverage of general practice over this sphere of care. The resilience of general practice as an economic and political form, however, is not to be underestimated. Although the National Audit Office reported in 2008 that the new contract was beginning to evidence some of the intended benefits, its most notable achievement to date has been to raise GP incomes by nearly 60 per cent in three years and to improve GP recruitment. The consistency of care had improved but it had cost much more than anticipated, productivity had fallen somewhat, and there had been little improvement in the development of services in deprived areas; PCTs still lacked adequate means of performance management of GP practices (NAO, 2008).

A visit to the local doctor is often the first port of call when a person feels unwell.

General practice continues to remain popular with the public. The national survey of local health services in 2008 showed high levels of patient satisfaction with the nature of the service they received, though access to those services continued to be a problem, with persistent local variations (Healthcare Commission, 2008). The position of general practice also continues to be affirmed in policy statements. While signalling further regulation of general practice and the extension of performance management through the contract, the Darzi review echoed the NHS *Plan* several years earlier in referring to general practice as 'the bedrock of our primary care system' (DH 2008b, p. 18). In policy commentary, general practice has been referred to as 'the lynchpin of primary care' (Sibbald, 2000, p. 14), and an authoritative analysis of general practice concluded 'that UK general practice is indeed a major jewel in the NHS crown' (Moon and North, 2000, p. 175). The Audit Commission (2002) report also drew attention to the comprehensiveness of cover afforded by general practice and its celebrated gatekeeping role to more specialized services, which is often seen as a major factor in the relative cost-effectiveness of the NHS. It is yet to be seen whether this role will be modified by the increased emphasis on patient choice of secondary provider.

gatekeeping   this term portrays the key role which general practitioners have traditionally played in managing the access of patients to secondary and other health care services

Yet general practice has been a source of government frustration, particularly around variations in the quality of services and in the drive to improve flexibility of access to primary care. As Maynard (2002, p. 19) commented wryly, 'Like pub food, general practice varies enormously from the excellent to the deadly'. Lurking in the concerns about quality are issues of accountability and control, and these have become more pronounced as primary care has assumed more strategic importance for the NHS as a whole. The relationship between the government and general practice has therefore been an ambiguous one, conditioned by what might be called the historic settlement of 1948 which saw the creation of the NHS and institutionalized the modern form of general practice.

While the history is complex, general practice can be said to have emerged in the early nineteenth century from the jumbled ranks of apothecaries and surgeons providing services to the expanding urban middle classes. Despite being incorporated in the medical establishment though the Medical Registration Act of 1858, general practice continued to occupy a lowly position in the medical hierarchy for the ensuing century. The national insurance reforms of 1911 provided the beginnings of a more secure economic position for general practice through the system of capitation payments based on patient lists, while continuing to allow GPs considerable autonomy in carrying out their business.

Nervous about the role of the state and the pre-eminence of hospital medicine (Moon and North, 2000), GPs initially resisted the plans for the creation of the NHS. This was finally overcome by the concession to allow them to retain their status as independent contractors. This essentially means that GPs (albeit through a collective agreement) would contract with the state to provide a range of care for patients but not be directly employed by it; capitation payments remained central to what became an increasingly complicated system of remuneration as successive governments attempted to 'buy' service development in primary care. This contractual context and the evolution of particular work practices of doctors in primary care had led one commentator to talk about 'the invention of general practice' (Marinker, 1998). This is a useful term in underscoring the proposition that general practice is the dominant but not the only way in which medical labour in the community might be organized.

It is difficult to underestimate the importance of the independent contractor status for the emergent mentality of general practice and the consequent impact on the development of primary care nursing. For example, GPs, through the General Medical Services Committee, mounted a determined and successful campaign against the proposals of the famous Cumberledge Report (DHSS, 1986) for community nursing (Sibbald, 2000), which flew (too) directly in the face of the economic and power relations in general practice and was sidestepped by the government. The 1990 GP contract and the

GP fundholding, introduced in 1990, meant that GP practices were able to hold budgets to purchase care for their patients; it was abolished in 1999

◄ development of GP fundholding (GPFH) expanded the profile of primary care and nursing services, but these were shaped by the interests of general practice (Wilson, 2000).

More recently, in 2008, the British Medical Association (BMA) on behalf of GPs launched a short, sharp and very effective campaign against early proposals in the Darzi review for the establishment of 'polyclinics'. In fact, in less than a matter of weeks the BMA managed to obtain over a million signatures for a petition calling for the proposals to be dropped: they were! While it was not entirely clear what kind of model was envisaged, essentially, as the label 'polyclinic' suggests, the intention was to bring together in one physical establishment a range of primary and community care services together with some secondary care. This implies the co-location of services and providers under some integrated management structure and possibly run by an independent organization. It is intended to provide better access to care, improved quality through the possibility of more local direct access to specialist and integrated care, and probably more effective use of resources, which is more difficult in the small-scale enterprises such as GP practices (Corrigan, 2005). The King's Fund undertook a policy analysis pointing up both the opportunities and the risks of this development in the United Kingdom context (Imison, Naylor and Maybin, 2008). The opposition of the BMA, however, reflected more the threats to the economic interests and independence of general practitioners in the primary care system. What emerged was a proposal for more GP-led health clinics, little more than an opportunity for the co-location of GP practices, which of itself does not guarantee joint working, integrated care or more flexible access.

It is therefore important to be aware that the organization of doctoring in the community as 'general practice' is a specific historical and political outcome. Recent policy developments signal an attempt to introduce more diversity in organization and provision to meet the particular circumstances of local communities and to adjust for the trends in the doctoring population. As we have seen, however, these have to contend with a deep reserve of potential resistance from general practitioners. There is no room for doubt that, while they care about the care they give, GPs also care about their businesses.

Policy overview

Following the publication of *Shifting the Balance of Power: Securing Delivery* (DH, 2001) primary care trusts were consolidated in April 2002 as the standard issue PCO throughout England. At the same time, the district health authorities and regional offices of the National Health Service Executive were also abolished, to be replaced by strategic health authorities. Parallel (but different) developments were in train in Scotland and Wales.

The creation of these organizations in primary care represented the realization of change prefigured by the new Labour government's first health White Paper, *The New NHS, Modern, Dependable* (DH, 1997). In policy terms, however, the increasingly sharper focus on primary care emerged a decade or so before the Labour programme which, while formally abolishing the marketization of health care, developed some of the emerging ideas for the structuring of primary care. The policy developments reflect the central dilemma for successive governments bequeathed by the politics of the 1948 NHS Act, whereby the providers remained essentially small private businesses, contracting their services to the NHS. Issues of development, direction, compliance, accountability and quality are difficult to manage in this sort of relationship and can only be crudely addressed in the contracting process, although the 2003 GP contract focused much more on quality through the Quality and Outcomes Framework (QOF) (see below).

However, the introduction of the internal market by the Conservative government, following the 1990 NHS and Community Care Act, established the distinction between purchasers and providers of care and most significantly introduced the system of GP fundholding. Successive waves of GPs took up this option such that, by the time fundholding was formally abolished in 1999, 75 per cent of patients were covered by these arrangements. Establishing GPs with purchasing power was intended to lever in more responsiveness and efficiency in the providers (hospital and community trusts) but also to modify the GP gatekeeping role, adding the responsibility for allocating resources to the power of referral to secondary care. This might be seen as the beginning of the incorporation of GPs into the process of service development.

However, as Peckham and Exworthy (2003, p. 76) note, 'reform was being conducted by primary care but not for primary care'. The notion of a 'primary care-led NHS' was coined in 1994 on the back of further development of the fundholding system; a government 'listening exercise' resulted in a White Paper, *Choice and Opportunity: Primary Care – The Future* (1996), followed by legislation in the last days of the Conservative government, the NHS (Primary Care) Act (1997). The thrust of policy was towards making the frameworks within which primary care services could be developed more flexibly, particularly in areas with client groups that had not been well served by the traditional arrangements for general practice (for example, economic migrants). Thus the Act allowed the setting up of what are known as **personal medical services (PMS) pilots**; significantly, it was the incoming Labour government of 1997 that implemented this policy, and PMS contracts continue to co-exist with the main contract, covering about 37 per cent of GPs.

personal medical services pilots were introduced following the 1997 NHS (Primary Care) Act. PMS operates through a local contract negotiated with, typically, a PCT to provide specific services to meet locally identified needs. Providers such as nurses, allied health professionals and community trusts could contract to provide the service

Primary care trusts

The creation of free-standing PCOs such as primary care trusts is one of the notable developments of health policy in recent years under the Labour government. In abolishing the internal market and GP fundholding, however, the government retained the distinction between purchasing – replaced by the wider concept of commissioning – and provision of services. This was embodied organizationally in the creation first in 1998 of primary care groups (PCGs) and then, by 2002, by a smaller number of more autonomous primary care trusts formed through mergers of the former. Further rationalization of PCTs has continued so that they typically cover large population areas; their governance arrangements have also evolved to reflect their responsibilities to the system as a whole rather than to local professional and community reference points.

The functions of PCTs were essentially the same as for their predecessors. These were about:

- improving (and addressing inequalities in) the health of their community;
- developing primary and community health services, through investing to improve the quality of care and the integration of services;
- commissioning secondary services. (DH, 1999)

The initial ethos of localism has become more difficult to sustain as PCTs encompass generally larger populations and a number of differing localities and communities. The burden of expectation placed on PCTs by government has been enormous, and the imposition of central targets has tended to unbalance the commitment to responsiveness to locally determined health needs. As noted at the beginning of the chapter, government policy is inducing further shifts in the focus of primary care trusts in the direction of commissioning health services rather than their provision. The Department of Health developed a competency framework for 'world class commissioning' by PCTs, revealing in the wake of this shift of role something of a deficit in the commissioning capability in these organizations.

Indeed, primary care trusts have appeared as organizers of local health systems rather than purveyors specifically of primary care, and they quickly took up the Darzi invitation to drop the reference to primary care in their titles. The notion of a primary care-led NHS has indeed become less prominent as the decade has progressed, subsumed if not replaced by the banner of a 'patient-led NHS'. A Department of Health (2005) guidance paper under that heading highlighted the need for a shift from the establishment of capability, structures, and so on, to a concern with content process, quality and patient experience for a service more responsive to patients. The motifs of 'choice', 'personalized care' and 'supporting self care', for example, were important organizing ideas.

In the context of a patient-led NHS, an 'innovation' in respect of primary care was the introduction of **practice-based commissioning** (PBC), which was intended to incentivize the development of services responsive to local needs. As with GP fundholding a decade earlier, this is more GP directed than patient led. There has been slow but substantial take-up of this 'voluntary scheme', which involves commissioning or purchasing with virtual as opposed to real cash budgets; the 'real' cash remains with the PCT. Groups or consortia of practices rather than the individual practice have operated as the commissioning unit, though there are some of these. Most PBC is targeted at the demand management for hospital services using PbR and, as part of this, in redesigning patient pathways, providing some services at practice level, and in drug prescribing. Practices are able to reinvest any notional savings in new or enhanced services with the approval of the PCT. This contrasts with fundholding in that there is no obligation to reinvest any savings accrued to the 'profits of the GP practice'. Developments in primary care services such as PBC are highly dependent on the engagement of GPs, and this is susceptible to contractual matters, pay and the reaction to other reform issues.

The Darzi review essentially underscored the drift of the patient-led NHS (DH, 2008a). It endorsed the world-class commissioning assurance framework and recommended the renewal and expansion of PBC, with more careful distinctions to be drawn between

practice-based commissioning was introduced in 2004. It allows individual but more likely groups of GP practices to commission/ 'purchase' a range of services (a range agreed with the PCT) for their practice populations against a notional budget. The intention is that, with financial and provider performance information, practices will seek to lever improved service design in both services commissioned in secondary care and those provided at the practice level. In principle, efficiency savings in the budget will release resources for the development of other services by the practice/consortium (in contrast to GP fundholding, where surpluses could be retained by the practices) multi-professional (practice) commissioning and the role of GP practices in enhancing the range of services. It echoed the emphasis on care closer to home and the issues around long-term conditions and preventative health care.

The approach to general practice was mixed. The early mooted proposal for the setting up of polyclinics was seen off by a determined and expert campaign mounted by the BMA. A watered-down version in the form of a proposal for (150) GP-led health clinics effectively evaded issues around power, direction and collaboration in general practice and deferred to the oppositional force of the GPs. On the other hand, the QOF was to be extended and to include incentives for clinical effectiveness, responsiveness and preventative work by GPs; there was to be more choice of GP for patients, and historic protective income payments were to be phased out. More significantly, GPs were to be subject to a new quality and safety regime through the Care Quality Commission, with an accreditation scheme for practices. While the emphasis was on quality and patient experience, the approach was essentially more of the same, but extending control and regulation into the historically fraught area of general practice. Proposals for the delivery and accountability of community services through the development of new integrated care organizations and social enterprises seems likely to undermine the overall dominance in the out-of-hospital care system by general practice, but history demands caution in this respect.

Towards integrated care?

Interestingly, as primary care came to prominence in the 1990s, it increasingly overshadowed its policy twin, community care, which had arguably been the organizing concept in social policy in the 1980s and early 1990s. As Lewis (1999) observes, both concepts have recent and similar histories, but paradoxically they have been dealt with separately in policy terms, whereas on the ground their implications for users, patients and professionals are closely linked.

The watershed in community care policy occurred with the implementation (in 1993) of the 1990 NHS and Community Care Act, following thirty years or so of policy debate driven at root by the economic costs of long-stay hospitals. The 1990s also saw the development of the market in the provision of social care in the community and some trialling of new forms of provision. The main target groups continued to be older people, people with learning disabilities and those with mental health problems. Older people moved increasingly centre stage as the dubious notion of 'bed-blocking' (i.e. delayed discharge) in the acute sector achieved greater policy prominence.

The model of community care which emerged in the form of 'care management' arguably reflected the needs of government more

> **Activity 12.3**   **Responsive primary and community care services**
>
> In your community placement or next visit to GP or health centre, look for signs of the Darzi vision for more responsive and flexible services in primary and community care.
>
> - What services are being offered other than appointments to see a GP?
> - Is there any evidence of attempts to engage patients or service users in service design?
> - Are there any signs that the practice or centre is promoting greater and more informed choice?
> - Are there specialist clinics taking place?
> - Search the NHS Choices website for information about the performance of the practice.

than those of users (Gorman and Postle, 2003). It also tended to weaken the position of nurses working in the community, as the lead responsibility for the negotiation of care packages with users and carers fell to social services. In addition, the reforms entailed an increasingly sharper distinction between health care and social care; the significance was that, while the former remained free at the point of delivery, social care involved charging and means testing. There were, thus, system pressures towards a tighter definition of what counted as health care in the community and on the roles of those providing it.

While the economic and policy fault line between health and social care seems fairly intractable, it has been overlaid more recently with the concept of 'out-of-hospital care' and crystallized in the Darzi outline proposals for a renewed commitment to integrated care. While 'out-of-hospital care' may comprise a spectrum of primary and community services and care groups, the core dynamic for this notion is the belated discovery of 'long-term conditions' (LTCs) (see also chapter 7). Conditions such as diabetes, heart failure and respiratory disease were seen to be having a disproportionate impact on acute in-patient days, emergency admissions, health care spend and, not least, the political goals concerning waiting times (Hewison and Cox, 2009). As the number of individuals suffering some form and degree of chronic illness(es) is huge, so is the scale of the challenge of service redesign. The model being developed – albeit with the customary local variation – hinges on the development of integrated, multi-professional care pathways appropriate to different levels of disease progression, co-ordinated typically by nurses (currently community matrons) – crucially, a model in which the structure of care is driven by the patient with the intended outcome of more individualized care.

Community meetings can help local people shape the provision and delivery of health care services.

As Hewison and Cox (2009) note, there is a pivotal opportunity for nurse-led teams to take responsibility, notwithstanding the funding issues, for all the health and social care needs of patients. Indeed, it is difficult to see how the broader out-of-hospital care strategy will succeed without nurses at the centre. However, Kelly and Symonds (2003) argue that the history of community nursing since the early nineteenth century is one of somewhat passive adaptation to emergent discourses such as those of the new community – and primary – care. As Malin et al. (1999) suggest, community nurses, albeit lacking the power resources of other groups, have been largely reactive and apolitical with respect to issues of the organization of care. This, then, is also a pivotal point for nursing leadership, in terms both of the challenge facing the professions and of the sustainability of patient-centred care.

Activity 12.4	Community care in action

During your practice placement, seek an opportunity to attend a multi-disciplinary discharge care planning meeting.

(a) Reflect on the roles of the professionals, patient/user and close relatives in determining the plan outcome.

(b) Consider the sense in which the outcome might be described as care by the community.

The focus of the next section is on the opportunities and potential for nurses and nursing in the changing context of primary care and community services.

5   Nursing, general practice and primary care

Although nursing roles in primary care have by no means been static, to date these have tended to reflect the interests, changing responsibilities and workloads of GPs. New nursing roles such as that of 'nurse practitioner' were conditioned by the circumstances of particular GP practice interests and as a result varied considerably in title and content. Such roles tended to embody an ambiguous notion of nurse autonomy – that is, nurses were subject to the overall control of the doctor while working without direct supervision. On the whole, GPs have successfully resisted genuine autonomy in nursing practice, even in areas where medical issues are not relevant (Ashburner and Birch, 1999), and, by default, have thus determined the paths of nursing development.

The initial reforms around the 'primary care-led NHS' were designed to lever changes in the wider health care system and did not on the whole disturb the settled power relationships in which general practitioners were both central and dominant. While it is almost always a mistake to overestimate the impact of policy change on power relations, the later focus on reforms in primary care and the more recent thrust of the Darzi review on the nature of primary and community care services seem more likely to unhinge the traditional backdrop of power and the centrality of general practice. While it is primarily symbolic, the fact that primary care trusts rapidly took up the Darzi invitation to drop 'primary care' from their titles is significant, as primary care is increasingly subsumed as a subsector of 'out-of-hospital care'. GP-directed services, themselves increasingly diverse under PBC developments, are just one aspect of a wide spectrum of non-institutional health and care services supported by a variety of organizational provider types and mixes of professionals 'out of hospital'.

As noted, many of these have the potential to be nurse led. The model for the management of long-term conditions incorporating medical input in multi-professional teams is an example which engages with the traditional territory of general practice. Darzi also proposed to encourage staff in community health services to set up social enterprises (not-for-profit organizations) as one of a number of means of providing such services as PCTs divest themselves of the provider function. PCTs are obliged to consider such applications from staff and to award contracts if the business case stands up. While nurses are by no means the only group among the 250,000 staff in community health work, they are the most numerous, and could be expected to take a major role in such developments. On the other hand, the development of GP-led health centres and the encouragement of minor and routine surgical procedures at the practice level is likely to reinforce more traditional GP–practice nurse relations.

Contemporary developments around the reconfiguration of services will mean that teamwork remains important but is unlikely to be focused on the traditional, GP practice-centred, primary care health team model, in which the GP was more typically an absent landlord, exercising power from a distance but with little real engagement as a team player. Teams are more likely to be fluidly constructed around particular projects such as patient groups, localized health care issues or integrated care pathways which will cut across traditional primary–secondary and provider organization lines and where medical leadership is no longer the default position. As Wilson (2000) argues, networks of professionals may represent forms of collaboration and communication more appropriate for the new context while continuing to draw on teamwork skills.

Whether the opportunities for nursing presented by the new context are realized depends on many interacting factors. Not least is the 'political' organization of nurses. In order to influence the direction of change, nurses in primary and community services will be required to develop a more united front and shared analysis than in the past. This is difficult, not least because of the way nursing in general practice has been shaped by medical practitioners; individual nurses have an interest in their specific positions as nurse practitioners or practice nurses and an identity with the 'practice'. The relationship between community nursing and general practice also has a chequered history, and, while a social enterprise model in community services presents opportunities, it may also underscore the division with practice-based nursing. There is thus a key role now for nursing leadership at all levels in the 'out-of-hospital' care environment to develop and articulate nursing strategy.

Activity 12.5	Commissioning for a deprived locality

Parkside is a one-time council housing neighbourhood, with a population of about 10,000, located on the edge of a prosperous borough. The original generation of residents were relocated there in the 1960s following urban development in a nearby large city. Local authority reorganization in the 1970s transferred responsibility for the area to a council historically dominated by middle-class interests. The neighbourhood now comprises a mixture of council and other social housing and some private housing purchased under tenant discount schemes in the 1980s. It includes both high- and low-rise accommodation which is now showing its age; shopping and other facilities are few and transport links poor. The neighbourhood is predominatly white; 45 per cent of the population is over fifty-five and 40 per cent is retired and/or on benefits. Lone parenting characterizes a fifth of all households. Levels of chronic respiratory and heart disease and diabetes are relatively high, as are rates of teenage pregnancy and substance misuse.

Primary care services have been provided by the same practice for thirty years, but the two remaining partners are due to retire within six months. So far there has been no interest in the practice as a business concern, and the PCT is contemplating other ways of commissioning a primary care service.

Drawing on the Darzi first-stage review and the review of primary and community services, what suggestions would you make for the provision of such a service to the residents?

Think about, for example:

- Who should provide the service?
- Who should drive it locally?
- Where should it be provided?
- How should the community be involved?

Summary and Resources

Summary

- Primary care moved towards the centre of health care policy in the last decade but is being eclipsed by the wider 'out-of-hospital' agenda.

- The institution of general medical practice has been a crucial determinant of the shape of primary care and nursing in primary and community services and will continue to be a key stakeholder.

- Primary care organizations established to introduce more strategic management and development of primary care services have evolved into organizations which manage local systems in which primary care services are only one of number of responsibilities. In this process, the commissioning and the provision of primary and community services have become more sharply distinguished.

- The newly developing scenario in primary and community services will present opportunities for nursing development and nurse-led services, but medical domination of the politics of nursing in the community will continue in the absence of more proactive nursing organization and leadership at the local level.

Questions for Discussion

1 The distinction between primary and secondary care is taken for granted among commentators and practitioners alike and is firmly rooted in health policy. Is it still relevant in a patient-centred service?

2 A 'primary care-led NHS' has been a key policy slogan of health service reform since 1997; what evidence would you point to from your practice experience which would support or detract from service change driven by, and in, primary care?

3 From cases you may have observed, evaluate the continuing significance of the distinction between health and social care for the care of patients or clients.

Further Reading

A. Kelly and A. Symonds: *The Social Construction of Community Nursing*. Basingstoke: Palgrave Macmillan, 2003.
Kelly and Symonds present a challenging insight into primary care through their principal focus on the development of community nursing and the discourses and policies which have shaped it over time.

N. Malin, J. Manthorpe, D. Race and S. Wilmot: *Community Care for Nurses and the Caring Professions*. Buckingham, Open University Press, 1999.
This book offers an excellent overview of the development of community care policy and practice over the past three decades and discusses a number of key practice issues, with particular emphasis on the implications for health care professionals.

G. Moon and N. North: *Policy and Place: General Medical Practice in the UK*. London: Macmillan, 2000.
This text analyses policy and politics in the NHS in terms of the impact on and influence of general medical practice in the community. The discussion offers an insight into the power relations between elements of the medical profession, and nurses in particular, and the reflection of these in the development of primary care in Britain.

S. Peckham and M. Exworthy: *Primary Care in the UK*. Basingstoke: Palgrave Macmillan, 2003.
This text provides a comprehensive and authoritative discussion of the development of primary care policy in the UK. It also discusses the organization of primary care and a number of key contemporary issues such as inter-professional working.

For further resources on this topic, go to the website at www.politybooks.com/sociologyfornurses.

References

Ashburner, L., and Birch, K. 1999: 'Professional control issues between medicine and nursing in primary care'. In A. L. Mark and S. Dopson (eds), *Organisational Behaviour in Health Care: the Research Agenda*. Basingstoke: Macmillan, pp. 63–76.

Audit Commission, 2002: *A Focus on General Practice in England*. London: Audit Commission.

Corrigan, P. 2005: *Size Matters: Making GP Services Fit for Purpose*. London, New Health Network.

Dawson, B., 1920: *Report on the Future Provision of Medical and Allied Services*, Cmd 693. London: HMSO.

DH (Department of Health), 1996: *Primary Care: Delivering the Future*. London: HMSO.

DH 1997: *The New NHS: Modern, Dependable*. London: HMSO.

DH 1999: *Primary Care Trusts: Establishment, the Preparatory Period and their Functions*. London: DH.

DH 2000: *The National Plan*. London: HMSO.

DH 2001: *Shifting the Balance of Power: Securing Delivery*. London: DH.

DH 2005: *Creating a Patient-Led NHS: Delivering the NHS Improvement Plan*. London: DH.

DH 2008a: *High Quality care for All: NHS Next Stage Review Final Report*. London: DH (Darzi Report).

DH 2008b: *NHS Next Stage Review: Our Vision for Primary and Community Care*. London: DH.

DHSS (Department of Health and Social Security) 1986: *Neighbourhood Nursing: a Focus for Care. The Cumberlege Report. Report of the Community Nursing Review*. London: HMSO.

Gorman, H., and Postle, K. 2003: *Transforming Community Care: A Distorted Vision?* Birmingham: Venture Press.

Healthcare Commission 2008: *National Survey of Local Health Services*. London: Healthcare Commission.

Hewison, A., and Cox, D. 2009: 'Long term conditions, policy and practice'. In E. Denny and S. Earle (eds), *The Sociology of Long Term Conditions and Nursing Practice*. Basingstoke: Palgrave Macmillan.

Houghton, M. 2002: 'We bought our own GP'. *Nursing Times*, 98(13), 28–9.

Imison, C., Naylor, C., and Maybin, J. 2008: *Under One Roof: Will Polyclinics Deliver Integrated Care?* London. King's Fund.

Kelly, A., and Symonds, A. 2003: *The Social Construction of Community Nursing*. Basingstoke: Palgrave Macmillan.

Lewis, J. 1999: 'The concepts of community care and primary care in the UK: the 1960s to the 1990s'. *Health and Social Care in the Community*, 7, 333–41.

Malin, N., Manthorpe J., Race, D., and Wilmot, S. 1999: *Community Care for Nurses and the Caring Professions*. Buckingham: Open University Press.

Marinker, M. 1998, 'The NHS in the 1960s and 70s: the invention of general practice'. In K. Bloor (ed.), *Radicalism and Reality in the National Health Service: Fifty Years and More*. York: Centre for Health Economics, University of York.

Maynard, A. 2002: 'Crisis in general practice'. *The Guardian*, 22 August [Letter].

Moon, G., and North, N. 2000: *Policy and Place: General Medical Practice in the UK*. London: Macmillan.

NAO (National Audit Office) 2008: *NHS Pay Modernisation: New Contracts for General Practice Services in England*. London: HMSO.

Offe, C. 1984: *Contradictions of the Welfare State*. London: Hutchinson.

Peckham, S., and Exworthy, M. 2003: *Primary Care in the UK*. Basingstoke: Palgrave Macmillan.

Sibbald, S. 2000: 'Primary care: background and policy issues'. In A. Williams, *Nursing, Medicine and Primary Care*. Buckingham: Open University Press, pp. 14–26.

Williams, A. 2000: *Nursing, Medicine and Primary Care*. Buckingham: Open University Press.

Wilson, A. E. 2000: 'The changing nature of primary health care teams and inter-professional relationships'. In P. Tovey (ed.), *Contemporary Primary Care*. Buckingham: Open University Press, pp. 43–60.

13 Hospitals and Institutions

Philip Shelton and Elaine Denny

Key issues in this chapter

- The emergence of the hospital
- The hospital: the best place for care?
- Institutionalization
- Institutions within the community

By the end of this chapter you should be able to . . .

- define the nature of an institution;
- understand the historical development of hospitals, asylums and other institutions;
- explore issues of discharge;
- understand the nature of institutions within the community;
- be aware of contemporary issues around institutions for nursing practice;
- recognize the challenges of medicalized death in hospital.

1 Introduction

institutionalization the long-term incarceration of individuals, whether compulsory, coercive or voluntary, for the purpose of treatment, care and social control

What is an institution? In what way does the institution have an effect on the delivery of care and the ways in which patients receive care? Is a hospital the best place to be in order to get better? This chapter will consider the growth of institutions as ways of caring for the sick. It will also chart their recent history, demonstrating the relationship of hospitals to the medicalization and **institutionalization** of health care, including the specialization of hospitals. The consideration of the latter will explore the structured relationships in hospitals, with particular emphasis on the place of the patient within these structures. There will also be critical discussions of the effectiveness of the modern hospital/institution in caring for the sick and for the dying. The NHS and Community Care Act (Department of Health, 1990) reshaped the organization and subsequent delivery of health and social care in the public, private, informal and voluntary sectors. The impetus was for convalescent and long-term care to take place within community settings, either residential or the person's own dwelling, thus freeing up secondary services for acute patients. The decrease in reliance on hospital beds has been compensated for only partially with the growth in the number of places in residential services. The implications of this for nurses will also be explored in this chapter.

2 What is an institution?

In sociological terms, the nature of institutions can be viewed in a number of ways depending on context and function. Scott and Christensen (1995, p. 33) suggest that 'institutions consist of cognitive, normative, and regulative structures and activities that provide stability and meaning to social behaviour'. In other words, institutions are more than just the buildings that create a hospital, an asylum or a university. They also comprise the practices, procedures and values that give them an identity. It may be worth reviewing chapter 1 here, particularly the discussion of theories of social structure and the importance of structures, rules and social roles.

While Scott and Christensen focus on the psychological, social and political elements of organizational life, Erving Goffman distinguishes between an institution and a 'total institution'. The latter he defines as 'a place of residence and work where a large number of like-situated individuals, cut off from the wider society for an appreciable period of time, together lead an enclosed, formally administered round of life' (1961, p. 11). According to King and Raynes (1968), the following are features of institutionalization:

1   depersonalization;
2   social distance (between staff and inmates);
3   block activities (when all activities are rigidly organized at group level, with little opportunity for individual preference);
4   a lack of variety in daily routine.

Other important factors are the appearance, size and structure of the accommodation, the furnishings and the atmosphere. Victorian edifices may rapidly induce gloom and despondency in those who come to live there, while a well-designed, bright, attractive modern

Are hospitals total
institutions?

building can have quite the opposite effect. However, in a resource-
limited service such as the NHS the desire to provide the personal
domestic-like features of a small establishment has to be balanced
against economic factors.

So whereas for most of us different activities, such as going to
work, socializing or playing sport, are carried out in different
settings, possibly with different people, within a total institution
all aspects of life are carried out under one roof or in one complex.
Other characteristics of institutions include activities being planned
to suit a rational goal, a privilege system where small rewards and
punishments can be built around obedience to staff, and situational
adaptations where either rebellion can serve to raise morale or
inmates are converted to taking the staff's view of themselves and
attempt to act the role of the perfect inmate.

For Goffman, tuberculosis sanatoria, army barracks and mental
asylums, amongst other organizations, constitute total institutions.
These settings are not conducive to long-stay patients becoming
independent and reaching their full potential, for reasons explored
in section 5.

Nurses do not usually view themselves as working in institutions,
as they are familiar with the routines of the hospital setting, may
find the rules conducive to the smooth running of the ward, and
do not always appreciate how alien it all seems to the patient.
However, in institutions for older people, those with mental
health problems or those with learning difficulties, procedures
and practices have traditionally been very inflexible, with no
scope for patients to express individuality or to deviate from
routines set by the staff. This can be viewed as a very controlling
environment, and, whilst they do not necessarily agree about what
constitutes an institution, sociologists would see the need to

examine the extent to which institutions can be seen as places of either care or control.

This section has examined both sociological definitions of the institution and the inflexibility of total institutions. It has highlighted the idea that institutionalization is not compatible with the notion of individualized care.

3   Types of institution

The emergence of the general hospital

According to Dainton (1961), from as early as 1155 hospitals were developed by religious orders as institutions for the sick. Hospitals in their earliest form both provided care for the sick and acted as homes for orphans and others who were unable to care for themselves. The dissolution of the monasteries (including their infirmaries) from 1535 to 1540 by Henry VIII and the resulting loss of their medical expertise acted as an impetus to the growth of the medical profession, which then developed outside its religious origins. The first indication of the organization of health services was the founding in 1518 of the Royal College of Physicians, which then began licensing London doctors.

In 1601 the Poor Law was introduced whereby parishes became responsible for the care of old and chronically ill poor people and fatherless children. This led to the development of workhouses, some of which had a separate infirmary for the sick. The well-to-do, with servants to carry out their nursing, and able to afford a doctor to visit them, were treated in their own homes.

In the eighteenth century, social changes brought about by industrialization and the urbanization of the population led to increasing numbers of both rich and poor. For the rich, philanthropic endeavours were a way of demonstrating their wealth, and subscribing to the building of voluntary hospitals and other public buildings, such as schools, libraries and public baths, provided a visible and lasting monument. In the rapidly growing cities, to which the poor were moving in large numbers because of the lure of work in the new industries, the care of the sick and vulnerable was not compatible with the need for wage earning, and these groups found themselves increasingly institutionalized. Poor living conditions and poverty led to a downturn in the health of the nation, especially with regard to infectious diseases, as previously isolated individuals and communities were brought into contact with one another (Vetter, 1995). The new voluntary hospitals were, however, very discriminating over who they would admit, and so most people were dependent on family or Poor Law institutions when sick.

Consequently both voluntary and Poor Law hospitals expanded and increased in number during the nineteenth century. Doctors who were members of the Royal Colleges dominated the voluntary hospitals, which developed into centres for research and teaching. Lobbying by the Poor Law Board, some members of the medical profession and philanthropists finally achieved an administrative separation of sick people and people with mental health problems from the workhouse and into infirmaries or asylums.

So a two-tier system existed, with voluntary hospitals caring for surgical patients and accident victims, and Poor Law infirmaries housing the chronically and terminally ill, people suffering from infections, and anyone else not catered for by voluntary hospitals.

The emergence of the asylum

In 1808 the County Asylums Act gave permissive powers to the justices of each county to build asylums and replace the few psychiatric annexes to voluntary general hospitals. The Poor Law Amendment Act (1834) required relief to be provided within institutions only, which meant that, to receive any help from the state, the destitute were obliged to enter the workhouse, which led to the construction of a huge network of workhouses.

The Lunatics Act of 1845 made the provision of asylums the responsibility of each county, and the number rose from nine in 1827 to ninety-one by 1910. They also grew in size, from an average of 166 patients in 1827 to 1,072 in 1910 (Busfield, 1986). It is said that following the 1845 Act the sex ratio in the asylums altered, from being predominantly male to predominantly female, a situation that remains to this day. This was because the main category of patient was the pauper lunatic, and more women than men found themselves destitute; they were labelled lunatics in order to allow them to be removed from being a drain on the parish rates.

The early mental hospital is a different institution from the general hospital in both its architecture and its locality. The asylum was located in the countryside, often remote from the nearest town, and tended to be self-sufficient. Inmates, as they were called, helped to nurse the old and frail and worked on the farms and in the kitchens of the asylum. This originally provided a contrast to disorganized privately run asylums in the cities, which were often a source of tuberculosis and disease (Hardey, 1998).

By the end of the nineteenth century a nationwide system of asylums and hospitals had been created in the USA and in many European countries and their colonies, as well as in Britain. Whilst the hospitals and the asylums shared characteristics, it was the latter which were to prove the most problematic. They housed both 'lunatics' (people with mental health problems) and 'idiots' (people with learning disabilities), and before the Mental Deficiency Act (1913) little attempt was made to differentiate the needs of these two very different groups. Contained within the same institutions were people suffering from neurological disorders, including epilepsy and dementia, and a variety of other individuals whose behaviour had prompted sharp moral and social rejection. Extramarital sex (by women) and homosexuality and masturbation (by both sexes) (Darby, 2003) had been characterized as types of 'moral insanity', which could provide a pretext for admission to an institution. The incarceration of this latter group is an obvious example of the use of institutions for the purpose of custody and social control rather than benevolent care and protection.

Foucault, writing on the origins and political functions of institutions, including hospitals (1973) and mental institutions (1967), suggests that institutions were born from a political imperative to segregate those sections of the population perceived as 'unproductive' – among them the sick and those with mental health problems or learning difficulties – within the developing capitalist economies of the eighteenth, nineteenth and twentieth centuries.

The emergence of the children's hospital

In the eighteenth century the presence of children in hospital was rare; there was strong opposition to their admission from prominent doctors on the grounds that a child should not be separated from its mother, and mothers would not be able to have the time from work to be admitted with their children (Dainton, 1961). Interestingly, the idea that children and mothers should not be separated was abandoned during the twentieth century and only revived following research on the needs of children in hospital in the 1960s. It was also recognized amongst the medical profession that children were more likely to develop infectious diseases (Higgins, 1952), which made hospitals reluctant to admit them. Instead, dispensaries were formed by doctors that enabled children to be treated in their own home. However, physicians did not always provide adequate supervision, which delayed their patients' recovery. In addition the opportunity to study the effect of diseases on children was missed.

By the nineteenth century the limitations of the general hospital were apparent, and medical advances meant there was a need for more specialist hospitals. In contrast to general hospitals, which had the backing of charitable laypeople aided by doctors, specialist hospitals were founded and controlled by doctors. The first British children's hospitals were opened in 1851 by Dr Charles West, who was convinced of the need for a hospital to provide care for children, despite the traumas of separation. In addition, whilst specialist hospitals, including those for children, were founded on the principle of helping the sick and advancing medical practice, other motives were a lack of opportunity for promotion within the voluntary hospital system and the chance for self-advancement in a new area.

The medical profession had developed into a unified profession by 1858. The elite were the voluntary hospital consultants, who had the opportunity to experiment on patients and develop skills in surgery, among other interventions. The old workhouse infirmaries were staffed by salaried doctors and were associated with care as opposed to cure. Specialist hospitals had developed to fill the gaps in provision left by the other hospitals' selectivity in admissions. By the inception of the NHS in 1948, however, many voluntary hospitals had lost much of their funding from donations and were variable in the standards of care they offered. It was hospitals attached to medical schools that became the new elite institutions. The asylums were redesignated psychiatric hospitals, reinforcing the idea of a medical model of treatment rather than custody and restraint.

Activity 13.1   **Care or control?**

(a)   Think about the ways in which hospitals, as institutions, are about social control as much as they are about care (you might want to consider the control of patient routine, behaviour, and so on).

(b)   To what extent, then, is the role of a nurse about control of the patient?

(c)   Consider the ways in which institutions regulate and reinforce their own institutional norms. How might this impact on your ability to care for the patient?

---

4   Hospitalization

When the general public is questioned about health care, it is hospitals and acute interventions that are most commonly raised. For most people the NHS is its hospitals, and what happens inside them will colour their perceptions of it. Hospitals are the very visible face of the NHS; they are where cutting-edge technology and heroic surgery take place. They are also the focus of political debates on the NHS and the health sector by which politicians' success in running the service will be judged. Indeed, in the 2001 election campaign Tony Blair declared 'schools and hospitals first' – not, you will note, 'education and the NHS first'. Hospitals are also important for providing clinical experience for students of the health professions.

The changing nature of hospitals

On its inception in July 1948, the NHS incorporated around 3,000 local authority or voluntary hospitals in varying states of repair and possessing diverse facilities. The NHS historian Charles Webster

(2002, p. 40) states that it 'was saddled' with old, defective hospitals that were wrongly located and ill-adapted to the needs of the patients within them. Particularly poor were the massive institutions catering for people with mental illness, learning disability and the elderly infirm.

Harrison (2008) has described the transformation of the hospital, via the district hospital vision of the 1960s, to the new superhospitals being built in the twenty-first century. District hospitals were the product of the 1962 Hospital Plan, which envisaged a hospital for every 100,000 to 150,000 people as a way of supplying most health care needs to the nation in an equitable manner. These would be supplemented with a few regional centres providing more specialist services. According to Harrison, two main developments changed the thinking about the suitability of the district hospital. First was the move towards care in the community and the seemingly conflicting trend to more specialization and sub-specialization, requiring more centralized facilities than could be offered in the district hospital. So the current trend is for fewer, larger, more specialist hospitals to deliver complex care, with more treatment being offered as day cases, or within primary care and the community – what has come to be know as 'care closer to home'. Harrison cites the case of accident and emergency services as an example, arguing that: 'Until very recently, the emergency function was regarded almost as a sideshow to the main business of the hospital' (ibid., p. 37). Patients admitted as emergencies would be placed under the care of whichever team was 'on take' and could be seen in the department by a junior doctor with no knowledge of the patient's condition. Now A&E is a specialism in its own right, with a career pathway, and the expectation is of an A&E consultant on site at all times. However, this is only feasible in units covering large catchment areas, and so the move has been to downgrade or close units and concentrate more specialized A&E services in larger, better staffed and equipped centres – a trend that has also occurred in cancer and obstetric services. This move, albeit on the grounds of safety and quality of care, has generally been treated with suspicion by a public that perceives any closure of 'their' services as driven purely by cost cutting.

hospitalization period of time as a patient confined to a hospital

Although the primary purpose of **hospitalization** is to care for the person's health and well-being, it also involves loss of both personal and physical privacy and the imposition of a number of restrictions. For example, not only are patients subject to the routines of the ward, they often find themselves in close proximity to one another, while intimate contact between health care provider and patient is unavoidable. There have been attempts to make certain wards more

palliative care care to meet the needs and expectations of patients (and of their families) who have a progressive life-threatening illness

patient-friendly, particularly in paediatrics and **palliative care**. For example, the NHS Plan (Department of Health, 2000) suggests that children and young people should be provided, free of charge wherever possible, with a range of equipment appropriate to their age, including a bedside TV with headphones, telephone and radio. In addition there should be facilities available for more active play, if the child wishes and their condition allows.

However, hospitalization inevitably restricts normal activity. Some restrictions, such as those imposed by bed rest or traction, may be therapeutically desirable, while others, such as visiting times, may be related more to organizational concerns. We may have had our own personal experience of hospitals at some point in our lives, or know someone who has, and it is worth remembering that when a person becomes hospitalized they have to contend not only with their illness but also with an environment which is alien to them, and where they are expected to entrust their care to strangers.

Whilst surgery and treatment can be stressful, an additional aspect of hospitalization is Illich's (1979) concept of iatrogenesis (see chapter 3), which suggests that a patient's health may deteriorate as a direct consequence of becoming hospitalized; for example, a poor hospital diet, or more likely an inadequate diet, can lead to malnutrition, or any misdiagnosis can lead to a delay in treatment.

The process of hospitalization can reflect aspects of institutionalization in that the patient is subject to the routine of the ward. However, for most people the length of time spent in hospital is relatively short, so it is difficult to argue that the patient's identity is being wholly subsumed within institutional life, unlike the area of mental health, as the next section illustrates.

5   Institutionalization and the asylums

The process of institutionalization described in section 13.2 has typically been played out in asylums. Whilst external factors, such as the nature of the buildings themselves, can influence institutionalization, Erving Goffman (1961) – influenced by theories of social action (see chapter 1) – broke new ground in the sociological understanding of institutions by focusing on the experiences of 'inmates' (patients). He made detailed observations of contact among inmates themselves and between inmates and the staff of the institution and suggested that these interactions symbolized power relationships, status differences and unstated expectations. He argued that what he termed the institutional 'underlife' (1961, p. 180) assumed an importance greater than the formal procedures and policies of the institution. He also coined the phrase 'total institution'. Whilst clearly no institution is completely disconnected from life outside, the use of this phrase does convey something of the flavour of the dominating and all-pervasive nature of the institution in the world of the inmate.

In many institutions the activities of daily life such as sleep and work take place under one roof governed by one authority. Each phase of a person's daily routine is rigidly fixed and carried out in the company of others, who are all treated alike. Enforced activities are part of an overall plan designed to fulfil the official aims of that institution. Inmates, who have restricted access to the world outside, are on admission stripped of 'habitual' supports, such as personal possessions (Goffman, 1961). It takes little thought to realize how well hospitals or homes providing continuing care can fit this pattern.

Most of these problems are not major and are often the result of staff becoming socialized within the prevailing culture of the institution, colluding in the provision of routinized, traditional and often uncaring and unevaluated practices. However, evidence to support this notion of total institutions emerged in Britain particularly during the late 1960s, when a series of enquiries into allegations of ill-treatment in long-stay hospitals, for example Ely Hospital, Cardiff, in 1969, were given prominence within the press.

Activity 13.2

Are care homes for older people fit for purpose?

The process of institutionalization

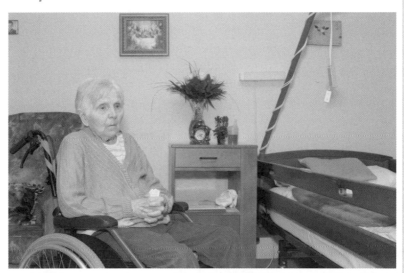

'Clothing is anonymous. One's possessions are limited to toothbrush, comb, upper or lower cot, half the space upon a narrow table, a razor . . . [other] things are assiduously gathered, jealously hidden or triumphantly displayed. (Cantine and Rainer, cited in Goffman, 1961, p. 269)

(a) Would it surprise you to learn that this extract is cited from prison literature? How far do you believe that it may describe the patient experience?

(b) Does it apply equally to all patients and all hospitals or hospital wards?

Scandals, which have included physical and sexual abuse, have been well documented (Martin, 1984), and the impact of their reporting has been to undermine public confidence in institutional provisions for those with chronic health problems and other long-term dependency needs.

Whilst Goffman documented the negative aspects of institutions, including loss of liberty, loss of autonomy, and depersonalization, he did not want to abolish the asylums entirely. However, within the UK, mounting criticism from influential professionals, spiralling public costs, changing demographics, and growing public outcry led the government to seek alternatives to large-scale institutional care.

6 Deinstitutionalization and the shift to community care

The idea of shifting the provision of care from institutions to the community had been considered by various governments over a number of years. The NHS and Community Care Act (Department of Health, 1990) was passed at a time when eleven years of neo-liberal political philosophies had led to a recasting of the definition of the purpose of public policy, placing an emphasis on individual responsibility and choice. As we have seen from the previous section, there were longstanding criticisms of the institution. Initially, community care was aimed at the elderly, the mentally ill and people with learning disabilities. However, the term has since been extended in official usage in two ways: to cover all sections of the population needing care and to recognize the diversity of non-institutional care that might be available.

Delayed discharge

bed blocking a pejorative term for 'delayed discharge' which depersonalizes the patient

delayed discharge a term for 'bed blocking' which recognizes that difficulties with discharge lie with the system and not the individual

This diversity was also meant to provide the solution to the complex problem of what is commonly referred to as **bed blocking**. However, because the latter term is associated with placing the onus on the individual, the practice will be referred to as **delayed discharge**. One reason why delayed discharge occurs is a steady decline in the number of acute hospital beds and its consequences or blockages in the system. This reflects a number of factors, in particular:

- the switch for older people, people with mental illnesses and those with learning disabilities from long-stay beds to care in the community;
- medical advances allowing for shorter lengths of stay (King's Fund, 2001);
- the congestion of beds, exacerbated by the inability of social services to provide care within a residential setting.

Activity 13.3   **A nursing student's experience on the ward: an example of 'bed blocking'**

> 'And once the patient is in hospital, because there's a process we couldn't get the social workers on the ward, because the social workers needed to assess people before they could be discharged and we were waiting weeks and months, sometimes just for a social worker to come out and do an assessment. So obviously we couldn't set up a social package for the person to go home. People were tying up beds you know, on the medical ward because the social workers weren't there to complete the package or relatives were, it's free while they were in hospital.' (Shelton, 2003)

(a)   What does the term 'bed blocking' imply compared with 'delayed discharge'?

(b)   What do you think might be some of the other reasons for the delay?

(c)   What are the implications for the patient?

Community care is often perceived differently by local authorities and health authorities. For example, 'To the former it meant a reduction in the amount of residential accommodation, while to the latter, it could refer to alternatives to hospitals such as residential accommodation, nursing homes or sheltered housing' (Allsop, 1995, p. 103). This situation can be very stressful for the nurse, particularly if the patient's operation has been a success but there is no residential home or 'care package' in place. One of the consequences for the patient if they remain in the hospital is iatrogenic in that there is the risk of infection such as methicillin-resistant staphylococcus aureus (MRSA). Postponement can also lead the patient to experience declining mobility and loss of confidence in relation to regaining their independence once home (Glasby, 2003). For long-stay patients, delayed discharge can have an adverse affect on their ability to become deinstitutionalized, making subsequent rehabilitation to independent living all the more problematic. Clearly the need for discharge planning is paramount, and the role of nurses in this process is crucial.

There are a range of institutions to which a patient can be transferred; the focus here is on four types of institutional care: residential care, nursing care, group homes and hospices. The next two subsections discuss some of the differences between institutions and explore institutional experiences.

Residential care homes, nursing homes and group homes

Residential care homes are registered with the local authority and intended for older people who, even with domiciliary support, cannot manage to live in their own homes but do not need intensive nursing care. All provide accommodation, meals, personal care, supervision of medication, and care during normal short illnesses, but not constant nursing care. The NHS is responsible for providing community health services (for example, district nursing, chiropody and incontinence supplies) to people in residential homes on the same basis as to people in their own homes. Nursing homes are registered with a strategic health authority and are required to have a registered nurse on duty twenty-four hours a day. Nursing homes care for those who are more dependent: for example, a nursing home would be more suitable for a person needing some form of continuing treatment, such as long-term care of a fistula.

While most people in nursing homes will be permanent residents, the use of these institutions as temporary accommodation in order to ease the problem of delayed discharge has been proposed. What has been termed 'intermediate care' would thus free up acute beds when a person's discharge is being delayed while they wait for social service assessment, or because they are not quite ready for independent living. A scheme in Liverpool uses beds in health authority-accredited homes for terminal and intermediate care. These beds are acquired on an *ad hoc* basis, and not more than five are used in one nursing home at any time (Last, 2000).

However, a survey of sixty primary care groups and trusts in 2000 found that the biggest perceived obstacle to the development of intermediate care was obstruction from acute hospitals and consultants, who would not welcome the transfer of resources from the acute to the primary care sector (Light and Dixon, 2000).

The deinstitutionalization of care has also affected individuals with learning disabilities, and now an increasing number live within the community. Community settings for people with learning disabilities can take many forms, ranging from independent living to living in supported accommodation. Group homes can also vary in size, although small-scale staffed housing is now the most common form of accommodation for people with learning disabilities in the UK (Perry et al., 2000).

The deinstitutionalization of people with learning disabilities is thought to increase community participation, community integration and quality of life (Myles et al., 2000) as well as to encourage personal development and increased activity levels (Perry et al., 2000). However, research evidence suggests that, whilst people with learning disabilities may be physically located within communities, they are still socially excluded from mainstream society, remaining 'socially outside, looking in' (Myers et al., 1998, p. 393). The location of group homes (for people with learning disabilities and mental health problems) has also often been met with resistance by local communities, resulting in the now well-established 'NIMBY' (not-in-my-back-yard) syndrome (Repper and Brooker, 1996; Cowan, 2003). Indeed, many studies have identified the problem of bullying and victimization of people with learning disabilities by members of their local communities (Mencap, 1999), including that which is perpetrated by children (Whittell and Ramcharan, 2000).

A group of young people with learning disabilities enjoy a day out shopping.

Activity 13.4

Life in a care home for older people

This case study is based on the audio diary of a fit, seventy-year-old woman (Deddie) who went 'undercover' as a resident of a care home for the BBC's *Today* programme.

Day 1
Her room at the home has a wardrobe, a bed, a chest of drawers and an en suite bathroom. It is 'very plain' but 'perfectly clean'.

Upon her first look in the lounge, she finds five residents and a television. 'The TV was on the whole time, no one was watching and, apart from chatting to the lady sitting beside me, no one spoke. We were alone for nearly an hour with no carer coming in.'

Dinner is served at 5 p.m. and Deddie has beans on toast, followed by stewed apricots and a cup of tea. She's in bed by 9.30 p.m., the earliest she has been to bed in years.

Day 2
Deddie is woken up at 5.45 a.m. by a carer coming into the room. 'The carer came in, switched the light on, changed the water in

my room, muttered it was cold, fiddled with the radiator and went out. Didn't speak to me or anything', she records. 'Not one of the night staff introduced themselves or spoke to me. It's very strange, quite lonely.' Breakfast is served at 9 a.m. Deddie notices the staff are 'very jolly and very kind'.

Day 3

'If I was helpless in here, I would feel quite safe and cared for.'

Before dinner Deddie revisits the lounge. 'Most are asleep but one, who is difficult to understand, speaks and I go over and talk to her. She says she is lonely.'

As she goes to bed she says: 'I felt there was a tremendous air of boredom in the lounge. They are surrounded by people but you get the feeling that they are bored.'

Day 4

Deddie has noticed that all the residents in the lounge are 'properly dressed and clean, and their nails are nicely cut and their hair brushed'.

It is sunny outside but Deddie spends the entire day reading in the lounge, the monotony punctuated only by meals.

Day 5

When the drug trolley is being wheeled around after breakfast, Deddie notices the nurse is 'transfixed to the television' and frequently leaves the trolley unattended. 'Apart from giving out the pills and medicines, she never spoke to anyone.'

On leaving the home, Deddie said that she was sad to leave the other residents.

(a)   How would you describe the care in the home?
(b)   What is the good and the unacceptable practice?
(c)   What can be done to enhance quality of life for residents?
(d)   How much can be done at little or no cost?

Source: Adapted from http://news.bbc.co.uk/go/pr/fr/-/today/hi/today/newsid_7408000/7408110.stm.

Hospices

A hospice is a registered charity catering for people with life-threatening and life-limiting conditions who require both respite and palliative care. There are specialist hospices which cater solely for children.

Hospices have been in existence for many centuries, but the hospice movement in the UK is associated with the opening of St Christopher's Hospice in South London by Dame Cicely Saunders in 1967. It was a response to the poor quality of care for dying people, both in institutions and at home, in a health system where acute interventions and cure dominate and death may be seen as a failure. Glaser and Strauss (1965) described restricted and poor communication with dying people and the individual routes towards death in hospital, which they termed 'dying trajectories'. They suggested that the uncertainty of some 'dying trajectories', set in the highly medicalized and routinized context of the hospital, posed problems for staff managing wards. In his classic contribution, Sudnow (1967) suggested that, once a patient had been defined as 'dying', medicine seemed to have little to offer, and medical and social contact were withdrawn from the dying person in a 'social death' which preceded biological death. Depersonalization of the dying can still be identified as a feature of hospitals and nursing homes in contemporary UK society, and reflects a shift in the way in which death and dying are conceptualized that began around the middle of the nineteenth century. Until well into the twentieth century most people would have encountered the death of a sibling or parent by the time they were adults, as life expectancy was low and child mortality high. So the process of dying and death was familiar, and customs and practices to deal with it were embedded in the social relations of a culture to be played out publicly. This is still the case in some parts of the world, and there is nothing inevitable about the way death is managed. With falling death rates the process of death became a less familiar occurrence, and the outpouring of grief that frequently accompanied it less acceptable in public, so that death is now largely hidden within the institution and the bereavement experience takes place behind closed doors. Death has become more of an individual event, with fewer collective customs and rituals and with more secrecy surrounding it. Death and dying remain taboo subjects, and this lack of open discussion has heralded an era of fear and denial that has influenced the way in which dying people and their families are treated within health care. Care of the dying has been professionalized, and what was once the duty of family is now the province of a medical and nursing specialism – palliative care. This way of managing death is not, however, universal, and on your placements you may well come across cultural approaches to death and dying that differ from those with which you are familiar.

The hospice movement grew outside of the NHS in order to develop its own model of care, different from the institutionalized care of those dying in hospital. By 1997 there were over 200 hospices, yet, despite this increase (particularly in domiciliary and out-patient care) death has become more institutionalized. The proportion of patients dying at home fell from a peak of 60 per cent in the 1960s to 24 per cent in 1997 (Bosanquet, 1997). In fact, as illness progresses, the number of patients and their relatives wanting death at home decreases (Hinton, 1994). Again this reflects the notion of death as a medicalized event that takes place away from the public gaze.

Critics of the growth in the number of hospices claim that it has been unplanned and unco-ordinated. They have been built wherever the funding can be raised, resulting in there being greater provision in wealthier areas rather than where need is greatest. There is also the criticism that the focus of hospice care is cancer at the expense of other terminal illness, although this is not the case in specialist children's hospices. And the association with Christianity has led to calls for greater recognition of British multicultural society.

Questions have been raised about the 'medicalization' of hospices, with the increasing influence of doctors in the institutions and the status given to the medical perspective (James and Field, 1992). Seale (1989) had already doubted whether hospice care was significantly better than hospital care for the dying, but in a later piece of work on palliative care he concedes that 'satisfaction with that [hospice] care reported by respondents after the death is very high, and generally higher than that of respondents for patients in conventional care' (Seale, 1991, p. 151).

The poor standard of care that gave rise to the hospice movement also led to ideas being formulated around what constitutes 'a good death'. We can, however, question whose needs a good death serves (the dying person or the family and carers around them?) and by what criteria a death is judged to be 'good' or 'bad'. Kendall et al. (2009) point out that there is little evidence from dying people or their carers to answer this, and their work with end-of-life researchers suggests that gatekeeping by health professionals and ethics committees act as barriers. However, using focus groups with users and carers, they confirmed that many people with advanced illness do want the opportunity to participate in research. Research is particularly lacking around the dying child, and Todd (2009) has described the 'silence' of the death of someone with learning disability.

normalization
a therapeutic philosophy which emphasizes individual patient choice and the importance of 'homelike' environments

A challenge to institutions comes from therapeutic philosophies such as normalization, and these have had considerable impact on traditional models of institutional care. Underpinning this is the belief that the consumers of health care should have the same life choices as any other citizen and that the ways in which users of health care services may be different from others should be valued, rather than seen as evidence of deviance from assumed norms. Normalization has had its greatest impact in the field of learning disability, but its influence has also extended to the fields of mental health, physical disability and the care of frail elderly people.

In summary, there are institutional alternatives to conventional hospitals, particularly for those with long-term and life-limiting conditions. The process of deinstitutionalization is a complex phenomenon involving not only the building but also the environment, the atmosphere, staff attitudes and standards of care.

Activity 13.5   **The death of a patient**

In *Making Sense of Death, Dying and Bereavement* (2009) Joyce Cavaye describes her first experience as a student nurse of the death of a patient. She recalls feeling fear and embarrassment – 'fear because I hadn't seen a dead body before, and embarrassment at my own emotions'. She goes on: 'I remember vividly the sense of shock and fear I felt. Shock that Jane [the patient] had deteriorated and died so quickly – she seemed too bright and alert for that to have happened. Fear that I was facing the unknown and wasn't sure how to react to a dead body.' For many nurses starting their education, knowing how to behave at the death of a patient is the greatest fear that they have.

(a)   How similar are Joyce's fears to your own?
(b)   If you have experienced the death of a patient, how did the reality match your expectations?
(c)   Discuss your responses to (a) and (b) with a colleague from a different branch of nursing, a different age, or a different ethnic group to yourself.

Summary and Resources

Summary

- Institutions have been central to Britain's health and social care service provisions, and this will continue to be the case.

- Institutionalization occurs in both health and social care settings, depriving the patient of their autonomy.

- The role of the hospital in the NHS is changing, with larger, more specialized centres developing.

- Whilst community care attempted to counter the problems of life within large institutions, there remains the problem of ensuring that institutionalization is not simply re-created, albeit within smaller settings.

- Alternative institutional care is now offered within hospices and homes which attempt to provide more individualized care, but these community settings generate their own problems.

- The institutionalization of dying in Western societies has led to a reconceptualization of death as a private affair, with few collective rituals.

Questions for Discussion

1 What are the characteristics of an institution?

2 Would you say that hospitals are healthy places to stay? With reference to your branch of nursing, give reasons for your answer.

3 Think about the process of discharge for a patient you have nursed. What went well? What went badly? How could these problems have been overcome?

Further Reading

R. Jack (ed.): Residential versus Community Care: The Role of Institutions in Welfare Provision. London: Macmillan, 1998.
This provides a useful account of the ways in which institutional care in a community setting can parallel and reinforce patients' hospital experiences.

D. Pilgrim and A. Rogers (eds): A Sociology of Mental Health and Illness. 3rd edn, Buckingham: Open University Press, 2005.
This provides a comprehensive overview of sociological approaches to mental health and illness. It explores the ways in which mental

illness is viewed by the law and institutions and is an excellent introduction to the world of sociology applied to mental health.

W. Scott: Institutions and Organizations. 2nd edn, London: Sage, 2001.
If you are interested in current approaches to organization theory, this provides a comprehensive and historical overview with a review of empirical research.

To explore this topic further, see www.politybooks.com/ sociologyfornurses for additional useful resources.

References

Allsop, J. 1995: *Health Policy and the National Health Service*. Harlow: Longman.

Bosanquet, N. 1997: 'New challenges for palliative care'. *British Medical Journal*, 314, 1294.

Busfield, J. 1986: *Managing Madness: Changing Ideas and Practice*. London: Hutchinson.

Cavaye, J. 2009: 'The first death: a student's experience'. In S. Earle, C. Bartholomew and C. Komaromy (eds), *Making Sense of Death, Dying and Bereavement: An Anthology*. London: Sage, pp. 145–7.

Cowan, S. 2003: 'NIMBY syndrome and public consultation policy: the implications of a discourse analysis of local responses to the establishment of a community mental health facility'. *Health and Social Care in the Community*, 11(5), 379–86.

Dainton, C. 1961: *The Story of England's Hospitals*. London: Museum Press.

Darby, R. 2003: 'The masturbation taboo and the rise of routine male circumcision: a review of the historiography'. *Journal of Social History*, 36(3), 737–57.

Department of Health 1990: *Community Care in the Next Decade and Beyond: Policy Guidance*. London: HMSO.

Department of Health 2000: *The NHS Plan*. London: HMSO.

Foucault, M. 1967: *Madness and Civilization: A History of Insanity in the Age of Reason*. London: Tavistock Press.

Foucault, M. 1973: *The Birth of the Clinic*. London: Tavistock Press.

Glasby, J. 2003: *Hospital Discharge: Integrating Health and Social Care*. Abingdon: Radcliffe Medical Press.

Glaser, B. G., and Strauss, A. L. 1965: *Awareness of Dying*. New York: Aldine de Gruyter.

Goffman, E. 1961: *Asylums: Essays on the Social Situation of Mental Patients and Other Inmates*. Harmondsworth: Penguin.

Hardey, M. 1998: *The Social Context of Health*. Buckingham: Open University Press.

Harrison, A. 2008: 'The reinvention of the hospital'. *Health Service Journal*, NHS 60th anniversary supplement, 3 July.

Higgins, T. 1952: *Great Ormond Street 1852–1952*. London: Odhams Press.

Hinton, J. 1994: 'Can home care maintain a quality of life for patients with terminal cancer and their relatives?' *Palliative Medicine*, 8, 183–96.

Illich, I. 1979: *Limits to Medicine: Medical Nemesis: The Expropriation of Health*. Harmondsworth: Penguin.

James, N., and Field, D. 1992: 'The routinization of hospice: charisma and bureaucratization'. *Social Science and Medicine*, 34(12), 1363–75.

Kendall, M., Harris, F., Boyd, K., Sheikh, A., Murray, S. A., Brown, D., Mallinson, I., Kearney, N., and Worth, A. 2009: 'Key challenges and ways forward in researching the good death'. In S. Earle, C. Komaromy and C. Bartholomew (eds), *Death and Dying: A Reader*. London: Sage, pp. 211–20.

King, R., and Raynes, N. 1968: 'An operational measure of inmate management in residential institutions'. *Journal of Social Sciences and Medicine*, 2, 41–53.

King's Fund 2001: *General Election 2001 Briefings*. London: King's Fund.

Last, S. 2000: 'Bed spread'. *Health Service Journal*, 10 August, 22–3.

Light, D., and Dixon, M. 2000: 'A new way through'. *Health Service Journal*, 10 August, 24–5.

Martin, J. 1984: *Hospitals in Trouble*. Oxford: Blackwell.

Mencap 1999: *Living in Fear*. London: Mencap.

Myers, F., Ager, A., Kerr, P., and Myles, S. 1998: 'Outside looking in? Studies of the community integration of people with learning disabilities.' *Disability and Society*, 13, 389–413.

Myles, S., Ager, A., Kerr, P., Myers, F., and Walker, J. 2000: 'Moving home: costs associated with different models of accommodation for adults with learning disabilities'. *Health and Social Care in the Community*, 8(6), 406–16.

Perry, J., Lowe, K., Felce, D., and Jones, S. 2000: 'Characteristics of staffed community housing services for people with learning disabilities: a stratified random sample of statutory, voluntary and private agency provision'. *Health and Social Care in the Community*, 8(5), 307–15.

Repper, J., and Brooker C. 1996: 'Public attitudes towards mental health facilities in the community'. *Health and Social Care in the Community*, 4(5), 290–9.

Scott, W., and Christensen, S. (eds) 1995: *The Institutional Construction of Organizations: International and Longitudinal Studies*. London: Sage.

Seale, C. 1989: 'What happens in hospices: a review of research evidence'. *Social Science and Medicine*, 28, 551–9.

Seale, C. 1991: 'A comparison of hospice and conventional care'. *Social Science and Medicine*, 32, 147–52.

Shelton, P. 2003: 'The application of sociological knowledge to nursing practice for pre-registration students'. Paper presented at the British Sociological Association Medical Sociology Conference, York.

Sudnow, D. 1967: *Passing On: The Social Organization of Dying*. Englewood Cliffs, NJ: Prentice-Hall.

Todd, S: 2009: 'Silenced endings: death, dying and learning disabilities'. In S. Earle, C. Bartholomew and C. Komaromy (eds), *Making Sense of Death, Dying and Bereavement: An Anthology*. London: Sage, pp. 152–5.

Vetter, N. 1995: *The Hospital: From the Centre of Excellence to Community Support*. London: Chapman & Hall.

Webster, C. 2002: *The National Health Service: A Political History*. 2nd edn, Oxford: Oxford University Press.

Whittell, B., and Ramcharan, P. 2000: 'The trouble with kids: an account of problems experienced with local children by people with learning disabilities'. *British Journal of Learning Disabilities*, 28, 21–4.

Part IV

Policy Influences on Health and Health Care

When thinking sociologically, it is important to recognize that private concerns are public troubles. Relationships between patients/clients and health care workers, and happenings on the hospital ward, are not isolated concerns but are connected socially, culturally and structurally. What this means is that nurses should recognize policy influences on experiences of health and ill-health, the provision of nursing care, and the organizational structure and culture within which care takes place. This part focuses specifically on health policy, the management and organization of health care, and the impact of wider environmental issues on health.

In chapter 14, 'Health Policy', you are introduced to the development and implementation of health policies. Whilst health policy may seem far removed from nursing, it is central to modern societies worldwide and important for nurses. This chapter examines the policy process and policies relating to treatment and health care, public health, health improvement and the prevention of ill-health. It also considers how where you work, what you are able to do for patients/clients, and the ways in which your work is monitored and assessed are shaped by policy, and encourages you to think about how changes in health policy can affect your practice.

Chapter 15, 'The Management and Organization of Health Care', sheds light on the role of management in the complex organization and delivery of health care. The term 'management' is defined and both its significance for nurses and the role of nurses as managers are discussed. Some key sociological concepts are introduced, including 'bureaucracy', 'negotiated order' and 'power', and the importance of sociological research methods for understanding organizations is highlighted. This chapter asks you to reflect on how management continues to influence patient/client care and the role of nurses.

A wider perspective is taken in chapter 16, 'Health, Housing and the Environment'. Following on from the discussion of the biomedical and social models in chapter 3, it contrasts the medical and public health models. It outlines recent trends in housing policy and discusses the relationship between housing and health. In particular, it looks at the significance of the 'fitness standard' and shows how poor housing conditions and homelessness affect health. Overall, this chapter asks you to develop an awareness of the importance of housing and environmental threats to health and to think about the wider role of nurses in health improvement and the prevention of ill-health.

This part provides only a brief introduction to some of the wider sociological and policy issues that influence nursing. Its purpose is to show that nursing work (and all other health work) is influenced by a range of factors that affect who becomes ill and who dies, and by the conditions within which nursing care takes place.

14 Health Policy

David Cox

Key issues in this chapter

- Health policy and the nurse
- Policy and the NHS
- Policies on the organization and management of health care
- Health policies and the process of treatment and care
- Policies and public health

By the end of this chapter you should be able to . . .

- understand how nursing is affected by changing health policies;
- appreciate how health care has become a central issue for government policy;
- understand the ways in which policies on organization and management, treatment and care, and health promotion have evolved over time;
- discuss and analyse health policy changes and their effects on your practice.

1 Introduction

This chapter is about how the health services in which nurses work are developed and shaped through the political system and the implementation of policies.

At first this might seem far removed from learning about patients' needs or nursing skills. You may come home after a placement shift too tired even to watch the TV news or to pick up a newspaper! You might, however, be surprised to find how much coverage is given to health service and policy matters in the media: both the human stories and the policies about health care are widely covered. As your training and professional career develop, understanding the policy context of your work may help you when faced with difficult situations and problems, such as the delay in discharging one of your patients to community care. This individual's personal problem is also part of a wider national policy debate which, as a citizen and as a professional, you may be able to influence.

Activity 14.1   **Media watch**

Do a 'media watch' on health issues, preferably in the week in which you read this chapter.

(a)   Choose a week and try to listen to one daily news broadcast and monitor a local or national paper.

(b)   What health care issues arise? Who speaks for the NHS on these issues? What are the implications for individual nurses and for the nursing profession more generally?

(c)   What is the balance in attention given to adult acute care, mental health, children's health or learning disability care?

---

2   Health policy and the nurse

Health policy refers to the laws and directions from governments that seek to affect health and to regulate and ensure supply of state-run, voluntary or private health care services. In industrial countries health policy is a major area of political interest and public debate. Governments seek to respond to changing patterns of ill-health, the needs of ageing populations, new diseases, the availability of new and expensive drugs and therapies, the maintenance costs of old and inadequate buildings, and the rising expectations of a more critical public. The most dramatic examples of health policy are probably when it fails. Waiting times and patient safety in particular have become dominant themes in British health policy discussion, and governments put both money and direct instructions into trying to solve these problems.

Policy is about how the powers of government are used to shape the world in which we live and work. How are policies developed? Where do they come from? Governments are not all-powerful – they have to raise money from tax-payers and live with the realities of economic constraints. They are accountable to the voters for the success or failure of their policies. Their every move is scrutinized

---

Activity 14.2   **Influencing the policy-makers**

Access the Department of Health website (www.doh.gov) and locate a current consultation or health policy which interests you and relates to your future practice in your chosen branch of nursing.

(a) Using the summary section, outline to a colleague what the main issues are.

(b) Try to form your own opinions about the policy you have chosen and its advantages and possible risks for clients or patients and for clinical professionals.

---

by powerful and critical media. Moreover, they have limited control over the behaviour of individuals, private companies and even their own governmental organizations. Many policies do not get fully implemented because of other influences on decisions and actions or because of problems in the organizations that are charged with carrying them out.

A good example has been the determined drive over several years to cut health care-acquired infections. Much instruction, guidance and 'support' from the Department of Health has encouraged more rigorous hand-washing, 'deep cleaning' of wards, cohort isolation of infected patients, more careful prescribing of antibiotics, and screening of patients coming in from the community. This drive from the highest levels of government will have influenced your training and placement experience.

Modern governments not only issue priorities and policies to the health service, they have become more determined to see their policies implemented. They set tight targets on key issues such as waiting times and monitor them closely. NHS trusts that fail to implement policies will be subject to investigation and a poor performance rating, and senior managers may be removed.

As a nurse, where you work, what you are able to do for your patients and clients (for example, the expansion of nurse prescribing), the nature of health services (community-based care, day cases, etc.), the ways in which you keep records, and the systems by which your work is monitored and assessed are all shaped by the policy process and subject to change.

modernization
the imposition of national standards in health care, the encouragement of local managerial and professional initiative, more public involvement in health issues and NHS organizations, improvement in buildings, equipment and IT, more streamlined ways of diagnosing and treating illness, and new ways of working which break down barriers between professions

3   Policy and the National Health Service

Discussion of health policy in the UK since 1948 has been dominated by the problems and opportunities of government-led NHS funding, 'reform' and 'modernization' (see Klein (2006) for a discussion of the political drivers shaping the NHS over nearly sixty years). The idea of a national, comprehensive health service, funded out of general taxation and largely available free at the point of delivery on a basis of need, has been central to popular experience, professional work and public discussion.

A national health service is not the only way to organize and provide health care in a modern society. Other approaches include that of the USA, which has a variety of private and public hospitals and services with mainstream funding from private health insurance, underpinned by Medicare and Medicaid federal schemes for the elderly and the poor. In continental Europe the norm is for health services to be funded through compulsory health insurance schemes paid for by employers and employees. Both these types of system involve higher administrative costs but can produce very good services for those who can afford to pay or who have good insurance cover. But, as chapter 8 shows, such people represent a good risk for insurers and are less likely to need health care. Private insurance schemes mean that the poor, the chronically ill and anyone who is considered a high risk (or who becomes one) are much less well provided for. At the time of writing, no major political party in the UK has included a move towards a more privatized or insurance-based health care system in its election manifesto, and they have all reiterated their commitment to NHS principles. Furthermore, the significant improvement in NHS funding each year from 2002 has been maintained, and the main political parties in all UK countries are promising to retain the NHS's share of national expenditure. In 2002, the Labour government continued a push for NHS modernization and change built around

internal market   a policy whereby a large public sector organization is broken down into smaller, more independent provider hospitals or community units which compete for contracts from a commissioning or purchasing body

an **internal market** that was begun by the radical Conservative governments of Margaret Thatcher. They asked a leading banker, Derek Wanless, to review the basic funding model of the NHS and compare it to systems elsewhere. His report (Wanless, 2002) reiterated the benefits in terms of economy and efficacy of preserving the tax-based, free-at-point-of-delivery model of the NHS. This important report cleared the way for the government to increase NHS spending to bring UK health expenditure up to average European levels and to enable sustained investment in the new facilities and staff that would be needed to achieve the targets set out in the NHS Plan (DH, 2000). However, he recommended a 'fully engaged' model where the public were very aware of how to protect and enhance their own health. This health promotion emphasis is something to which Derek Wanless returned in a later report (Wanless, 2004).

There are some interesting differences in how major NHS reviews have been conducted. Mrs Thatcher asked the leading businessman from Sainsbury's, Sir Roy Griffiths, to make recommendations about the NHS workforce, and this led to the important introduction of 'general managers' as well as much better qualified accountants and better understanding of costs. He produced a 23-page letter based on some personal visits to NHS hospitals. Sir Derek Wanless was brought in as an independent financial expert for his comprehensive study and commissioned some impressive demographic, economic and epidemiological research. A more recent policy review published in 2008 to celebrate sixty years of the NHS is known as the *The NHS Next Stage Review.* It was led by Lord Ara Darzi, a famous surgeon, who was brought into the government specifically to give 'clinical leadership' to a policy review entitled *High Quality Care for All*, showing how the NHS should be established for the next sixty years. (DH, 2008) (see also chapter 12 for the implications for primary care).

How effectively can business principles be applied to health care and the management of health services?

This is a significant change in policy fashion and perhaps indicates government sensitivity to a negative reaction from clinicians and the public to repeated policy initiatives dominated by business perspectives, managers and accountants. In spite of considerable and sustained increased spending on the NHS, the government felt that its motives, for example, in concentrating specialized medicine and trauma services in large regional centres or in creating larger local health centres to deal with many routine out-patient appointments were misunderstood by the public and by professional trade unions and spokespeople.

The *Next Stage Review* process was driven by extensive consultation with members of the public in large focus groups around the country and with hand-picked and respected clinical leaders rather than managers and board directors. The outcome was in part the specification of eight clinical pathways, which established the optimum pattern of care meeting national standards of best practice locally. There was a determined attempt to shift the policy debate from discussion about money, markets and top-down managerial directives

towards a model of expert clinicians consulting with the public and
each other to establish excellent standards and pathways of care.

Activity 14.3   **The Darzi inheritance**

At the time of writing, it is hard to predict the outcome of the
Next Stage Review: will it mark a step change in NHS policy-making
or is it a lot of publicity without long-term substance? You can
now make your own assessment by working through the
questions below.

(a)   Use a web browser such as Google to see what the following
groups are saying about Lord Darzi and *The NHS Next Stage Review*
as you study this chapter.

(b)   Does it still feature strongly on the Department of Health website
or has a new government moved on and marginalized it?

(c)   What does the medical press say about this 2008 initiative?

(d)   What do the nursing press and the nursing professional bodies
say about it?

(e)   Acute surgical and medical care and developments in primary
care, often known as 'polyclinics', were featured strongly in
Darzi's proposals, but have mental health services, learning
disability services and children's services received similar
attention in the years since the report was published?

It is important to be aware that, in the UK, not all health care
is provided by the NHS. As chapter 11 shows, much health care in
Britain, as throughout the world, is provided informally through self-
care, through families and neighbours. Furthermore, there is a
significant private sector (16 per cent of UK health care) made up
of hospitals, private medical practices and nursing homes funded
through direct payment or private health insurance (King's Fund,
2001). In 1999 the Labour government initiated a policy of greater
collaboration with the private health sector, and there is support for
treating NHS patients in private hospitals where necessary and for
inviting private and overseas suppliers in independent treatment
centres to carry out some of the treatments needed by NHS patients.
An important element of this policy was to give patients a greater
choice about where they were treated and to increase capacity in the
supply of services even where the NHS was paying.

In the UK, governments have to pay close attention to NHS
funding, effectiveness and efficiency while trying to ensure that it
continues to satisfy the public that use it. While the NHS remains
popular overall, successive governments have tried to 'reform' the
way it operates, and the latest ideas on such reforms feature strongly

in party manifestos and conference speeches. Wherever you work in health care there will be more 'reforms' and policy changes in the pipeline. A good professional needs to be ahead of the curve on these changes, recognize the opportunities and think through how they might be used to improve services and benefit their patients.

4   The policy process

Governments are elected in part on the basis of party manifestos which outline the policies or courses of action that they intend to carry out. This will be done through acts of parliament, annual decisions on expenditure (comprehensive spending reviews), budgets, and much administrative detailed guidance issued by government departments such as the Department of Health. In a democratic society policies are widely discussed, with political parties and independent 'think-tanks' making proposals, and pressure groups (such as professions, patients' associations and big pharmaceutical companies) giving their views and lobbying or persuading governments and the public to their way of thinking. The press, TV and radio give extensive coverage to these debates, and there will be national and local consultations about service developments and changes.

This chapter will now look first at how health policies are changed and then at how they operate in three related areas – policy on health service organization, policy on treatments and care, and finally policies around public health, health improvement and disease prevention.

How are policies changed?

A review of previous chapters will suggest that some groups in society have less influence than others. This is a key aspect of inequality, and factors such as class, race, gender, age, sexual orientation and disability become dimensions of powerlessness (see part II of this book). Excluded groups have to organize and overcome structural difficulties if they are to have any influence on policies or challenge the status quo. Hence campaigns for equal rights for women, the labour and trade union organizations, movements for race equality, gay and lesbian pride organizations, campaigns by pensioners, the disability rights movement – all have tried to reshape the way decisions are made and resources are allocated and to influence policy, with varied success.

Chapters 3 and 4 show how important medical dominance has been for a century and a half in shaping health policy, both by influencing government and societal thinking about health and by ensuring medical control of key institutions, activities and practices. Nursing has for many years found itself to be in a subordinate position constrained by medical power and medical attitudes.

However, this can change, and, as professionals and as citizens/voters, often by working through pressure groups, nurses have opportunities to influence and reshape health policy in a way that emphasizes the values of nursing and care.

The care of sick children in hospital and in the community is one aspect which provides a good example of this process and of the influence of independent pressure groups that seek to influence and improve policies which affect their area of concern and interest. Action for Sick Children is a major charity which aims to improve services for children with health problems. It began over forty years ago as the National Association for the Welfare of Children in Hospital (NAWCH). Many policies that we as parents or child health nurses now take for granted were the result of the efforts of this campaigning organization to influence government and NHS bodies. Research in the 1950s seemed to show that separating young children from their parents could have long-term effects on their health and well-being (Bowlby, 1967). NAWCH brought together parents, journalists, sociologists and health care professionals to campaign for overnight rooms for parents, specialized children's wards, more specialist children's nurses and doctors, and a greater recognition of children's emotional and psychological needs.

Policy with regard to the care and health of children is likely to engage public and media interest, and the campaign to improve the care of children in hospitals had access to good research evidence and influential professionals as well as the support and patronage of relatively wealthy and influential members of the public. Campaigns for the 'normalization' of care for people with learning difficulties and the eventual closure of the isolating 'colonies' of special hospitals took many years to implement (for a definition of normalization, see chapter 13). Even though the professional argument had been won, funding for suitable teams of multi-professional staff and the building of suitable homes in the community took some years to come through.

Through pressure groups and professional bodies, nurses and members of the public can seek to change and modify policies, and, where there is a determined effort on behalf of particular patient groups, this can be very successful.

5 Evolution of policy on health care organization and provision

Rob Baggott (2004) describes how policy has evolved around the funding, organization and management of the British health care system. If you talk to people who have been involved as managers or nurses in the NHS for some time then you will probably hear complaints about too many organizational changes and targets being handed down from central government. UK governments of different political parties often say that they wish to leave the professionals – the doctors and nurses – to get on with treating patients. Yet politicians feel compelled to intervene, reorganize, develop new policies and closely monitor their implementation. Bringing a senior clinician such as Lord Darzi into the government in 2007 was a significant change of direction, but it remains to be seen whether other clinicians recognize this change or whether he comes to be seen as just another politician.

Policies on the organization and management of health care

The NHS was founded in 1948. Major structural reorganizations were initiated in 1974, 1982, 1990, 1997, 2002 and 2006. These policies have been concerned with improving the management, efficiency and quality of service through different patterns of organization, often reflecting ideas and practice from the private sector. Detailed accounts of these changes can be followed up elsewhere (see Baggott, 2004; Ham 2004).

A number of important changes known as 'system reform' have been introduced since 2002. NHS trusts have been encouraged to become foundation trusts (FTs). These have to be approved on very strict business criteria by a regulator known as a 'monitor', but thereafter are allowed a degree of independence from government directives. They can borrow money for new developments and attract new services funded by local NHS commissioners. They are non-profit-making public bodies with a large membership made up of patients, local residents, staff and local stakeholders. Members elect a governing body which gives overall direction to the trust, owns its assets and appoints a more conventional board of directors to do the day-to-day management. The first wave of the new FTs consisted of acute hospitals, including many prestigious teaching hospitals, but their numbers have increased to incorporate mental health trusts, and community trusts (providing local community services) are also envisaged. These FTs earn their income through a system of 'payment by results' whereby there is a standard treatment-based tariff payment for each patient referred by their GP. The idea is that, with greater patient choice, trusts will compete to attract more patients with higher quality services.

Meanwhile the local NHS bodies – primary care trusts (PCTs) – and groups of GPs known as 'practice-based commissioners' will be responsible for the local health care budget and seek to ensure that only patients who really need acute or specialist treatment are referred. It is intended that vulnerable people, rather than being admitted inappropriately through accident and emergency departments, should be cared for under programmes such as case management or crisis intervention teams in their own homes or in local community hospitals. Since 2006 the local PCTs have been encouraged to separate out any of their 'provider functions', such as community nursing, local mental health services or rehabilitative care, into new independent organizations so that they can concentrate on planning, commissioning and paying for all the health care needed by their populations. This is developed further in chapter 12.

While on placement it should be possible to seek out some of the more experienced members of staff and ask them their views. Let us consider someone appointed in 1980 as a mental health nurse (probably in a large mental hospital) and now perhaps considering retirement. She or he would have been trained in a small hospital-based school of mental health nursing and have worked initially in that same hospital. The hospital was within an area health authority which provided all secondary, hospital and community care for its area. The new nurse's role would have been near the bottom of a nursing hierarchy which was led by a director of nursing services. Professions were all-important, and at each level there were committees made up of senior representatives of each profession determining how the service should be run. The 1982 reorganization removed a layer of bureaucracy above the new district health authority (DHA), but this would not have impacted much on our nurse.

In 1983, however, the Thatcher government commissioned a report from Sir Roy Griffiths, managing director of Sainsbury supermarkets. The Griffiths Report (DHSS, 1983) brought the introduction of 'general' management, 'regardless' of professional discipline, into the NHS. Still part of the DHA, the mental health hospital now became a unit, with a unit general manager reporting to a district general manager. The new general managers and a number of processes of co-ordination and control began to challenge the full autonomy of the teams of professionals. The service became more cost-conscious, better financial and performance information was required and, while overall expenditure continued to rise, efficiency savings had to be made each year, and 'cuts' might result from spending reviews when budgets were in danger of being overspent.

Between 1990 and 1997 the Conservative government's new policy of the internal market had an effect on the mental health service, as elsewhere. The local mental health service became an 'NHS trust', a bit like an independent company, although still in the NHS and not allowed to make a 'profit'. To treat patients and survive, the trust had to attract funding contracts through a commissioning or purchasing process from the district health authority. Financial discipline was increasing: only patients covered in the main contract or from specially agreed 'extra-contractual referrals' from other districts could be treated.

A new Labour government in 1997 promised to end the internal market, improve funding and encourage partnership working in the NHS. However, the NHS trusts continued with a modified system of contracting through 'service and financial frameworks' negotiated by district health authorities and, more recently, as legally binding contracts by PCTs, thus perpetuating a modified form of internal market.

These managerial changes (discussed further in the next chapter) demonstrate the pressure on successive governments to implement health care policies which control costs and meet public expectations as well as a restless search for new structures and a growing reliance on management processes which would then be balanced by attempts at clinical engagement. The changing political and ideological climate means that all governments in advanced countries are confronted with similar dilemmas.

Health policies and the process of treatment and care

Alongside these reorganizations, there has been a steady growth of policy initiatives concerned with the actual processes of treatment and health care and the patient experience. These policies have a much more direct impact on what happens to patients in terms of access to services and the treatments they experience, while they also influence the way nurses and other health professionals work. For example, policies have been developed and implemented on how long patients wait in accident and emergency departments. Successive governments have tried to reduce the time spent waiting for outpatient appointments, diagnostic tests and elective operations, and tight targets have been set for access to general practitioners and practice nurses in primary care practices (see chapter 12). These matters become part of health policy because, in the national and centralized NHS, governments are held directly responsible for such standards of service. Delayed treatments rapidly become matters of political controversy; governments set targets and then have to put pressure on local NHS managers and clinicians to achieve them or be seen to fail.

What happens to patients is of course important to them, and traditionally this was determined by resources available locally and the clinical discretion of trained professionals deciding on priorities and using their expertise and judgement. Since the development of *The Patient's Charter* (DH, 1996) and many promises made by later governments, patient expectations, treatments, targets and

performance monitoring ◄ performance monitoring have become subject to direct political
regular checks by involvement. The organizational and managerial changes discussed
superior bodies within above have made this much more possible, but it is the way in which
the NHS hierarchy on key health policy has become much more 'up close and personal' that is
targets such as financial interesting.
balance, waiting times
and discharge delays

Quality of care is in part defined by the ability to meet the satisfaction of patients and clients in terms of waiting lists, patient information, cleanliness of facilities and attitudes of staff. The mental health nurse is now much more involved in consulting users and carers and designing services around their needs and aspirations. You will find that this commitment to working in partnership with clients or patients and their carers is now an integral part of modern nurse training in all four branches.

In *The New NHS: Modern, Dependable* (DH, 1997), the incoming government laid out its plans for the NHS. One important theme was the idea of common national standards implemented locally. The objective was to ensure that best practice was available throughout the country and to set standards for the 'quality' of service delivered by the NHS. There are a number of dimensions to this set of policies, but they were outlined in the paper *A First Class Service* (DH, 1998), which made clinical quality a top priority for NHS trusts. The concept of clinical governance was introduced along with two new institutions: the National Institute for Clinical Excellence – now known as the National Institute for Health and Clinical Excellence (NICE) – and an independent regulator of health care quality – initially, the Commission for Health Improvement (CHI), then the Healthcare Commission. From 2009 this body has been merged with the Commission for Social Care Inspection and the Mental Health Act Commission to form one integrated health and care regulator, reporting independently to parliament and known as the Care Quality Commission (CQC).

Clinical audit, a method of comparing patient outcomes whereby fellow professionals critically assess practice, had been instituted in the NHS since the 1990s, but the information was confidential (mainly within the medical profession). A number of scandals, notably the Bristol child heart surgery investigation, and research which showed that patient outcomes varied across the country, for example in cancer treatment, meant that a coherent set of policies about the process of treatment and care could be introduced.

NICE was established as a government-backed expert body which began to evaluate the efficacy, cost-effectiveness and patient acceptability of new drugs and treatments. It issues guidelines which, while not mandatory, set the standards against which local health care practice will be evaluated. There has been much controversy about the speed with which NICE approves new drug treatments and its use of cost-effectiveness calculations to decide whether expensive drugs, especially those used at the later stages of cancer care, at the early stages of Alzheimer's syndrome or for wet macular degeneration, should be recommended for widespread use.

At the same time comprehensive and compulsory National Service Frameworks (NSFs) have been developed by the Department of Health using expert opinion. These set out the standards to be achieved within a number of key service areas. NSFs have been issued for mental health, care of the elderly, chronic heart disease, and diabetes. The pathway approach of the *Next Stage Review* is a development of this approach, using expert groups and consultation with professionals

clinical governance the process whereby a health care organization works to ensure a high and rising standard of treatment and care for patients and users

National Institute for Health and Clinical Excellence (NICE) a body of experts who evaluate the evidence on new and existing treatments, drugs and clinical procedures and determine whether they are worthwhile clinically and economically

Care Quality Commission (CQC) the independent regulatory body for health care

and the public to specify the optimum care pathway from diagnosis to rehabilitation for people needing common forms of health care treatment. These pathways often cross several health and social care organizations and professional specialists, and it can be in the handovers between different clinicians and different organizations that mistakes can be made.

Activity 14.4   **NICE guidance and patient pathways**

Look up the NICE website and choose a treatment or drug that you know about from your clinical placement. Look at the evidence that NICE has used to make its recommendation.

(a) Why is your chosen drug or treatment recommended
• clinically?
• in terms of patient acceptability?
• in term of cost effectiveness?

(b) Use a search engine to see what organizations or professional bodies have expressed views on this treatment/drug. What arguments have they put forward to recommend its adoption?

(c) See if you can locate a treatment or drug that has been turned down and follow through the arguments and identify the reasons that NICE give for not supporting its use.

(d) Think about whether you would personally pay privately to use a drug or treatment that is not recommended by NICE.

Your nurse education and training is influenced by health policy.

These are powerful health policies which guide practice, investment, training and local plans and give a strong sense of direction to critical areas of health care. For example, the NSF on chronic heart disease has saved many lives by earlier intervention and led to much-increased prescribing of cholesterol-reducing drugs called statins. There is no doubt that aspects of your own syllabus and placement experience will have been affected by NSFs, the guidance from NICE and the recommendations from the Darzi review of health care pathways.

However, as discussed earlier, issuing policy does not guarantee implementation within very complex organizations. For example, there has been considerable media coverage of complaints from cancer specialists and mental health charities that aspects of policy have not been fully implemented across the country and that investment earmarked for cancer care or mental health or children with disabilities has been siphoned off into meeting other priorities or to cover previous deficits.

From 2009, the Care Quality Commission (CQC) will carry out a process of checking, enforcement, inspection and performance monitoring for all NHS trusts, private health care suppliers, nursing and care homes, and primary care centres. The CQC sends expert teams in to visit trusts regularly and requires them to produce self-assessments against government-determined health care standards and targets. Trusts returns and assessments are cross-checked against a large collection of statistical data. The commission then inspects both their performance and their internal clinical governance arrangements and processes. Are waiting list targets being met? Have relevant NSFs been implemented? Are staff appropriately trained and retrained? Are arrangements for clinical governance in place? Are treatments and practices reviewed regularly? Are these quality matters regularly reported to the board?

Governments will defend such policies of inspection on the grounds of 'accountability'. Health care professionals and managers are responsible for spending large amounts of public money and carry out work which is of the utmost importance to patients and their families. How else can the government and thus the public be assured that standards are being upheld and the best possible practice is being carried out across a large and complex system? To encourage improved performance, trusts are evaluated annually, with extra opportunities and money going to successful 'high performing' trusts, whilst those with merely adequate or poor performance will be subject to greater intervention and scrutiny, with the ultimate possibility of new managers being brought in from elsewhere.

Policies on public health, health improvement and prevention

Thus far we have concentrated on health care policies – how best to ensure treatment for people who fall ill. However, there is an important aspect of health policy concerned with preventing illness and trying to ensure the good health of the population.

These policies are associated with prevention through measures to enhance individual and community health and interventions such as vaccination or smoking cessation clinics. Finding ways to shift thinking and behaviour from treatment to prevention has been the holy grail of health policy. Research by McKeown (1979) suggests that the major improvements in the health of populations in the industrialized world have been the result of environmental improvements, especially to water supplies and housing, together with economic prosperity, rather than the remedial intervention of medicine and health care systems (see chapter 3 for a further discussion of the social causes of ill-health). If all the population lived in warm, dry, well-lit housing in a cleaner and safer environment, if economic policy improved household incomes and greater equality reduced stress, then there would be less pressure on the health service and people would enjoy healthier lives. Similarly, from a more individual perspective, if health education encouraged people to stop smoking, eat sensibly, breastfeed their babies, reduce alcohol intake, practise contraception and safer sex, drive more carefully and take regular exercise, then fewer people would suffer from cancer, chronic heart disease, diabetes, accidents, mental health problems, obesity, and HIV and other sexually transmitted diseases.

Health education and promotion campaigns have been a feature of health policy for many years, with public health organizations producing materials and encouraging behavioural change through advertisements, training programmes, support to teachers, advice to companies, legislation such as banning smoking in public places, and so on. Some of this will have permeated your nursing course; for example, you will be encouraged to use your influence as a nurse to advise and support patients and clients in search of a healthier lifestyle. Activity 14.5 asks you to consider health promotion for young people.

Key documents such as *Choosing Health* (DH, 2004) have sought to emphasize health promotion and set targets for improving health. While not having the immediacy and popular impact of policies on health care and never attracting the level of funding and professional interest that responding to ill-health requires, health promotion remains a significant aspect of health policy.

Furthermore, the government has given some emphasis to health promotion and improvement in the way the NHS and partner agencies are directed, in the setting of targets and in monitoring and evaluation. Local NHS bodies have directors of public health and are tasked to enter into partnership with other agencies, especially the local authorities, schools and voluntary organizations, in working towards health improvement. Thus activity to cut smoking or avoid heart disease might be co-ordinated across an area or a particular estate and projects around diet, exercise and support programmes introduced. Similarly, the monitoring and performance rating of NHS bodies will include scores on the number of people who have quit smoking, the incidence of venereal disease or the rate of teenage pregnancies.

Activity 14.5   **'Our future?' health and young people**

Drinking and
smoking is
widespread
among
teenagers.

(a)   Brainstorm a health promotion strategy for young people living
on an outer-city housing estate with poor services, few leisure
facilities, and high rates of teenage pregnancy and
unemployment.

(b)   Consider a health promotion strategy for young people with *either*
learning disabilities *or* mental health difficulties. How would this
strategy differ from (or be similar to) the strategy identified for
question (a)?

(c)   Should you aim to spread 'health messages' among young people
regarding safer sex, obesity, smoking, and so on, or try to
persuade local and central government to target the estate's
underlying problems?

Once again it is possible to see how the context of health care
and the work of nurses is directly affected by the health policies
adopted by successive governments, and how the desire to ensure
implementation drives down to directing the work of local
practitioners. Community and practice nurses are involved in work
around smoking cessation, sexual health and advice on diet and
exercise. While this is fully in line with good professional practice,
they are aware that their results are being assessed and will be one
of the factors that lead to a successful or unsuccessful performance
rating of the local NHS.

Summary and Resources

Summary

- Health policy is of major importance in British politics, and the nurse's professional practice is carried out within a legal, organizational, financial and health care system determined through the policy process.

- The NHS has been central to health policy in the UK since 1948, and there have been successive reorganizations in pursuit of a better and more efficient service.

- Policies are the product of a political process to which, as a citizen and as a professional, the nurse can make a contribution.

- Health policies have increasingly been about the detailed management of the health service, improving patients' access to treatment and the very process of clinical care itself, trying to ensure universal best practice and patient satisfaction.

- There is a longstanding emphasis in health policy on trying to improve the health of the population through public health measures and health promotion so as to enhance well-being and prevent illness.

Questions for Discussion

1. How can the quality of health services be improved and what should the balance be between quality outcomes assessed by clinical experts and quality as measured by patient satisfaction?

2. Can patients and clients make an effective choice between different hospitals, community services or treatment methods, or should they accept the judgement of trained professionals as to what is best for them?

3. What will you say to friends and relatives when they ask you whether the services that you have worked in and seen on placement are safe, comfortable and effective in meeting their needs?

Further Reading

S. Harrison and R. McDonald: *The Politics of Health Care in Britain*. London: Sage, 2008.
A useful and up-to-date thematic account of the underlying political issues that shape health care. It covers resources and rationing, professionalism, clinical knowledge, organization and management, and the policy process.

S. Peckham and E. Meerabeau: *Social Policy for Nurses and the Helping Professions*. Maidenhead: Open University Press, 2007.
This text relates key issues in social policy to nursing by the use of examples and case studies for different client groups. It considers the development of social policy in preventing illness and reducing health inequalities. It also covers professional regulation.

R. Baggott: *Health and Health Care in Britain*. 3rd edn, Basingstoke: Macmillan, 2004.
A thorough account of all aspects of health policy, ideal for exploring issues in depth or obtaining an understanding of how the NHS and health policy have developed.

C. J. Ham: *Health Policy in Britain*. 5th edn, London: Palgrave, 2004.
A comprehensive guide produced by a leading authority and government adviser on health policy.

To explore this topic further, go to www.politybooks.com/ sociologyfornurses.

References

Baggott, R. 2004: *Health and Health Care in Britain*. 3rd edn, Basingstoke: Macmillan.

Bowlby, J. 1967: *Child Care and the Growth of Love*. 2nd edn, Harmondsworth: Penguin.

DH (Department of Health) 1996: *The Patient's Charter and You: A Charter for England*. Leeds: DH.

DH 1997: *The New NHS: Modern, Dependable*, Cm 3807. London: HMSO.

DH 1998: *A First Class Service: Quality in the New NHS*. London: HMSO.

DH 2000: *The NHS Plan: A Plan for Investment*, Cm 4818. London: HMSO.

DH 2004: *Choosing Health: Making Healthy Choices Easier*, Cm 6374. London: HMSO.

DH 2008: *High Quality Care for All: Final Report*, Cm 7432 [Darzi Report]. London: HMSO.

DHSS 1983: *NHS Management Inquiry* [Griffiths Report]. London: Department of Health and Social Security.

Ham, C. J. 2004: *Health policy in Britain*. 5th edn, London: Palgrave.

King's Fund 2001: *General Election 2001 Briefings*. London: King's Fund, 8.

Klein, R. 2006: *The New Politics of the NHS: From Creation to Reinvention*. 5th edn, Oxford: Radcliffe.

McKeown, T. 1979: *The Role of Medicine: Dream, Mirage or Nemesis?* Oxford: Blackwell.

Wanless, D. 2002: *Securing our Future Health: Taking a Long-Term View: Final Report*. London: HM Treasury; www.hm-treasury.gov.uk/ consult_wanless_final.htm [last accessed 30 November 2008].

Wanless, D. 2004: *Securing Good Health for the Whole Population, Final Report*. London: HM Treasury.

15

The Management and Organization of Health Care

Alistair Hewison

Key issues in this chapter

- What is management?
- The contribution of sociology to our understanding of the management and organization of health care.
- The need for nurses to engage with management and leadership
- Organizational aspects of health care, including nurse leadership, the introduction of the modern matron and evidence-based practice
- The application of sociological concepts to the reality of everyday practice

At the end of this chapter you should be able to . . .

- define the term management;
- use sociological concepts to examine the activities contained in the chapter;
- summarize the main components of the structure of a typical NHS organization;
- discuss the role of the nurse as a manager;
- recognize the continuing influence of management in health care.

1 Introduction

When a football club is relegated, who is sacked or resigns? If a business is failing, who is deemed to be responsible? When an error is made in an NHS trust, who is expected to explain the circumstances to the media? In most circumstances the answer to these questions is the manager, or, to use a more recent title, the chief executive. How does this observation relate to nursing and health care? Essentially all organizations, both large and small, need to be managed in some way. In the case of health care, if the service is to be delivered, certain people in the organization need to make sure things are done on time and in the right way. However, this is not as straightforward as it might appear. Things go wrong, people make mistakes; sometimes a ward or department is so busy that information concerning patient care is not passed on and patients do not receive appropriate care. The focus of this chapter is what sociology can offer to help explain how such situations occur and to provide an indication of how things can be improved.

2 What is management?

The term 'manage' derives from the Italian word *maneggiare*, which means to control or to train, and was originally applied to the management of horses (Grint, 1995). One of the foremost writers on management summarizes a view that many have of this activity: 'Management is a curious phenomenon. It is generously paid, enormously influential, and significantly devoid of common sense' (Mintzberg, 1996, p. 61). Yet without management and organization, would it be possible to provide patient care? If nurses do not know who is in charge, which patients they are looking after on a particular shift, which patients are for surgery that day, or which patients need medication at a particular time, problems will ensue.

The aim of this chapter is to offer a working definition of management and to examine the contribution of sociology towards increasing our understanding of the management and organization of health care. In this chapter management is defined as an expression

agency the capacity individuals have to shape their social world ⟵ of human **agency**, the capacity actively to shape and direct the world, rather than simply to react to it. Management therefore has five elements:

1. deciding/planning what is to be done, and how;
2. allocating time and effort to what is to be done;
3. motivating or generating the effort to do it;
4. co-ordinating and combining disparate efforts;

5   controlling what is to be done to ensure that it conforms with what
was intended. (Hales, 1993, p. 2)

This is relevant to people working in all organizations, including
health care. As Iles (2005, p. 5) observes: 'As soon as we ask someone
else to do something, rather than undertaking it ourselves, we
become managers. We rely on someone else to perform that task in
the way we would do it.' Nurses soon find they have to ask others,
such as care assistants, parents, carers, and members of the multi-
disciplinary team, to undertake a range of tasks, and so are involved
in management from an early stage in their career.

3   Management in health care

It has been argued that, from its inception in 1948 until the
introduction of the recommendations arising from the Griffiths Report
(DHSS, 1983), the NHS was 'administered' rather than managed
(Connelly, 2000; Harrison, 1988; Harrison et al., 1992). The Griffiths
Report ushered in a structure in which there were 'general managers'
and an 'executive' board. The managers were seen as fulfilling the role
that a manager in a commercial company would play, that is,
undertaking the five key aspects of management identified earlier to
ensure the service was delivered. The impact of the Griffiths Report
was assessed by a number of researchers employing a particular

ethnography   a research ◄— sociological approach called **ethnography** which examined its origins
approach which involves
the direct observation of
the activity of members of
a group or organization

and implementation (see, for example, Cox, 1991; Owens and
Glennerster, 1990; Strong and Robinson, 1990). They found that the
report had a profound effect on nursing. Many senior nurses lost their
positions, and those retained were there to provide advice to whoever
was now managing nursing. Furthermore, in a third of health districts
senior nursing advice was dispensed with altogether (Strong and
Robinson, 1990). It caused widespread disruption and uncertainty,
particularly in the higher levels of the nursing hierarchy, and most
units were reorganized in such a way that nursing management was
eliminated (Owens and Glennerster, 1990). This was a traumatic period
for nursing management.

The Griffiths Report was followed by the White Paper *Working for
Patients* (DH, 1989), which led to the establishment of an internal
market in health care in which contracts between providers of
services, such as hospitals and clinics, and purchasers of services,
such as health authorities and general practitioners, formed the basis
of the organization and structure of the NHS in the 1990s (Salter,

modern matron   a nurse   1998). Subsequently, the publication of *The NHS Plan* (DH, 2000)
who is easily identifiable
to patients, accountable
for a group of wards and
in control of the resources
necessary to organize the
fundamentals of care

indicated the way the government envisaged health care being
managed for the following five years. It was anticipated that nurses
would take on significant leadership and management respon-
◄— sibilities in the NHS, reflected in the creation of the **modern matron**

nurse leadership
programme   a
programme of leadership
development for nurses at
ward and senior level
instituted following *The
NHS Plan*

posts and the establishment of the national nurse leadership programme.

The modern matron post was introduced to ensure there was a senior nursing management presence in the ward areas of hospitals with a specific remit to improve cleanliness and raise nutritional standards (DH 2001a). It is difficult to determine the impact of this role as the evidence is mixed, partly because it has been implemented in different ways in different trusts (Savage and Scott, 2004). The matrons did have some effect in improving quality (Dealey et al., 2007), though in many instances their potential was unrecognized (Savage and Scott, 2004). This is not entirely surprising, because when the role was first mooted it was not clear precisely what it would entail (Snell, 2001) and consequently judging 'success' is problematic. However, the need for nursing leadership and management remains a policy concern and is reflected in the Darzi Report (DH, 2008) (see below and chapters 12 and 14).

In relation to nurse leadership, by 2003 more than 32,000 nurses had taken part in the Leading Empowered Organizations (LEO) programme (Faugier and Woolnough, 2003a). This represents a considerable investment in the development of nursing leadership and was part of a wider suite of programmes that was introduced in the wake of *The NHS Plan* to help ensure leadership skills were embedded in all levels of nursing (Govier, 2004). While it is interesting to note that many nurses enjoyed the LEO programme and got a lot from it, one study reports that those who attended were unable to provide examples of how their practice had changed as a result (Werrett, Griffiths and Clifford, 2002). It was also found that the leadership role for many nurses was not supported in their organization (Faugier and Woolnough 2003b). This indicates that, in terms of leadership, the aims of the plan have not been fully met. This is reflected in the continuing prominence given to leadership as an essential part of the management and organization of health care (see below).

The organization of UK health care since 2000

The overall approach indicated by *The NHS Plan* (DH 2000) was refined and developed in subsequent years, resulting in a great deal of change in the structure and delivery of the service (DH, 2005). The main elements of how the NHS is supposed to operate are summarized in box 15.1, which illustrates the wide range of activities in which different parts of the service are engaged. However, it must be appreciated that there has also been a process of devolution, and so the systems in England, Scotland, Wales and Northern Ireland are all different to some degree (Greer and Trench, 2008).

Most recently the Darzi Report (DH, 2008) has been published. Lord Darzi, the parliamentary undersecretary of state for health, conducted a large consultation exercise involving over 2,000 clinicians, patients, members of the general public and politicians. Following this he produced a very detailed review which sets out a further programme of reform in health care. A central theme of the report is that it seeks to place a new emphasis on enabling NHS staff to lead and manage the organizations in which they work (ibid., p. 13). Indeed, there is a stated commitment to invest in programmes to prepare clinicians, including nurses, for clinical and board leadership. The intention is that nurses will be practitioners, partners and leaders in the NHS.

This all serves to underline the importance of nurses having an understanding of management and organization in health care. If they are to lead and manage practice, and assume the roles and responsibilities envisaged by Darzi, then knowledge of what is involved is crucial. In what follows, some of the concepts from sociology which provide useful insights on the way health care organizations function are considered. 'Medical sociologists, with their traditional preoccupation with macro and micro themes and issues in health care, are well placed to bring a distinctive and well informed perspective to bear on policy, implementation and management issues' (Hunter, 1990, p. 215). Similarly, Albrow (1997) concludes, sociology regards

Box 15.1   The government's view of health reform

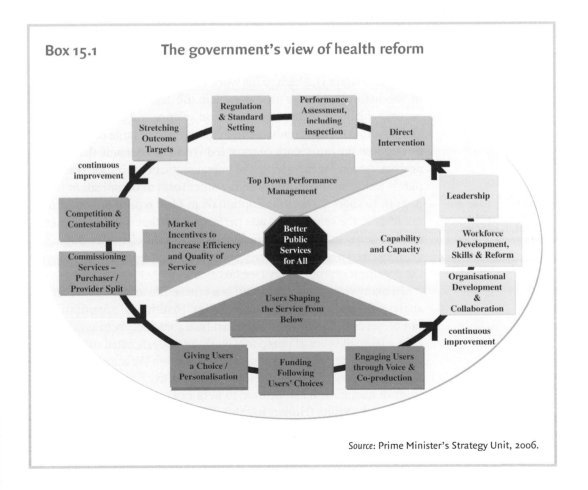

Source: Prime Minister's Strategy Unit, 2006.

organization as the outcome of social activity. Organizations are human creations, and sociology studies their origins and continued existence, which can never be taken for granted.

4   Sociology and the management of health care

This 'distinctive and well-informed perspective' derives from a number of concepts that can help us make sense of how organizations and the people working in them function. Five are examined below. These are bureaucracy, the division of labour, negotiated order, the informal organization, and power.

Bureaucracy

This term is often used to describe rule-bound organizations where it is difficult to get any explanation or response because of 'red tape'. If a process or person is referred to as being 'bureaucratic' it generally indicates that this is negative and unhelpful. In an extreme form bureaucratic organizations fail to do what they are supposed to do because rules and regulations are applied so rigidly that employees lose sight of what their job is.

bureaucracy   a structure found in large organizations, based on the specialization of tasks, rules and regulations, systems and authority

Bureaucracy, as a sociological concept, was originally developed by Max Weber, one of the first sociologists to consider the role of individuals in relation to the structural determinants of social action (see also chapter 1). Much of his work was concerned with the notion of 'rationality', which he used to explain the development of Western society which was increasingly based on science and calculation (Jary and Jary, 1991). This, combined with the growth of large organizations throughout the nineteenth century, led Weber to conclude that the decisive reason for the advance of bureaucratic organization was its purely technical superiority over any other form of organization (1947, p. 214). In short, it was a description of an ideal type of organization –

ideal type   a model of a phenomenon which identifies its essential elements

not ideal in the sense that it was perfect or one that should be aimed for, but rather that its structure contained specific elements that characterized it as a bureaucracy and which were necessary to manage the organizations of the day (see box 15.2).

In many respects, the hospital is a crucial illustration of Weber's analysis of rationalization (Turner, 1987). Health care organizations can be described as 'professionalized bureaucracies' because they have a large number of personnel working in designated roles that are governed by rules and procedures. Although Weber's concept of rational bureaucracy does not form the definitive framework for the study of hospitals, it can be used to help explain organizational failure and conflict (Hillier, 1987). For example, it is now generally accepted that the best time to give many types of tablet is with meals. Drugs are usually dispensed in caring institutions during medication rounds of one form or another. If the nursing staff wish to change the

Record-keeping is an important part of health care work.

Box 15.2   **The main components of a bureaucracy**

- Rules govern the exercise of authority.

- There are boundaries of specialism and areas of competence within which authority is exercised.

- People in the organization hold an office within the hierarchy.

- Staff or office-holders lower in the hierarchy are responsible to staff at a higher level.

- Staff undertake training that prepares them for their specific role within the hierarchy.

- Administrative acts, decisions and rules are formulated and recorded in written form.

- The office-holder is expected to act objectively and administer in compliance with the rules.

Source: Adapted from Blundell and Murdock, 1997, and Weber, 1947.

time of the medication round to coincide with meals, such a proposal would need to be considered and agreed to by a wide range of staff. Medical staff would have to change their prescribing habits; the pharmacy staff would need to alter their system for ensuring ward or department stocks of medication were up to date; the mealtime routine would have to be changed. This would also involve gaining the agreement of the catering staff, and the way the drug round was conducted would have to be changed. All of these actions are likely to require both discussion by a range of groups of staff in different meetings and examination of the implications of the change before it occurs. This all takes time, and there are many potential barriers to the change.

Activity 15.1   **Introducing self-medication in a bureaucracy**

As part of the treatment programme it has been decided by clinical staff that clients need to manage the administration of their own medication.

(a)   Think about this and identify the potential barriers to the introduction of a self-medication scheme for clients in a psychiatric unit.

(b)   Who would need to discuss such a proposal? Can you think of any committees that would be required to rule on this?

(c)   How would a bureaucratic structure affect the speed of decision-making in this case?

Once you have thought about the issue in this way it becomes clear how the concept of bureaucracy can be useful in explaining seemingly strange rules and procedures in health care. Bureaucracy can be observed in the barriers that sometimes exist between different wards and departments and the lack of co-operation that ensues. Also prolonged discussion concerning, for example, patients' hygiene needs can result in the development of a whole classification system to determine whether patients being cared for in the community require a 'nursing' or a 'social' bath. At a more basic level, nurses can become so concerned with all of the forms that need to be filled in when a patient is admitted that they have less time to spend with that patient delivering care. This is not a criticism of the individual nurse who is trying to complete her work; rather it is an indication of how an understanding of the concept of bureaucracy can help explain some of the more puzzling aspects of nursing practice. Activity 15.2 further illustrates how it can be applied to make sense of the organization as a whole.

Activity 15.2   Organizations as bureaucracies

(a)   Describe the structure of an NHS organization of which you have knowledge. Who is the chief executive? Is there a board? How many levels are there in the hierarchy above ward/department level?

(b)   Identify the rules and policies that are deemed to be the most important.

(c)   When you have done this, try to assess to what extent the organization matches Weber's ideal type of bureaucracy. In what ways does this help you understand how the organization functions?

The division of labour

One of the features of a bureaucracy noted earlier is that there are boundaries of specialism and areas of competence within which authority is exercised. Another way of thinking about this is to consider the division of labour (see also chapter 4). This is one of the oldest concepts in sociology (Scott and Marshall, 2005), and it has several applications. For example, it can refer to the technical division of labour – that is, allocating work to people because they have the skills expertise and training to do it – or assigning people to different tasks on an assembly line. It is also used to direct attention to the social division of labour, whereby the social class a person is from determines the work they do. A third element is the sexual division of labour, where different work is undertaken by men and women simply on the basis of gender. The focus here is on the technical division of labour and its continuing relevance to health care. If applied in a fairly basic way, this concept can be used as a simple device for dividing up the nursing work that needs to be done among the team. The delegation of particular tasks, or the allocation of the care of a group of patients, involves considering who has the appropriate level of skills and technical ability to look after which patient. In the wider healthcare organization, though, it can have other applications.

> **division of labour** the allocation of work tasks to groups or individuals according to the nature of the task

Giddens (2006) suggests that, with the development of industrialism, the division of labour became vastly more complex and that in the modern world it is international in scope. This is particularly evident in a large and complicated environment such as health care.

The development of this extremely specialized division of labour resulted in a situation in the mid-1990s where there was a mixture of pay and grading systems in the NHS, some with significant defects (DH, 2004). Consequently a scheme called *Agenda for Change* (DH,

Activity 15.3   **The division of labour in an NHS acute trust**

The extract below is taken from a Department of Health factsheet produced in 2005. Its purpose is to inform the public about the role of an NHS acute trust. Once you have read it, consider the questions that follow.

> Hospitals are managed by acute trusts, which make sure that they provide high quality health care and that they spend their money efficiently. They also decide on a strategy for how the hospital will develop, so that services improve.
> Acute trusts employ a large part of the NHS workforce – nurses, doctors, pharmacists, midwives and health visitors – as well as people doing jobs related to medicine – physiotherapists, radiographers, podiatrists, speech and language therapists, counsellors, occupational therapists and psychologists. There are many other non-medical staff employed by acute trusts, including receptionists, porters, cleaners, specialists in information technology, managers, engineers, caterers and domestic and security staff.
> Some acute trusts are regional or national centres for more specialized care. Others are attached to universities and help to train health professionals. Acute trusts can also provide services in the community, for example through health centres and clinics or in people's homes.
> (www.info.doh.gov.uk/nhfactsheets.nsf/vwHelp/ Acute%20trusts?OpenDocument#whatis)

(a)   List as many of the different professions/occupations you are aware of in health care that are not referred to here. How many can you identify in total?

(b)   Why might different acute trusts have a different division of labour?

(c)   Why are some groups of staff paid more than others?

(d)   How is this organized?

(e)   Does the division of labour provide the good service for the patients mentioned in the factsheet?

1999) was introduced in order to modernize the NHS pay system. However, in doing so it retained elements of the technical division of labour. The aim of the *Agenda for Change* proposals was to create a single job evaluation scheme that would cover all roles in the health service to support a review of pay and all other terms and conditions (DH 2001b; NHS Executive 2001). Yet three pay scales were created: one for doctors and dentists, one for other professional groups and one for all remaining staff. This reflects a continuing emphasis on task specialization and the allocation of those tasks to various categories of workers (Watson, 1995). This can be viewed as unproblematic in that different levels of skill are necessary for different types of work. But it can become more complex when questions are raised as to the value of the different contributions within this division of labour (see Allen, 2001, for an interesting discussion of this issue).

On a purely practical level, an awareness that this scheme is in operation in health care is important for nurses. The ability to demonstrate competence in different aspects of work is now central to the pay banding system in health care. This involves a broad range of knowledge and skills. Of particular relevance in terms of management and organization, however, are planning and organizational skills and responsibilities for policy and service development implementation (DH, 2004). If nurses, and other health care workers, are to progress up the pay bands, they need to be able to develop the necessary new skills and competences. This is an example of how the technical division of labour is put into practice as part of a bureaucractic system.

Given the size and complexity of the NHS, it cannot be explained or understood in terms of individual concepts. Sociological analysis involves drawing on a range of ideas and frameworks to learn more about how organizations function. One of those which was developed, in part, to account for the limitations of bureaucracy is the **negotiated order** approach.

negotiated order a means of organizing the outcome of interactions between people

Negotiated order

In contrast to the ideal type of bureaucracy, the concept of negotiated order emphasizes the importance of negotiation between individuals. Bond and Bond (1986) locate the concept of negotiated order within a broad interactionist tradition. This is that social phenomena, particularly organizational arrangements, emerge from the ongoing interaction among people. It involves negotiation and renegotiation over actions and decisions and stresses the fluidity and uncertainty of social arrangements.

Negotiating care Two classic pieces of sociological work which illustrate the application of the negotiated order approach to understanding health care are examined below.

From work conducted in psychiatric hospitals Strauss et al. (1963) found that the way care and treatment were organized was the outcome of constant negotiation on the part of the people involved. Whereas bureaucracy would suggest that all that is necessary is to follow the rules, the authors discovered that this is only part of the picture. For example, in the hospitals they studied they found that there were different ideologies of treatment advocated by different doctors, ranging from medication and electric shock-based approaches at one extreme through to psychotherapeutic or counselling-based ones at the other. As they observed:

> On occasion the diagnosis and treatment of a given patient runs against the judgement of the nurses and aids, who may not go along with the physician's directives, who may or may not disagree openly. They may subvert his therapeutic programme by one of their own. They may choose to argue the matter. They may go over his head to an administrative officer. Indeed, they have many choices of action – each requiring negotiative behaviour. In truth, while physicians are able to command considerable obedience to their directives at this particular hospital, frequently they must work hard at obtaining cooperation in their programming. (Strauss et al., 1963, p. 154)

This situation is compounded by the fact that in many circumstances there is a lack of certainty concerning the patient's illness. There is still a great deal that is unknown about psychiatric illness in particular and illness in general. This creates the space for disagreement and negotiation about care and treatment. Discussion of treatment programmes and decisions about the most appropriate way to treat patients are not fixed and are often unsystematic. They are the outcome of negotiation between various interested parties, including nurses, doctors, patients, carers, social workers, and so on.

As Strauss et al. (1963) conclude, the hospital is a locale where staff are enmeshed in a complex negotiative process in order to accomplish their individual and organizational objectives. The

Can all patients participate in negotiating their own care?

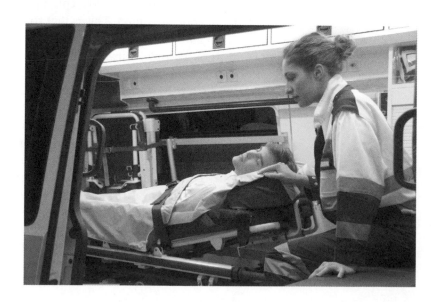

dynamics of how this is accomplished on a day-to-day basis are illustrated in the work of Stein (1967), who characterized it as the 'doctor–nurse game'. This is described in chapter 4 and is a particular type of negotiation. In playing the game the intention is that the work can be done without creating too much friction. The role of the nurse has moved on a good deal since 1967, and in 1990 Stein, Watts and Howell noted that, in an increasing number of hospital settings nurses feel free to confront and even challenge physicians more directly on issues of patient care.

Activity 15.4	Negotiating patient care

Negotiating patient care

The next time you are involved in a handover report or case conference on one of your clinical placements, think about the way decisions are being made about patient/client care.

To what extent are decisions the outcome of a formal process and based on 'objective' clinical evidence, and to what extent are they the outcome of informal discussion? Whose views prevail and why?

The informal organization

This process also takes place between and among groups throughout the organization. For example, there may be a formal process for obtaining blood results; however, if the nurse has a friend who works in the laboratory she may simply give her friend a call to get the results. This is just one of many ways people in organizations can 'work around' the system. This is known as the **informal organization**, which is the network of relationships that spontaneously establish themselves between members of an organization on the basis of their common interests and friendships (Huczynski and Buchanan, 2007). The importance of this concept can be illustrated through a brief consideration of research which has investigated the introduction of **evidence-based practice** (EBP). EBP is a priority in health care, yet some of the factors that can affect its implementation are the attitudes, beliefs and relationships of practitioners (McInnes et al., 2001). For example, Dopson et al. (2002) found that, for many health professionals, there are grey areas of practice where there is limited current evidence, and so they rely on trusted colleagues for advice. The professional network is central to when and how evidence is accepted, and practice changes as a result. Diffusing evidence into practice is a construct of debate and agreement among practitioners (Fitzgerald et al., 1999). This demonstrates how group relationships and norms of behaviour exist outside the official structure and also that the informal organization can be in conflict with the aims of the formal organization (Mullins,

informal organization the relationships, networks and norms of behaviour that people who work together develop outside the formal organizational structure and processes

evidence-based practice the conscientious, explicit and judicious use of current best evidence in making decisions about the care of individual patients (Sackett et al., 1997)

2005). So, although the UK government has increasingly proclaimed the importance of developing and implementing health and social care policy and practice that is evidence-based (Glasby, Walshe and Harvey, 2007), without an understanding of how the informal organization works this is unlikely to become a reality.

Inherent in the process of negotiation and the informal organization is the way that **power** is exerted. This is another concept which is central to sociological analysis. One of the elements of the negotiated order approaches is the relative power of people in the setting and, indeed, the power of the setting to shape or influence events.

> **power**   the ability to control or influence other people with or without their consent

Power

The notion of power is extremely complex and, as Johnson and Gill (1993) note, despite its obvious importance, the literature on power seems to suffer from ambiguous definitions and applications deriving from conflicting philosophical assumptions. Also, debates about power are often conducted in highly esoteric language. However, detailed discussions concerning the nature of power which are useful sources for further study in this area include Clegg (1979, 1989), Etzioni (1975), Lukes (1974) and Mintzberg (1983). Consideration of the nature of power is also a particular concern of many of the sociologists referred to in other chapters in this book. Central to much of the work of Weber and Marx, for example, was the analysis of organizations as social settings characterized by power struggles. It is beyond the scope of this chapter to examine this work in detail; rather, the intention is to take an example from sociology that can be applied to health care organizations and used to increase understanding of the way they function.

Individuals have power over others for all sorts of reasons, such as their gender, social class and ethnicity (see chapters 5, 8 and 9 respectively). The focus here is on the nature of power as a social resource in organizations. French and Raven (1959) produced a useful typology of social power which has continued relevance in the context of contemporary health care. They identified five sources of power within organizations that can serve as a basis for people to exert 'social power' (see box 15.3).

Different people within health care organizations have power over others arising from the sources identified by French and Raven. In a ward team there is a ward sister or charge nurse who is the appointed leader and should possess legitimate power. Members of the ward team will defer to the ward manager's right to exert influence over them. But what if members of the team do not believe that the manager is equal to the task? If there is a perception that the individual concerned has been appointed without having amassed sufficient experience and knowledge (expert power) and is not a popular individual (lacks referent power), team members are less likely to accept his or her authority. This can result in a dysfunctional team.

In order to be a skilled manager it is necessary to be able to use these sources of power in a balanced and constructive way. For example, coercive power, if not used sparingly, will very quickly have detrimental effects on any team. If a ward manager seeks to blame an individual when errors occur and punishes him or her with a public rebuke, the individual concerned is less likely to report any errors in the future for fear of being treated in a similar manner. This can have serious consequences. If a drug administration error is not reported because the nurse is worried about being told off and

---

Box 15.3　　　**The sources of social power**

Reward power is based on a person's perception that his or her leader or supervisor has the ability and resources to confer rewards of various kinds on those who comply with directives. These may be pay rises, promotion, increased responsibilities or the granting of privileges.

Coercive power is based on fear and the employee's perception that the leader or supervisor has the capacity to punish or bring about undesirable outcomes for those who do not follow directives. This can include withholding of privileges, allocation of undesirable duties or responsibilities, withholding of support, and use of disciplinary procedures.

Legitimate power is based on the person's perception that the manager or supervisor has a right to power because of his or her role or position in the organization. It is a recognition of the authority vested in managers at particular levels of the hierarchy of the organization.

Referent power is based on the employee's identification with the manager. The manager exercises influence because of the perceived attractiveness or popularity he or she has. Other terms in this form of social power are respect, esteem and charisma, which all convey the way the manager is regarded by others.

Expert power is based on the recognition by the employee of the specialist knowledge or expertise of the manager or supervisor. It arises from perceptions on the part of employees of the credibility of the manager. Evidence of this can include particular qualifications and skills.

Source: Based on French and Raven, 1959, and Mullins, 2005.

humiliated, the patient concerned is at risk. The need to have systems whereby risk and potential errors are identified and discussed to avoid harm to patients is central to clinical governance (DH, 1998), the government's strategy for quality in the NHS. However, if power is misused within the ward, such disclosure will not occur.

What types of power might be in action in this scene?

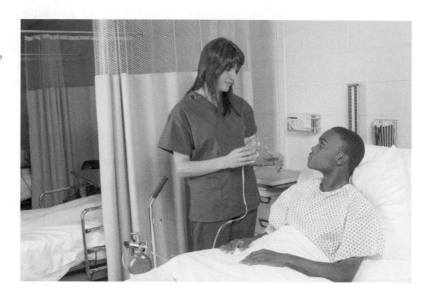

Another set of power relationships of which it is important to be aware are those which exist between nurses and their patients. Nurses can exercise power over patients because in many situations they are perceived as the experts with legitimate power. There is an emphasis in current approaches to nurse education on communication and working in partnership with patients/clients. The expectation is that nurses will discuss the needs their patients have and then construct care plans to meet those needs. This is not always possible: patients may feel that 'nurse knows best' and defer to the perceived expert and legitimate power. Also, nurses may use the power they have to 'control' the activities of patients (May, 1992a, 1992b).

It is vital that all those involved in the management and delivery of care understand the power relationships that exist, as these must be managed if the needs of the patients are to be met. Hospitals are large, powerful institutions with a complex division of labour, and sociology has a major part to play in the understanding of health care organization (Green and Thorogood, 1998). Nurses constitute the largest group of employees in health care organizations (Salter, 1998) and so have the potential to exert considerable power by sheer dint of numbers. This alone would suggest that it is worth considering the nature of power within health care. As nurses take on more management responsibilities, insights from sociology can help ensure that these duties are performed in pursuit of the patient's interests, rather than for the purposes of internal organizational power struggles.

Activity 15.5   **Power relationships at work**

When you are on placement, take a little time to observe how power relationships operate. Focus primarily on the nursing team and assess who is able to exert power and why.

(a)   Which of the staff do you recognize as having 'expert' power? Is coercive power used? If so, why? How is power exerted over patients?

(b)   Consider how a knowledge of social power may influence your approach to managing the nursing team in the future.

Summary and Resources

Summary

- Health care organizations are large and complex and will not function unless they are managed. The importance of management in the organization and delivery of health care is reflected in the structure of NHS organizations.

- Key concepts from the study of sociology, such as bureaucracy, the division of labour, negotiated order, the informal organization and power, can provide useful insights into the way health care organizations operate. Similarly, research methods developed in the discipline of sociology have been used to shed light on important aspects of health care organizations.

- Nurses are increasingly involved in management from an early stage in their careers, and so an understanding of how organizations work is important. The study of sociology is helpful in developing the composite knowledge base all managers need.

- Management is a prominent feature of the government's plans for health care over the next few years. Health policy is predicated on notions of the NHS being effectively managed and organized. Sociology provides a means of studying this development.

Questions for Discussion

1   Why is it important for health care organizations to be managed effectively?

2   What are the advantages and disadvantages of nurses being managers in health care?

3   Are people born managers or can they be trained?

4   Is it possible to manage the National Health Service?

Further Reading

J. Barr and L. Dowding: *Leadership in Health Care*. London: Sage, 2008.

A. A. Huczynski and D. Buchanan: *Organizational Behaviour: An Introductory Text*. 6th edn, Harlow: Pearson Education, 2007.

L. J. Mullins: *Management and Organisational Behaviour*. 7th edn, Harrow: Financial Times/Prentice Hall, 2005.

S. Peckham and L. Meerbeau: *Social Policy for Nurses and the Helping Professions*. 2nd edn, Maidenhead: Open University Press, 2007.

K. Walshe and J. Smith (eds): *Health Care Management*. Maidenhead: Open University Press, 2006.

T. J. Watson: *Sociology of Work and Industry*. 4th edn, London: Routledge, 2003.

References

Albrow, M. 1997: *Do Organizations have Feelings?* London: Routledge.

Allen, D. 2001: *The Changing Shape of Nursing Practice: The Role of Nurses in the Hospital Division of Labour*. London: Routledge.

Blundell, B., and Murdock, A. 1997: *Managing in the Public Sector*. London: Butterworth Heinemann.

Bond, J., and Bond, S. 1986: *Sociology and Health Care*. Edinburgh: Churchill Livingstone.

Clegg, S. R. 1979: *The Theory of Power and Organization*. London: Routledge.

Clegg, S. R. 1989: *Frameworks of Power*. London: Sage.

Connelly, J. 2000: 'A realistic theory of health sector management: the case for critical realism'. *Journal of Management in Medicine*, 14(5/6), 262–71.

Cox, D. 1991: 'Health service management – a sociological view: Griffiths and the non-negotiated order of the hospital'. In J. Gabe, M. Calman and M. Bury (eds), *The Sociology of the Health Service*. London: Routledge, pp. 89–114.

Dealey, C., Moss, H., Marshall, J., and Elcoat, C. 2007: 'Auditing the impact of implementing the modern matron role in an acute teaching trust'. *Journal of Nursing Management*, 15(1), 22–33.

DH (Department of Health) 1989: *Working for Patients*, Cm 555. London: HMSO.

DH 1998: *A First Class Service: Quality in the New NHS*. London: HMSO.

DH 1999: *Agenda for Change: Modernising the NHS Pay System*. London: DH.

DH 2000: *The NHS Plan: A Plan for Investment, a Plan for Reform*, Cm 4818–1). London: HMSO.

DH 2001a: *Implementing the NHS Plan: Modern Matrons*, HSC 2001/010. London: DH.

DH 2001b: *Agenda for Change: Modernising the NHS Pay System*. Leeds: NHS Executive.

DH 2004: *NHS Job Evaluation Handbook*. 2nd edn, London: DH.

DH 2005: *Health Reform in England: Update and Next Steps*. London: DH.

DH 2008: *High Quality Care for All: NHS Next Stage Review Final Report* [Darzi Report]. London: DH.

DHSS 1983: NHS Management Inquiry [Griffiths Report]. London: Department of Health and Social Security

Dopson, S., Fitzgerald, L., Ferlie, E., Gabbay, J., and Locock, L. 2002: 'No magic targets! Changing clinical practice to become more evidence based'. Health Care Management Review, 27(3), 35–47.

Etzioni, A. 1975: The Comparative Analysis of Complex Organizations. 2nd edn, New York: Free Press.

Faugier, J., and Woolnough, H. 2003a: 'Lessons from LEO: part two'. Nursing Management, 10(3), 22–4.

Faugier, J., and Woolnough, H. 2003b: 'Lessons from LEO'. Nursing Management, 10(2), 22–5.

Fitzgerald, L., Ferlie, E., Wood, M., and Hawkins, C. 1999: 'Evidence into practice? An exploratory analysis of the interpretation of evidence'. In A. L. Mark and S. Dopson (eds), Organisational Behaviour in Health Care: The Research Agenda. Basingstoke: Macmillan, pp. 189–206.

French, J. R. P., and Raven, B. 1959: 'The bases of social power'. In D. Cartwright (ed.), Studies in Social Power. Ann Arbor: University of Michigan Press, pp. 150–67.

Giddens, A. 2006: Sociology. 5th edn, Cambridge: Polity.

Glasby, J., Walshe, K., and Harvey, G. 2007: 'What counts as "evidence" in "evidence-based practice"?' Evidence & Policy, 3(3), 325–7.

Govier, I. 2004: 'Advancing excellence in leadership'. Nursing Management, 10(9), 13–15.

Green, J., and Thorogood, N. 1998: Analysing Health Policy: A Sociological Approach. London: Longman.

Greer, S. L., and Trench, A. 2008: Health and Intergovernmental Relations in the Devolved United Kingdom. London: Nuffield Trust.

Grint, K. 1995: Management: A Sociological Introduction. Cambridge: Polity.

Hales, C. P. 1993: Managing through Organisation. London: Routledge.

Harrison, S. 1988: Managing the National Health Service: Shifting the Frontier? London: Chapman & Hall.

Harrison, S., Hunter, D. J., Marnoch, G., and Pollitt, C. 1992: Just Managing: Power and Culture in the National Health Service. Basingstoke: Macmillan.

Hillier, S. 1987: 'Rationalism, bureaucracy, and the organization of health services: Max Weber's contribution to understanding modern health care systems'. In G. Scambler (ed.), Sociological Theory and Medical Sociology. London: Tavistock, pp. 194–220.

Huczynski, A. A., and Buchanan, D. A. 2007: Organizational Behaviour: An Introductory Text. 6th edn, Harlow: Prentice-Hall/Financial Times.

Hunter, D. 1990: 'Organizing and managing health care: a challenge for medical sociology'. In S. Cunningham-Burley and

N. P. McKeganey (eds), *Readings in Medical Sociology*. London: Tavistock/Routledge, pp. 213–36.

Iles, V. 2005: *Really Managing Health Care*. 2nd edn, Maidenhead: Open University Press.

Jary, D., and Jary, J. 1991: *Collins Dictionary of Sociology*. Glasgow: HarperCollins.

Johnson, P., and Gill, J. 1993: *Management Control and Organizational Behaviour*. London: Paul Chapman.

Lukes, S. 1974: *Power: A Radical View*. London: Macmillan.

McInnes, E., Harvey, G., Fennessy, G., Seers, K. and Clark, E. 2001: 'Implementing evidence-based practice in clinical situations'. *Nursing Standard*, 15(41), 40–4.

May, C. 1992a: 'Nursing work, nurses' knowledge, and the subjectification of the patient'. *Sociology of Health & Illness*, 14(4), 472–87.

May, C. 1992b: 'Individual care? Power and subjectivity in therapeutic relationships'. *Sociology*, 26(4), 589–602.

Mintzberg, H. 1983: *Power in and around Organizations*. Englewood Cliffs, NJ: Prentice-Hall.

Mintzberg, H. 1996: 'Musings on management'. *Harvard Business Review*, July–August, 61–7.

Mullins, L. J. 2005: *Management and Organisational Behaviour*. 7th edn, Harlow: Prentice-Hall/Financial Times.

NHS Executive 2001: *Agenda for Change: Modernising the NHS Pay System*. Leeds: NHS Executive.

Owens, P., and Glennerster, H. 1990: *Nursing in Conflict*. Basingstoke: Macmillan Education.

Prime Minister's Strategy Unit. 2006: *The UK Government's Approach to Public Service Reform*. www.cabinetoffice.gov.uk/media/ cabinetoffice/strategy/assets/sj_pamphlet.pdf [last accessed 03 November 2008].

Sackett, D. L., Richardson, W. S., Rosenberg, W., and Haynes, R. B. 1997: *Evidence Based Medicine: How to Practice and Teach EBM*. Edinburgh: Churchill Livingstone.

Salter, B. 1998: *The Politics of Change in the Health Service*. Basingstoke: Macmillan.

Savage, J., and Scott, C. 2004: 'The modern matron: a hybrid management role with implications for continuous quality improvement'. *Journal of Nursing Management*, 12(6), 419–26.

Scott, J., and Marshall, G. 2005: *Oxford Dictionary of Sociology*. 3rd edn, Oxford: Oxford University Press.

Snell, J. 2001: 'Thoroughly modern matron'. *Health Service Journal*, 1 March, 28–31.

Stein, L. I. 1967: 'The doctor–nurse game'. *Archives of General Psychiatry*, 16, 699–703.

Stein, L. I., Watts, D. T., and Howell, T. 1990: 'The doctor–nurse game revisited'. *New England Journal of Medicine*, 322(8), 546–9.

Strauss, A., Schatzman, L., Ehrlich, D., Bucher, R., and Sabshin, M. 1963: 'The hospital and its negotiated order'. In E. Freidson (ed.), *The Hospital in Modern Society*. Basingstoke: Macmillan, 147–69.

Strong, P. M., and Robinson, J. 1990: *The NHS: Under New Management*. Milton Keynes: Open University Press.

Turner, B. S. 1987: *Medical Power and Social Knowledge*. London: Sage.

Weber, M. 1947: *The Theory of Social and Economic Organization*. New York: Free Press.

Watson, T. J. 1995: *Sociology, Work and Industry*. 3rd edn, London: Routledge.

Werrett, J., Griffiths, M., and Clifford, C. 2002: 'A regional evaluation of the impact of the Leading an Empowered Organisation leadership programme'. *NT Research*, 7(6), 459–70.

Health, Housing and the Environment

Douglas McCarrick

Key issues in this chapter

- The effects of housing on health
- Housing status and health
- Housing and environmental issues
- Housing, environment and the role of the nurse

At the end of this chapter you should be able to . . .

- understand the contrasting perspectives of medical and public health models;
- have an understanding of trends in housing policy;
- recognize how housing conditions and homelessness affect health;
- discuss the significance of government measures of housing quality;
- be aware of the importance of housing and environmental threats to health for nurses.

---

1 Introduction

Public health largely preventive health measures targeting populations and environmental improvements (in contrast to individual, curative medical approaches)

This chapter is concerned with two major aspects of **public health** – housing and its environment – and recognizes that the relationship between health and housing is a complicated but nevertheless crucial one. The effects of housing and other environmental factors on health and the significance of housing provision for particularly vulnerable social groups will be considered; the latter requires a review of housing policy. The chapter will also consider the importance of these issues for nursing.

At the time of writing housing has become a major social issue. Rising fuel costs have raised concerns about the ability of older people to heat their homes adequately. A crisis in the banking sector and the restrictions on credit have blocked prospective house buyers gaining mortgages and led to both a growth in repossessions and, more generally, a fall in house-building. The latter reflects the economy sliding into recession, with greater unemployment, homelessness and poverty, with their associated health threats, projecting a bleaker future in the medium term.

The economic crisis demands recognition of the social influences on health and ways of thinking about health other than the medical model. The public health approach addresses issues as they relate to communities or populations. It often takes a more preventive position towards ill-health, seeking to avoid its causes in communities, and thus is often concerned with health threats in the environment. The public health view

salutogenic focusing on health as positive and on resources for maintaining health rather than on factors which threaten morbidity and mortality

of health is typically **salutogenic**, since it focuses on health rather than illness, takes a wider focus on a population or a community, and is concerned with epidemiological perspectives and prevention. This contrasts with the medical approach, which is largely individualistic, concerned with the signs and symptoms of disease, and oriented towards cure. The public health perspective therefore leads to an examination of how housing and other elements of the environment contribute to causing ill-health.

2 The effects of housing on health

There are several ways in which housing can be seen to influence health. If a house has no clean water supply or has holes in the roof, these defects will clearly pose health threats to those who live there. Yet houses are much more than physical structures (Davey Smith, Dorling and Shaw, 2001). They can be particularly important for those who spend long periods of time at home – for example, mothers with young children, carers, the unemployed, and sick and disabled people (Blackburn, 1991).

The places we live in can pose physical threats to health through their condition, their design, or the materials from which they are constructed. Residents can face dangers of overcrowding or from the people who share their homes, or even from the creatures which also inhabit them. Insecure homes, in terms of tenure or crime, can mean psychological or physical threats. Gas and electricity connections can carry their own menace. Each of these aspects of housing merits the

Activity 16.1   **Housing and health?**

Inner-city
terraced housing

How might housing affect health? Write down three ways in
which you think housing might affect the health of the people
who live there.

attention of health professionals, who, at least, need to be aware of
the hazards in people's homes and, at best, might be in a position to
help do something about them.

There is some evidence that housing improvements lead to an
improvement in health. For example, Howden-Chapman et al. (2007)
recorded self-reported improvements in health following a home
insulation project.

Activity 16.2   The significance of housing conditions on health

Consider the following graph, compiled by T. H. C. Stevenson, the medical officer of health for Liverpool in 1911.

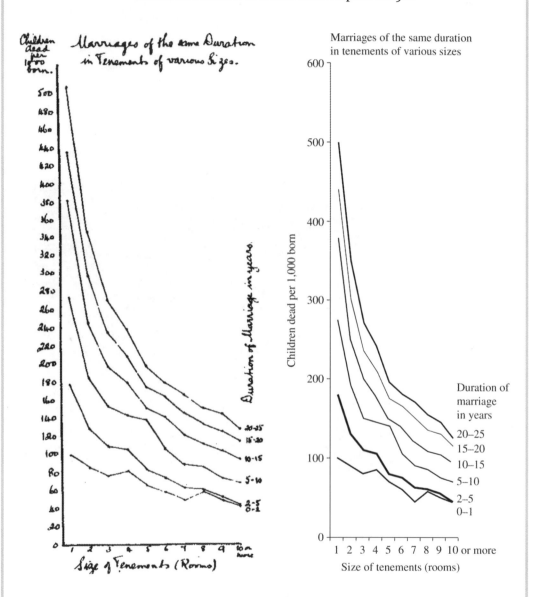

(a) Along the horizontal axis is the size of apartment – getting larger to the right. What does the vertical axis measure?

(b) Stevenson has provided several graphs in this one representation. They show the duration of marriage in the families being examined. What do these graphs tell us?

Researching health and housing

While it seems common sense that houses in poor condition will affect the health of the people who live in them, it is also important to recognize that, although living conditions have long been reported to affect health, demonstrating that relationship has considerably challenged researchers. Are poor people who live in poor housing unwell because of their housing conditions or because of factors related to their poverty? Social life is a complex phenomenon, and some have suggested that 'it is almost impossible to show a clear causal link between bad housing and ill health largely because of the "confounding variables" problem; it is almost impossible to separate housing out from such linked factors as poverty and poor diet' (Burridge and Ormandy, 1993, p. 72).

The Acheson inquiry (Acheson, 1998), which the New Labour government established to review the association between social exclusion and health, confirmed the belief that there were links between cold, damp houses and ill-health (also see discussion in chapter 8). Such conditions are also especially threatening to those already vulnerable – babies, the sick and older people.

In spite of the difficulty of investigating the relationship between housing and health, various researchers have identified strong and significant links between them which are independent of other variables, such as smoking, income and employment status. Some of the key findings are summarized in box 16.1.

The condition of people's homes is the main housing influence on their health. The '**fitness**' of a home for human habitation has been established in law. Hygienic toilet and food preparation areas, some form of heating and a water supply are among the accepted requirements for 'fitness'. The current fitness standard is incorporated in the 'Decent Homes' definition, introduced by the 2000 housing **Green Paper** *Quality and Choice: A Decent Home for All* (DETR, 2000). It includes many housing features and implies a high quality of accommodation (see activity 16.3). Unfortunately, despite significant progress, especially in the social housing sector, many homes do not meet that standard. Figures from 2003 show some improvement, with 972,000 local authority homes as 'non-decent'. However, the government's higher standards for judging homes meant that there were nearly 7 million dwellings which failed to provide their inhabitants with a decent home (ODPM, 2003, p. 5) (see box 16.2). Local authorities were given finance to provide assistance with some of these matters, although they faced declining funding and the criteria for receiving help became increasingly restrictive. More recently government had recognized that the poorer quality homes are in the private rented sector, and it is to that area that attention of policy has begun to turn.

fitness (for human habitation)   the legal standards for minimum requirements in housing services and conditions

Green Paper a discussion document issued by government as a first step towards legislation

---

Box 16.1 **Key research findings: housing and health**

- Four million British households suffer fuel poverty (the need to spend 10 per cent of household income on energy to maintain an adequate standard of warmth), resulting in 25,000 to 45,000 winter deaths per year (*English House Condition Survey 1996: Energy Report*, cited in Olsen, 2001).

- The presence of damp causes emotional distress in women and reports of respiratory and gastrointestinal problems and infections in children (Davies and Kelly, 1993).

- Wheezing and other respiratory problems, aches and pains, nerves, diarrhoea, headaches and fever are more prevalent in children who live in damp and mouldy homes (Wilkinson, 1999).

- Damp homes cause overcrowding in the more habitable parts of the accommodation and increase psychological stress (Etherington, 1983).

- High-rise accommodation causes social isolation and provides no play space for children (ibid.).

- Poorly insulated homes can create noise and neighbour disputes, generating a sense of persecution and anxiety (ibid.).

Box 16.2 **Decent homes**

For a dwelling to be considered a 'decent' home it must:

- meet the statutory minimum for housing (i.e., be fit);

- be in a reasonable state of repair;

- have reasonably modern facilities and services;

- provide a reasonable degree of thermal comfort.

Source: ODPM, 2003.

Despite assistance as the economic situation changes, greater health risks are likely to be generated in the private sector by difficulties in providing and maintaining better homes and the financial challenges for tenants on insecure or falling incomes. Community nurses and other health professionals are likely to face housing-associated health risks and declining living conditions in their daily work.

Activity 16.3   **'Fit' for human habitation?**

ITEM A: The 'fitness' standard

Decent homes should be in a reasonable state of repair, be reasonably modern and have reasonable thermal comfort. They also should be 'fit for human habitation' and have:

- a piped water supply;
- a wash basin with hot and cold water, a fixed bath or shower, and an internal WC;
- drainage and sanitation facilities;
- cooking and food preparation facilities, a sink with hot and cold water, and waste disposal facilities;
- adequate natural and satisfactory artificial light, heating and ventilation.

In addition, they should be:

- substantially free from rising damp, penetrating damp and condensation;
- structurally stable and of adequate repair. (Ministry of Health, 1946)

ITEM B

Unfit for human habitation?

(a)   Some houses have been classed as 'unfit for human habitation'. How would you judge a house as adequate for human beings to live in?

(b)   Below what minimum standards of provision and quality do you think a house would have to fall in modern Britain to make it 'unfit for human habitation'?

House design, construction and location

The condition of a person's home is not the only way in which that domestic environment can impact on health. Homes can also pose threats to health through their design, the materials of which they are made or the location they occupy. Fuller-Thomson, Hulchanski and Hwang (2000) identify four housing characteristics relevant to health:

1   physical and chemical conditions
2   biological threats
3   physical characteristics of the house
4   social characteristics of housing.

Poorly designed or badly lit kitchens create risky environments. Stairs, especially if handrails are inadequate, pose the obvious threat of falls for children and older people. In 2001 the Department of Trade and Industry reported that seventy-six people were killed in domestic accidents each week in Britain, and compared this with sixty-six deaths weekly on the roads. Among the casualties are the victims of scalding, fires, accidental collisions, carbon monoxide poisoning, falls and DIY accidents; again, the most vulnerable groups are children and older people (DTI, 2001). In a written parliamentary answer the minister for public health noted that non-fatal domestic accident figures were not collected centrally but estimated 2.7 million accidents resulting in A&E hospital visits in 2002 (Primarolo, 2008).

The risks from lead in paint and pipes, asbestos roofing and insulation, and radon gas are widely accepted (Wilkinson, 1999), although only a small proportion of homes are affected. Poor wiring is also a major contributor to the domestic fires which take hundreds of lives each year. With a bitter irony, among those most at risk are those already homeless and relying on accommodation in buildings of multiple occupation (homeless hostels).

While the UK water supply is generally sound, there have been incidents of supply becoming contaminated. For example, in 2008 the water supply in Northampton was contaminated by the parasite cryptosporidium, leaving over 100,000 households without fresh water for several weeks. In some areas the water we receive from our taps may be fluoridated to improve dental health, and, while the

White Paper   a later discussion document in which government proposals are set out and which invites more limited consultation

◄ White Paper *Saving Lives: Our Healthier Nation* (DH, 1999) strengthened this element of public health, it is worth noting that this policy is not uncontested, with claims that fluoridation itself poses different health threats (Hillier et al., 1996).

Some households are at threat from infestations of insects or rodents, although these are much less common in Britain that they have been in the past (NPTA, 2008). Current proposals among some local councils to cut back on waste collection may increase health risks from rodents.

Housing and mental health

Conway (2000) has pointed out that mental ill-health and housing are related and that there is a reciprocal relationship between housing conditions and mental health. While poor housing can create health threats, illness can lead to vulnerability of domestic security. Mental ill-health can cause a home to be poorly maintained and become a physical health threat; it can also result in sick leave and unemployment, jeopardizing rent (or mortgage) payments and therefore leading to eviction (or repossession).

The difficulties of demonstrating in research the relationships between health and housing have been referred to above. However, the situation is even more complex, since 'the effect of poor housing on health may be indirect or take several years to manifest itself' (Marsh et al., 2000, p. 412). Housing can affect both mental and physical health in a number of ways. The condition of a house, where it is located, its design and the materials of which it is constructed can all impact on the health of its inhabitants.

Changes in policy bring their own dangers. It might be noted that housing policy has been concerned with the quality of housing since the movements for slum clearance, and to that has been added more recent targets for the provision of adequate numbers of homes. While density of housing has also been an interest of statutory regulation, attention has been drawn to the drive for more homes, resulting in smaller homes and the significance of restricted living space for the mental health of their residents (Evans, 2003).

3   Housing status and health

Trends in housing provision

In Britain there are principally three forms of housing:

- owner-occupied homes
- privately rented homes
- the social housing sector.

social housing
housing provided by local authorities and housing associations to tenants with special needs usually unable to afford their own homes

Other forms of accommodation, such as houses of multiple occupation, student halls of residence, various residential institutions and others, make up a small proportion of the total housing stock.

The balance of provision across these sectors changed remarkably through the twentieth century, reflecting the different political approaches to housing the nation. In 1914, 90 per cent of houses were privately rented, with only 10 per cent making up those in owner occupation (Conway, 2000). The trend has been a massive increase of owner-occupied housing over the century, encouraged by successive governments, with 70 per cent of homes falling into this category since 2001. Local authority provision expanded as a central

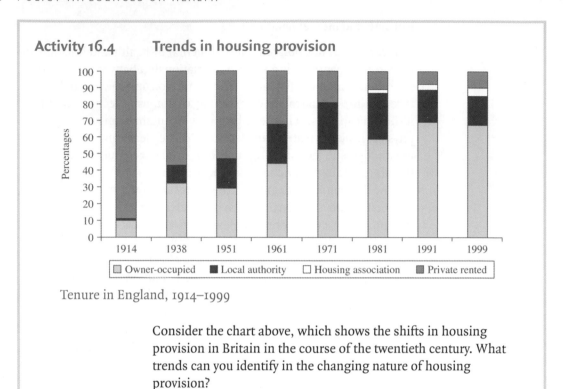

Activity 16.4   Trends in housing provision

Tenure in England, 1914–1999

> Consider the chart above, which shows the shifts in housing provision in Britain in the course of the twentieth century. What trends can you identify in the changing nature of housing provision?

element of the post-war welfare state until it accounted for 29 per cent of housing in 1971. Despite the retreat from council housing under Thatcher's governments in the 1980s, led by the right to buy scheme of the 1980 Housing Act (ibid., p. 31), in 2001 council housing still made up 13 per cent of the nation's total housing stock. The attack on council housing has continued under subsequent Conservative and Labour governments: in 2007–8, only 300 council houses were built nationally. By 1997 private rented homes made up only 10 per cent of the total, and a new form of not-for-profit housing provision, social landlords, made up a growing 5 per cent. Shelter and others are describing a housing crisis and have claimed that there are now 5 million people on social housing waiting lists. The indicated intention of the Brown government in 2008 to free councils to build once again will face the difficulties of the global economic position. There continues to be ideological resistance to the strategy of transferring local authority housing into private or charitable ownership. The current shape of British housing shows about 8 per cent of homes are in the private rented sector and both local authority and housing association provision at about 10 per cent.

The 2000 Housing Green Paper focused on helping owner-occupiers (though this was largely to be through creating 'a strong and stable economy') and 'promoting a healthy private rented sector' (DETR, 2000). Hills (2007) and others have recognized that progress towards the decent homes standard had been slowest in the private rented sector, and concerns about Britain's poor record on hypothermia prompted government action. Although deaths from hypothermia make up a small proportion even of older people's deaths in Britain, they have been linked to cold weather and excite public and political attention. The Green Paper therefore promoted 'a reasonable degree of thermal comfort' (ibid.), confirmed in the 2004 Housing Act, and in 2006 the new housing health and safety rating scale (HHSRS) was implemented to include measures of adequate heating. The HHSRS shifted the focus from house 'fitness' to the effects of housing defects in terms of threats and severity. The *English House Condition Survey 2003* (DCLG, 2006) had indicated 1.7 million private sector homes with low energy efficiency compared with 327,000 in the social sector, though there are significant regional differences, and improving these became a 'decent homes' priority. The government's home energy efficiency scheme offers support with insulating homes for those threatened with fuel poverty and may be a resource to which community health carers can direct service users.

Defining homelessness

homelessness without appropriate accommodation; this can range from living in undesirable conditions to being roofless

The 1977 Housing (Homeless Persons) Act had placed a statutory responsibility on local authorities to house the homeless. The definition of homelessness in the Act was extensive, incorporating ideas of overcrowding, of being in a home which was insecure, and of being in a home where you were the victim of domestic violence or sexual abuse (see box 16.3). This wide view of homelessness, however, came under pressure during the Thatcherite years with the notorious comment of one Conservative minister that the real homeless were 'the sort you step over when you come out of the opera' (Sir George Young, minister for housing, reported in the *Mail on Sunday* during 1991). By the time this construction of homelessness had been articulated there had already been a diminution of the responsibility of local councils with the Housing Act 1985, which contained the concept of people making themselves 'intentionally homeless'. The Act absolved councils of their erstwhile statutory duty if applicants were judged to be responsible for their own plight. By 1990 about 5,500 households were denied assistance, since they were deemed 'intentionally homeless' (DoE, 1991).

These policies had direct implications for health. The housing policies of the Thatcherite period had seen a reduction in the provision of social housing and an increase in homelessness, with its consequent health threats (see box 16.4). The 1996 Housing Act offered another wide definition of homelessness, suggesting that,

---

Box 16.3   **The continuum of homelessness**

- Without a roof

- In homeless accommodation

- In insecure housing

- Shortly to be released from an institution

- Sharing accommodation in intolerable relationships

- Living in unsatisfactory accommodation

- Sharing involuntarily

Source: Conway, 2000.

---

if there was no accommodation to which a person was entitled or if it was not reasonable for the person to live in the accommodation currently occupied, then he or she was 'homeless'. But the local authorities' responsibility to assist a homeless person were still restricted by conditions. Paragraph 188(1) of the Act states the criteria of condition, eligibility and priority:

> If the local housing authority have reason to believe that an applicant may be homeless, eligible for assistance and have a priority need, they shall secure that accommodation is available for his occupation pending a decision as to the duty (if any) owed to him under the following provisions of this Part. (OPSI, 1996)

While homelessness has reduced during New Labour's terms of office, the first quarter of 2008 still saw 15,680 applications accepted by local authorities as representing 'statutory homelessness' (DCLG, 2008). The trends in England demonstrate a high application level in 2003–4 of 135,430 of those recognized by local authorities as 'unintentionally homeless and in priority need' compared with a projected figure of 63,170 for 2007–8.

Although the Homelessness Act required local authorities to take preventative action and homelessness has fallen, young people are disproportionately represented in the figures. In 2006 the government did announce several measures to tackle youth homelessness, including advice and mediation services. However, while children are a priority in assessing homelessness cases, it has been pointed out that joint working between housing and children's services does not recognize how other government policies on worklessness, anti-social behaviour, family policy and the care system might impact on young people's precipitation into homelessness (Jones, 2008).

Homelessness, rooflessness and ill-health

Homelessness affects health in several ways. People who are living on the streets face particular threats, but there are also threats to physical and mental health from living in hostels and in the restricted access to health services (see box 16.4).

Box 16.4   Health problems and homeless people

Families in temporary accommodation	*Single homeless people*
Poor diet	Chronic chest and breathing problems
Infections	Malnutrition/digestive problems
Child accidents	Infestation and skin complaints
Poor child development and behaviour	Musculo-skeletal and foot problems
Dental, eyesight and hearing problems	Stress and depression
Obstetric risks in pregnancy	Risk of violence/assault
Babies of low birth weight	

Source: Conway, 2000.

The condition brings isolation, stress and depression; rooflessness restricts access to proper food preparation and hygiene facilities as well as bringing vulnerability to cold and pollution. Rough sleepers, says Skellington (in Dallos and McLaughlin, 1993, p. 262), 'are especially vulnerable to diabetes and epilepsy[, and] bad diet and living in poor environments has meant that homeless people become particularly susceptible to chest infections'. Problems with their feet, and a greater incidence of tuberculosis, have also been noted among the roofless. It has been reported that the life expectancy of homeless people is far below the national average; homeless people are 150 times more likely to be fatally assaulted, thirty-four times more likely to commit suicide, eight times more likely to die in an accident and three times more likely to die of hypothermia or pneumonia than the average person (WMHRU, 1994).

Homelessness and ill-health have been shown to be related. The partnership website Homelesslink (www.homeless.org.uk) comments, 'Homelessness services report that mental health problems and personality disorders are prevalent among their clients'. Bines (2000) demonstrates that physical health problems were more common among the single homeless than the population at large and that people in hostels and (temporary) bed and breakfast accommodation were eight times more likely to experience mental ill-health. For those sleeping rough the proportion rose to eleven times.

Those threats recognized there has been considerable progress under New Labour in supporting those sleeping rough. The Rough

Sleepers Unit (RSU) was established in 1999 with aims to support those sleeping out, to help them rebuild their lives and to prevent sleeping rough as a future social phenomenon. Targets for reducing these numbers set by Blair's administration were met ahead of time in 2001, and in 2008 the RSU reported numbers in England of under 500.

Homelessness, diversity and inequalities in health

Risks of homelessness and to health are not proportionally distributed across society. The reduced opportunities to find alternative housing have also meant that people who find themselves in unwanted situations have fewer escape routes. Diaz (2000) reported that in 1999 Shelter estimated 400,000 individuals were accepted as homeless by local councils; 60 per cent of these households had children and 25 per cent had lost their homes because of relationship breakdown. The people who become homeless are therefore often already vulnerable. Currently Shelter (2008) claims that 1.7 million households are on social housing waiting lists and that twice as many households were accepted by local authorities as homeless in 2007 than in 1997. There is a difficulty in arriving at accurate numbers for the homeless. Methodologies vary: charities estimate, local authorities count only those presenting as households, figures for nightly and yearly homelessness are both used. Yet it is arguable that under New Labour the trends have been to reduce homelessness, families in bed and breakfast accommodation, and rooflessness. However, it is likely that the current trend towards recession will place added pressures on families and exacerbate family breakdown.

Darke (1989) argues that women are especially disadvantaged with respect to housing. She claims that women relate to houses differently to men, spending more time in that environment and giving it more social importance, yet house design rarely takes into account the domestic and caring tasks which often fall to women within them. The disadvantages faced by women (and children) are exacerbated by the lack of alternatives to abusive situations (see chapter 11). Homeless people are at increased risk of injury and attack, and Gilroy and Woods (1994) have indicated that women will try to avoid sleeping rough because of the threat of sexual attack.

Oppenheim (1990) found that every indicator of poverty showed that black groups were more at risk of homelessness. A Shelter report (Garvie, 2004) echoed these findings, commenting that, though representing about 8 per cent of the population, in 2004 minority ethnic groups represented 20 per cent of the homeless population overall. Most recent figures suggest that minority ethnic households are proportionately three times more likely be statutorily homeless than white households, with black African and Caribbean families at even greater risk within that category (ETHNOS, 2005).

For black women the situation may be even more acute, since they have been identified as four times more likely to be homeless (Sexty, 1990). Gilroy and Woods (1994, pp. 107–14) suggest:

> Because of racist attacks/racial harassment, instead of the home being a sanctuary, for many Black women it is, or can be, a prison. . . . leaving a violent home may well mean embarking on a long ordeal of racism, homelessness, near destitution as well as fighting immigration laws.

Garvie (2004) argued that minority ethnic families are more likely to be overcrowded, often experiencing 'hidden' homelessness created by larger or extended families in smaller homes or the accommodation of new migrants. Such conditions generate domestic tensions and pose physical and mental health threats.

The homes they live in may also have especial significance for older people. It is likely that older residents will spend longer in their homes, with a proportionate increase in the influence their housing conditions will have on their health. The community care policies developed over the 1980s and 1990s were largely welcomed as a shift from institutionalization. However, among the criticisms of under-resourcing of services there was also a claim that housing matters were inadequately considered (Heywood, Oldman and Means, 2002).

These are, of course, issues which must concern nurses involved in the discharge of patients into the community. Houses which are not appropriate for older people may pose health threats through cold, falls or isolation and depression. Homelessness not only reflects and generates health problems; the situation is compounded by difficulties in engaging health services which are critically required. Community nurses and practice nurses may find they rarely encounter homeless patients, in spite of their health care needs; indeed, research has suggested that 37 per cent of homeless people are not registered with a GP (Diaz, 2000). Conway (2000) remarks on the difficulties of access to health services, explaining this in part by the mobile nature of the homeless population, but also commenting on the attitudes of doctors, who may see homeless patients as more expensive to treat than housed patients. It has been suggested this leads to a 'cycle of reluctance' whereby an unwillingness to treat homeless people leads to an unwillingness on their part to seek aid (Fisher and Collins, 1993). More recent research (Homeless Link, 2009) paints an improved but far from ideal picture for those in hostels and attending day centres.

The twentieth century saw increasing involvement of the state in housing provision and significant changes across the **housing sectors** away from private rented accommodation towards state housing and owner-occupation. In the 1980s, in particular, governments retreated from direct provision of housing, and this led to increasing homelessness. The twenty-first century opened with a continuation of

housing sectors
the forms of housing provision in Britain: social housing, private rented accommodation and owner occupation

the policy of encouraging owner-occupation and the provision of social housing through housing associations rather than local councils; however, there are signs that the government may see local authorities again playing a significant role in housing provision. Nevertheless the entry into recession in 2008 may find these policies wanting in coping with the new financial pressures on home-owners, purchasers, local authorities and housing associations as the expected greater housing need emerges.

Homelessness can describe a range of inappropriate housing situations. Homelessness affects health, and rooflessness is especially health threatening since it is compounded by poor access to health services.

4   Housing and environmental policies

Along with health, education and a minimum income, housing was recognized as a key element of the welfare state that was established after World War II. In the post-war consensus, Labour and Conservative governments vied with each other to build more local authority housing each year. This situation lasted until the 1970s, when governments began the retreat from collective state provision of housing and other services.

The Blair government did acknowledge housing and environmental issues as important to health. The Green Paper *Our Healthier Nation: A Contract for Health* (DH, 1998a, p. 12) stated:

> The government recognises that the social causes of ill health and the equalities which stem from them must be acknowledged and acted upon. Connected problems require joined-up solutions. This means tackling inequality which stems from poverty, poor housing, pollution, low educational standards, joblessness and low pay.

In July 2000 the Labour government pledged to ensure all social housing meets standards of decency by 2010, but despite politicians' aspirations towards 'joined up' government the primary care trusts (PCTs) include social services representation by right, but no

housing policy
government policy on housing provision and control

housing representation. **Housing policy** has to deal with improving existing homes and encouraging the provision of new homes, and the government is on target to meet the decent homes standard for social housing. However, into the new millennium, government policy has been oriented towards fiscal conservatism and reliance on the private sector to provide housing and on housing associations to supply social housing. Indications are that there are still 8 million homes in the private sector which do not yet meet the new standard. Government has provided grants to bring poor housing up to scratch, but these have also been facing gradual but significant reductions.

The Housing and Local Government Act 1989 established mandatory renovation grants by which any home which was found unfit for human habitation was brought fully up to standard, and minor works assistance, which helped home-owners over sixty get the work done which would allow them to remain living at home. The Act also endorsed home improvement agencies which acted as agents for householders seeking government help for improving their properties – they helped with the forms, helped tender for contractors, supervised work, and so on. In addition there was a disabled facilities grant (DFG), introduced in 1990, to assist in the access to and adaptation of homes for residents with disabilities. Since then the trend in housing policy has been towards less funding and the provision of discretionary local authority grants only. The 1996 Housing Grants, Construction and Regeneration Act even removed the right to a grant for people living in unfit homes. However, although critical of the limited nature of government help to that point, Heywood, Oldman and Means (2002) argue that the value of what had been provided, especially to older people, should not be underestimated.

Homes are set within communities, and the local environment – ambience, facilities and resources – matters for health. A poor living environment has been defined as including badly managed spaces, neglected buildings and vacant sites, graffiti, vandalism, scruffy gardens and rubbish dumping. It has been suggested that 3.3 million households in England are located in poor quality environments (DCLG, 2006).

Nurses who work in the community should be aware of the provision in their local areas. Renovation grants are available for fitness matters, insulation, heating, fire escapes, roofs, gutters, windows, doors, drains, unsafe gas and water pipes, damp-proofing, installing an inside toilet or bathroom, improving ventilation or dealing with rot. A decade ago *Modernising Social Services* (DH, 1998b) announced a 'prevention grant' of £100 million over three years to help keep older people in their homes, and this policy of prioritizing 'community care' continues into the Brown premiership. Home safety checks, handyperson schemes, and speedier access to aids and adaptations may be available through local authorities. Insulation and draught-proofing are also presently available through other government schemes.

Health Action Zones were established as experiments in establishing health-promoting partnerships in areas of health inequality. They were 'trailblazers' to tackle key health and social problems such as the incidence of coronary heart disease, cancer, mental health, teenage pregnancies, drug abuse and other issues, including housing. They had mixed success, although they did help maintain the focus on health inequalities, and their work became incorporated into the PCTs (Benzeval, 2003).

How does where
you live influence
your health?

Healthy Living Centres have been encouraged to involve a range of
local agencies in building better neighbourhood health. About 350
centres have been set up across the country. They have come to
represent the mainstream of government policy – locally based
resources to assist people to give up smoking, take more exercise and
eat more healthily. The Health Improvement Programme (HImP)
requires each PCT to engage the local community in identifying its
health needs for the plan. Though the requirement to produce a local
plan has reinforced collaboration and local consultation, arguably the
success of that involvement has been limited. The New Deal for
Communities was an area-based initiative to tackle a number of social
inequalities, including health. While some progress has been made in
some areas, the approach has fallen short of meeting its health
targets (Beatty et al., 2008).

Saving Lives: Our Healthier Nation (DH, 1999) proposed the collection of good local information on health which would allow the assessment of how effective its health promoting activities were. These 'public health observatories' in each NHS region identify and monitor local health needs, set up disease registers and promote research. The observatories have a virtual identity through the internet.

Much of the government's approach to local provision encourages local agencies to collaborate; however, there has not as yet been a great deal of extra funding for these ventures. It is arguable that area-based initiatives have a poor history of success, and the success of present area schemes for improving the health of disadvantaged communities has been mixed (Thomson, 2008).

Housing is a crucial element of a healthy environment. The first intervention by the state in housing was in terms of public health objectives. Housing policy has continued to recognize the influence housing has on health, and renovation grants were intended to create better home environments for the inhabitants of poor housing. Small adaptations to people's homes and insulation grants can also have an affect on the quality of life of the most vulnerable. The government is keen to encourage agencies to collaborate to improve people's health, and the public health observatories provide accurate information on local health needs. There is some question, however, about the effectiveness of area-based initiatives.

5   Housing and the environment: the role of the nurse

As nursing has increasingly recognized the complexities of health and become committed to holistic care, the significance of housing has become apparent. Directions in health policy also require a widened pubic health role for nurses, including community health assessment and a focus on disadvantaged groups (DH, 1999).

There is a growing need for nurses, whatever their professional context, to be aware of the housing and community conditions of the people they care for. Those who work in hospitals, perhaps somewhat removed from the immediacy of people's lives, need some understanding of the living conditions of patients, the possible contributory factors to ill-health and the health threats which they may face on discharge. While it is understandable that hospital-based professionals may prioritize emptying beds, partnership with social services in setting up the support systems required for someone to return home safely might be more effective once the complications of establishing a healthy home are better understood.

Nurses who work in the community are likely to have a more immediate insight into the health issues of people's homes, though there may be an issue of how far they regard these as 'their business'. Nevertheless, there have been appeals for a wider approach to health care in nursing (see Fisk, 1998).

Housing is central to a healthy life. Bad housing contributes to ill-health and can jeopardize rehabilitation. The importance of the local environment has increasingly been acknowledged in legislation, and community nurses in particular are considered to have important health promotion roles. There are resources nurses might explore for help. The disabled facilities grant, for example, may be called upon to make a home safer for a disabled resident. Primary care trusts have budgets and responsibility for health promoting activities in their areas. Local authorities control budgets for adapting houses and removing some of the health risks they pose. New technology, such as remote controls, timers and security lights, may also help create safer homes. For those on low incomes, local authority grants or remortgaging with a private company might provide funds older people need for house repairs, and government grants for creating warmer homes might be available to vulnerable households. There may also be a nurse or health visitor dedicated to working with homeless people.

The debate about state intervention in health, and especially in housing, will go on. Nurses have a calling to care for the ill and will therefore continue to pick up the casualties if no good answers are found, and good housing has a huge potential for maintaining good health. Holistic nursing recognizes the limitations of the medical model and values the insights the public health perspective offers. Arguably, it is nursing's responsibility to understand the effects of housing on health as nurses are peculiarly placed to see the effects of poor health. They know better than most the needs for resources for the most vulnerable. Nurses understand how social conditions shape health and, through practice and research, can extend their influence into those areas of policy which create healthier homes and environments for their patients.

Activity 16.5	Hospital discharge

Mavis is a 68-year-old woman who is on your ward following a fall near her home. You have been asked to help in making arrangments for her discharge, as the bruises are healing and there were no internal injuries found. She was only admitted from the emergency department as her temperature was a little low. Mavis is a widow who lives in a housing association flat with her son, who does not work because of periodic bouts of severe depression. The pair moved there after Mavis's husband died and they could no longer afford the upkeep of their big family home. She says that she knows very few people in the area and her son's illness means it is difficult to make friends.

You know of the area where Mavis lives, as your grandparents formerly lived there. Although it is considered 'inner city', it used to be a nice neighbourhood with a community feel, but you have heard that it has become run down since then. Mavis's fall was the result of some rubbish being left in the open area outside the block of flats which she did not see in the dark as she came home from the shops one evening.

(a) What aspects of Mavis's housing and environment may have impacted on her and her son's health?

(b) What information would you need from Mavis about her housing in order for you to make a discharge plan?

(c) If her housing was found not to be of an adequate standard, what services could you refer Mavis and her son to?

Summary and Resources

Summary

- The chapter considered housing policy and focused on housing as a health resource and as a public health approach to health improvement.

- Our homes affect our health in many ways, from overcrowding, cold or pest-infested conditions to homes which isolate us and are detrimental to our mental health.

- Homelessness has been both a target for housing policy and a consequence of it. We have seen how homelessness affects health and the difficulties homeless people have often experienced in gaining access to health services.

- Nurses recognize the effects housing has on the health of patients being treated or facing discharge. Nurses can call upon local councils to provide assistance for residents, either to improve homes or to adapt them for their health needs.

Questions for Discussion

1   Consider the situation of patients facing discharge to poor properties. What might nurses do about the problems they face?

2   In what ways should homes be suitable for the following people: women, older people, people with mental illnesses, people with learning disabilities?

3   What might be the advantages and disadvantages of state-provided housing (council housing)? As well as considering the interests of the householder, examine the advantages and disadvantages for society as a whole. Consider the same questions in the case of charitable provision of housing.

Further Reading

J. Conway: *Housing Policy*. Eastbourne: Gildredge Press, 2000. This chapter owes a lot to this excellent and eminently accessible book. It covers housing policy, homelessness and health issues, recognizing the range of social factors involved. It includes some useful internet sites.

F. Heywood, C. Oldman and R. Means: *Housing and Home in Later Life*. Buckingham: Open University Press, 2002.

An excellent consideration of this specific sector of housing need. It considers the physical and psychological importance of housing to older people and raises critical questions for housing provision and inter-professional working for good community care.

M. Stafford and M. McCarthy: 'Neighbourhoods, Housing and Health'. In R. G. Wilkinson and M. Marmot (eds), *Social Determinants of Health*. 2nd edn, Oxford: Oxford University Press, 2006.
The chapter offers a very full discussion of the significance of where we live for the health we experience. It presents statistical information and draws attention to the complex perspectives of housing and health.

To extend your understanding of this topic, go to www.politybooks.com/sociologyfornurses for additional resources, questions for discussion and further reading.

References

Acheson, D. 1998: *Independent Inquiry into Inequalities in Health* [Acheson Report]. London: HMSO.

Beatty, C., Foden, M., Lawless, P., and Wilson, I. 2008 *New Deal for Communities: A Synthesis of New Programme Wide Evidence*. London: Department for Communities and Local Government.

Benzeval, M. (2003) *The Final Report of the Tackling Inequalities in Health Module*. London: Queen Mary and Westfield College.

Bines, W. 2000: *The Health of Single Homeless People*. York: Centre for Housing Policy, University of York.

Blackburn, C. 1991: *Poverty and Health*. Buckingham: Open University Press.

Burridge, R., and Ormandy, D. 1993: *Unhealthy Housing: Research, Remedies and Reforms*. London: Spon.

Conway, J. 2000: *Housing Policy*. Eastbourne: Gildredge Press.

Dallos, R., and McLaughlin, E. 1993: *Social Problems and the Family*. London: Sage.

Darke, J. 1989: 'Problem without a name'. *Roof*, March/April, 31.

Davey Smith, G., Dorling, D., and Shaw, M. 2001: *Poverty, Inequality and Health in Britain: 1800–2000: A Reader*. Bristol: Policy Press.

Davies, J. K., and Kelly, M. P. 1993: *Healthy Cities: Research and Practice*. London: Routledge.

DCLG (Department for Communities and Local Government) 2006: *English House Condition Survey 2003: Regional Report*. London: DCLG.

DCLG 2008: Statutory Homelessness: First Quarter 2008; www.communities.gov.uk/publications/corporate/statistics/homelessnessQ22008 [last accessed 5 November 2008].

DETR (Department of the Environment, Transport and the Regions) 2000: *Quality and Choice: A Decent Home for All*. London: HMSO.

DH (Department of Health) 1998a: *Our Healthier Nation: A Contract for Health*. London: DH.

DH 1998b: *Modernising Social Services*, CM 4169. London: HMSO.

DH 1999: *Saving Lives: Our Healthier Nation*. London: DH.

Diaz, R. 2000: *Health and Housing*. London: Shelter.

DoE (Department of the Environment) 1991: *Homelessness Statistics*. London: HMSO.

DTI (Department of Trade and Industry) 2001: *Home Surveillance System Report*. London: HMSO.

Etherington, S. 1983: *Housing and Mental Health*. London: MIND/Circle 33 Housing Trust.

ETHNOS 2005: *Causes of Homelessness in Ethnic Minority Communities*. London: Office of the Deputy Prime Minister.

Evans, G. W., 2003 'The built environment and mental health'. *Journal of Urban Health*, 80, 536–55.

Fisher, K., and Collins, J. 1993: *Homelessness, Health and Welfare Provision*. London: Routledge.

Fisk, L. 1998: 'Housing primary care in the community'. In M. Allott and M. Robb (eds), *Understanding Health and Social Care*. London: Sage, pp. 155–162.

Fuller-Thomson, E., Hulchanski, J. D., and Hwang, S. 2000: 'The housing/health relationship: what do we know?' *Reviews on Environmental Health*, 15(1–2), 109–33.

Garvie, D. 2004: *The Black and Minority Ethnic Housing Crisis*. http://england.shelter.org.uk/professional_resources/policy_librar y/policy_library_folder/the_black_and_minority_ethnic_housing_ crisis [last accessed 4 November 2008].

Gilroy, R., and Woods, R. 1994: *Housing Women*. London: Routledge.

Heywood, F., Oldman, C., and Means, R. 2002: *Housing and Home in Later Life*. Buckingham: Open University Press.

Hillier, S., Inskip, H., Coggon, D., and Cooper, C. 1996: 'Water fluoridation and osteoporotic fracture'. *Community Dental Health*, 13, 63–8.

Hills, J. 2007: *Ends and Means: The Future Roles of Social Housing in England*. London: ESRC Research Centre for Analysis of Social Exclusion.

Homeless Link 2009: *Policy Briefing: Drugs and Alcohol*; www.homeless.org.uk/policyandinfo/issues/briefings/ drugsandalcohol [last accessed 6 June 2009].

Howden-Chapman, P., Matheson, J., Crane, H., Viggers, M., Cunningham, T., Blakeley, C., Cunningham, A., Woodward, K., Saville-Smith, D., and O'Dea, D. 2007: 'Effect of insulating existing houses on health inequality'. *British Medical Journal*, 334(7591), 460.

Jones, P., 2008: *Joint Working between Housing and Children's Services: Preventing Homelessness and Tackling its Effects on Children*. Children's Services Network; www.csn.info/csn/briefing-detail.jsp?&id+ 1857&md=0&section= briefing [last accessed 4 November 2008].

Marsh, A., Gordon, D., Heslop, P., and Pantazis, C. 2000: 'Housing deprivation and health: a longitudinal analysis'. *Housing Studies,* 15(3), 411–28.

Ministry of Health 1946: *Report of the Standards of Fitness for Habitation Sub-committee of the Central Housing Advisory Committee.* London: Ministry of Health.

NPTA (National Pest Technicians Association) 2008: *National Rodent Survey 2007/8.* www.npta.org.uk/assets/pages/rodent_report.html [last accessed 4 November 2008].

ODPM (Office of the Deputy Prime Minister) 2003: *English Housing Condition Survey.* London: Office for National Statistics.

Olsen, N. D. L. 2001: 'Prescribing warmer, healthier homes'. *British Medical Journal,* 322, 748–9.

Oppenheim, C. 1990: *Poverty: The Facts.* London: Child Poverty Action Group.

OPSI (Office of Public Sector Information) 1996: *1996 Housing Act.* London, HMSO; www.opsi.gov.uk/Acts/acts1996/ ukpga_19960052_en_1 [last accessed 4 November 2008].

Primarolo D. 2008: Parliamentary written answer, 2 June, Hansard; www.theyworkforyou.com/wrans/?id=2008-06-02f.207287.h [last accessed 5 November 2008].

Sexty, C. 1990: *Women Losing Out.* London: Shelter.

Shelter 2008: *The Housing Crisis.* http://england.shelter.org.uk/ housing_issues/the_housing_crisis [last accessed 5 November 2008].

Thomson, H. 2008: 'A dose of realism for healthy urban policy: lessons from area-based initiatives in the UK'. *Journal of Epidemiology and Community Health,* 62, 932–6.

Wilkinson, D. 1999: *Poor Housing and Ill Health: A Summary of the Evidence.* Edinburgh: Scottish Office.

WMHRU (West Midlands Health Research Unit) 1994: 'Health and Homelessness'. *Health Watch,* March, Birmingham: West Midlands Health Research Unit.

Conclusion

Elaine Denny and Sarah Earle

Developing your sociological imagination

This book has sought to develop your 'sociological imagination' – something which we hope you will find useful, both in meeting the diverse needs of your patients and in your pursuit of a career within nursing. We have described sociology here as multi-paradigmatic. This means that sociology can provide you with a set of theories, concepts and methodological tools which you can apply to everyday issues within clinical practice. It does not usually provide you with an 'answer' but, rather, with ways of knowing, the ability to question everyday assumptions and the capacity to look beyond common-sense explanations.

Reading through the book you have probably found that some parts, or chapters, are more meaningful to you than others. This will, of course, depend upon your previous knowledge as well as your personal and clinical experiences. Each chapter has been written to ensure that its sociological relevance is applicable to all branches of nursing, but you may find that some of the issues resonate more powerfully and that some issues are more interesting than others. For example, if you are pursuing a career in learning-disability nursing, then chapter 7 may seem particularly relevant. Similarly, those of you wishing to pursue children's nursing may find chapters 6 and 11 of more interest, and those of you studying mental-health nursing may find chapter 13 of especial significance. As you progress through your career it is likely that this will change and that all of the issues raised within the book will take on a particular importance.

The sociology of health is already a vast, and increasingly a growing, area of study. It has been described by Sarah Nettleton (2006) as disparate and eclectic, and the range of issues we have addressed are a reflection as much of the field itself as of our own preferences and expertise as editors and authors. The sociology of health has a very strong empirical tradition, and most of the research in this area deals with issues that are familiar to us all, as either lay individuals or health professionals. However, it is precisely this which ensures that the sociology of health can be applied so well to clinical practice. The book is not exhaustive and, indeed, there are numerous omissions. It has not been our intention to provide such an account of the sociology of health, but to outline some of the key debates within sociology and to show how these are of relevance to the various branches of nursing. We hope that the book has provided you with a solid grounding in the sociology of health to enable you to continue thinking sociologically.

Each of the chapters has been written as a springboard for supplementary study in that area. Further study of sociological theory, for example, will reveal a wider range of theoretical perspectives than those described in this book. Postmodernism is one such theory. It suggests that there is no one valid 'truth' or 'reality', and can very usefully be applied to the relationships between patients and so-called medical experts, and to the subsequent shifts in knowledge and power between the two. A guide to classic and contemporary theories in sociology can be found in McDonnell et al. (2009). Further exploration of feminist theory will also, in fact, reveal a choice of feminist theories, ranging from the radical to the reformist. There are many feminist texts available, but you may find the volume by Gayle Letherby (2003) particularly useful.

This book has also introduced you to sociological research methods. These are useful not only because nursing is an increasingly evidence-based profession but because, one day, you too may engage in research and find sociological methods of value. A further study of research methods will enable you to assess the research findings of others better and, thus, be more competent to evaluate the extent to which such findings should influence your own practice. Sociology also offers a rich set of methodologies that can be applied to help you understand the experience of being a patient. The book by Judith Green and Nicki Thorogood (2004) is useful, as is that by Joanne Neale (2007).

A deeper study of public health will enable you to understand the effects that environment can have on your patients. In this book we have focused on the role of housing as a health resource and have considered issues of class and poverty, but these are only some of the facets of public health. It is worth considering other issues – for example, education and the concept of 'healthy schools', the workplace and occupational health, or the relationship between public spaces, leisure and health. The volume edited by Cathy Lloyd et al. (2007) examines participatory and community approaches to public health and also includes the impact of globalization on public health. You may wish to pursue the study of risk and think about health promotion and the problem of dangerous behaviours. You may also wish to think about how nurses and other health professionals can manage the uncertainties of clinical practice. The dilemma of protecting sick and, often, vulnerable patients whilst at the same time promoting empowerment and choice could also be usefully explored. The book edited by Alan Patterson and Iain Wilkinson (2007) explores how risk is constructed for various client groups, such as mental health users and pregnant women.

As we said at the beginning of this book, sociology can be applied to everything and, indeed, it is possible to have a sociology of anything. The different sociological theories, concepts and tools outlined here can be, and have been, applied to any area of nursing or clinical practice. We hope that you have enjoyed learning about the sociology of health and that you continue to apply sociology to your own nursing practice.

References

Green, J., and Thorogood, N. 2004: *Qualitative Methods in Health Research*. London: Sage.

Letherby, G. 2003: *Feminist Research in Theory and Practice*. Buckingham: Open University Press.

Lloyd, C., Handsley, S., Douglas, J., Earle, S., and Spurr, S. (eds) 2007: *Policy and Practice in Promoting Public Health*. London: Sage.

McDonnell, O., Lohan, M., Hyde, A., and Porter, S. 2009: *Social Theory. Health and Healthcare*. Basingstoke: Palgrave Macmillan.

Neale, J. 2007: *Research Methods for Health and Social Care*. Basingstoke: Palgrave Macmillan.

Nettleton, S. 2006: *The Sociology of Health and Illness*. 2nd edn. Cambridge: Polity.

Patterson, A., and Wilkinson, I. 2007: *Health, Risk and Vulnerability*. London: Routledge.

Index